The Relevance of Public Finance
for Policy-Making

De la Pertinence des Finances Publiques
dans l' Elaboration des Politiques Economiques

The Relevance of Public Finance for Policy-Making
De la Pertinence des Finances Publiques dans l' Elaboration des Politiques Economiques

Proceedings of the 41st Congress
of the International Institute of Public Finance
Madrid, Spain, 1985

Edited by
Hans M. van de Kar
Barbara L. Wolfe

Wayne State University Press, Detroit, 1987

Library of Congress Cataloging-in-Publication Data

International Institute of Public Finance. Congress
 (41st: 1985: Madrid, Spain)
  The relevance of public finance for policy-making—
De la pertinence des finances publiques dans
l'elaboration des politiques économiques.

   English and French; résumés in French.
   Includes bibliographies.
   1. Finance, Public—Congresses. 2. Policy sciences
—Congresses. I. Kar, Hans M. van de. II. Wolfe,
Barbara L. III. Title. IV. Title: De la pertinence
des finances publiques dans l'elaboration des politiques économiques.
HJ113.I73   1985   336   87-6197
ISBN 0-8143-1910-6
ISBN 0-8143-1911-4 (pbk.)

HJ
113
.I73
1985

OFFICERS OF THE BOARD OF MANAGEMENT 1986
MEMBRES DU COMITÉ DE DIRECTION 1986

Président/President
Karl W. Roskamp, Etats-Unis/USA

Futur Président/President elect
Victor Halberstadt, Pays-Bas/Netherlands

Vice-Présidents Exécutifs/Executive Vice-Presidents
Hans van de Kar, Pays-Bas/Netherlands
Guy Terny, France

Vice-Président/Vice-President
Boris Boldirev, URSS/USSR

Trésorier/Treasurer
André van Buggenhout, Belgique/Belgium

Membres du Comité/Board Members
Aldo Chiancone, Italie/Italy
Horst Hanusch, République Fédérale d'Allemagne/Federal Republic
of Germany
Robert H. Haveman, Etats-Unis/USA
Vladimir Ilyin, URSS/USSR
Gerold Krause-Junk, République Fédérale d'Allemagne/Federal
Republic of Germany
Joergen Lotz, Danemark/Denmark
Peter Medgyessy, Hongrie/Hungary
Kenneth Messere, Royaume-Uni/United Kingdom
Masazo Ohkawa, Japon/Japan
Rémy Prud'homme, France
José Raga Gil, Espagne/Spain
Vito Tanzi, Etats-Unis/USA
Johannes Weitenberg, Pays-Bas/Netherlands

Censeurs/Auditors
Armin Bohnet, République Fédérale d'Allemagne/Federal Republic of
Germany
Marcel Zimmer, Belgique/Belgium

Secrétaire Administrative/Executive Secretary
Mrs. Birgit Schneider, République Fédérale d'Allemagne/Federal
Republic of Germany

International Institute of Public Finance

A Brief Survey of Historical and Current Matters

The International Institute of Public Finance was founded in Paris in 1937. It held two conferences before the Second World War, and members have since met at least once a year from 1947 until the present. The Institute now has over 800 members from some 50 countries, and annual conferences are normally attended also by some non-members with a special interest in the particular topic.

The aims of the Institute are scientific. Its objectives include in particular: the study of Public Finance and Public Economics, the research and publications in both of these areas, the establishment of scientific contacts and exchange of knowledge and experience between persons of all nationalities. The Institute is exclusively and directly concerned with the furthering of public interest. The activities of the Institute have been recognized on an international level by the Economic and Social Council of the United Nations, which conferred upon it the Statut Consultatif B.

The Institute provides a forum for those concerned with problems of public economics, broadly defined. It has over the years aspired to sustain high academic standards. In the selection of topics and their investigation it has directed itself towards matters of practical importance and towards issues of implementation, as well as of principle. The membership embraces both academic economists whose prime interests are in teaching and research, and public officials who face the problems "on the ground": the unifying characteristic is acceptance of a proper standard of intellectual rigor.

Membership is essentially individual though corporate subscriptions are welcome. The Institute is proud of the involvement in its activities of members from countries of all kinds of political persuasion and all levels of economic development.

The Institute is governed by a Board of Management whose decisions require approval by the general assembly of members, with a President and Vice-Presidents elected for a period of three years. The Institute is administered by an Executive Committee (present membership, Professor Karl W. Roskamp, President, Detroit; Professor Hans van de Kar, Leyden; Professor Guy Terny, Paris).

All questions concerning the Institute should be directed to:

Mrs. B. Schneider, Executive Secretary
International Institute of Public Finance
University of Saarland
D-6600 Saarbrücken 11
West Germany

Institut International de Finances Publiques

Un aperçu de son passé et de ses activités actuelles.

L'Institut International de Finances Publiques fut fondé à Paris, en 1937. Il tint deux congrès avant la dernière guerre mondiale. En 1947, il put réunir à nouveau ses membres et, depuis, ceux-ci se sont rencontrés au moins une fois par an aux quatre coins du globe. L'Institut compte, aujourd'hui, plus de 800 membres appartenant à 50 pays et ses congrès annuels sont régulièrement suivis non seulement par ceux-ci mais également par des non-membres intéressés par tel ou tel sujet.

Les buts poursuivis par l'Institut sont purement scientifiques. Ses objectifs incluent en particulier: l'étude des finances publiques et de l'économie publique, la mise en oeuvre de recherches et la publication de travaux dans ces domaines ainsi que l'établissement de contacts scientifiques et l'échange de connaissances et d'expériences entre des personnes de toute nationalité. L'Institut est guidé exclusivement et directement par le souci de l'intérêt général. L'Institut a vu sa mission reconnue, sur le plan international, par le Conseil économique et social des Nations-Unies, qui lui a conféré le statut consultatif B.

L'Institut offre un terrain de recontre pour les spécialistes intéressés par les problèmes d'économie publique, au sens large du terme. Le maintien d'un niveau scientifique très élevé est pour ses responsables une préoccupation permanente. Dans le choix des sujets et la manière de les traiter, il s'attache aussi bien aux problèmes théoriques qu'aux problèmes pratiques et à leurs solutions. Ses membres sont des spécialistes universitaires et de la recherche scientifique et des hauts fonctionnaires qui assument d'importantes responsabilités. Tous sont d'un niveau intellectuel notoirement reconnu.

L'Institut est composé essentiellement de membres individuels et il réunit dans ses activités des personnalités de pays relevant de tous les systèmes d'organisation politique et de tous les niveaux de développement économique.

La direction de l'Institut est assurée par un Comité de Direction conformément aux orientations définies par l'Assemblée Générale des membres. Son administration incombe à un Comité Exécutif actuellement composé du:
Président, le Professeur Karl W. Roskamp, Détroit,
Vice-Présidents, les Professeurs
Hans van de Kar, Leyden, et Guy Terny, Paris

Toute question relative à l'Institut est à addresser à:

Madame B. Schneider, Secrétaire Administrative,
Institut International de Finances Publiques
Université de la Sarre
D-6600 Saarbrücken 11
(R.F.A.)

Contributors

Aaron, Henry J., *Senior Fellow, The Brookings Institution, Washington, DC, USA.*

Boldyrev, Boris, *Professor, All-Union Extramural Financial and Economic Research Institute, Moscow, USSR.*

Bovenberg, A. Lans, *Economist, International Monetary Fund, Washington, DC, USA.*

Burtless, Gary, *Senior Fellow, The Brookings Institution, Washington, DC, USA.*

Danziger, Sheldon, *Professor, University of Wisconsin-Madison, USA.*

de Groot, Hans, *Social and Cultural Planning Bureau, Rijswijk, The Netherlands.*

Endres, Alfred, *Professor, Technical University of Berlin, Federal Republic of Germany.*

Gilbert, Guy, *University of Paris X-Nanterre, France.*

Goode, Richard, *Guest Scholar, The Brookings Institution, Washington, DC, and Professorial Lecturer at the School of Advanced International Studies, John Hopkins University, USA.*

Goudriaan, René, *Social and Cultural Planning Bureau, Rijswijk, The Netherlands.*

Hansson, Ingemar, *University of Lund, Sweden.*

Haveman, Robert, *Professor, University of Wisconsin-Madison, USA.*

Hoffman, Ronald, *Senior Economist, Department of the Treasury, Washington, DC, USA.*

Hoyt, William, *Assistant Professor, University of Kentucky, USA.*

Ilyin, Vladimir, *Professor, All-Union Extramural Financial and Economic Research Institute, Moscow, USSR.*

Ishi, Hiromitsu, *Professor, Hitotsubashi University, Tokyo, Japan.*

Kay, John A., *London Business School, London, UK.*

Krause-Junk, Gerold, *Professor, Hamburg University, Federal Republic of Germany.*

Llau, Pierre, *Professor, GREFI, University of Paris X-Nanterre, France.*

McLure, Charles E., Jr., *Senior Fellow, Hoover Institution, Stanford, California, USA*

Mentré, Paul, *Inspector General of Finance, Ministry of Finance, Paris, France.*

Mishan, Ezra J., *Professor Emeritus, London School of Economics, UK.*

Musgrave, Richard A., *Professor, University of California, Santa Cruz, USA.*

Peacock, Alan, *Professor, Heriot Watt University, Edinburgh, Scotland, UK.*

Raga Gil, José T., *Professor, University Complutense, Madrid, Spain.*

Sichev, Nikolai, *Professor, All-Union Extramural Financial and Economic Research Institute, Moscow, USSR.*

ix

Smolensky, Eugene, *Professor, University of Wisconsin-Madison, USA.*
Tanzi, Vito, *Director, Fiscal Affairs Department, International Monetary Fund, Washington, DC, USA.*
Tarschys, Daniel, *University of Uppsala, Sweden.*
Trías Fargas, Ramón, *Professor, University of Barcelona, Member, Spanish Parliament, Spain.*
van Tulder, Frank, *Social and Cultural Planning Bureau, Rijswijk, The Netherlands.*
van de Kar, Hans M., *Associate Professor, University of Leyden, The Netherlands.*
Wolfe, Barbara L., *Associate Professor, University of Wisconsin, Madison, USA.*

*Message from His Majesty
the King of Spain
Juan Carlos I
to the
International Institute
of Public Finance*

"PALACIO MARIVENT NO SIENDO
POSIBLE MI PRESENCIA EN EL ACTO DE
APERTURA DEL XLI CONGRESO DEL
INSTITUT INTERNATIONAL DE
FINANCES PUBLIQUES QUIERO A
TRAVES DE ESTE MENSAJE EXPRESAR
MIS MEJORES DESEOS DE EXITO PARA EL
MISMO PUNTO QUIERO TAMBIEN HACER
LLEGAR A TODOS LOS PARTICIPANTES
MI MAS SINCERA FELICITACION Y UN
SALUDO CON EL MAYOR AFECTO JUAN
CARLOS R."

Welcoming Address to the 41st IIPF Congress
Madrid, Spain

by President Karl W. Roskamp

After twelve years we have the privilege of holding another Congress in Spain. Whereas in 1973 we were invited to come to the friendly city of Barcelona, it is now the splendid Spanish capital itself which offers us its hospitality. We are thankful to our gracious Spanish host for the cordial welcome they extended to us. They indeed made outstanding efforts to prepare our Congress in their attractive city. For this I say, muchas gracias a mis amigos españoles.

During the past years the Congresses of the International Institute of Public Finance have often dealt with concrete problems encountered by different nations in their desire to enhance the well-being of their citizens through Public Finance measures. Here in Madrid, we shall do something different. We shall be concerned with a wider problem, namely, the Relevance of Public Finance for Policy-Making. I believe the choice of this topic is an important and timely one, because it is in these days that many people of good will and understanding are frequently puzzled by the difference between the policy prescriptions emanating from the theory of Public Finance and those actually implemented in practice through the political choice process. In many places it is felt that a considerable gap has arisen between the two. The 41st Congress gives us an opportunity to reflect on this problem and to review the troops. I believe the discussions will be most stimulating for the simple reason that they must touch upon some fundamental issues in our field.

Lingering in the background of many of the topics to be discussed, there will be the perennial problem of the desirable relationship between the individual and the state. Depending on how this relationship is viewed, the nature of Public Finance decisions will vary. There may be a pure individualistic variant as one polar case. Another possibility is to view the state as an independent entity with an existence of its own. Between these two fall all those cases one encounters in reality. A new interest in the theory of constitutions and work in the area of public choice has in recent years thrown new light on some basic issues encountered here. Public Finance experts were quick to work the new ground. Clearly, as ideas about the relationship between the individual and the state change, so will be the tasks one expects Public Finance to perform.

The world in which we live is a dynamic one. As time passes there will be changes in the ideas and aspirations of individuals and nations alike. There will be changes in the understanding of the working of an economy. Public Finance is embedded in this dynamic process and it will be invariably affected. I do not wish to anticipate the topics you are going to discuss during this Congress. I am sure that your important work in these congenial surroundings, here in Madrid, will be most productive and that it will shed new light on many issues.

Let me extend to all of you a very cordial welcome to the 41st Congress of the IIPF. I wish you much success and a very pleasant stay in this great country.

Preface

The 41st Congress of the International Institute of Public Finance was held in Madrid, Spain, August 26–30, 1985. The topic of the Congress was "The Relevance of Public Finance for Policy-Making". This rather broad topic was narrowed down in three Working Groups, where participants actively explored the gap between theoretical and empirical findings in public finance on the one hand and questions raised in actual public policy on the other hand.

The first Working Group dealt with the state of public finance theory and its usefulness for policy-making. Selected issues, such as the economic theory of fiscal policy, public choice theory, and the theory of optimal taxation were addressed in order to assess their contribution to the solution of practical problems.

In the second Working Group the focus was on empirical findings. The results, for instance, of studies of the economic effects of taxation on capital formation and on labor supply were evaluated, as were the findings of budget-incidence studies, studies of public sector growth and of public productivity. The need of policymakers for facts and figures about the efficacy of public finance instruments was considered with respect to areas such as the environment and public infrastructure.

The third Working Group related actual advice and its impact and therefore tried to assess, in retrospect, the causes of success or failure of major efforts in the field of tax reform, social security reform, and expenditure control.

The Scientific Committee for the 41st Congress received advice and support from numerous people in drafting the scientific programme; the chairman of the Scientific Committee gratefully acknowledges the help of Norbert Andel, Richard Bird, Sijbren Cnossen, Willem Drees, Francesco Forte, Otto Gado, Victor Halberstadt, Heinz Haller, Horst Hanusch, Robert Haveman, Fritz Neumark, Alan Peacock, Horst Claus Recktenwald, Karl Roskamp, Kurt Schmidt, Burton Weisbrod, Dirk Wolfson, and Barbara Wolfe.

The secretarial staff of the public finance department of the Erasmus University and—later—of the University of Leyden were of great help in taking care of the immense correspondence. Special thanks for secretarial and organizational assistance go to Saskia ten Asbroek and Birgit Schneider. In close contact with José Raga Gil of the Local Organizing Committee they also skillfully took care of the Congress Desk in Madrid. With regard to the provision of the excellent conference facilities in Madrid, the Local Organizing Committee chaired by Alberto Monreal Luque deserves special thanks.

Assistance in the editing and other efforts necessary for the publication of the Proceedings volume was provided by Saskia ten Asbroek, Rémy Prud'homme, Karl Roskamp, and Elisabeth Vessilier. The editorial assistance of Elizabeth Evanson is appreciated. The University of Wisconsin-Madison and the University of Leyden deserve thanks for their support in preparing the volume.

Hans M. van de Kar, University of Leyden, The Netherlands
Barbara L. Wolfe, University of Wisconsin-Madison, U.S.A.
editors

The Scientific Committee for the 41st Congress:

Hans M. van de Kar (the Netherlands), Chairman
Natalia Gajl (Poland)
José Raga Gil (Spain)
Daniel M. Holland (USA)
Helga Pollak (FRG)
Rémy Prud'homme (France)
Hirofumi Shibata (Japan)

Contents

The Nature and Relevance of Public Finance

Hans M. van de Kar
Barbara L. Wolfe

The purpose of the 1985 IIPF conference in Madrid was to evaluate the usefulness of public finance from the perspective of policy implementation. Participants endeavored to put themselves in the position of their clients, the policymakers, rather than simply exchange views among themselves. An evaluation of the usefulness of public finance is particularly important at a time when, because of historical changes, public finance and its practitioners have both come under attack.

During the twenty-five-year period of nearly continuous growth that followed World War II, the scope and depth of public finance theory significantly increased. It became more and more specialized, reflecting the enlargement and complexity of the public sector. The subfields of urban economics, health economics, economics of education, housing, environment, regulation and others evolved. This development resulted in an apparent separation of public macroeconomics or fiscal policy (in Musgrave's terminology, the stabilization branch) from public microeconomics. Traditional public finance, which is very broad in scope, appeared to be transformed into public (sector) economics with a microeconomic focus on efficiency and equity aspects.

One of the goals of the 1985 Madrid conference was to consider whether public finance was indeed still relevant for the solution of practical policy questions, in view of the fact that the economic decline of the 1970s brought entirely new challenges in its wake. Citizens increasingly voiced criticisms of the size and efficiency of the public sector, and also began to question the perspicacity of those who had helped design the prevailing policies—public finance theorists. What had become an extensive public sector was blamed for causing economic stagnation, for not being able to alleviate the consequences of poor economic performance, and for not restoring economic growth.

On the microeconomic level, public economists are today under pressure to increase the efficiency of the public sector, and that pressure has

The Relevance of Public Finance for Policy-Making. Proceedings of the 41st Congress of the International Institute of Public Finance. Madrid, 1985, pp. 1–10.

intensified as the economy continues to stagnate and budget deficits are at unacceptable levels. Even though greater efficiency has been given high priority, suggestions for program retrenchment and reorientation have met predictably strong resistance from those who benefit from those programs.

On the macroeconomic level, public finance experts are faced with the need to stimulate growth, and at the same time they are expected to stem the large budget deficits. The continuing lag in economic growth and employment has not helped their public credibility. In the face of these demands, among others, the question arises of whether the public is not expecting too much from the public finance profession. It is therefore appropriate to take stock, to evaluate what advice can be offered to enhance decision-making, to understand the successes and failures of the past, to investigate whether the traditional insights are adequate and efficacious in periods of slackening economic performance.

What can reasonably be expected from public finance economists? First, they should evaluate and explain the efficiency and equity implications of existing policies and alternative options. Second, they should do so within the context of the objectives and limitations of the politicians and other "clients," and also within the existing institutional framework, thus giving consideration to the interconnections between policies and their institutional constraints in the effort to produce suggestions for institutional reform. Three, they should anticipate future directions. Much like the marketing function of a business firm which includes product development, the public finance specialist may have to design new or modified strategies and programs in the public sector to deal with anticipated changes, such as the aging of the population or regional displacement of industries. This may require providing policymakers with alternative proposals and indicating areas of priority. Four, they should caution against objectives that are inconsistent or unattainable.

The papers that follow evaluate the relevance of public finance for policy-making. Their general theme is an exploration of the gap between the theoretical and empirical findings in public finance on the one hand and questions raised by public policy on the other. The first set of papers deals with the state of public finance theory—the development of theories and related policy options in response to anticipated and recognized policy needs. The second set concentrates on empirical findings, focusing on the testing of theories and policies. The last group investigates the causes of success or failure of policy recommendations in the past.

1. Developing Theory and Policy Options

A summary of section one of this volume might be stated as: "Public finance has developed analytical tools and the methodology to apply them, but the lack of empirically verified and reliable estimates of the relevant behavioral relationships inhibits use of these tools."

Most of these papers evaluate current public finance theory from the perspective of those who offer advice and examine the usefulness of advice based on this theory. There is a certain irony in some of the papers, which seems to suggest that although our theories have reached a very high level, in a substantial number of cases we have little advice to give—that any advice based on our theories must go hand in hand with empirical knowledge, and that we need much more such knowledge. At this juncture arises the fundamental philosophical problem of the relationship between theory and empirical knowledge—between a priori and a posteriori reasoning—to which some of the greatest thinkers have devoted much effort without producing definite answers. In the sciences in general, and ours in particular, issues have been raised but not resolved. In the macro area, *Hoffman* argues that unresolved issues "constitute obstacles to a consensus about how the economy responds to short-run counter-cyclical fiscal and monetary policy changes." These include conflicting analytical issues, not just empirical verification.

Bovenberg also points out the limitations imposed by current empirical knowledge, but regards general equilibrium models as a very useful and promising tool for policy analysis. He provides evidence concerning their value in giving us insight into the likely consequences of alternative policies. The models have a great deal of potential, since they can employ a variety of assumptions to obtain estimates of the range of likely outcomes. They can be used for medium-run outcomes as well as short-run and long-run equilibrium. He also discusses some of their shortcomings: sensitivity to assumptions, and the fact that the modeling technology has in some ways outrun our knowledge of the partial equilibrium relationships. In this way he sets the stage for the *Smolensky, Hoyt, and Danziger* paper in the next section. And his views are consistent with the idea that our theories are farther advanced than is empirical verification—that they require empirical knowledge that is largely unavailable at present. He does, however, cast a positive light on our ability to perform tests for ranges of outcomes.

Mishan's discussion of cost-benefit analysis, a method frequently used within public policy decision-making, also highlights the difficulties of empirical knowledge and the contrast between the theory of such analysis and its actual implementation. A number of problems accompany benefit-cost analysis, including how to deal with uncertainty, how to take into consideration future generations, and how to incorporate intangibles. This form of analysis remains a contribution to decision-making, but has serious limitations. Its limitations are not primarily conceptual; they arise in the course of analysis, and result from the severe difficulties of securing empirical estimates.

The paper on optimal taxation offers a somewhat different theme concerning the relevance of public finance theory for policy. *Krause-Junk* suggests that theory offers few insights that can be used beyond those already understood under traditional public finance. Optimal tax theory is a mathematical system of analysis to design a tax system that minimizes the welfare costs of the inevitable distortions. Unfortunately, most of its recommendations are unworkable in practice, being either inequitable or impractical. The recommendations that are useful are consistent with those we already knew, before the contribution of optimal tax theory. Hence the view that optimal taxation is a cul-de-sac—or not very useful to public policy. This is also the view of the President of the IIPF, Karl Roskamp, who in his welcoming address questioned the assumptions of theoretical models. He wonders whether the desire for consistent, elegant mathematical models sometimes renders public finance experts oblivious to the fact that feasibility and applicability to problems in the actual politico-economic world are all important. What happens to optimal taxation theory if consumers are not the postulated docile neoclassical actors, smoothly maximizing their utilities within whatever after-tax income constraints a supposedly benevolent government imposes?

A more optimistic view of the usefulness of public finance theory is presented by *Kay* in his analysis of tax committee reports in developing countries. He finds the reports in general agreement on the merit of moving to fewer income tax rates, to a more comprehensive base that includes fringe benefits, and toward taxing household units rather than individuals. The negative aspect of his review is that few of these recommendations have been carried out, at least in the near term. Nevertheless, the reports provide blueprints that are likely to be more useful than detailed changes in current legislation.

In a number of ways, the papers of *Aaron* and *McLure* are similar to that of Kay. Each reports on the current search for changes in policy in the United States. Aaron uses public finance theory to evaluate options in funding social security—a topic of general concern in industrialized countries today. He points to two central problems. One is the need for empirical knowledge to accurately predict both the growth of social security payments and the tax base, predictions which require correct estimation of population change and earnings growth. Second, Aaron describes the problem of determining what will occur if a particular tax system is established in a country, given that no country has consistently followed basic tax principles. McLure's frustration concerns the politics of changing tax policy: the role of interest groups and the limited role of tax policy advisers. Both McLure and Aaron refer to the eternal problem of converting theory into policy in the face of conflicting objectives.

Musgrave also highlights a difficulty in applying public finance theory to policy matters. He focuses on two traditional objectives of public finance: horizontal and vertical equity. The dilemma he examines is the impracticality of applying the well-developed theory of tax equity. For example, achieving horizontal equity requires knowledge of individual preference functions, which are virtually unknowable except at possibly very great expense. He argues that we do not have the knowledge to apply well-established public finance principles—again, the theory is available, but is of limited practical use owing to our lack of empirical knowledge.

2. Empirical Evidence

The first group of papers in Part II reviews and evaluates the empirical evidence on several major theories of public finance, including budget incidence studies and general equilibrium computer-based simulations, which attempt to evaluate the overall effect of the fisc (Smolensky, Hoyt, and Danziger); analysis of the labor-supply effects of taxes and transfers (Burtless and Haveman); and the capital-formation effects of capital income taxation (Hansson). Their general theme is that while we have become more sophisticated in our methodology for estimating the effect of the fisc or changes in the fisc, our estimates still must rely on weak estimates of behavior, which have major impacts on our policy conclusions. The result is large variation in empirical estimates.

Burtless and Haveman review the evidence on the labor-supply effects of taxes and transfers (one potential use of general equilibrium models). Early studies, relying primarily on survey models, concluded that there was no labor-supply effect. The 1970s witnessed large microdata studies in the United States, using regression analysis and actual experimental data (the negative income tax experiments). Subsequently, experimental as well as longitudinal data were evaluated and more sophisticated econometric techniques were developed and employed in computable general equilibrium models. Even with the use of this new methodology, widely divergent estimates of the labor-supply responses to incentives remain. These divergences largely reflect the underlying assumptions of the models used. The authors argue against the higher (alarmist) estimates on several grounds, including lack of replication of these results and the basic inconsistency of such findings with longer-run observed trends in labor supply, at least in the United States. Even apart from the very high elasticities, there are substantial differences among the remaining behavioral estimates.

Hansson considers the evidence on the effects of tax policy on capital formation (another application of general equilibrium models). His paper, more theoretical than the others in this section, observes that there is a great deal of variation among the estimates of the likely response of capital formation to alternative taxes. While focusing on the results of general equilibrium models, he concludes that a decrease in capital taxes increases capital formation, but that the estimates of the magnitudes, even controlling for the openness of an economy, differ rather widely. The sources of these differences again are largely the divergences in estimated responses—elasticities of labor supply, elasticity of substitution between inputs, etc.—and the sensitivity of the models to alternative specifications. Nevertheless, Hansson concludes that the evidence cited does provide a useful range of estimates of the expected effects of alternative taxation structures.

After discussing budget incidence studies, *Smolensky, Hoyt, and Danziger* argue that in order to resolve the remaining key issues regarding the overall impact of the fisc, a radically new methodology is needed; namely, computable general equilibrium models. Because these models permit inclusion of individual responses to the fisc in terms of labor supply and savings, substitution of inputs in production, and secondary effects of taxes and excess burden, they increase the ability of public economists to evaluate the effects of introducing new taxes and transfers. But, as suggested above, these authors as well as Burtless, Haveman, and Hansson raise questions concerning the validity of such simulation models, since they require and are sensitive to a number of assumptions.

A quite different picture of empirical validation is presented by *Endres*. He finds consistent evidence in favor of the theories suggested by economists for regulating the environment. When applied by government, the results in terms of efficiency in pollution control are as predicted. The frustration in this area is, according to Endres, that the recommendations made by public economists are rarely followed. Both self-interest and ideology influence actual policy—a finding echoed in several of the papers in the last section.

Rather than evaluate an existing empirical literature on an aspect of public finance, *Goudriaan, de Groot and van Tulder* are interested in direct evidence on public sector productivity. They offer a method to empirically test that productivity—a desirable but rarely attempted objective. The authors seek to provide facts and figures, using data from the Netherlands in the period 1975–1983. Their study includes both intermediate production and final products. They find very large differences in productivity trends across public subsectors. From these findings, they argue that their approach has the potential of improving budget allocations as well as the overall productivity of the public sector.

3. The Role and Impact of Advice

In this last section, several authors endeavor to assess the relationship between the advice of public financiers and actual policy-making (Goode,

Tanzi, Ishi). The successes and failures of consulting efforts in the past, including such "classics" as the Shoup Mission in Japan, are analyzed. The impact of a permanent advisory institution is highlighted (Llau and Gilbert). Other authors take a broader view, using the changes in the political framework and/or political economic thinking to explain the dynamics of tax and fiscal policy (Trias Fargas and Raga; Boldyrev, Ilyin, and Sichov). Political and institutional constraints that impede the pursuit of policy advice are also considered (Peacock; Tarschys; Trias Fargas and Raga).

Given that many of the early developments in public finance dealt with taxation, it is not surprising that most of the evidence on the usefulness of public finance is in the tax area. Perhaps more surprising is the concentration on developing rather than developed countries; apparently it is somewhat easier to assess the evidence in less developed nations than in more industrialized ones. Yet, even in the simpler economic systems of developing countries, many obstacles to tax reform are encountered. *Goode*, drawing on his experience at the IMF Fiscal Affairs Department, first mentions the intellectual and analytical difficulties of appraising an existing local situation, owing in part to the lack of reliable data. He also refers, however, to other forms of inappropriate advice—an economically sound report without the necessary instruction manual for the client will miss its target.

In addition, Goode draws attention to the environment in which policy recommendations are supposed to be implemented, identifying political and bureaucratic barriers and weaknesses in administration and compliance. A policy adviser must take these factors into account.

Tanzi compiles an impressive list of the common characteristics shared by major tax policy missions. Cultural biases of experts seem to be inevitable, as is overoptimism concerning what taxation can accomplish. Advice that follows current fashion, and neglect of the rigidities in the existing tax administration, are additional obstacles highlighted by Tanzi.

Many of the common denominators found by Goode and Tanzi also appear in *Ishi's* analysis of postwar tax reform in Japan. This commonality underlines the observation that it is indeed possible to point to general causes for success or failure of policy advice, at least in the area of taxation. Many of these factors have to do with the relationship between the adviser and his client, whether politician or bureaucrat.

The public finance adviser should first of all understand the needs of the policymaker in a technical sense. His primary function is to choose the instruments, while the policymaker chooses the policies. But a successful adviser is more than a technician: he or she should also be a good salesperson, remaining aware of clients' motivation and the limitations of technical knowledge. The wheeling and dealing of politics may only permit second- or third-best options, from a technical point of view.

This relationship between the political situation and the prestige and impact of policy advisers is a main theme of the paper by *Trias Fargas and Raga*. They investigate this relationship during the 1970s, when the energy crisis dominated economic life and the transition from authoritarian regime to democracy was the main event in Spain's political life.

Peacock provides newcomers to the trade of policy advice with cautions and recommendations. He notes that a policy adviser often has to choose either to act as a hired gun or to make a fool of himself when nobody listens to his ideas. He stresses that a well-meaning policy adviser risks becoming frustrated: first by the cynicism of his wiser and sadder colleagues, second by the policymaker who is not always satisfied with the advice, even if it is technically sound. Peacock follows Machiavelli when he shows (in a payoff matrix) that the best (or least worse) position for a policy adviser is when his advice is correct but not taken. He then will receive credit from his clients, and his professional colleagues will not be jealous.

The well-directed but somewhat cynical warnings of Peacock are underlined by *Tanzi*, who spells out five basic ingredients for successful tax reform—ingredients which, however, lie for the most part beyond the control of the policy adviser. The first requirement is that the government taking the advice should have a long time horizon, since the benefits of a reform belong essentially to the future, while the costs are always immediate. Another requirement is that there should be at least one powerful figure in government who pushes for the reform and remains in power long enough to nurse it through its initial stages. Third, tax reform must be recognized as more than a change in tax policy: it should also be accompanied by reorganization at the administrative level. Tanzi's fourth and fifth requirements are that the policy adviser should have an excellent knowledge of the domestic economic conditions and that the local tax administrators should support the reform proposals, as they are often in a position to block reform. Ishi describes how the Shoup Commission handled such obstacles adequately in postwar Japan, one of the few examples of a tax reform study that has enjoyed successful implementation. Apart from the professional excellence of the Shoup report and the wide local support it gained, an important factor in its success was the fact that its reform proposals came immediately after the social and economic dislocations of World War II.

Llau and Gilbert also focus on the constraints that impede the impact of tax theory on tax policy. The subject of their analysis is not a tax mission but a permanent advisory institution in France, the Conseil des Impôts. The authors assess the impact of this institution on several actual tax policy measures taken since 1971, including simplification and broadening of the tax base. Their contribution shows how thin and blurred is the borderline in practice between theory and policy, even in the well-developed area of taxation.

In the relatively new field of the economics of regulation it is even harder to distinguish theory and policy when considering actual developments. This is illustrated by *Mentré* (a policymaker), who tries to identify recent developments in various countries by classifying the forms of regulation and deregulation.

Also relatively new in public finance is the study of theories and policies of retrenchment. *Tarschys* contributes to that discussion. He ventures to describe how, in various countries, fiscal stress is handled by adapting traditional budgetary procedures. The relationship between theory and actual policymaking is spelled out against this background. It appears that the familiar theories of budgetary reform offer little support when governments are faced with the acute need to implement systemic expenditure cuts. Furthermore, it appears that under austerity, policy advice is at first even more neglected than under normal circumstances, but that its impact grows when cutbacks become persistent. Tarschys spells out how governments have to invest in analysis in order to master the art of contraction.

Taken together, what do all of these papers have to say about the usefulness of public finance in its traditional domain, e.g., covering the micro- and macroeconomic aspects of government actions? First, we now have well-developed theories and methodological means to provide policymakers with a framework and qualitative scenarios through which reasonably informed policy decisions can be formulated. These are most advanced in the tax area. Second, public finance does quite well in influencing future directions of policy by laying out blueprints for general reform rather than exact specifications. Third, public economists have provided useful advice, especially when they consider social conditions and institutional constraints. Fourth, public finance would be much more useful if there were systematic efforts at empirical testing of behavioral relationships (elasticity of labor supply, elasticity of capital formation to taxes, etc.) across countries. We as public finance advisers would do well to broaden our advice to include the need for such systematic research (and its associated data collection efforts). Fifth, public finance has been most relevant when it provides advice on the basic structure rather than small, piecemeal elements. This may be because in the case of detailed changes it is easy to identify the gainers and losers.

To conclude, in many areas of its traditional domain—tax and expenditure incidence, distortionary impacts, tax integration and administration, fiscal effects—public finance can legitimately claim to have been and to be useful for policymaking. Its theoretical and (to a lesser extent) empirical knowledge bases have expanded, and techniques for performing simulations promise to become powerful tools for the development and testing of new policy options. Tax policy, including the development of new taxes, has profited from the knowledge and advice of public finance experts, and in the future may be more finely tuned to policy objectives through our improved ability to understand the full implications of any alternative tax structure. The usefulness of public finance recommendations has been and is being constrained, however, by insufficient empirical knowledge. Our theories seem always to be several steps ahead of our empirical learning, owing either to lack of adequate data, or of estimable models, or of resources devoted to such activities. One could of course argue that the development of internally consistent theory is a positive achievement by itself and, at least in the long run, is likely to increase the effectiveness of the profession, but this was not the question addressed by this conference. Its purpose was to test the relevance of public finance from the point of view of the policymaker. And it is in this respect that the public finance profession is handicapped by the absence of reliable estimates of behavioral responses. If public finance is to increase its usefulness, efforts will have to be made either to improve the synchronization of theoretical and empirical knowledge or to advance the empirical knowledge frontier, especially in the area of behavioral relationships, by allocating more resources toward such pursuits.

There has been a trend, especially in the United States, to move away from broad studies whch consider all three of the traditional areas of public finance in evaluating fiscal systems—allocation, distribution, and stabilization—toward increased specialization, with a greater focus on microeconomics and less on macro, or stabilization. A symptom of this development is the publication of public finance textbooks that have no section on macroeconomic stabilization policy (Stiglitz and Rosen[1]). Such shifts reflect a trade-off: While a broader, more traditional approach provides a more comprehensive picture of the effects of fiscal measures, specialization offers the potential of a much deeper theoretical and empirical understanding of the operation of individual sectors or behaviors, taking into account unique characteristics (e.g., market failures, institutions, etc.). The profession should recognize this trade-off as it seeks to increase the usefulness of public finance to policymakers.

---

[1] Joseph Stiglitz, *Economics of the Public Sector* (New York: Norton, 1986); Harvey Rosen, *Public Finance* (Homewood, Illinois: Richard Irwin, 1985).

Part I

Developing Theory and Policy Options

Macroeconomic Analysis and Stabilization Policy: Searching for Consensus

Ronald Hoffman*

I. Introduction

My assigned topic for this meeting is to discuss the relationship between macroeconomic analysis and policy from the viewpoint of one who advises policy makers. I begin by noting that in his Economic Report of January 1980, President Carter wrote that inflation was the nation's number one economic problem and that a mild recession, with a moderate rise in the unemployment rate, was expected to occur early in the year. A working group of U.S. government economists was assigned to develop and analyze a fiscal stimulus package that might forestall the expected recession. The staff analysis concluded against the adoption of such a package. To my knowledge that is the last occasion in which a countercyclical fiscal stimulus proposal has been seriously considered by an American president's administration.

Indeed, the following year, in his January 1981 Report, after the election but before the inauguration of President Reagan, Mr. Carter called for an "anti-inflationary program of fiscal restraint," while also recommending a (supply side?) tax reduction to provide longer-run incentives for saving and investment.[1] The context for these recommendations was an annual percentage change in real GNP of −0.3 percent for 1980 and 2.6 percent for 1981. Thus, it appears that by January 1981, Mr. Carter was no longer a countercyclical fiscal activist.

In his first Economic Report (January 1982), President Reagan wrote that although his administration viewed the current recession with concern, it was important to avoid the "stop-and-go" countercyclical policies of the

*The author is a senior economist of the U.S. Treasury Department.

This paper expresses the personal views of the author and does not necessarily imply, reflect or represent Department policy. As noted, portions of this paper are taken from previous work done with Mickey D. Levy and Angelo Mascaro. In addition, their helpful comments on this paper are gratefully acknowledged, and although it would be preferable not to implicate them in the errors that may remain, that may be impossible.

The Relevance of Public Finance for Policy-Making. Proceedings of the 41st Congress of the International Institute of Public Finance. Madrid, 1985, pp. 13–31.

past, and to concentrate on constructing a sound, stable framework for long-term growth. Thus he proposed permanent spending reductions and tax cuts.

I offer these observations of recent history as description, not analysis. But in my opinion they express a similarity of economic policy *intent* on the part of two quite different administrations. As a matter of interpretation I surmise that Carter's departing suggestion of fiscal restraint and pro-capital tax incentives reflected the longer-run perspective espoused by Reagan; this is in contrast to the conjecture of some, which construes the Reagan "supply-side" tax cut as a disguised policy of short-run countercyclical demand stimulus. To the extent that this perception is correct, I believe that it is pertinent to the theme of this conference: "The Relevance of Public Finance for Policymaking," and to the focus of this session: "Public Finance Theory, Stabilization, and Growth." Indeed, from my perspective, these titles imply the question: How is the apparent shift away from a countercyclical "fine-tuning" disposition by economic policy makers (in the United States, at least) linked to the analytical base of macroeconomics?

The theme of this paper is that the current state of macroeconomic analysis appears to caution against an activist role for macroeconomic policy. This caution stems from the view that, as yet, we do not know enough to justify activist policies, but it is also consistent with an alternative view that we now know enough to judge that such intervention is bound to fail.[2]

The paper begins with a sketch of some unresolved analytical issues that are obstacles to a consensus about how the economy behaves in response to the presence (or absence) of short-run countercyclical fiscal and monetary policy changes. Some current suggestions for a cyclically neutral deficit policy are noted briefly.[3] Then attention is focused on the longer-run matter of the growth of government debt that is implicit in the realization and projection of persistently large deficits. Here the discussion moves to the effects of policy on capital accumulation and inflation and leads to a consideration of the monetary-fiscal policy "mix" question. In this context, stabilization policy is interpreted somewhat differently than in public finance discussions as usually construed. The paper cautions that a leading proposal to encourage private capital formation by manipulating the fiscal-monetary policy mix relies on the questionable use of inflation, and that a much publicized spectacular example, where, with a persistent primary deficit, lower inflation results from looser rather than tighter money, depends on extreme assumptions. Monetary policy expansive enough to cause persistent inflation—and thus an inflation tax—may be viewed more generally as a type of tax policy. The paper concludes that although the notion of a manipulatable fiscal-monetary mix for either short- or longer-run stabilization purposes sounds attractive, it is not yet a policy derivable, except under extreme or unusual circumstances, from a credible theoretical framework.

II. A Sketch of Some Macroeconomic Policy Issues

Macroeconomic policy consists of fiscal policy and monetary policy.[4] Fiscal policy relates to choices about government spending and taxing—and therefore about the deficit—while monetary policy relates to the actions of the Federal Reserve (central bank) to manage the money supply. But the macroeconomic effects of these two components of macroeconomic policy are controversial and the dispute concerns both goals and methods. Although in most respects the deficit is considered part of fiscal policy, decisions about the deficit are affected by and have effects on monetary policy.

A. Monetary Policy

The dispute about the role of monetary policy has two dimensions: the goals to be achieved and the methods to be used in the efforts to reach those objectives. The methods controversy is, generally speaking, a contest between "activist" and "nonactivist" (discretion versus rules) strategies. But the distinction between an active policy and a commitment to a rule becomes, in practice, a matter of degree—when, for example, an active policy allows only infrequent discretionary changes as dictated by specified criteria, or when commitment to a rule is not absolute, but allows for change, again subject to specified criteria.

The issue about the appropriate goal is whether and in what way monetary policy can and should address itself directly to improving the performance of real macroeconomic variables such as real output and the unemployment rate, or whether it should focus its concern on achieving price stability. Those who accept the first view tend to suggest that the Federal Reserve actively manage the money supply to accomplish, as a primary objective, a real economic performance goal, e.g., a target rate of unemployment. This policy has a history of leading to accelerating inflation—which eventually causes its abandonment. But the policy continues to command support among some academic economists and policy makers (e.g., see Rivlin [34][5]).

Proponents of the alternative view share the position that changes in money growth have their permanent effects substantially on inflation rather than on real economic growth. According to this view the Federal Reserve should focus on providing a stable and predictable macroeconomic environment, in nominal terms, e.g., nominal GNP, in which real economic activity would encounter a minimum of disturbance due to nominal fluctuations.

However, even those who agree with this viewpoint may disagree on what targets or operating procedures the Federal Reserve should follow in order to provide a stable and predictable macroeconomic environment.

There are varying degrees of confidence in the predictability of the relation-ship between the monetary base and the money supply (money multiplier) and the relationship between changes in the growth rates of money and nominal GNP (velocity changes). Some proponents argue that the Fed (central bank) should establish a rule for the growth of the monetary base (which is more or less under the Fed's control) and stick to it over the business cycle. This view is based on the idea that the money multiplier and velocity are relatively predictable across business cycles, but are rela-tively unpredictable within a cycle (e.g., see Fellner [12] and the reference to Fellner in Stein [37]). Others would say that the Fed should announce and maintain, over a period of several years, a path (within a range to accommodate fluctuations in velocity) for one or another of the monetary aggregates (e.g., M1). (Beryl Sprinkel, among others, has taken this posi-tion.) This procedure bypasses the monetary base as a target, and avoids unpredictability of the money multiplier. Still others argue that because velocity is relatively unpredictable, the Fed should announce and monitor a nominal GNP target range—the range to accommodate velocity fluctua-tions. (Robert Gordon [16] has espoused this viewpoint.)

On these issues, no firm consensus exists either among researchers or policy makers. For instance, a current debate is whether U.S. monetary policy during the period of fall 1979 to summer 1982 was or was not a "monetarist" experiment and, if it was, whether it was "successful" and should be resumed or "unsuccessful" and be abandoned. (See B. Friedman [13]; Pierce [32]; M. Friedman [15]; and Eisner and Pieper [11].) And, although the Fed continues to announce targets for the monetary aggre-gates, many "Fed watchers" are inclined to believe that nobody knows what the monetary policy is, or on what basis it might be changed. The Reagan administration has asked the Fed to announce a target path of slowly decel-erating money growth, but the Fed has not responded to the request. Some evidence collected by William Poole [33] suggests that, since October 1982, the Fed has been managing the Federal funds rate but the Fed denies this, even though some applaud them for doing so.

Resolution of these conceptual and operational issues concerning mone-tary policy matters is important to the stabilization policy issue. While monetary and fiscal policies tend to be conducted independently, each af-fects the outcome of the other, and the policy mix is perceived to be an important determinant of economic performance. I will say more about this matter later.

B. Fiscal Policy

A similar lack of consensus concerns the macroeconomic aims of fiscal policy and its ability to fulfill them. The so-called Keynesian view is that changes in some measure of the deficit can be manipulated to alter aggregate demand and smooth fluctuations in nominal GNP [3]. Being able to do so depends on the ability to forecast fluctuations far enough in advance to overcome the lags inherent in the process of enacting changes in taxes or spending programs, and to estimate the timing and magnitude of the impact of such discretionary changes. Both tasks are difficult to accomplish with any precision, particularly, predicting the time profiles of the multipliers and the amount of the discretionary change in real terms that actually will occur when the policy action is implemented [11].[6] The argument in favor of using fiscal policy for stabilization is based on the idea that relatively small temporary changes in income taxes generate predictable responses in spending [3]. But according to Eisner [9, 10], temporary tax cuts appear to be ineffective—because they are temporary.[7] The "Lucas critique" (Lucas [22])—that parameters estimated under one policy regime are substantially inaccurate as predictors of results of a policy change, because responses of market participants are based on expectations that are influenced by those changes—and the economic theory on which the "critique" is based suggest that all such efforts are at best in vain, and at worst destabilizing.

Thus, discretionary fiscal policy has been challenged on the grounds that such efforts—in varying degrees of frequency of "fine-ness" of tuning—have turned out to be procyclical and therefore destabilizing, that they impose the cost of inefficient resource allocations, and in any case are neither necessary nor sufficient to achieve their goal. This suggests to some (as noted above) that monetary policy is the better choice as a countercyclical instrument.

According to this view, deficit policy should be neutral with respect to cyclical stabilization.[8] Indeed policy strategy might be guided by an idea that Robert Lucas [23] attributes to Milton Friedman—that thinking about policy should be regarded as a problem in selecting stable, predictable policy rules. But defining a cyclically neutral deficit and constructing and implementing a budget that provides such a deficit is no simple task.

Stein [37] for example has suggested that a cyclically neutral deficit can be estimated from the nominal GNP path that is set as a target for monetary policy (space limitations prohibit discussion of other examples[9]). He emphasizes that while the purpose of such a policy is to provide stability and predictability, infrequent changes would be an acceptable part of such a policy. Such a suggestion is compatible with the view that the level of and change in the deficit may affect the structural parameters of the velocity relationship, and thus must be a consideration for monetary policy. (Gordon [17] refers to the deficit as a "constraint" on velocity.)

Focusing on the countercyclical neutrality of deficit policy does not deny that the level and composition of government spending and taxes, resulting from the interplay of economic conditions and decisions about national objectives, affect the allocation of resources and the distribution of income, and thus influence the structure of the economy.[10] Certainly, the budget elements operate as aggregate supply constraints that also affect the outcome of monetary policy, by influencing the way nominal GNP growth is shared between real output growth and inflation. Also, the level of the cyclically neutral deficit path, for example in relation to GNP, is important because of its implication for the accumulation of the stock of government debt. This matter is discussed in Section III.

III. Policy, Inflation and Capital Accumulation

Apart from the countercyclical issue discussed in the foregoing sketch, deficit policy has an allocative role that can be important for the stability and incline of the growth path of the economy. Certainly this subject is at the center of the current debate about U.S. economic and budget policy.

A risk associated with persistent large deficits is that, in the longer term, the share of GNP allocated to private capital formation will be reduced and real economic growth will be inhibited.[11] To the extent that an annual real deficit absorbs a larger share of annual real saving, and unless there is a balancing increase in the saving rate,[12] less is available to finance enough investment to maintain even a constant capital-to-output ratio. And, more important, the mounting stock of federal debt may grow faster than GNP and may absorb an increasing share of the stock of total outstanding credit (debt) relative to GNP. In addition to its potential for slowing growth, an incessant build-up of the federal debt-to-GNP ratio breeds the fear of and the potential for higher inflation.

These conclusions are found in recent research by several economists who examine projections of the debt-to-GNP ratio from diverse angles and obtain results with enough similarity to indicate a consensus. (See B. Friedman [14], de Leeuw and Holloway [8], Tobin [40], Gramlich [18], Miller [28], Sargent and Wallace [35], and Brunner [4]). These analyses indicate that in the long run the capital/output ratio is related to the ratio of government debt-to-GNP, that a prolonged increase in the government debt-to-GNP ratio is reason for concern about capital accumulation and/or inflation, and that a crucial element in the analysis—indeed for the longer-run stability of the economy—is whether the real interest rate is greater or smaller than the growth rate of real GNP.

The relationship between capital accumulation and inflation is a particularly significant issue for macroeconomic policy in the U.S.[13] The issue arises in the search for a low interest rate - high capital accumulation rate policy,[14] in which it is generally agreed that the path of future government deficits is to be lowered by slowing the growth of federal spending rather than by raising taxes.

As Brunner [4] points out, a noninflationary monetary policy is necessary but not sufficient for a low interest rate policy—it is also necessary to limit the growth in the government debt-to-GNP ratio. Expressing the interest rate as the sum of the real rate, an inflation premium, and a risk premium illuminates the problem: an inflationary monetary policy will raise expected inflation, while persistent but unsustainable growth in the government debt-to-GNP ratio will create uncertainty about future policy adjustments (e.g., reduced expenditures, increased taxes, or higher inflation) which will increase the risk premium embedded in the real rate.

Some major features in the analytical debate on this policy issue can be observed by examining two somewhat contending points of view. One view is espoused by James Tobin [41], who argues for tighter fiscal policy to allow the increase in money growth necessary to reduce interest rates and increase investment. In contrast, Thomas Sargent and Neil Wallace [35] argue for a lower deficit policy in order to *avoid* the money growth that inevitably would bring inflation. Both positions are based on models in which interest rates are determined in markets for stocks of financial assets, rather than being determined by the annual flow of saving and investment.

A. Tobin's Policy Mix

Tobin supports his policy prescription with an analysis based on an inventive, simple model he developed with William Buiter. To be sure, Tobin and Buiter (T-B) [44] do not assert that their model shows unambiguously that "tighter" fiscal policy and "looser" monetary policy will reduce the interest rate and increase capital formation—rather, they make the more modest point that according to their model these results can occur.

The T-B model is a type of portfolio balance model which involves demand functions for three assets—real capital, bonds, and money—and implies an underlying IS-LM framework. Thus the model focuses attention on the effect that fiscal and monetary policy has on asset prices and stocks. It also provides a role for expectations about price changes and a potential role for changes in those expectations. However, these characteristics are significantly circumscribed by several apparently innocuous but actually crucial choices in the construction and manipulation of the model.

In my opinion these modeling decisions are unwarranted. Once certain changes are made to incorporate more reasonable choices, the model's *qualitative* results become questionable, and its ability to support the policy conclusions attributed to it is weakened substantially. Therefore I suggest caution to those who are asked to accept policies that propose to enhance capital formation by increasing money growth to balance a lowered deficit path. This caution stems mainly from the way the T-B model treats inflation and expectations, and the implications these have for capital formation. In particular the model implies that increased inflation and inflationary expectations cause investors to increase investment in real capital.[15]

The T-B model does not acknowledge that during periods of inflation such as the late 1970s, existing assets that do not play a significant role in producing domestic real output can very often be preferred stores of value for some investors. As a result, in the T-B model, when increased actual and expected inflation cause investors to move out of bonds and money, their only alternative is to buy more real capital, thus bidding up its price. Since investment in output-producing (real) capital is a positive function of the price of real capital, the model implies that higher expected inflation stimulates more investment and higher future output. Because the model unrealistically restricts the avenue by which investors may attempt to escape from inflation, it implies a faulty prediction. For instance, it is not equipped to address the problem of stagflation that characterized the U.S. economy in the late 1970s. More importantly, this deficiency allows the model to overlook the economic distortion of the inflation tax and, therefore, to suggest that a policy of money-financed deficits is a suitable means to encourage capital formation.

The theoretical implication that inflation stimulates investment, and the efficacy of the associated policy proposal (that money-financed deficits can be used to encourage capital formation) can be denied by altering the model to include claims on real assets that do not produce real domestic output. This classification includes items such as gold, old unpotable wines, warehoused works of deceased artists, and real estate held for capital appreciation, as well as investments abroad.[16]

T-B say that it is not inflation *per se*, rather it is the future policy responses associated with inflation that discourage investment. This might be read to suggest a policy that allows inflation to creep upward or, at the extreme, to run unabated. Indeed, T-B show that in their steady-state model one possible outcome is that a higher rate of steady-state inflation can be accompanied by a higher capital-output ratio. But this result must implicitly assume the absence of any economic inefficiency being induced by a regime of permanent inflation.

It is important to note that the T-B steady-state analysis assumes that in the long run the deficit allows the economy to find a stable equilibrium. Whether the deficit path is stable depends in part on whether the real growth rate exceeds "the" real interest rate.[17] To be sure, in the T-B model the real debt-to-GNP ratio implied by the deficit path can be stabilized by allowing inflation to reduce the real value of the debt.[18] That is, the inflation tax "stabilizes" the economy.

T-B conclude their analysis by offering an answer to the question whether there is a long-run investment-oriented strategy that does not rely on deficits and inflation to diminish savers' preferences for liquid forms of wealth. Their answer is that the government—Federal Reserve Banks—could invest in private debt and equity securities. That is, presumably the government would issue money and debt and use the proceeds to purchase private securities, so that government debt would not "tie up" private savings. This plan seems to combine debt monetization and government ownership of privately managed businesses. In effect it would allow private business to acquire funds at the "government rate," similar to a federal credit program, except that it may apply to equity as well as debt.

Analysis of this inventive, "market-auxiliary" proposal is beyond the scope of this paper. However, we note that on other occasions Tobin has suggested recourse to a market-auxiliary arrangement. For instance, he has proposed an incomes policy to complement the "loosening" of the monetary policy component of the "policy-mix" in order to restrain inflation (see [42]).[19] In any case, T-B conclude that inflationary bias seems to be endemic in modern capitalist democracies, that it is foolish to think that the problem will be solved by adherence to monetary and fiscal rules, and that new additional policy instruments are required if inflation is to be controlled without slowing the growth of capital accumulation.

B. Tobin's "Capital Demise" Model

One interpretation of the T-B recourse to additional policy instruments is that they are not confident about the odds that a long-run capital accumulation policy can be based on the use of inflation to repudiate the debt. Indeed Tobin [43] analyzes the effect of an increase in the debt-to-GNP ratio under the assumption that monetary policy holds the base money-to-GNP ratio constant at the level required to maintain a constant (target) rate of inflation (4 percent).

The analysis is based on a simple growth model, similar to the one that implicitly underlies the T-B steady-state exercise referred to above. Although it is not readily apparent from the exposition of the model, the comparison of the real growth rate and the interest rate—given the size of the primary deficit—is a crucial determinant of the stability of the system.

Here Tobin shows that when the federal debt grows faster than output, it absorbs an increasing share of resources which are otherwise available to finance investment in the real productive capital that, in turn, is the source of improved productivity and living standards. As a result there is a slowdown of real economic growth which can lead to eventual impoverishment. As Tobin says, where the condition for steady-state equilibrium does not hold, "the economy is in real trouble" because net investment is negative and the capital output ratio declines at an increasing rate.

In this analysis Tobin's assumptions disavow an attempt to use inflation as a method for driving down the real interest rate,[20] and thus endeavor to stabilize the economy when the primary deficit is too heavy a load to be carried by real growth (given the real interest rate). However, as a theoretical matter it is my impression that such an attempt would fail in models of this type unless the inflation rate was rather substantial. The application of this result to the T-B model suggests the inadvisability of a program that would purport to encourage investment in real capital by inflating away the value of the government debt.

C. The Sargent-Wallace View of Policy Mix

Inflating away the value of the federal debt is also the concern—but not a policy recommendation—of Sargent and Wallace (S-W) [35]. They question the monetarist conclusion that a permanent deficit can be maintained without inflation; that is, they challenge the proposition that monetary policy (open market operations) can permanently control inflation even in a "monetarist economy."

The S-W challenge takes place on a specially constructed court, the specifications of which are as follows. (1) The economy is monetarist in that (a) the monetary base and the price level are closely connected; (b) the natural or equilibrium growth rates of population and real output are equal, and this rate and the real interest rate on govenment bonds are independent of monetary policy; and (c) the monetary authority can raise revenue through seigniorage. (2) The policy-mix "game" is defined by a dominant fiscal policy path; that is, the permanent primary deficit (the difference between tax revenues and government spending exclusive of debt interest) path is given and independent of current or future monetary policy.[21] S-W note that their analysis does not deny that monetary policy can permanently affect inflation when monetary policy can "go first" and effectively discipline fiscal policy. (3) The real rate of interest exceeds real output growth, so that, other things remaining unchanged, the federal debt-to-GNP ratio rises simply because borrowing must be increased to pay interest on existing debt.

The latter condition indicates the instability of the situation; eventually a limit to the acceptable debt/GNP ratio is reached (when interest payments absorb all of GNP, if not before.)[22] Thus, although the monetary authority may attempt to control inflation by restraining the growth of base money, it eventually must capitulate and increase the growth of money in order to generate seigniorage to finance the persistent deficit.

In general, the government's annual budget can be expressed as a cash-flow requirement which states that spending must be financed by the sum of tax revenues and issues of bonds and base money. This statement can be rephrased, with variables defined per unit of real GNP, as a relationship that equates the annual growth in the stock of bonds to the sum of the primary deficit plus interest on the government debt, minus the sum of the annual growth in the stock of base money plus the seigniorage earned as a result of the impact of inflation on the monetary base.[23]

By manipulating this relationship it can be shown that a stable equilibrium, where the government debt-to-GNP ratio is constant, can exist if the real rate of growth exceeds the real interest rate. If the reverse is true, nominal GNP growth in excess of the long-run trend can offset the margin of the interest rate over the growth rate. But in the long run, real output growth and inflation will tend toward their steady-state values and the difference between the real interest rate and the growth of real output becomes crucial. Indeed, in the steady state, where the ratio of base money to GNP is constant, if the real interest rate exceeds the growth rate, the debt-to-GNP ratio will grow without limit unless the inflation rate grows fast enough to generate the necessary seigniorage. Further algebraic manipulation shows that the required inflation rate is positively related to the primary deficit-to-GNP ratio, the government debt-to-GNP ratio and the difference between the real rate of interest and the real rate of growth, and negatively related to the ratio of base money to GNP.[24]

Thus, in the S-W model (and, some fear, a potential practice in the United States in the future) fiscal policy is dominant in the sense that it exists as a constraint for monetary policy. In this case the concept of the fiscal-monetary mix is that, given an exogenous fiscal policy, monetary policy becomes endogenous and is not available to pursue an anti-inflationary regime.

The S-W model with a simple quantity-theory-type money demand function (constant growth in base velocity) provides the straightforward result that a tight monetary policy during the period in which the real per capita government debt increases will result in a higher permanent inflation rate during the subsequent period. This is the case because—given the real interest rate, the real growth rate, the interest rate greater than the growth rate, the primary deficit and the date at which the maximum debt-to-GNP ratio is determined—a tighter monetary policy (lower money growth rate) implies a higher permanent maximum level of the debt-to-GNP ratio. The higher is that ratio from the time the maximum is reached onward, the more rapid is the required permanent money growth rate and therefore the higher the permanent inflation rate.[25]

To examine the current effect of expectations of future inflation, S-W modify their model by replacing the quantity-theory money demand with a

Cagan-type function in which desired real money balances vary inversely with expected inflation. From this model S-W derive the result that not only does tighter money in the present imply higher permanent inflation in the future, but—their "spectacular example"—it can also result in higher inflation "now," in the present (i.e., during the period prior to the date at which the monetary policy regime changes).

To the extent that the economy responds symmetrically to an increase in money growth, the S-W (and Liviatan [21], [SWL]) analyses seem to imply that a loose money growth policy would be desirable, in a dominant primary deficit regime, as a way to finance the deficit and to lower inflation as well. Moreover, a reader of S-W may note that the inflation rates are rather low in both the tight and easy money illustrations. But closer inspection of the SWL analysis indicates that very specialized assumptions, in which price-level inflexibility can cause the model economy to diverge along an unstable price-level path of accelerating disinflation, are required to preserve their conclusions. If, instead, prices are allowed to exhibit enough flexibility to respond to discrete changes in money growth, then the path of inflation mimics that of monetary growth. In this case the monetarist world reappears; the spectacular results such as those presented by SWL fail to emerge.

Thus, it is prudent to note that an attempt to implement a policy based upon the SWL spectacular examples could easily lead, at best, to a standard monetarist result in which easy money led to high rather than low inflation, or, at worst, to a highly unstable environment characterized by monetary policy-induced swings in inflation and in real growth as well. As a practical matter, the presence of short-term price inertia may allow a rapid money growth policy to have a transitory influence on real growth rather than on inflation, as a result of informational impediments and of uncertainties about the policy change. But while the lag between money and inflation can be long and variable, we know of no evidence which suggests that the lag is infinite or perverse—eventually the public "catches on" and the inflation rate accelerates under the rapid money growth policy.

Karl Brunner [4] also concludes that the S-W analysis makes clear the inflationary danger of an unrelenting primary deficit. He grants the analytical importance of the question whether the real interest rate is greater or less than the growth rate, but he argues that it would be unwise to take comfort in the fact that the growth rate exceeds the interest rate.[26]

Brunner makes some simple calculations based on the steady state expression relating the debt-to-GNP ratio to the primary deficit-to-GNP ratio, the base money-to-GNP ratio, the rates of inflation, real interest, and real output growth, and the difference between the latter two.[27] Assuming that base money per unit of GNP = .05 and the real interest rate minus the growth rate = (.02 − .03), he estimates that the steady-state inflation rate would range between 8 percent and 88 percent, depending on whether the primary deficit-to-GNP ratio is .01 or .05, where the government debt-to-GNP ratio is set at .5 (alternatively, the range of inflation rates is 17 percent–97 percent if the debt/GNP ratio is set at .33).

Brunner's conclusion is that a noninflationary monetary regime is likely to capitulate to a fiscal regime of persistent, large deficits, in an attempt to restrain growth in the debt/GNP ratio. He notes that since the calculations assume that the growth rate exceeds the real interest rate, the context is a non-Ricardian/Barro world where government debt is considered to be wealth, and therefore an increase in the government debt-to-GNP ratio can have real effects. His calculations show that under the assumption of a low steady-state inflation rate the projected increases in the debt/GNP ratio could be expected to be substantial enough to raise the real rate of interest. This may cause the interest rate to exceed the growth rate and to shift output away from investment and into consumption goods, with a subsequent negative effect on real output growth. Moreover, an increase in the interest rate which causes it to exceed the growth rate need not result in a cessation of real effects from the rising debt-to-GNP ratio (i.e., the system need not "become Ricardian" just because the interest rate exceeds the growth rate)

IV. Conclusion

The conclusions of this paper can be summarized briefly. Unresolved issues in macroeconomic analysis constitute obstacles to a consensus about how the economy responds to short-run countercyclical fiscal and monetary policy changes. This has led to a search for a cyclically neutral deficit policy. An important aspect of such a policy is its implication for the path of capital accumulation. A risk associated with persistent large deficits is that the government debt-to-GNP ratio might rise enough to reduce private capital formation and inhibit economic growth.

There are reasons to be skeptical of Tobin's proposal to encourage private real capital accumulation by loosening monetary policy when and because fiscal policy is tightened. This skepticism is based on an examination of the Tobin-Buiter model which is the theoretical support for the policy proposal. This model has several questionable features, and the absence of an inflation hedge that does not produce real output is a particularly important one. In the end it appears that the pro-capital results of the model stem from an unconvincing reliance on the dubious benefits of inflation.

The Sargent-Wallace analysis does not consider the capital formation issue; rather, it focuses on the extent to which a dominant primary deficit policy constrains monetary policy and on the inflationary implications of that constraint. The basic message from S-W is the warning that such a fiscal policy can foster a reliance on rapid inflation, a view consistent with other commentators on this subject. More questionable is the S-W spectacular example, wherein a "looser" monetary policy is associated with lower inflation than a "tighter" monetary policy would be, and the magnitude of the inflation rate is rather low in either case. The example requires very special assumptions, without which the S-W model implies an inflation rate which could quickly rise to over 100 percent.

The S-W analysis provides a method for exposing the extent to which an inflation tax is required to finance a conventional deficit when that deficit rises as a result of increasing interest costs, given a permanent primary deficit. Thus in this view monetary policy may be considered to be a veil behind which resides a flat tax that is used in preference to a legislated "conventional" tax.

In contrast, the Tobin-Buiter analysis suggests the possibility that under special circumstances an inflationary monetary policy can be relied upon to encourage increased capital formation. And it appears that their analysis is offered in support of an inflation policy to crowd-in private investment—a policy that implicitly relies on the use of a fiat tax, rather than more conventional "tax preferences" or direct subsidies.

Thus, stabilization policy is a mixture of fiscal and monetary policy, but the policy-mix issue is not exactly what it seems to be, particularly in the longer run. In reality, a monetary policy that is expansive enough to cause persistent inflation may be viewed more generally as a type of tax policy. The analytical use of the primary deficit facilitates our ability to see this. However, focusing on the primary rather than the conventional deficit can obscure the fact that a choice has thereby been made to resolve a given deficit with a fiat tax rather than with a spending reduction or a legislated tax increase.

Notes

1. President Carter also proposed a tax-based incomes policy to help slow inflation. The Reagan administration has explicitly rejected such proposals.
2. In the bluntly put view of Robert Lucas [23:259], "As an advice-giving profession we [economists] are in way over our heads."
3. Given space limitations and the policy orientation of this paper, I do not discuss explicitly the fundamental analytical question of whether the macroeconomy is appropriately modeled as a disequilibrium system or alternatively as an equilibrium system, and the related matter of the nature of the equilibrium concept at issue (e.g., stable deterministic versus stable stochastic). Similarly I only note here, but do not discuss further, that this question is prior to (more basic than) a conjecture regarding the reason that a given market appears not to have

cleared at some particular moment or over some time period, and that the variety of such conjectures includes cyclical fluctuation versus structural shift in some variables (such as employment), the existence of market imperfection (such as sticky wages), and response to actual or expected policy intervention. Consequently I do not discuss the implications that these matters have for the development of accurate estimates of the long-run dynamic paths of the significant endogenous macroeconomic variables, including the formation of expectations. Also I only allude to the fact that economic policy is developed under the severe constraint of the absence of adequate dynamic models, and that as a consequence, short-run analysis of policy change is hazardous because such analysis ignores outcomes that occur after the short run and therefore ignores the potential cost against which the policy gain must be assessed.

4. This section is drawn from Hoffman and Levy [19].

5. The Fed is advised to emphasize "goals for real output and employment growth consistent with a nonacceleration of inflation." Also see House Resolution 1569, which would require the Fed to set targets for real output as well as inflation and nominal GNP.

6. While acknowledging that monetary policy was tight, Eisner and Pieper present evidence that suggests that fiscal restraint unrecognized in official statistics deserves blame for the severity of the recession.

7. Observers of the U.S. policy debate might note (and perhaps question) that in the past several years *cuts* in the deficit have been advocated on the grounds that failure to do so would prevent, abort, or stifle the recovery from the 1982 recession. This counter-countercyclical viewpoint appears to be based on a confusion between the level of aggregate demand and its composition, and on the mistaken presumption that interest rates are determined by flow variables rather than by supply and demand for stocks of assets. However, see Mankiw and Summers [24] for an analysis that concludes that in the short run a personal tax cut may be contractionary—it depresses aggregate demand—because consumer spending generates more demand for money than do other components of G.N.P.

8. To the extent that Barro's [1] analysis applies, this policy issue does not arise because federal debt is not wealth; the present value of future taxes required to service and retire the debt neutralizes the bonds issued to cover the deficit.

9. de Leeuw and Holloway [8] have developed a cyclically adjusted budget concept, based on the trend level of real GNP as projected through the mid-expansion points in postwar business cycles, and have made estimates using U.S. data. Balancing this "mid-expansion" budget over the cycle would be neutral in the sense that federal debt would remain approximately unchanged. An alternative is to set deficit policy to stabilize the government debt-to-GNP ratio (see Congressional Budget Office [5]).

10. For a discussion of why the deficit—even adjusted to reflect the effect of inflation and interest rate changes on the real market value of the federal debt stock and to distill from the actual deficit the "passive" deficit that results from below-trend economic activity (i.e., some measure of the cyclically adjusted deficit)—is, as a residual, incapable of providing unambiguous information about either the short-run or long-run macroeconomic effects of fiscal policy, see U.S. Treasury Department [45]. For a discussion of fiscal policy that focuses consideration on the composition of the spending and revenue sides of the budget, see Council of Economic Advisers [6].

11. The extent to which capital accumulation contributes to growth is an unresolved empirical question, the discussion of which is beyond the scope of this paper.

12. Net capital inflow from abroad may increase enough to maintain the capital/output ratio.

13. This discussion is drawn from Hoffman and Mascaro [20].

14. More precisely, the objective is to increase capital accumulation, and a policy that raises the real interest rate because it raises the marginal productivity of real capital is not incompatible with a pro-capital-accumulation policy.

15. Space requirements force a focus on this issue; a more complete discussion of the limitations of the T-B model is in Hoffman and Mascaro [20].

16. As a hedge against inflation, the existence of such assets moderates the extent to which the so-called Mundell-Tobin real balances effect might be brought into play. In general this hypothesis holds that inflation reduces the real interest rate by reducing the value of real money balances, and hence wealth, thus increasing savings.

17. The precise definition of the relevant real interest rates depends on the specification of the model to be analyzed. This is discussed briefly below. For an extensive discussion see Barth, Iden, and Russek [2].

18. For example, the steady-state value of the real debt-to-GNP ratio can be expressed in terms of the policy parameters for government spending, taxes, and the share of bonds in the total of bonds and money; the real return on bonds; and the inflation rate. From this relationship it is clear that changes in government spending and taxes can be offset by changes in the inflation rate.

19. See Okun and Perry [31] for an analysis of the advantages and disadvantages of tax-based incomes policies (TIPS).

20. The model is sophisticated in that the federal government is able to borrow at a relatively low net rate (because it receives a good-credit-risk discount from the market and it taxes nominal interest income and therefore gains revenue from inflation).

21. McCallum [27] points out that a pure bond-finance policy is feasible, without inducing inflation, when the deficit is defined inclusive of interest payments. For this same case of the conventionally defined deficit, Liviatan [21] shows that the S-W spectacular result is reversed—a tight monetary policy is associated with *less* inflation.

22. Recall that in Tobin's "capital demise" model (discussed above), the rising government debt-to-GNP ratio results in a falling capital-output ratio. McCallum [27] examines the S-W hypothesis in a somewhat different theoretical structure and obtains a result which suggests an upper limit to bond finance of a persistent primary deficit, and which also may suggest an inconsistency with the Ricardo/Barro hypothesis (that individual utility maximizers will increase saving by enough to purchase the bond issue).

23. For the details of these equations see Hoffman and Mascaro [20] and the reference to Brunner [4] cited therein.

24. This negative relationship between the inflation rate and the base money-to-GNP ratio simply means that to raise a given amount of revenue from the inflation tax, the tax rate (inflation rate) can be lower, the higher is the tax base (money stock per unit of GNP). This relationship should not be confused with the positive relationship between the growth rate of the money stock and inflation.

25. Alternatively, the exercise can be formulated so that a specified maximum level of the debt-to-GNP ratio is used to determine the time at which the monetary policy regime changes, in which case tight money now implies that the limiting value of the debt-to-GNP ratio is reached sooner and thus the growth rate of base money and therefore the inflation rate must be raised sooner.

26. Darby [7] criticizes the S-W finding by challenging their necessary assumption that the real interest rate exceeds the growth rate, and presents U.S. data showing that the relevant interest rate—the after-tax real yield on government bonds—is likely to be below the real rate of growth. Miller and Sargent [30] rebut Darby on the grounds that increases in the debt/GNP ratio will raise the real interest rate on government bonds, relative to the real growth rate, so that eventually the assumed fiscal policy will drive the interest rate above the growth rate. Regarding empirical estimates of the real interest rate and real growth rate also see Barth, Iden, and Russek [2].

27. The algebraic expression for these calculations is the steady-state version of the equation referred to above, in note 23. As indicated in the text, this latter expression describes the cash flow reuqirements of the government budget, and thus is common to all analyses that examine the relationship among growth, government debt, and inflation. In symbols, the algebraic expression is $b = [1/(r - n)][m(p + n) - x]$, where b = the federal debt-to-GNP ratio, r = the real interest rate, n = the growth rate, m = the ratio base money to GNP, p = the inflation rate, and x = the primary deficit-to-GNP ratio.

References

[1] Barro, Robert, "Are Government Bonds New Wealth", *Journal of Political Economy*, 82, November/December 1974: 1095–1117.

[2] Barth, James; Iden, George; and Russek, Frank, "The Economic Consequences of Federal

Deficits: An Examination of the Net Wealth and Instability Issues," a paper presented to the Southern Economic Association Meetings, Atlanta, Georgia, November 1984.

[3] Blinder, Alan, and Solow, Robert, "Analytical Foundations of Fiscal Policy", in *The Economics of Public Finance*, The Brookings Institute, 1972, 3–115.

[4] Brunner, Karl, "Deficits, Interest Rates, and Monetary Policy," paper presented at the Cato Institute's Third Annual Monetary Conference, Washington, D.C., February, 1985.

[5] Congressional Budget Office, *The Economic Outlook*, Washington, D.C., February 1984.

[6] Council of Economic Advisers, "The Economic Report of The Council of Economic Advisers" in *The Economic Report of The President*, Washington, D.C., February 1985.

[7] Darby, Michael, "Some Pleasant Monetarist Arithmetic," *Federal Reserve Bank of Minneapolis*, Winter 1985, 32–37.

[8] de Leeuw, Frank, and Holloway, Thomas, "Measuring and Analyzing the Cyclically Adjusted Budget", in *The Economics of Large Government Deficits* Conference Series, no. 27. Boston, Mass., Federal Reserve Bank of Boston, 1983.

[9] Eisner, Robert, "Fiscal and Monetary Policy Reconsidered", *American Economic Review*, 59, December 1969: 897–905.

[10] ———, "What Went Wrong", *Journal of Political Economy*, 79, May/June 1971: 629–641.

[11] ———, and Pieper, Paul, "A New View of the Federal Debt and Budget Deficits," *American Economic Review*, 74, March 1984: 11–29.

[12] Fellner, William, testimony in *Legislation for Alternative Target for Monetary Policy*, Hearings before the Subcommittee on Domestic Monetary Policy of the Committee on Banking, Finance and Urban Affairs, House of Representatives, 98th Congress, 1st Session, April 26, 1983, 110–118.

[13] Friedman, Benjamin, "Lessons from the 1979–82 Monetary Policy Experiment", *American Economic Review*, 74, May 1984: 382–387.

[14] ———, "Implications of the Government Deficit for U.S. Capital Formation", in *The Economics of Large Government Deficits* Conference Series, no. 27. Boston, Mass., Federal Reserve Bank of Boston, 1983.

[15] Friedman, Milton, "Lessons from the 1979–82 Monetary Policy Experiment", *American Economic Review*, 74, May 1984: 397–400.

[16] Gordon, Robert, testimony in *Legislation for Alternative Targets for Monetary Policy*, Hearings before the Subcommittee on Domestic Monetary Policy of the Committee on Banking, Finance and Urban Affairs, House of Representatives, 98th Congress, 1st Session, April 26, 1983: 136–156.

[17] ———, "The Conduct of Domestic Monetary Policy", National Bureau of Economic Research, Working Paper 1221, October 1983.

[18] Gramlich, Edward M., "How Bad are the Large Deficits?" in *Federal Budget Policy in the 1980's*, Urban Institute Press 1985.

[19] Hoffman, Ronald and Levy, Mickey D., "Economic and Budget Issues for Deficit Policy", *Contemporary Policy Issues*, 3, Number 1, Fall, 1984–5: 96–114.

[20] Hoffman, Ronald, and Mascaro, Angelo, "The Fiscal-Monetary Policy Mix", paper presented to the Western Economic Association Conference, July 1985.

[21] Liviatan, Nissan, "Tight Money and Inflation", *Journal of Monetary Economics*, 13, January 1984: 5–15.

[22] Lucas, Robert "Econometric Policy Evaluation: A Critique", in Lucas, *Studies in Business Cycle Theory*, MIT Press, 1981, 104–130.

[23] ———, "Rules, Discretion, and the Role of the Economic Advisor", in Lucas, *Studies in Business Cycle Theory*, MIT Press, 1981, 248–261.

[24] Mankiw, N. Gregory, and Summers, Lawrence H., "Are Tax Cuts Really Expansionary?" National Bureau of Economic Research, Working paper No. 1443, Cambridge, Mass.

[25] Mascaro, Angelo, and Meltzer, Allen, "Long- and Short-Term Interest Rates in a Risky World", *Journal of Monetary Economics*, 11, 1983: 485–518.

[26] McCallum, Bennett, "Monetarist Rules in the Light of Recent Experience", *American Economic Review*, 74 May 1984: 388–391.

[27] McCallum, Bennett, "Are Bond Financed Deficits Inflationary? A Ricardian Analysis", *Journal of Political Economy*, 92, February 1984: 123–135.

[28] Miller, Preston, "The Inflation Risk in Projected Deficits," background paper prepared for the first annual Conference Board Economic Policy Forum, November 28, 1983.

[29] ——, "Higher Deficit Policies Lead to Higher Inflation", *Federal Reserve Bank of Minneapolis, Quarterly Review*, Winter 1983.

[30] Miller, Preston, and Sargent, Thomas, "A Reply to Darby", *Federal Reserve Bank of Minneapolis, Quarterly Review*, Winter 1985.

[31] Okun, Arthur, and Perry, George, eds., *Brookings Papers on Economic Activity, Special Issue, Innovative Policies to Slow Inflation*, 2:1978, The Brookings Institution, Washington, D.C.

[32] Pierce, James, "Did Financial Innovation Hurt the Great Monetarist Experiment?", *American Economic Review*, 74, May 1984: 392–396.

[33] Poole, William, *CEA memo*, 1985.

[34] Rivlin, Alice, ed., *Economic Choices, 1984*, The Brookings Institution, Washington, D.C., 1984.

[35] Sargent, Thomas, and Wallace, Neil, "Some Unpleasant Monetarist Arithmetic", *Federal Reserve Bank of Minneapolis, Quarterly Review*, Fall, 1981, 5: 1–17.

[36] Sidrauski, Miguel, "Rational Choice and Patterns of Growth in a Monetary Economy", *American Economic Review, Papers and Proceedings*, 57, May 1967: 534–44.

[37] Stein, Herbert, *An Agenda for the Study of Macroeconomic Policy*, Washington, D.C., American Enterprise Institute, 1982.

[38] ——, in *On Key Economic Issues*. AEI Studies, no. 399. Washington, D.C., American Enterprise Institute, 1984.

[39] ——, "Maybe Interest Rates Are Too Low", *Wall Street Journal*, August 17, 1983: 13–15.

[40] Tobin, James, "Budget Deficits, Federal Debt and Inflation in Short and Long Runs", in Albert T. Sommers, ed., *Toward a Reconstruction of Federal Budgeting*, The Conference Board, 1983.

[41] ——, in *On Key Economic Issues*. AEI Studies, no. 399. Washington, D.C., American Enterprise Institute, 1984.

[42] ——, "Okun on Macroeconomic Policy: A Final Comment", in Tobin, ed., *Macroeconomics, Prices and Quantities, Essays in Memory of Arthur M. Okun*, The Brookings Institution, 1983: 297–300.

[43] ——, " 'Crowding Out' Dynamics: A Simple Model", unpublished paper, December, 1984.

[44] Tobin, James, and Buiter, William, "Fiscal and Monetary Policies, Capital Formation and Economic Activity", in George M. Von Furstenberg, ed., *The Government and Capital Formation*, Cambridge, Mass., Ballinger: 73–151. 1980

[45] U.S. Treasury Depaartment, *The Effects on Prices of Financial Assets: Theory and Evidence*, U.S. Treasury Deprtment, Washington, D.C., 1984.

[46] ——, *Blueprints for Basic Tax Reform*, Washington, D.C., 1977.

Résumé

Le thème de ce rapport est que l'état actuel de l'analyse macroéconomique conseille d'être très prudent si on veut lui faire jouer un rôle actif dans la politique macroéconomique. Cette prudence repose sur la considération que, jusqu'à présent, nous n'en savons pas assez pour justifier des politiques actives; elle est aussi compatible avec la considération que maintenant nous en connaissons suffisamment pour estimer qu'une telle intervention ne peut manquer d'échouer. Ce rapport débute par l'exposé de ces problèmes d'analyse non résolus qui constituent des obstacles à un consensus sur la manière dont l'économie répond à court terme aux modifications de politique contracyclique d'ordre financier et monétaire. On indique brièvement les suggestions habituelles en vue d'une politique de déficit cycliquement neutre. Ensuite, on centre l'attention sur l'accroissement à long terme de la dette publique, lequel résulte forcément de la réalisation et de la projection de déficits constamment élevés. La discussion s'oriente alors vers les effets de la politique sur l'accumulation du capital et l'inflation et conduit à examiner la question d'une politique "mixte" monétaire et financière. Dans ce contexte, la politique de stabilisation est interprétée d'une manière un peu différente de celle des discussions de finances publiques, telles qu'elles sont généralement menées. Ce rapport conclut que, bien que la notion d'une politique mixte active financière et monétaire paraisse attrayante pour atteindre des objectifs de stabilisation à court ou long terme, il ne semble pas que, jusqu'à présent, cette politique puisse s'appuyer sur un cadre théorique crédible, sauf sous des hypothèses extrêmes et inhabituelles. Les principales analyses qui ont été développées à l'appui d'une telle politique ont dû se fonder sur des hypothèses extrêmes et des taux élevés d'inflation.

The General Equilibrium Approach: Relevant for Public Policy?

A. Lans Bovenberg*

I. Introduction

Applied general equilibrium analysis simulates the interaction of decentralized optimizing agents and government policies. The models are firmly rooted in the clearly specified theoretical framework of microeconomic theory. They attempt to give the Walrasian general equilibrium structure, as formalized by Kenneth Arrow and Gérard Debreu (see, e.g., [1] and [5]), operational content in order to evaluate alternative policy options. Arnold Harberger [18] introduced general equilibrium analysis to the field of public finance. Others have since extended his approach to study several public finance issues. For example, John Shoven and John Whalley [30] introduced numerical solution techniques, developed by Herb Scarf, to solve for disaggregated models with several tax instruments. For a survey of more recent extensions and applications, see [31].

This paper evaluates these extensions from the point of view of the policy maker. It focuses on the models whose primary purpose is the evaluation of fiscal reform rather than trade policy (see [31]), energy policy, or development policy (see, e.g., [7]). Section II examines some of the relative advantages of the applied general equilibrium framework while summarizing some results contained in recent literature. The weaknesses are discussed in section III, along with an evaluation of attempts to overcome them. It is argued that in order to enhance policy relevance, modelers should pay more attention to market distortions, structural rigidities, slow adjustment and distributional consequences.

In section IV, the importance of some of these elements is illustrated by simulating the incidence effects of a corporate income tax in a dynamic

*The author is an economist at the International Monetary Fund. He gratefully acknowledges the helpful comments of S. Devarajan, D. Wolfson, I.C.R. Byatt and other participants of the I.I.P.F. 41st Congress in Madrid. The views expressed in this paper are those of the author and do not necessarily reflect the official views of the International Monetary Fund.

The Relevance of Public Finance for Policy-Making. Proceedings of the 41st Congress of the International Institute of Public Finance. Madrid, 1985, pp. 33–43.

version of the Harberger model with imperfectly mobile capital, an added rigidity. Adjustment costs in the installation of sector-specific capital give rise to slow adjustment and redistribution of wealth. Section V concludes that the applied general equilibrium framework is a potentially useful instrument to examine how policy effects depend on behavioral responses of economic agents.

II. Strengths

This section summarizes and illustrates some of the relative advantages of the applied general equilibrium framework for policy making. In contrast to most econometric modeling, general equilibrium models explicitly derive the behavior of decentralized agents from basic parameters of taste and technology. Thus, when policy is changed, the elasticities can be expected to remain more stable than the coefficients of econometric models that are estimated on the basis of the old policy regime (see [27]). While microsimulations also simulate rational economic behavior, they abstract from the feedback from other markets. General equilibrium analysis, on the other hand, explicitly accounts for the interaction among markets. Thus, it can identify the most important links between markets that should be incorporated to avoid misleading policy advice. For an explicit comparison of the partial equilibrium and general equilibrium results on the distribution of tax burdens, see [8].

The use of a general equilibrium framework forces policy makers to consider changes in behavior and changes in market prices that their policy induces. Two examples illustrate the potential importance of these induced changes. First, public policies that aim at redistributing welfare may be undermined. Using a general equilibrium study for the Netherlands, Keller [24] and Wolfson [35] show that the changes in factor prices associated with a policy aimed at redistributing welfare by expanding the public sector significantly benefit skilled labor at the expense of unskilled labor. In a decentralized market economy, a more efficient distribution policy should focus on the redistribution of endowments (e.g., by education), rather than on transferring income through the public sector. The redistribution of earning abilities prevents the skills supplied by the relatively affluent from remaining scarce. Furthermore, such a policy does not require high implicit marginal tax rates on the relatively poor that promote social dependency.

Second, changes in behavior induced by increases in tax rates can erode the tax base. Using a model for the United States, Fullerton [13] examines the "Laffer curve" for broad-based labor taxes. Given reasonable estimates for labor supply elasticities and marginal tax rates, his results suggest that cuts in labor tax rates would not increase tax revenue. Stuart

[33], on the other hand, found that the Swedish government was operating in the "prohibitive" range, in which decreasing tax rates would yield an increase in revenue.

These results demonstrate how applied models can provide some quantitative insights regarding the empirical importance of qualitative effects that have been established by a priori theorizing. In addition, the model simulations reveal which market feedbacks and behavioral features are crucial for the order of magnitude of the effects. Thus, the parameters whose estimation should receive priority in empirical work are identified. To illustrate, Goulder, Shoven, and Whalley [16] report that the consequences of domestic tax policy in the United States do not significantly depend on the specification of foreign trade. They find, however, that the modeling of international capital flows can either substantially increase the domestic welfare gain (in the case of corporate tax integration), or turn a significant gain into a large loss (in the case of the introduction of a consumption tax). Given the demonstrated sensitivity of the results with respect to capital flows (see also [23]), more empirical and theoretical research to enhance our understanding of international capital flows in general and the effects of taxation in particular seems appropriate.

An important and recurring theme in the literature is the welfare costs of tax instruments. The estimation of these costs by completely removing taxes and replacing them by lump-sum taxes suggests rather low average efficiency costs. Ballard, Shoven, and Whalley [3], however, report that the marginal welfare costs from raising existing distorting taxes can be substantial. For the United States, they estimate that the marginal excess burden of one dollar of additional tax financing amounts to 15 to 50 cents. Given higher marginal tax rates, Hansson and Stuart [17] find even higher estimates for the Swedish economy, ranging from $0.69 to $1.29. These studies conclude that policy makers should take these costs into account when considering tax financing. Another policy implication is that substantial efficiency gains can be realized by lowering marginal tax rates and broadening the tax base, rather than by modifying the entire tax structure.

Focusing on only a few tax distortions in analytically tractable models can lead to misleading policy advice. In principle, applied models can simultaneously account for several tax instruments. Thus, they can contribute to the understanding of the interaction among various distortions. To illustrate, in an intertemporal equilibrium model for the United States, Jorgenson and Yun [22] specify differential tax treatments of capital income earned in the corporate sector and the noncorporate sector. These are the tax distortions considered by Harberger [18] and Shoven [29]. In addition, Jorgenson and Yun examine discrepancies in the treatment of capital income from long-lived and short-term assets, as well as double taxation of saving. (For a similar approach, see [15].) They find that equalizing the effective tax rates between the corporate and the noncorporate sector, while fixing government expenditures, reduces welfare of their representative household.

When the public authorities only have a restricted set of tax instruments to enhance social welfare, a general equilibrium model can help to provide some intuition concerning the relationship among structural features of an economy (such as behavioral parameters), social welfare functions, and a closer to optimal structure of prices, taxes, and public production (see, e.g., Heady and Mitra [20]). In this way, it can contribute to our understanding of equity/efficiency trade-offs, as well as to an estimation of the social costs of limitations on a government's tax powers. Furthermore, the models provide a potentially powerful framework to estimate the shadow prices of goods and factors that are used for the evaluation of public projects in distorted economies (see [6]).

III. Weaknesses

Given the strengths mentioned above, this section examines some limitations of the applied general equilibrium framework. The richness of most model structures, particularly the dynamic ones, does not allow for the simultaneous estimation of all parameters. The typical modeler chooses analytically convenient functional forms and uses econometric estimates out of the empirical literature (see [21], however, for a more econometric approach). Thus, the models can be used to explore the policy implications of empirical findings on decentralized behavior.

Given the limited information concerning parameters, functional forms, and model specifications, and in the absence of statistical information regarding these sources of uncertainty, the simulated policy effects should be interpreted with appropriate judgment and care. This is especially the case when policy impacts turn out to be rather sensitive to particular parameters. To illustrate, different types of government financing (such as debt, capital taxes, etc.) can have markedly different consequences, depending on the intertemporal preferences (such as mutual caring within families) and the liquidity constraints that underlie savings behavior (see, e.g., [11], [25]). Econometric research has not yet been able to discriminate between competing hypotheses concerning these issues (and similar issues such as international capital mobility; see section II). Policy makers need to be aware that the predictive value of the point estimates can be extremely limited. The development of the general equilibrium framework as a predictive tool has outpaced the availability of information on behavior and other detailed data. The potential of the models may be more fully realized when more and better information becomes available.

A weakness of almost all models is the specification of financial behavior and portfolio decisions. Typically, an exogenous financial structure of firms independent of taxes is assumed. For an attempt to model portfolio behavior in a general equilibrium framework, see [32]. For monetary phenomena, see [12]. Additional work on financial behavior and the behavior under uncertainty seems to be worthwhile. The same holds true for tax evasion, an important issue policy makers face and that the models have not yet begun to address.

Regarding the specification of the tax system, it is typically assumed that marginal tax rates equal average tax rates, which can be misleading. For countries with an elaborate welfare system, the high marginal tax rates implicit in transfer programs (and their consequences) need further study. For the United States, Fullerton and Gordon [14] find that, following the dramatic shortening of asset lives for depreciation allowances in 1981, average tax rates provide a poor characterization of the marginal rates on capital income.

The perfect competition framework of the models is challenged by Harris [19]. He demonstrates the feasibility of incorporating industrial organization features of imperfect competition and scale economies out of recent theoretical work on product markets in an empirical general equilibrium model. He finds that ignoring imperfect competition features results in seriously underestimating the benefits of trade liberalization. The policy implications are that efforts to promote free trade are well founded on grounds of gains in efficiency. Thus, market structures significantly affect policy effects. This may not only apply to product markets but to noncompetitive labor markets as well.

In order for the models to be used more fruitfully for the study of welfare effects in a far from first-best world, incorporation of additional market imperfections and distortions is needed. In this respect, the public finance models have lagged behind the theoretical and development literature on rent-seeking accompanying trade restrictions (see, e.g., [7], [26]), nontariff barriers (such as voluntary import constraints), segmentation of labor and financial markets, fixed prices and rationing (see, e.g., [28]).

Most public finance models have emphasized aggregate welfare effects. More attention to distributional effects, however, would enhance the policy relevance of the models. Typically, aggregate welfare measures are quite arbitrarily computed as the sum of compensating variations. While other summary measures have been proposed (see, e.g., [9]), in the absence of an explicit social welfare function there always remains an element of arbitrariness. Thus, a detailed account of who gains and who loses is needed.

By retaining Harberger's assumptions concerning instantaneous adjustment, most models tend to overestimate efficiency effects, while underestimating distributional impacts. With a proper modeling of segmented markets and other factors that impede adjustment, larger changes in relative prices are required to achieve quantity adjustment. Relative price movements, however, not only reallocate resources, they also redistribute income.

Integrating distributional consequences with theories about political behavior and information on the political power structure can contribute to a deeper understanding of the political pressures that policy makers face. Political forces must allow for the redistribution implied by price adjustment when relative prices clear markets. Political pressures can result in market intervention (such as protectionism and price controls) in an attempt to preserve the status quo, thereby preventing adjustment.

In order to inform policy makers of the political pressures that particular policies (or external shocks) may generate, a disaggregation of households according to socioeconomic characteristics or sources of income is required. Most public finance models disaggregate households according to their income level. Policies that have similar consequences for the overall distribution may have dramatically different effects on the composition of the rich and the poor, and thus can have quite divergent political implications.

An example of an appropriate disaggregation is provided by Auerbach and Kotlikoff [2]. Focusing on intergenerational incidence, they disaggregate the households according to age. They demonstrate that the introducton of a consumption tax to replace a wage tax entails a significant redistribution between retirees and younger cohorts. This occurs because the agents are locked into their patterns of work and retirement, and thus retirees are dependent on capital income. Other policies that redistribute resources across generations (such as social security and government debt) can be evaluated in properly disaggregated models (see [25]).

IV. An Illustration

In this section the importance of slow adjustment is illustrated within the setting of an intertemporal equilibrium version of the Harberger model in which capital is not perfectly mobile. This illustration is chosen because the structure of the Harberger model is quite well known, and it underlies the theoretical framework of most applied general equilibrium tax models. The model simulations also provide an opportunity to illustrate the important relation between slow adjustment and distributional effects using a timely and relevant tax policy issue—a reduction of the corporate income tax.

Starting from an initial steady state, a balanced budget reduction of the corporate income tax compensated for by an increase in labor taxes is simulated. An intertemporal equilibrium is characterized by decentralized intertemporal optimizing behavior with perfect foresight. All households maximize additive separable utility functions over an infinite time horizon. Inertia in the capital allocation between the corporate and noncorporate sector is captured by marginal adjustment costs that rise with the rates of industry-specific investment. With dynamic optimizing behavior, these adjustment costs give rise to Q-theory type of investment functions. Q is the ratio of the market value and the replacement value of capital (see, e.g., [34]). With unanticipated policy shocks, rental rates differ across industries and initial adjustment is absorbed by the financial market valuations of sector-specific capital. Given perfect foresight, these valuations reflect the future earnings. With sector-specific investment guided by these valuations, investment behavior is forward-looking. Assuming stability, the investment responses cause the interindustry capital allocation to adjust gradually over time so that capital is mobile in the long run. A complete description of the model and the solution technique is available in [4].

The parameters are given in the note to Table 1. They are a crude representation of the U.S. economy. The adjustment costs parameter is taken from [34]. The implications of a larger investment elasticity with respect to Q that is implicit in slower rising adjustment costs are explored in case II. Case III simulates perfect capital mobility, while infinitely elastic saving behavior is examined in case IV. The role of larger substitution elasticities in demand is analyzed in case V. Case IV assumes a lower initial steady-state ratio of gross investment and the value of the capital stock reflecting smaller depreciation rates. The sensitivity analysis illustrates how one can analyze the relation between structural features of an economy and policy effects.

The simulation results presented in the table suggest that in the absence of adjustment costs (Case III), the policy change is in the interest of all wealth holders. With Summers' [34] estimate for the investment elasticity, however, real human wealth declines (Case I). With smaller depreciation rates (Case VI), labor suffers larger losses. Even with infinitely elastic saving (Case IV), the adjustment costs embody enough rigidity in the economy to prevent labor from gaining. Furthermore, the rigidities cause a substantial redistribution of wealth among the two types of capital and a significant reduction of economy-wide welfare effects.

The policy implications are that in the presence of real-world inertia, unanticipated tax reforms tend to induce a significant redistribution of wealth, implying potential political pressures. In addition, the efficiency gain might be more moderate than is suggested by the traditional public finance models that deal with sectoral capital taxes and ignore these inertia (see, e.g., [15] and [22]).

From the numerical simulations, it appears that incorporating the adjustment costs implicit in the Q-theory of investment is relevant for policy.

Table 1

Numerical Results for a Permanent Decrease in the Corporate Income Tax from 25 Percent to 24.25 Percent

Case	I Bench-mark	II $\sigma_x = 1$	III $\sigma_x = 0$	IV $\sigma_c = 0$	V $\sigma_H = 5$ $\sigma_I = 5$	VI $xg'(x) = 0.047$
			(Percentages)			
Economy-wide welfare effect	0.043	0.048	0.058	0.044	0.043	0.036
Welfare effect, aggregate capital	0.80	0.64	0.33	0.75	0.80	0.77
Welfare effect, corporate capital	1.46	1.13	0.33	1.41	1.63	1.41
Welfare effect, non-corporate capital	0.14	0.15	0.33	0.09	−0.03	0.13
Welfare effect, labor	−0.016	0.003	0.037	−0.010	−0.016	−0.037

Note: Benchmark parameter values: rate of time preference = 0.03; population growth = 0.01; productivity growth = 0.01; capital share in gross production = 0.25; production share corporate sector = 0.5; initial ratio investment and value capital stock $xg'(x) = 0.067$; tax rates on capital = 0.25; tax rate on labor = 0.25; elasticity marginal utility $\sigma_c = 1$; elasticity of adjustment costs in investment (the inverse of the elasticity of investment with respect to Q) σ_x = 2; substitution elasticities in demand σ_H, $\sigma_I = 1$; substitution elasticity in production between labor and capital = 1. In cases II–VI, parameters are changed according to headings.

Welfare effects are computed as the change in lifetime resources needed to produce the change in welfare realized in the alternative tax regime.

Thus, further study on the nature and on the empirical significance of these adjustment costs should be an important research priority.

V. Conclusions

By explicitly modeling the mechanisms through which policy affects decentralized decisions, applied general equilibrium models provide a useful analytical framework for sound policy discussion. Policy makers are encouraged to make explicit their assumptions concerning decentralized behavior, thereby revealing differences in the perception of economic and political behavior as well as conflicting political preferences. In addition, the general equilibrium framework indicates which linkages between markets and agents are crucial for the effects of policy.

In this paper it is argued that general equilibrium modeling provides a powerful analytic framework that has not yet been fully explored for policy analysis. Several policy-relevant issues such as the relation between inelastic behavior, adjustment costs, distributional effects, market intervention, and political pressures can be studied within the framework. Given recent advances in economic theory, computer technology, solution techniques (models can be solved on microcomputers) and the gathering and organization of disaggregated data (social accounting matrices have been constructed for numerous countries), the models have the potential to become more useful for policy analysis.

Taking into account the weaknesses of the models (section III), however, the quantitative results should only be seen as indicative of the rough order of magnitude of the policy effects, given particular assumptions about economic behavior as well as about political and institutional responses. Given the limitations of any prediction that depends on political and economic behavior of people, policy makers should not expect the models to give precise predictions. The models find their use for policy analysis not so much in prediction as in analyzing how medium-run and long-run adjustments depend on behavioral and technical assumptions. While it is assumed that the model solutions exert a certain pull on the economy, the simulations should always be supplemented with what one believes and knows about the economic, institutional, and political world, and how that complex real world relates to the stylized model. Besides practical and political judgment, the analysis of simple analytic general equilibrium models remains extremely important. In order to evaluate the numerical results provided by large models, policy makers should understand the main mechanisms that drive the simulations. A good example of an appropriate modeling strategy is described in Dixon et al. [10]. These modelers have built a small version of their larger model in order to enhance the understanding of the important causal linkages. Numerical simulation of large models can never replace sound economic reasoning. The best they can do is to add to economic intuition. General equilibrium analysis should induce policy makes to start, rather than stop, thinking.

References

[1] Arrow, K., and Hahn, F., *General Competitive Analysis*, San Francisco, Holden-Day, 1971.

[2] Auerbach, A., and Kotlikoff, L., "National Savings, Economic Welfare, and the Structure of Taxation", in *Behavioral Simulation Methods in Tax Policy Analysis*, ed. M. Feldstein, Chicago, University of Chicago Press, 1983.

[3] Ballard, C., Shoven, J., and Whalley, J., "General Equilibrium Computations of the Marginal Welfare Costs of Taxes in the United States", *American Economic Review*, 75, March 1985: 128–30.

[4] Bovenberg, A. L., "Capital Accumulation and Capital Immobility: Q-Theory in a Dy-

namic General Equilibrium Framework," unpublished Ph.D. dissertation, University of California, Berkeley, 1984.

[5] Debreu, G., *Theory of Value*, New York, John Wiley, 1959.

[6] Dervis, K., Martin, R., and van Wijnbergen, S., "Shadow Pricing, Foreign Borrowing, and Resource Extraction Policies in Egypt", World Bank Working Paper, Washington, D.C.

[7] Dervis, K., de Melo, J., and Robinson, S., *General Equilibrium Models for Development Policy*, New York, Cambridge University Press, 1982.

[8] Devarajan, S., Fullerton, D., and Musgrave, R. A., "Estimating the Distribution of Tax Burdens", *Journal of Public Economics*, 13, April 1980: 155–82.

[9] Diewert, W. E., "The Measurement of Waste and Welfare in Applied General Equilibrium Models", mimeo., University of British Columbia, Vancouver, 1982.

[10] Dixon, P., Parmenter, B., Sutton, J., and Vincent, D., *ORANI: A Multi-Sectoral Model of the Australian Economy*, Amsterdam, North-Holland, 1981.

[11] Evans, O., "Tax Policy, the Interest Elasticity of Saving, and Capital Accumulation: Numerical Analysis of Theoretical Models", *American Economic Review*, 73, June 1983: 398–410.

[12] Feltenstein, A., "Money and Bonds in a Disaggregated Open Economy", in *Applied General Equilibrium Analysis*, ed. H. Scarf and J. Shoven, New York, Cambridge University Press, 1984.

[13] Fullerton, D., "On the Possibility of an Inverse Relationship between Tax Rates and Government Revenues", *Journal of Public Economics*, 19, October 1983: 3–22.

[14] Fullerton, D., and Gordon, R., "A Reexamination of Tax Distortions in General Equilibrium Models", in *Behavioral Simulation Methods in Tax Policy Analysis*, ed., M. Feldstein, Chicago, University of Chicago Press, 1983.

[15] Fullerton, D., King, A., Shoven, J., and Whalley, J., "Corporate Tax Integration in the United States: A General Equilibrium Approach", *American Economic Review*, 71, September 1983: 677–91.

[16] Goulder, L., Shoven, J., and Whalley, J., "Domestic Tax Policy and the Foreign Sector: The Importance of Alternative Foreign Sector Formulations to Results from a General Equilibrium Tax Analysis Model", in *Behavioral Simulation Methods in Tax Policy Analysis*, ed. M. Feldstein, Chicago, University of Chicago Press, 1983.

[17] Hansson, I., and Stuart, C., "Tax Revenue and the Marginal Cost of Public Funds in Sweden", mimeo., University of California, Santa Barbara, 1983.

[18] Harberger, A., "The Incidence of the Corporation Income Tax", *Journal of Political Economy*, 70 (3), June 1962, 215–40.

[19] Harris, R., "Applied General Equilibrium Analysis of Small Open Economies with Scale Economies and Imperfect Competition", *American Economic Review*, 74, December 1984, 1016–32.

[20] Heady, C., and Mitra, P., "Restricted Redistributive Taxation, Shadow Prices and Trade Policy", *Journal of Public Economics*, 17, February 1982: 1–22.

[21] Jorgenson, D., "Econometric Methods for Applied General Equilibrium Modeling", in *Applied General Equilibrium Analysis*, ed. H. Scarf and J. Shoven, New York, Cambridge University Press, 1984.

[22] Jorgenson, D., and Yun, K.-Y., "Tax Policy and Capital Allocation", mimeo., Harvard University, Cambridge, Mass., 1984.

[23] Keller, W. J., *Tax Incidence: A General Equilibrium Approach*, Amsterdam, North-Holland, 1980.

[24] Keller, W. J., "Effects of Education, Technology, and Public Expenditures on the Distribution of Income", *Journal of Public Economics*, 15, 1981: 235–49.

[25] Kotlikoff, L., "Taxation and Savings: A Neoclassical Perspective", *Journal of Economic Literature*, 22, December 1984: 1576–1629.

[26] Krueger, A., "The Political Economy of the Rent-Seeking Society", *American Economic Review*, 64, June 1974: 291–303.

[27] Lucas, R. E., "Econometric Policy Evaluation: A Critique", in *The Phillips Curve and Labor Markets*, ed. K. Brunner and A. Metzler, Carnegie-Rochester Conference Series on Public Policy, Vol. 1, Amsterdam, North-Holland, 1976.

[28] Neary, J., and Roberts, K., "The Theory of Household Behavior under Rationing," *European Economic Review*, 13, January 1980: 25–42.

[29] Shoven, J., "The Incidence and Efficiency Effects of Taxes on Income from Capital", *Journal of Political Economy*, 84, December 1976: 1261–83.

[30] Shoven, J., and Whalley, J., "A General Equilibrium Calculation of the Effects of Differential Taxation of Income from Capital in the U.S.", *Journal of Public Economics*, 1, February 1972: 281–322.

[31] Shoven, J., and Whalley, J., "Applied General Equilibrium Models of Taxation and International Trade: Introduction and Survey", *Journal of Economic Literature*, 22, September 1984: 1007–51.

[32] Slemrod, J., "A General Equilibrium Model of Taxation with Endogenous Financial Behavior", in *Behavioral Methods in Tax Policy Analysis*, ed. M. Feldstein, Chicago, University of Chicago Press, 1983.

[33] Stuart, C., "Swedish Tax Rates, Labor Supply, and Tax Revenues", *Journal of Political Economy*, 89, October 1981: 1020–38.

[34] Summers, L., "Taxation and Corporate Investment: a Q-Theory Approach", *Brookings Papers on Economic Activity*, 1981, 1: 67–127.

[35] Wolfson, D., "Pen and Tinbergen on Income Distribution", *De Economist*, 127, July 1979: 446–58.

Résumé

Ce rapport évalue l'importance de l'analyse d'équilibre général pour l'analyse politique. Il discute les forces potentielles d'un cadre d'équilibre général appliqué et résume quelques uns des enseignements que l'on peut en tirer en politique publique. Après examen de certaines de ses insuffisances, le rapport expose de récents efforts pour surmonter ces limitations. On avance qu'en incorporant d'autres imperfections du marché et des facteurs qui empêchent un rapide ajustement, on rehausserait la pertinence des modèles pour élaborer une politique. En outre, il faut mettre davantage l'accent sur les effets de distribution. Si on simulait les conséquences distributives de l'impôt sur le revenu des sociétés dans la version d'un équilibre intertemporel du modèle de Haberger, où le capital n'est pas parfaitement mobile, on illustrerait l'importance des rigidités de la modélisation. Le rapport conclut que les modèles d'équilibre général appliqué sont potentiellement d'utiles instruments pour chercher comment le comportement économique et politique affecte les conséquences d'une politique.

Is Cost-Benefit Analysis a Bastard Science?

Ezra J. Mishan

As Minerva rose fully formed from the head of Jupiter, so cost-benefit analysis entered the world as the sturdy offspring of a single parent, welfare economics: indeed, in original intent and in continued application it may be rationalized by the criterion commonly attributed to Kaldor and Hicks in 1939. Insofar as the term "bastard science" is pertinent, it is not so much the pedigree of the subject that is at issue as its scientific legitimacy. Such warrant as there is for skepticism in this connection may be extended as well to practically the whole field of economics. Among infidels such as myself, it has long been accepted that the "science" of economics can never come within bowling distance of the physical sciences in the numerical accuracy of its predictions. Econometric studies applied to those parts of macroeconomic theory that are currently believed to be relevant to economic policy serve also as salutary reminders of year-to-year numerical revision by economists of familiar economic relationships in hectic endeavors to keep abreast of behavioral, institutional, technological, and political changes which are inescapable features of the modern dynamic economy. As for the irrepressible flow of theoretical refinements in microeconomics—in theories of consumer behavior, in factor price theorems, in golden-path formulations, in general equilibrium theory, and so on—which undoubtedly possess some aesthetic or heuristic value, their influence on economic policy is so slight as to be virtually indiscernible.

In contrast, the theory and practice of cost-benefit analysis (CBA) does have a perceptible influence on economic policy. Estimates of the net benefits conferred by public projects or programs do enter as a significant component in the political decision-making process. For this reason, at least, doubts about the validity of cost-benefit techniques are of more than academic interest. They are a matter of public concern.

The Relevance of Public Finance for Policy-Making. Proceedings of the 41st Congress of the International Institute of Public Finance. Madrid, 1985, pp. 45–54.

I. Defects in the Application of CBA

I shall say least about the criterion itself, for whether or not the public, in its ethical capacity, regards the fulfillment of the Kaldor-Hicks, or net-benefit, criterion as an acceptable criterion, it is a fact of life that governments themselves regard a cost-benefit calculation as a relevant agendum in many of their decisions. The economist may therefore legitimately restrict his attention to those techniques which, if pursued consistently, will produce estimates of the required net-benefit magnitude.

In principle, then, he is engaged in a piece of positive economics and need claim no more than that his resultant net-benefit estimates are as close an approximation to the hypothetically correct ones as are within his power to achieve—given the time and resources at his disposal.

As it happens, however, economists cannot truthfully claim as much. Owing in part to the influence of a number of well-known guidebooks sponsored by international agencies (OECD, U.N., World Bank) purporting to offer expertise to planners in "third-world" countries, the very concept of net benefit—properly understood as the algebraic sum of individual valuations (positive and negative) of the economic change in question—has become obfuscated as a result either of political predilection or of recourse, for practical convenience, to recommended formulae or rules of thumb. Terms such as "the shadow price of labor" or "the shadow price of investment" are often enough mistaken by students for basic cost-benefit concepts and so serve to distract the mind from a more comprehensive conception of the issues involved.

Again, excessive absorption in technique—in methods of setting up and solving problems—occasionally results in popular formulations that are at odds with the essential concepts. Only recently, and with manifest reluctance, economists are coming to abandon a calculation of the value of life based upon an individual's expected future production and consumption[1] and, indeed, have not yet given up valuing health, or disease in much the same way, nor yet given up valuing the worth of a university degree by reference chiefly to expected earnings differentials.

If, therefore, we conclude that CBA is not wholly a respectable method of procedure, it is partly because of the political biases of writers and partly because, even among otherwise competent professionals, enthusiasm sometimes triumphs over judgment. Moreover, application of CBA is still inhibited by residual theoretical confusion while, at the same time, its status remains uncertain and will continue to do so until the limitations inherent in any economic calculation of net benefits are clearly recognized.

II. Remediable Errors in Economic Calculation

The brief exposition which follows aspires to impart perspective chiefly by differentiating between remediable and irremediable weaknesses in an ideal calculation of net benefits, as defined.

Those which I take to be remediable arise from fuzziness of conception or from intellectual error. Fuzziness still surrounds the exact conceptual measure of benefit (or loss) to be adopted since, as every economist should know, the individual's valuation of a change, from the existing situation (1) to a new or proposed situation (2), can differ according to whether we employ CV^{12} (the compensating variation in moving from the given situation 1 to an alternative situation 2) or CV^{21} (the compensating variation in moving, instead, from the alternative situation 2 to the given situation 1), where the measure CV^{21} is by definition equal to the measure EV^{12} (the equivalent variation, as defined by Hicks, in moving from 1 to 2). In consequence, it is easy to construct hypothetical examples in which, for a community of two or more persons, $\Sigma CV^{12} > 0$ at the same time as $\Sigma CV^{21} > 0$, or else $\Sigma CV^{12} < 0$ at the same time as $\Sigma CV^{21} < 0$.

Demonstrations of this seeming paradox were originally illustrated within the simplified format of a general equilibrium context. And within that context the paradox was apparently resolved in 1973, when it was shown that the existence simultaneously of both $\Sigma CV^{12} > 0$ and $\Sigma CV^{21} > 0$—the seemingly contradictory ranking of two equilibrium collections of goods—invariably indicates that the combination of individual welfares produced by each of the two equilibrium collections of goods is also a distinct (efficient) distribution of a single hypothetical collection of goods. Hence no allocative ranking of the original collections of goods is possible; only a distributional ranking is possible.[2]

Later on, it was also shown that within a *partial* economic context, one more relevant to CBA, the same "paradox"—both $\Sigma CV^{12} > 0$ and $\Sigma CV^{21} > 0$—can still arise. The crux of the "contradiction" within this partial context, however, no longer turns on the two different equilibrium set of prices generated by the alternative equilibrium collections of goods (as it does within the general equilibrium model). It arises instead from the introduction of one or more collective goods or bads in the changeover from a given situation 1 to an alternative situation 2. Thus, inasmuch as each individual's valuation of any nonmarket good or bad turns on whether he is deemed to have *to pay* for the nonmarket good (or the removal of the nonmarket bad), or else *to receive payment* in lieu of the nonmarket good (or in lieu of the removal of the nonmarket bad), it is again easy enough to contrive hypothetical, though quite plausible, examples in which both $\Sigma CV^{12} > 0$ and also $\Sigma CV^{21} > 0$.

A unique aggregate valuation in the movement from the partial equilibrium in one situation to the partial equilibrium of the alternative situation
would therefore require prior determination of property rights. For only
when the relevant property rights are assigned can we determine who is to
pay compensation for infringing them whenever a nonmarket bad is created
in moving from one situation to the other. Nonetheless, it has been argued
on pragmatic grounds that, in the absence of legally defined property
rights, recourse to the CV[12] measure—at least within a partial economic
equilibrium context—is likely to be satisfactory.[3]

Again, the belief that the validity of the net-benefit estimate depends
upon the assumption of constancy of tastes over the project's time span is
unwarranted. Only if the net-benefit figure were to be interpreted as an
index of the change in social welfare would the assumption be necessary.
But the net-benefit criterion, whether or not it commands a consensus,
need not be supposed—nor can it in fact be reasonably supposed—to carry
this implication. Net benefit is defined so that it can be part of a positive
economics, bereft of any commendatory overtones.

When we turn to intellectual errors, three are commonly found in the
literature on consumer surplus. The first is quite elementary and resides in
the argument that a net consumer surplus figure is obtained by subtracting
from the area of a positive surplus resulting, say, from a fall in the price of
good x, the "negative" surpluses associated with the "negative" areas created
by the leftward shifts of the demand curves for substitute goods (and doing
the reverse for goods that are complementary with x). In fact, any change in
the price of good x, *ceteris paribus*, entails a general reshuffling of expenditures on all the other goods in order that the consumer avail himself of the
opportunity for gain (or for reduction of loss). But, as evident from Hicks'
general formula of 1942, the areas resulting from such reshuffling of expenditures on other goods (whose prices are unchanged) have no bearing on the
net gain or loss as measured by the price change of good x.[4] Any constraints
imposed on the individual's chosen reshuffling reduces to that extent his
consumer gain, there being (in the limiting case) no consumer gain whatever
if he is prevented from changing in any way the original pattern of his
expenditures.

Second, there is the alleged path-dependency problem: when the prices
of two or more goods change, the resulting consumer surplus aggregate is
said to depend, in general, on the order in which the consumer surpluses
are measured.

That a path-dependency mathematical theorem exists is true, but that
it can properly be applied to this consumer surplus problem is false. What
has been overlooked is that in the measuring procedure adopted by the
economist, he is constrained to add the consumer surpluses of two or more
price changes in a particular order. So far as the consumer himself is

concerned, however, he experiences a unique change in his welfare in consequence of a *simultaneous* change in the price of a number of goods. The economist is therefore at liberty to add the relevant consumer-surplus areas in any order as, in any case, he does in project evaluation where such areas are derived from estimates of market demand curves, these serving as a proxy for an ideal aggregation of compensated demand curves.

However, and here we come to the third common error, the appropriate *ceteris paribus* for the demand curves of the two or more goods whose consumer surpluses for a simultaneous fall in their prices requires special attention to any adopted sequence for their suggestion. For if, in the *ceteris paribus* of each of the relevant demand curves, the *original* price in each of the other one or more goods is held constant, the resulting consumer surplus calculation will be an overestimate if the goods are substitutes, and an underestimate if they are complements. *Per contra*, if the *subsequent* price of the other one or more goods is entered in the *ceteris paribus* of each of the demand curves, the resulting consumer surplus calculation will be an underestimate if the goods are substitutes and an overestimate if they are complements.[5]

As Hicks [2] shows, using his illuminating example of a simultaneous introduction into an area of three substitute sources of energy, coal, gas, and electricity, the *ceteris paribus* of each of the three demand curves taken in any given sequence is different from those of the other two.

III. Accepting Political Constraints while Avoiding Political Adulteration

A source of confusion to the student of CBA arises from failure to recognize that when the economist undertakes to estimate the net benefits of the various projects proposed by policymakers, he does so in the knowledge that they will generally determine also how the funds are to be raised (taxation and/or borrowing), how the benefits over time are to be allocated (the proportion to be consumed or invested in private or public projects), and in the knowledge that economic resources may currently be far from ideally allocated. Thus, the economist's calculation of the streams of net benefits of alternative projects are constrained by political decisions and by circumstances that he cannot control.

If, for example, the economist is to calculate the value of some important raw material necessary to the project in question, adherence to the basic maxim of the net-benefit criterion (each individual's own valuation) is inconsistent with the use, instead, of the world price of that raw material. In this example, the basic maxim is consistent only with the *opportunity cost* to the particular economy of the raw material to be imported—which, in the last resort, is equal to the value to consumers there of the goods that have now to be forgone in order to make available the foreign currency necessary to pay for the raw material in question.

Thus, if Pakistan raises $50,000 in order to pay for the tractor from the United States by reducing its imports of, say, copper wire, the opportunity cost of the tractor is not (necessarily) the international price of the copper wire (much less the international price of the tractor itself). The opportunity cost of the tractor exceeds $50,000 according to the height of the tariff on the copper wire, the imports of which have to be reduced to pay for the tractor. The existence, then, of an ad valorem tariff that triples the c.i.f. price of copper wire in Pakistan from $50 a coil to $150 a coil to the consumer means that the saving of $50,000 from reducing copper imports inflicts a loss of domestic value of (at least) $150,000, which is, therefore, the opportunity cost of the tractor to the Pakistani economy.

On the other hand, although the existing and expected political and institutional constraints have indeed to be accepted by the economist in such calculations, the net-benefit criterion itself—if it is to serve the community with impartiality—has to turn on valuations that arise only from constant application of the basic maxim, a procedure that characterizes *economic* calculation. Such a criterion cannot, therefore, be adulterated with *politically* determined valuations or parameters. True, the adoption of a politically chosen rate of discount is wonderfully convenient for the economist, but such adoption constitutes a clear violation of the *raison d'être* of an economic calculation. Therefore a positive net benefit figure arising from the adoption of such politically chosen discount rate can no longer be assumed to realize an excess of individual gains over losses as revealed by the individuals themselves.

Admittedly, it may sometimes be expedient, in view of the extreme difficulties of particular kinds of economic calculation, to resign oneself to rough estimates of the ideal measure, as for instance ideally weighted relevant rates of return or ideally weighted social rates of time preference. But no surrender to political exigencies is involved in conscientious attempts to approximate the economically ideal, given the constraints on time and resources. Yet a clear conception of the ideal economic calculation is all the more necessary as enabling us to form a judgment about the degree of error involved in adopting a proximate measure.

The caveat against employment of politically determined parameters mentioned above applies equally to the employment of distributional, ethnic, regional, or other weights. The economist may be under the impression that the effect of such weighting will be to favor projects conferring greater "utility," or satisfaction, on the community. In the event, however, the weights proposed are almost invariably politically determined: in the UNIDO manual[6] for instance, political weights are explicitly recommended as a means of promoting the government's objectives.

What is undeniable, however, is that the use of politically determined weights and parameters acts to produce quantitative rationalization for the politically inspired policies and programs of the party or regime in power. Indeed, instead of serving as a check against current political ambitions, such politically "doctored" calculations (contrived from political weights and parameters) serve to reinforce them—at least until the public's faith in the "objectivity" of the economist's method of calculation has been undermined.[7]

As a postscript, I might add that the search for an appropriate discount rate or for a general accounting formula, even for a given population, is naïve. For the opportunities for growth over the relevant time span—through use of the combinations of the relevant rates of return—both of the sums raised for the projects and also of the expected disposal of future net benefits of the projects can vary enormously as between different projects and different economic circumstances. Clarity of conception would therefore favor rules for compounding forward of alternative net-benefit streams to a terminal value rather than persisting in the attempt to create increasingly comprehensive and elaborate discounting formulae.[8]

IV. Irremediable Limitations on CBA Applications

Finally, there are three irremediable limitations to the accuracy of cost-benefit estimates.

1. Once the stream of benefits and costs extends beyond a given population or, more generally, extends over generational time, the reduction of the gains and losses to a single net-benefit magnitude—whether it is discounted present value (which is still popular) or a compounded terminal value (as I have proposed)—can no longer be assumed to conform with the familiar definition of a Kaldor-Hicks (or potential Pareto) improvement. Such an assumption would be warranted only if no distinguishable generation suffered a net loss, a condition that cannot be guaranteed. And where such condition is in fact not met, an *actual* Pareto improvement is realized only if actual (costless) *inter*generational transfers are undertaken and accompany actual (costless) *intra*generational transfers.

Therefore, where this condition is *not* met—where, say, some distinguishable generation suffers a net loss in addition to the virtual certainty that some persons in each generation will suffer a loss—a positive figure for the discounted present value (or for the compounded terminal value) of the stream of net benefits over generation time may no longer be interpreted as a Kaldor-Hicks or potential Pareto improvement. Instead, it has to be interpreted as the magnitude of a *potential* Kaldor-Hicks improvement of a *potential* potential Pareto improvement—a criterion of economic betterment that is less likely to be ethically acceptable or even politically acceptable.[9]

2. Uncertainty of the magnitudes of future benefits and costs of any

future period increases rapidly with their distance from the present, and the more so with the novelty of the project. Although there is a variety of methods for coping with uncertainty, it should be obvious that none of them can remove the uncertainty or even go far in reducing it.

The alternative projects that are to be ranked are usually subjected to a common terminal date which, in the case of publicly financed projects, is not likely to be short. Other than the more stable forms of investment, such as those in public utilities, the actual net benefit or loss in, say, the fifth year can be expected to deviate markedly from the best or most likely estimate made for the fifth year—the expected error of the actual from the best estimate of net benefit in the tenth year being generally more than twice the error in the fifth year, and so on.

The techniques proposed for dealing with uncertainty are arbitrary (in that they are not known to command wide support in the community), often cumbersome or impractical; and in fact sophisticated techniques are seldom used in any actual cost-benefit study. Even simple proposals to employ a sensitivity analysis, by having experts attach a probability to their guesses, respectively, of the most likely of a high and of a low price in the nth period or year of each of several important inputs and outputs, begin to founder in consequence of the sheer range of the net-benefit probability distribution thereby generated for any project having a time span of six or more years.

3. Coverage presents an even more intractable problem. Ideally, every effect on the welfare of society has to be included, whether it falls into the category of the environmental, the aesthetic, the sentimental, or the patriotic. Although on a formal level we may conceive each distinguishable effect being brought "into relation with the measuring rod of money" (by imagining each individual affected to set an exact payment for accepting the change), there are practical limits to the usefulness of quantitative survey methods in cases of high feeling or strong convictions. In addition, socially significant externalities may emerge over the future which the economist cannot anticipate. And even where he is able to anticipate one or more such externalities, he may be unable properly to evaluate them in the absence of people's experience of them.

Hence, the more complex and farreaching are the changes wrought by the project or program, the more likely are the potential net benefits (positive or negative)—both of the intangible effects and of the unanticipated consequences—to swamp the economist's *measurable* net benefits.

It is for these three reasons, if no others, that the economist recognizes that the most scrupulous cost-benefit study can never be more than a contribution—a somewhat flawed and possibly also a misleading contribution—to the political decision-making process. It is a matter of prudence, therefore, that the conscientious economist make a point of stressing such limitations in his cost-benefit studies and of describing the possible range of intangible but potent effects that have perforce to be omitted from the economic calculus.

Notes

1. Recidivist tendencies are exemplified in a number of recent articles in which the weight of the technical apparatus has broken through the safety net of good sense. I am thinking in particular of the papers of Usher (1973), Conley (1976) and Arthur (1981). For my comments on these and other over-ingenious constructs, see Chapter 5 (containing references to these papers) in the volume edited by Jones-Lee [3].

2. For a simple exposition of the relevant analysis, see Chapter 48 of my *Normative Economics* [4].

3. For reasons given in Chapter 26 of my *Cost-Benefit Analysis* [5].

4. For a short verbal explanation, see Chapter 24 of my *Normative Economics* [4].

5. The analysis can be found in Chapter 25 of [4].

6. See Dasgupta, P. *et al.*

7. Nor can a distributionally weighted net-benefit criterion ensure that the successful project does not involve a regressive distribution. Again, the market itself operates, albeit imperfectly, in a manner analogous to the (unweighted) net-benefit criterion. The introduction therefore of a *weighted* net-benefit criterion for the public sector would create difficulties if only because one of the continually recurring policy problems includes that of determining the allocation of resources between the public and the private sectors of the economy.

8. A general critique of the discounting method is given in Chapter 37 of [5].

9. Since an intergenerational project discounted in the usual way to a positive net benefit can be one that inflicts heavy risks or losses on future generations, unanimous agreement to discount such losses to a figure below some very modest benefits conferred on earlier generations would not be reached by a committee composed of members of each of the generations affected. In such cases, the economist should replace a single net benefit figure by the whole intergenerational pattern of expected benefits and losses, leaving the decision to the political process.

Bibliography

[1] Dasgupta, P., Marglin, S. and Sen, A., *Guidelines for Project Evaluation* United Nations, New York. 1972

[2] Hicks, J. R., "Consumer's Surplus and Index Numbers", *Review of Economic Studies*, 1942.

[3] ———, *A Revision of Demand Theory*, The Clarendon Press. Oxford, 1956.

[4] Jones-Lee, M. W., ed., *The Value of Life and Safety*, Amsterdam, North-Holland, 1982.

[5] Mishan, E. J., *Introduction to Normative Economics*, Oxford Univ. Press, Oxford, 1981.

[6] ———, *Cost-Benefit Analysis: An Informal Introduction*, Allen & Unwin, 3rd ed., London, 1982.

Résumé

Le cynisme avec lequel l'analyse coût-avantage est parfois considérée peut être aussi bien étendu à presque toutes les branches d'économie appliquée. Le principal défaut présenté par ce sujet est, à mon avis, la faiblesse de jugement manifestée par les méthodes recommandées par la plupart des auteurs. Un autre défaut est un reliquat persistant de confusion et d'erreur intellectuelle. Cependant, si l'on remédiait à ces deux défauts, la confiance que l'on peut accorder à cette technique ne serait limitée que par les limitations auxquelles on ne peut échapper car elles sont inhérentes à tout calcul économique de gains et pertes futurs pour la société. Pour cette raison, au moins, les conclusions d'une étude coût-avantage devraient être prises en considération, au mieux, comme une modeste contribution au processus de prise de décision politique qui est inclus dans le jugement que l'on porte sur la valeur sociale d'un projet ou programme public.

Optimal Taxation: A Beautiful Cul-de-sac?

*Gerold Krause-Junk**

I. The Problem

Income taxes and consumption taxes have one sad thing in common: they discriminate against earned income. This is obvious with respect to the income tax, at least if one considers income in the income tax sense. But it is just as true of the general consumption tax, as long as income is entirely or partly spent on consumption.

Under the usual assumptions of a neoclassical world, this discrimination is harmful.[1] The taxpayer trying to respond rationally attains a utility level even lower than it had to be with respect to the final tax payment, as compared with a nondiscriminatory tax regime. This utility loss is the well-known "excess burden," Musgrave [14].

Generally, nondiscriminatory taxation is ruled out for distributive reasons. Using just about every indicator of individual well-being—income, consumption, property, etc.—distributional policy reasonably could adopt as its criterion for a distribution of the individual tax burden, allocative losses are the inevitable price of distributional policy, just as distributional abstinence would have to accompany allocative neutrality.

But it is unsatisfactory to stop at this stage of knowledge, because not all allocationally suboptimal solutions are likely to be equally bad. What is sought is a second-best solution. This is where "Optimal Taxation" (OT) comes in. It is under this label that, beginning with the pioneering article of Mirrlees [13], a good deal of public finance literature of the last decade has been devoted, developing and analyzing models attempting to derive welfare-maximizing tax rules—or some conditions thereof—based on the assumption that only certain "realistic" taxes, such as income or consumption taxes, are permitted. Some authors even claim to have established a "new" public finance (Stiglitz and Boskin [23], Stern [22]) because, in comparison

*The author is Professor of Economics at the International Tax Institute of the University of Hamburg. He wishes to thank his colleagues J. H. von Oehsen and W. Laux, partners in many stimulating discussions.

The Relevance of Public Finance for Policy-Making. Proceedings of the 41st Congress of the International Institute of Public Finance. Madrid, 1985, pp. 55–66.

with "traditional" public finance, which lacked "guiding principles" [22, p. 353], the welfare-theoretical basis of OT is properly laid out and the analysis is stringent and straightforward. The notion of "new" (or "OT") versus "traditional" public finance might be followed for the purpose of this paper, though some doubts seem to be appropriate as to whether OT really provides a new conception of the ideal tax system. What traditional normative public finance theory recommended was necessarily based on some preferential ordering of social states, i.e., on a social welfare function, even if it did so implicitly.[2] Whether OT results are somehow novel, is a question to be postponed to the final part of this paper, after we have discussed the basis of OT.

II. Optimal Income Tax

We first consider an income-tax-only world. If people act according to the marginal calculus, it is the marginal tax burden which, under the allocative goal, has to be kept as low as other goals may permit. There is really no problem in a one-person world. The tax formula would simply have to be constructed in such a way that the tax burden falls on infra-marginal rather than on marginal income. That might also be done in a world of two, or few, taxpayers, even if the tax formula would look somewhat awkward, displaying zero-marginal tax rates at all income levels which are actually occupied by taxpayers. Of course, the more persons there are, the more questionable is the assumption that all taxpayers act only according to the marginal calculus—or, to put it differently, the less room is left for infra-marginal taxation. In a world of continuous incomes, an overall zero-marginal tax rate is equivalent to the distributionally unacceptable poll tax (to which the formal income tax would degenerate, so to speak).

But OT has demonstrated that—independent of the assumed welfare function, as long as Pareto improvements are considered welfare-raising—a zero marginal tax rate is optimal with respect to the highest as well as the lowest actual income. The former seems to be obvious: if the highest income person in the equilibrium position must pay taxes on an additional income unit, he would refrain from earning more income, thus society or the state would gain nothing from this "hypothetical tax".

Similarly, a positive marginal tax rate on the lowest actual income would create an unnecessary allocative burden. Let us consider the last unit of actual income of the lowest-income person. The thereupon levied tax could be substituted by a distributionally neutral rise of the poll component of the income tax. Nobody would be harmed, but the lowest-income person would be taxed in an allocatively neutral manner. In fact, since the lowest-income person would move to a preferred position once his marginal tax is dropped, he would reach a higher utility level, ceteris paribus.

Certain difficulties arise if there are zero-corner-solutions at the bottom of the income hierarchy, i.e., if there are a number of people not working because their wage rate, even without tax, does not equal the marginal utility of their very last bit of leisure. Here it might be a good idea to have a marginal tax rate at the beginning of the tax schedule, since the people with the lowest utility level would not be negatively affected (they wouldn't work anyway), whereas the tax return could be used to grant them an additional lump-sum transfer. To put it differently: dropping the marginal tax for the whole set of lowest-income persons would not necessarily improve the position of the worst off; it would only improve the position of the person at the margin (who would now start working) (Seade [19].)

Not much can be said about the optimal tax schedule between the two endpoints. Consider, e.g., the second-highest income person. If one would assign to him a zero-marginal tax rate for allocative reasons, one would automatically, at least in the continuous case, grant a tax favor to the highest-income person, too. And that might not be acceptable for distributive reasons.

Generally, one can imagine a neutral tax treatment that would be more justified the more strongly a taxpayer would react to discriminatory taxation. If, e.g., a certain income class is known for its high sensitivity to marginal taxation, one might be inclined to grant it moderate marginal tax rates, even if that would mean some shortcomings on the distributional side. But, of course, to be certain about this, one would have to have a solid norm to balance allocational and distributional effects. And such a norm, at least a widely accepted one, simply does not exist.

So one might experiment with different welfare functions that exhibit a wide range of value judgments, from purest liberalism to strongest egalitarianism[3] and be content with whatever tax schedules might prove to be optimal. But that means, in my view, not much more than substituting one unknown for another, and pretending there is a degree of precision which in fact could not be followed in making any practical recommendation.

This can be clearly seen when the analyst tries to give his mathematical equations some economic meaning. I consider the "cul-de-sac" as fair figuration if, after a tremendous amount of analytical work, one arrives at the same rate of knowledge from which he reasonably could have started. So, according to Seade [20], who refers to the works of Mirrlees, Atkinson, Feldstein, and Stern, the marginal income tax rate to be attached to some person ought to be, ceteris paribus, the higher:

— the more pretax inequality there is (Mirrlees [13]);
— the more inequality-averse the government is (Atkinson [1]); and notably

— the less a typical consumer's labor supply responds to small (and compensated) changes in his marginal tax rate (Feldstein [9], Stern [21]).

I suppose nobody is surprised at this.

III. Optimal Consumption Tax

Let us now turn to the world in which only a consumption tax is permitted. For simplicity we assume that all income is consumed. Again, the allocative goal requires the burden on marginal income to be as low as possible, i.e., as low as the other goals will allow. If only the type of general consumption tax with uniform tax rates on all consumption goods (except leisure) is available, there is not much choice, because the lowest general tax rate consistent with the intended tax yield will suffice.

Now, in OT models it is not uncommon to combine the general consumption tax with a poll tax, so that in fact the tax rate can be optimized, since the poll tax would fill any gaps in tax revenues. This procedure seems to be cheating a bit as the inadequacy of the poll tax is a starting point of OT analysis. But, even if the poll tax as sole tax instrument is ruled out (for distributional reasons), it might be granted an auxiliary status. The optimal uniform tax rate is, of course, again a compromise between allocative and distributional considerations. Allocatively the tax rate ought to be low, as will be the tax return from the consumption tax; distributionally, the tax rate ought to be high, as long as one considers consumption (and so income) as an indicator of well-being.

Of more interest is the case of a (principally) differentiated consumption tax, i.e., a system of differential tax rates on the different consumption goods. Here no poll tax is needed to adjust the burden on marginal income of a single person, as long as his marginal and his average baskets of consumption goods differ. The trick is to differentiate the specific tax rates according to the shares of the different goods in the average and in the marginal baskets, respectively. So, if a given amount of individual tax is to generate only a minimum discrimination against income, taxation would have to be concentrated on those goods whose shares (after taxation) in the marginal basket are relatively small, as compared with the average basket.

Unfortunately, such a strategy is not entirely satisfactory, even under purely allocative considerations. Differentiation of tax rates usually generates distortions with respect to the individual consumption choice. So, the allocatively optimal tax-rate differentiation is reached when any further differentiation would result in an equal gain and loss—the gain in reducing the burden on marginal income, the loss in distortion of the consumer's choice.

The exact optimal tax-rate structure is, of course, highly sensitive to the individual utility function, as the following two special cases demonstrate.

1. If the structures of the marginal and of the average baskets are always equal, independent of the consumer price structure, then tax differentiation is not a way to reduce the tax burden on marginal income. Uniform tax rates are optimal.[4]
2. If there are no substitution effects between goods, i.e., all compensated cross-price elasticities are zero, one does not have to worry about consumer choice distortions and can, in fact, minimize the burden on marginal income by levying the tax on goods with the relatively smallest shares in the marginal basket (after tax).

But, of course, utility functions generally do not do us the favor of having properties which lead to rules as neat as the two described above. They will generally be nonseparable (1), and nonlimitational (and thereby conflicting with (2)). And so optimal tax rates, if directly related to the individual preference structures, are complicated expressions of countless substitution rates or, if (indirectly) related to the individual demand functions, no less complicated expressions of countless elasticities of individual demand. According to the "indirect" approach, described by Ramsey as early as 1927, the structure of different consumption tax rates is optimal, if a relatively equal infinitesimal (compensated) increase of all tax rates leads to a relatively equal reduction of demand for all goods and of supply of working time. The most general rule so far produced by the direct approach is a leisure-complementarity rule (Deaton [6], Krause-Junk, and Von Oehsen [11]), according to which a special consumption tax rate is, ceteris paribus, to be the higher, the closer is the leisure complementarity of the taxed good. The resulting formulae contain nothing less than every single (compensated) substitution rate between any two goods and any good and leisure. But even this calculation is restricted by a simplification that is anything but harmless: the assumption that there is just one untaxable good (and so a well-defined marginal basket of taxable goods), where the one untaxed good is leisure, of course. We will return to that point later.

Now let us assume that we have really found the allocatively optimal tax rates for a single person. That, of course, does not mean that these tax rates would be acceptable under distributive considerations. To put it as simply as possible: a low burden on additional earned income in exchange for an infinitesimal reduction of leisure, in general means a low burden on the differential income, earned by any person at higher levels of the income hierarchy.

But, of course, there are exceptions. Apart from any differences in the utility functions, there is one notable case: suppose that the man in a higher position earns his additional income not because he works more hours but because he enjoys a higher wage rate. And suppose, since his differential income has a different source from that which the other fellow may incrementally earn, that he also spends his additional income on quite different goods as compared with those goods the other one would buy if he worked more hours. Then a differential consumption tax might be able simultaneously to spare additional earnings due to additional working time while more heavily taxing other differential income. Again, this requires special utility functions which are most unlikely to be confirmed by empirical evidence. On the contrary, most goods of a leisure-substitution character, i.e., goods someone might buy if made to work an additional hour, are very likely to be luxuries, i.e., goods someone would buy if he received a higher wage rate or reached a higher utility level by any other means.

So we again arrive at the old conflict between allocation and distribution, and in my view it would be of little help to reformulate this conflict using some refined welfare and utility functions. All that possibly could result is something we knew to begin with: if leisure substitutes are luxuries as well, the proper tax-rate structure cannot be anything but a political choice.

IV. Optimal Tax Mix

Let us now look briefly at those worlds in which income taxes as well as consumption taxes are permitted. One might imagine the income tax (of the nonlinear type) to be dominant, as it is able both to set the proper burden on marginal income and to be neutral with respect to consumer choice. But, even within the general setting of OT models, there are at least two reasons why there might be room for an additional consumption tax. A general income tax cannot differentiate between persons of equal income and between incomes of different sources, and both might be desirable.

It is commonly understood that persons with equal income might reach completely different utility levels. So equity considerations may require a different tax treatment. This could be properly performed if the different utility levels systematically account for different consumption patterns rather than for different incomes. By the same token, no need exists for an extra consumption tax, if for a given price structure a certain income level always corresponds to a certain consumption pattern.[5]

Differential taxation of income from different sources might be appropriate if people can make choices on some of the sources but not others. If, for instance, working time is considered an individual choice, then of course taxation should try to avoid distortions of that choice. If, on the other hand, the individual wage rate is considered given, then income differentials due to differences in wage rates do not have to be of any concern to an allocation-minded tax authority. Generally there are no income sources which are absolutely fixed; otherwise we could achieve first-best taxation. But there are differences in the tax sensitivity of incomes from different sources, at least in the short run. So, if these differences correspond to different consumption patterns, a properly differentiated consumption tax might turn out to be allocatively superior to a general income tax. But it is very difficult to offer a practical example.

Perhaps the following case is illustrative. Both a general manager and a blue collar worker might be induced to work an extra hour, if they could purchase a fast car at a lower price. So a differentiated consumption tax with a low tax rate on fast cars seems to be appropriate. But the concept breaks down if, e.g., the general manager (and all persons high on the income hierarchy) would own a fast car anyway, and would like to use it for work as well as for leisure. Besides, if it really is possible to specify that certain sources of income should be taxed favorably, then a differential income tax (discriminating between different income sources) still seems more appropriate than any complicated method of indirect differential tax treatment through a consumption tax. In the above example, income tax liabilities should vary with wage rates and should not vary with working time if the latter can be influenced by the taxpayer and the former not. Alas, there generally are no income sources of the former type.

V. A Critical Summation

A critique must concentrate on the question of whether OT has given us any new theoretical results—i.e., results unknown to traditional public finance—and, if so, whether any traditional tax rules are to be changed accordingly. Before taking up that question, we will discuss a natural (but in our view misplaced) objection to OT.

One could argue that in a situation of world-wide unemployment, there could not be a theory more redundant than one which complains of an excess of voluntary leisure. Such a critique would, however, be beside the point. After all, OT only proves that the single taxpayer chooses an inefficient (short) working time because of the inefficient collection of a *given* tax. Nothing whatsoever prevents the fisc from reducing the individual tax burden and hence the efficient working time (as the tax reduction might have a positive income effect on leisure). Additionally, one has to take into account not only the substitution but also the complimentary effects between working hours of different persons. Workers who can determine their own mixture of working time and leisure seem to be job-creating rather than job-taking. Viewed in this way, a less discriminatory (optimal) tax might actually reduce unemployment.

Finally, one has to keep in mind that in OT models leisure is only an example of an untaxed good. Hence, the results generally would be valid if, instead of leisure, any other kind of untaxed good were considered. But OT, in my view, is not quite innocent when its results are misread in this fashion.

Are there any traditional tax rules which, in the light of OT, seem to have to be changed or even abandoned? As far as I see there are four possible candidates.

Candidate 1.

The optimal income tax schedule should display a certain, preferably smooth, overall progressivity.

This rule seems to be obsolete, as OT has proven that for a wide range of possible welfare functions the marginal tax rates at the bottom and at the top are supposed to be zero, so the optimal tax schedule will be regressive somewhere (Sadka [15], Seade [19]). But since, without any further specification of the welfare function, optimal regressivity is valid only with respect to the two highest income persons, the tax politician need worry little about that refinement. He can still favor an entirely progressive tax schedule, even if he knows that there might be some unexhausted welfare gain at the very top.

Candidate 2.

With respect to distributional targets, the intended tax yield ought to be raised by taxing income rather than consumption.

This view may not be shared by all traditional public finance economists, but in fact consumption taxation is traditionally considered to be at variance with a fair distribution of the tax burden.

There are OT models that more or less tell us that the opposite is true (Atkinson and Stiglitz [4, p. 432]). But those models usually compare a linear income tax with a system of differential consumption tax rates. And if, additionally, all income is assumed to be consumed, then a consumption tax proper might accomplish distributional ends which an income tax cannot. No traditional economist would disagree with this.[6]

Candidate 3.

The income tax must play the leading role in a rational tax system.

This rule again might not be supported by all traditional economists, but can be considered a common view of abilty-to-pay oriented public finance (Haller [10]).

OT generally seems to suggest a tax mix, putting great weight on consumption taxation. This follows directly from what was mentioned above, if only a linear income tax is admitted. But the time for a general flat-rate tax has not yet arrived, even in the most liberal countries. So the question is whether we have a case for consumption taxation even under a nonlinear income tax. According to OT one might say yes, if differences in the individual utility levels reflect different consumption patterns rather than different incomes, especially if people with a high income potential enjoy more leisure. Then, if certain consumption goods are leisure complements as well as luxuries (in the sense of being utility-superior) and if income taxation is not supposed to discriminate between different income sources (e.g., wage-rate or work-hours differences), then a well-designed consumption tax might have distributional as well as allocational advantages.

I personally doubt whether a consumption tax really should attempt to do this. Leaving aside all the problems a tax authority might have in sorting whether a taxpayer's time belongs to working hours or leisure, and earmarking the goods as to whether they belong with work or leisure, we must not overlook the following obstacle. It *is not* only leisure that would have to be considered as an alternative or substitute for income. What about the satisfaction or dissatisfaction with work; what about the personal risks which necessarily have to be taken with certain kinds of work; what about the different moral impacts? These and other reasons which might prevent people from using their utmost earning capacity would have to be taken into accounnt by an entirely neutral, or rather second-best tax system—which would turn out to be something, I think, that nobody would like.

Candidate 4.

For allocative reasons, a uniform consumption tax rate is superior to a set of differential consumption tax rates.

If a traditional economist might have been careless enough to formulate such a rule without taking proper precautions, then OT has definitely proved he is wrong. Starting with a uniform consumption tax rate, there generally should be some welfare potentials which could be exhausted by a proper tax-rate differentiation. But how? As I have mentioned, it is not only leisure that has to be considered as an untaxable good—it is work satisfaction, risk avoidance, promotional opportunities, immobility, and so on. Some of these entities in a complete utility function may in fact be separable from all consumption goods; others, such as leisure, may not. So

I could think of goods which are complements for leisure and substitutes for work satisfaction—perhaps a cigarette. Ought these goods to be taxed relatively high or relatively low, or should we really try to average this problem out? I would instead say that we should stick to the uniform tax rate—all the more so because individual utility functions are considered to differ and, basically, the tax authority would have to do this calculation for every single taxpayer. It would not be of any help to impose a certain utility function on a political basis—using it, so to speak, as a political standard, as has actually been proposed for distributional reasons (Haller [10]). To do so on efficiency grounds would be nonsense, since one cannot avoid excess burdens by supposing a utility function which individuals do not follow in practice.

To recommend consumption taxation without proper implementation of OT considerations might appear to impoverish tax policy, to renounce theoretical progress. But this can honestly be asserted only by someone who fails to take note of the economic damages which the complexity and the ambiguities of contemporary tax systems already have caused.

Notes

1. There is one notable exception: the taxation of residual gains, such as infra-marginal land rents. Such taxation is costless because it should not induce any taxpayer response.

2. The principle of the equal relative sacrifice seems to be implemented in a welfare function:

$$W = \min \{a_1U_1, a_2U_2, \ldots, a_nU_n\} \overset{!}{=} \max$$

$$\text{where } a_j = \frac{\Sigma U_j^*}{U_j^*}$$

= [inverse individual shares of utilities before tax].

3. Or, to put it allegorically, from Bentham to Rawls. But as Serge Christoph Kolm, in his valuable oral comment on this paper pointed out, the two names are not necessarily the two boundaries of the range of value judgments. One could in particular conceive of a far more liberal position than Bentham's.

4. Technically, if the utility functions are quasi separable (Deaton [6]).

5. Technically, if the utility functions are weakly separable (Deaton [6]).

6. Though he still might have serious objections to the use of consumption taxes as a distributional device. Just to mention two: (1) many goods which seem to be of the luxury class at one time turn out to be essentials only a few years later; (2) true luxury good taxation has special adverse effects on those persons who belong to a low-income class but strive for that little something extra.

References

[1] Atkinson, A., "How Progressive Should Income Tax Be?", in *Essays in Modern Economics*, ed. M. Parkin and A. Nobay, Longman Group Ltd., London, 1973.

[2]   Atkinson, A., "Optimal Taxation and the Direct versus Indirect Tax Controversy," *Canadian Journal of Economics*, 10, 1977: 590–606.
[3]   Atkinson, A., and Stiglitz, J., "The Design of Tax Structure: Direct versus Indirect Taxation," *Journal of Public Economics*, 6, 1976: 58–75.
[4]   Atkinson, A., and Stiglitz, J., *Lectures on Public Economics*, Mc-Graw Hill, London, 1980.
[5]   Cooter, R., "Optimal Tax Schedules and Rates: Mirrlees and Ramsey," *American Economic Review*, 68, 1978: 756–68.
[6]   Deaton, A., "Optimal Taxes and the Structure of Preferences," *Econometrica*, 49, 1981: 1245–60.
[7]   Diamond, P., "A Many-Person Ramsey Tax Rule," *Journal of Public Economics*, 4, 1975: 335–42.
[8]   Diamond, P., and Mirrlees, J., "Optimal Taxation and Public Production," *American Economic Review*, 61, 1971: 8–27; 261–78.
[9]   Feldstein, M., "On the Optimal Progressivity of the Income Tax," *Journal of Public Economics*, 2, 1973: 357–76.
[10] Haller, H., *Die Steuern*, J.C.B. Mohr (Paul Siebeck), Tübingen, 1964 (3rd ed. 1981).
[11] Krause-Junk, G., and Von Oehsen, J. H., "Besteuerung, optimale," Handwörterbuch der Wirtschaftswissenschaft, Gustav Fischer, Stuttgart and New York, J.C.B. Mohr, Tübingen and Vandenhoek and Ruprecht, Göttingen and Zürich, 9, 1981: 706–23.
[12] Lipsey, R., and Lancaster, K., "The General Theory of Second Best," *Review of Economic Studies*, 24, 1956: 11–32.
[13] Mirrlees, J., "An Exploration in the Theory of Optimal Income Taxation," *Review of Economic Studies*, 38, 1971: 175–208.
[14] Musgrave, R., *The Theory of Public Finance*, Mc-Graw Hill, New York, 1959.
[15] Sadka, E., "On Income Distribution, Incentive Effects and Optimal Income Taxation," *Review of Economic Studies*, 43, 1976: 261–67.
[16] Samuelson, P., *Foundations of Economic Analysis*, Harvard University Press, Cambridge, Mass., 1947.
[17] Sandmo, A., "Optimal Taxation: An Introduction to the Literature," *Journal of Public Economics*, 6, 1976: 37–54.
[18] Sandmo, A., and Dixit, A., "Some Simplified Formulae for Optimal Income Taxation," *Scandinavian Journal of Economics*, 79, 1977: 416–23.
[19] Seade, J., "On the Shape of Optimal Tax Schedules," *Journal of Public Economics*, 7, 1977: 203–35.
[20] Seade, J., "On the Sign of Optimum Marginal Income Tax Rate," *Review of Economic Studies*, 49, 1982: 637–43.
[21] Stern, N., "On the Specification of Models of Optimum Income Taxation," *Journal of Public Economics*, 6, 1976: 123–62.
[22] Stern, N., "Optimum Taxation and Tax Policy," *International Monetary Fund Staff Papers*, 1984: 339–78.
[23] Stiglitz, J., and Boskin, M., "Some Lessons from the New Public Finance," *American Economic Review, Papers and Proceedings*, 67, 1977: 295–301.

Résumé

La fiscalité optimale (OT) s'efforce de trouver des règles fiscales optimisant le bien-être, quand seulement certaines catégories ("réalistes") d'impôts sont admises. Ce rapport discute des impôts sur le revenu et la consommation et d'un mélange des deux. Généralement, les résultats dépendent fortement duquel des deux objectifs prédomine, celui d'allocation ou celui de distribution. Mais il semble évident qu'il faille débuter par là; c'est pourquoi, considérant l'énorme quantité de travail d'analyse qui a été réalisé, OT semble avoir abouti à un "cul-de-sac". On peut d'autant plus estimer cela vrai que ses recommandations de politique publique ne sont pas, apparemment, très différentes des croyances des finances publiques "traditionnelles". Par ailleurs, si l'on prend au sérieux son message—l'existence de biens non-fiscalisables mais qui doivent néanmoins être fiscalisés—on retombe sur un système fiscal monstrueux et absurde, un autre cul-de-sac.

Tax Reform in Retrospect: The Role of Inquiries

J. A. Kay*

Why do governments so frequently appoint commissions to inquire into their tax systems? It is very unusual, after all, for a government to promote an independent inquiry into its foreign policy, or its defense policy, or its macroeconomic policy. Tax policy may seem less clearly a political issue than some of these, but it is hardly less political than foreign policy. Tax policy may seem more technical than some of these, but it is hardly less technical than defense policy.

This paper will suggest that the motives behind government sponsorship of these inquiries may be somewhat disingenuous, since it will show that the degree of implementation of inquiry recommendations by the promoting governments is low. Indeed, the very concept of official independent inquiry into policy matters is a puzzling one, since what such inquiries do is principally to hear representations and undertake analysis, both of which governments are well equipped to do on their own behalf.

If we look at the use by government of inquiry into subjects other than taxation, we can identify several purposes. Two theories of the role of the inquiry might be put forward that are consistent with the low rate of implementation. The inquiry may serve the function of postponing an issue. For example, in 1976 the British government established a committee of inquiry to review the functioning of financial institutions. The reason was that the Labour party conference had approved a resolution calling for the nationalization of banks and various other organizations, which the Labour government of the day found deeply embarrassing. The establishment of a committee enabled it to take a—publicly—agnostic view of the issue until the committee's report was received. In the event, the committee did not report until after the next election, made no recommendations of significance, and none were implemented.

This function of public inquiry into policy sees it as a substitute for

*The author is a Professor, London School of Business, London, England. He thanks John Bossons, Charles McLure, Mariam Hedermann O'Brien and Remy Prud'homme for comments on an earlier draft of this paper.

The Relevance of Public Finance for Policy-Making. Proceedings of the 41st Congress of the International Institute of Public Finance. Madrid, 1985, pp. 67–81.

policy. An alternative purpose for independent inquiry arises when the government knows well what policy it wants to implement but, sensing that the policy will be unpopular, either with the public at large or with its own supporters, seeks to defend its position or deflect responsibility by praying the support of an independent inquiry in aid. The current British Conservative government has used such inquiries only infrequently, but one instance was its decision to set up an inquiry to review legislation governing restrictions on the opening hours of shops. There can be little doubt that the government wished to repeal such legislation but, knowing that such repeal would be opposed by some substantial interests and was difficult to reconcile with past assurances, it wanted the support of the independent inquiry. The committee duly recommended repeal, and the government went ahead with implementation.

But the record of implementation of tax policy reports is much poorer than this. Certainly, any programme of structural tax reform will require that a variety of vested interests be tackled, and there will be both gainers and losers. A Committee of Inquiry, particularly one which contains representatives of many of these interests, may provide support for an attack on them. But the record of implementation would suggest that it does not provide enough support. Governments are not necessarily more ready to tackle the political problems of structural reform after the report of the inquiry than they were before.

There is a third explanation of the purpose of taxation inquiries which deserves mention. Tax administrators are rarely the most enlightened and imaginative of civil servants. Although the process of policy review could in principle be carried out within government, as it would be in most other areas, it encounters considerable difficulty and resistance. Hence, there seems to be purpose in having that review carried out externally. Unfortunately, the obstacles to having a comprehensive review conducted also prove to be obstacles to having such a review implemented.

It is likely that each of these objects—the desire to procrastinate, the desire to win independent support for potentially unpopular policies, the difficulty of having effective review undertaken internally—has played its part in the establishment of the various reviews described here. But if these descriptions and intentions are correct, the value of the operation seems very limited: either there is no intention that recommendations be implemented, or there is an intention that is likely to be frustrated by the same factors which prevented implementation before the inquiry was established. Given this, it might seem that anyone tempted to become involved in such a review might be well advised to lie down until the feeling had passed.

But this skepticism would be exaggerated. In this paper, I shall argue that these inquiries have had a very substantial impact on general attitudes to the structure of taxation—on the climate of opinion in tax policy both in their country of origin and internationally. They have helped to create an intellectual consensus on directions of change and to transmit that consensus to a wider public of policymakers and tax professionals. This climate does have a real effect on policy, although often with a considerable lag. It is, for example, remarkable that the dominant intellectual influence on political discussion of tax policy now appears to be the concept of the comprehensive income tax—almost fifty years after it was first propounded and twenty years after the apogee of academic interest in it was reached, in the 1960s. The economic ideas of politicians and senior civil servants are, as Keynes remarked, rarely the newest; but, as he commented in the same passage, the long-term influence of ideas on policy is far greater than generally realized. In the concluding section of this paper I consider the implications of this appraisal for those who are engaged in independent inquiry into tax systems.

I. Taxation Inquiries

The Carter Commission was established in Canada in 1962. Its chairman was a chartered accountant, with five supporting members. Its brief was to review the whole tax system, and this occupied it for four years: its report, in six volumes, was presented in December 1966.

The Carter Report is the most comprehensive examination of the implications of a comprehensive income tax ever undertaken. It favors a single tax base which would include not only income and capital gains but also gifts received, with extensive averaging provisions. The income of corporations was to be imputed and taxed as the income of shareholders. This led to lower income tax rates, especially, it suggested, at the upper end of the income distribution. More generally, it proposed the substitution of a retail sales tax for the Canadian manufacturers' tax and a shift in the burden of taxation from personal taxes generally toward the corporate sector. The Canadian government published a white paper in response three years after publication of the report and introduced a tax reform package in 1971. The government actually abandoned federal gifts taxation. It did introduce a capital gains tax, although well short of taxation as income. The corporate income tax was not integrated, although partial imputation was introduced. No retail sales tax was introduced. The rate structure was rationalized and generally lowered.

The Asprey Committee was established by the Australian government in 1972. Its chairman was a judge, assisted by four others. Its 600-page report was published in January 1975. Its brief was to cover the whole Australian tax system, and its report concerned matters of technical detail as well as general principle. Its principal recommendations included the restructuring of the income tax schedule to provide fewer and wider rate bands; the reduction of the number of deductions and their replacement by rebates (of equivalent value to all taxpayers); the substitution of the value added tax (VAT) for the Australian wholesale sales tax; no wealth tax, but tougher gift and estates taxes combined with the introduction of a capital gains tax.

The move from deductions to rebates was made immediately, and successive Australian governments did reduce the number of bands in the rate schedule. Estate and gift duties have been reduced or abolished. Australia still has no VAT or capital gains tax, although their possible introduction was a central element in the discussion surrounding the July 1985 "tax summit".

The British Meade Report was not the product of an official committee of inquiry, but its composition and proceedings were similar; it was established and financed by the independent Institute for Fiscal Studies, with an academic, Professor J. E. Meade, as chairman. It began work in 1975 and its report was published in January 1978. Its brief related only to direct taxes. The Meade Report was to the expenditure tax what Carter was to the comprehensive income tax—an exhaustive analysis of consequences and implications—and its principal proposal is a move toward such a base. In conjunction with this, a reform of the corporation tax on a cash-flow basis is favored. Estate and gifts taxes are to be replaced by a progressive annual wealth accessions tax, which combines some features of an accessions tax and an annual wealth tax. The subsequent Conservative government introduced a major extension and liberalization of the rules governing personal pensions, but no further action has been taken to implement these recommendations.

The Irish Commission on taxation was established in March 1980. A particular issue in Ireland, and one which contributed to an awareness that an overall review of the tax system was appropriate, was widespread public demonstration over a perceived disparity between the burdens on PAYE taxpayers and the rest of the population. The chairman of the commission was a lawyer; ten other members were appointed from different economic sectors. The commission was required to consider the whole tax system, and completed its five-volume report by the end of 1985. Like Asprey, the commission gives attention to the detail as well as the general principles of the existing tax structure.

The Irish Commission's central recommendation was for a single rate of income tax, applying to both corporate and personal income, with full imputation of the company tax against the personal tax on dividends, supplemented by a progressive expenditure tax on the highest incomes. The tax base would be widened, and real capital gains would be brought within it. The six rates of VAT should be reduced to one, and fewer specific commodity duties should be imposed. As yet, no significant progress has been made toward the commission's direct tax objectives, although the number of direct tax rates has been reduced with somewhat wider bands and some simplification and restructuring of indirect taxes has taken place.

The McCaw Report was the product of a "task force" established by the New Zealand government. It was set up in July 1981 and reported only nine months later. Although its brief covered the whole tax system, its 300-page report includes little detail and the stated intention of the group was to attempt to meet the tight deadline imposed rather than to be comprehensive in coverage. The principal recommendations are for fewer, and lower, rates of income tax over a wider band, and for a rationalization of the wholesale sales tax with an eye to the prospective introduction of a VAT. Inflation accounting for tax purposes is advocated, with an element of imputation. The report opposes a capital gains tax, on either real or nominal gains. There has been some simplification of the rate structure; no other positive central recommendations were immediately implemented, but several received further consideration again, subsequent to the 1984 change of government. In particular the new government has decided to introduce a goods and services tax (GST), which is effectively a comprehensive VAT.

Canada, Australia, and New Zealand are all countries with a British parliamentary tradition. The United States has had no analogous independent committees, but two reports, "Blueprints for Basic Tax Reform," published in 1977, and "Tax Reform for Fairness, Simplicity and Economic Growth," issued in November 1984 (see the chapter by Charles McLure, in this volume), share similar objectives to those of the inquiries described. While both were administration documents, their principal authors were short-term appointees rather than career tax officials, and their function was to initiate public debate rather than to commit the administration to particular policies. "Blueprints" appeared in the final days of the Ford administration, and no action followed; "Tax Reform for Fairness, Simplicity and Economic Growth" was followed by the president's own proposals to Congress (generally known as Treasury 1 and Treasury 2, respectively). Treasury 2 follows a similar broad approach, although there are important differences of detail.

"Blueprints" was concerned only with direct taxes, and it put forward two alternative proposals for their reform. One, following Carter, implied movement towards a comprehensive income tax, with full integration of personal and corporate tax. Capital gains were to be adjusted for inflation and taxed as income. The proposals stopped short of Carter in not bringing gifts within the comprehensive income base. The alternative scheme provided for an expenditure tax on lines very similar to those of the Meade Report (see below). Under both groups of proposals the rate structure would be revised to involve fewer, wider rate bands with generally somewhat lower rates.

The working group which produced "Treasury 1" was established following the president's 1984 State of the Union message and was published in November 1984. The main proposals provided for a reduction in the number of marginal rates of tax from 14 to 3, accompanied by a general lowering of rates and widening of bands, and for a substantial reduction in the very wide range of deductions and exemptions available to U.S. taxpayers. Investment income and capital gains were both indexed and taxed as income. In the corporate sector, investment incentive provisions were removed, but depreciation was indexed and the overall corporation tax rate was reduced. An element of imputation of corporate tax liabilities against personal taxation on dividends was proposed. A variety of tax proposals based on Treasury 1 and Treasury 2 is currently before Congress.

It is evident that there are both common themes and differences in the range of recommendations. In subsequent sections I elaborate on a number of these, picking illustrative elements rather than attempting a comprehensive comparison.

II. The Choice of Tax base

All the reports consider the choice between income and expenditure as alternative tax bases. It is interesting to note that wealth taxes are implicitly or explicitly rejected in all cases: by Carter, on the grounds that it would discriminate inappropriately between human and tangible capital, by Meade, Asprey, and the Irish Commission principally on the grounds that it is more efficient, and more equitable, to tax either the accumulation of capital or the proceeds of it. For McCaw, the choice between income and expenditure is seen as relatively unimportant. The task force takes the view that over the life cycle there is no difference between the amount paid under the two regimes and that the effect of the choice is simply one of timing. The error in this argument is clearly enough explained in "Blueprints": "The choice is between an income tax that, *at each level of endowment*, favors early consumers and late earners over late consumers and early earners and a consumption tax that is *neutral* between these two types of individuals" (p. 52).

Sentiments similar to those of McCaw are to be found in Carter, which regards the continuous taxation of accretions to economic power as the best approximation to their idea of taxing economic power—wealth including human capital—itself.

For Asprey, the choice between income and expenditure taxation is seen as broadly equivalent to a choice between complexity and simplicity in tax structures. The expenditure taxes the report envisages are indirect rather than direct. It sees the income tax as an intrinsically complex structure but views this as a price which has to be paid for the potential merits of a tax which is capable of being fine-tuned to the needs of economic policy and the distribution and redistribution of income. It is generally skeptical about the value of such fine-tuning, and hence its broad approach is to support a tax structure based more on expenditure. "Blueprints" provides a survey of issues involved but refrains from making any choice between them.

Meade follows the "Blueprints" approach in examining the possibilities of both comprehensive expenditure and comprehensive income taxes, and in concluding that either would be superior to existing hybrids. Having reached this point, however, it goes beyond "Blueprints" and concludes that mainly practical considerations favor the choice of expenditure:

> Our examination of the problem in Chapter 7 has convinced us that it would be extremely difficult, if not impossible, to introduce all the features of a comprehensive income tax. In particular, we think that many of the measures which would theoretically be necessary to index the system for proper capital-income adjustments against inflation would not be practicable. . . . a basic argument for a move in the direction of an income tax is that it would enlarge the tax base. Apart from this possibility, it may be claimed that the balance of considerations points in the opposite direction, namely a move towards some form of expenditure tax (pp. 500–502).

The Irish Commission is less convinced of the arguments, either on equity or feasibility grounds, for a general substitution of expenditure for income taxes. Seeing the equity arguments as indecisive, it does not propose a change in the balance of direct and indirect taxes. It is, however, strongly persuaded of the practical advantages of expenditure over other bases for deriving tax efficiently and effectively from relatively wealthy tax payers. Hence it proposes the introduction of what is described by Meade as a "top-end expenditure tax."

McCaw reviews the general debate on income versus expenditure taxation, concluding that this offers no decisive conclusion on either theoretical or practical grounds. It notes, however, New Zealand's extreme reliance on the income tax, supported by neither any payroll taxes nor any general sales tax, and argues that this has put the income tax structure under unacceptable strain. For these reasons the report supports some shift to indirect taxes.

The U.S. Treasury Report considers both a direct expenditure tax and a value-added tax as alternatives to the existing income tax structures. It notes the advantages of a direct expenditure tax—which it describes as a consumed income tax, particularly in relation to the issues of capital/income measurement—but rejects it, partly on grounds of equity and concern for possible transitional and international problems. The value-added tax is rejected because of concern for its distributional and administrative costs in a country with no broad-based federal sales tax.

Although there are different views on the overall choice between income and expenditure, there is near unanimity in favoring extension and liberalization of rules giving expenditure tax treatment to life-cycle saving. Carter proposes more generous treatment for pensions and retirement saving, a suggestion which may seem odd to those who see the Carter Report as the strongest affirmation of the comprehensive income tax, but which can be understood more clearly if the arguments underlying that recommendation are as described above. Asprey puts forward two views without choosing between them—one a mild reorganization of existing provision for retirement savings, the other a very substantial extension, which would give tax exemption to all households to savings for life-cycle purposes up to $150,000. "Blueprints" and Meade explore the expenditure tax route. The Irish Commission supports higher limits on contributions for the self-employed and the introduction of individual retirement accounts on U.S. lines. The U.S. Treasury Report, while restricting income tax deductions generally, favors extending those relating to retirement benefits. The only exception is the McCaw Report, which advocated a critical review of existing superannuation provisions, and this is a recommendation on which action was taken.

III. Fringe Benefits

There is no subject on which there is such clear agreement on the appropriate direction of reform than the taxation of fringe benefits.

> The administration has not been sufficiently stringent in bringing employee benefits in kind into tax. Faced with high taxes on money income on the one hand, and the possibility of no tax on non-cash benefits on the other, employers and employees have found it attractive to substitute the one for the other. . . . To stop this trend we recommend that employers should either add the value of all non-cash benefits to the tax base of the employee or pay a high tax on the amount not allocated to employees (Carter Commission).

> The special rule . . . has not prevented the offering and accepting of fringe benefits in substitution for cash, under employment contracts. Some of these benefits are certainly taxed; but to the extent that they are valued for income tax purposes below what would be paid for them in cash outside the income-producing relationship, the equity of the system is seriously affected (Asprey Report, para. 7.15).

For "Blueprints" and for Meade, the issue is so obvious that it barely requires to be argued: both go directly to sets of measures designed to deal with the issue. The Irish Commission repeats a familiar theme: "The existing taxation treatment of fringe benefits is favourable in relation to that accorded to ordinary income. Reform is essential" (para. 12.1). McCaw reiterates: "The failure to tax such gains as fringe benefits . . . provides substantial incentives and opportunities for taxpayers to convert income from taxed to untaxed (or less taxed) sources. . . . This has happened in New Zealand, and the overall result has been, in the opinion of the Task Force, a significant diminution of the general acceptability of the tax system (para. 5.7).

The U.S. Treasury Report offers an exceptionally concise and lucid statement of the argument:

> The tax advantage now accorded some fringe benefits causes more of them to be consumed than if, like most goods and services, they could only be bought with after-tax income. This distortion of consumer choices would only be accentuated by widening the exemption of fringe benefits. Moreover, extending the scope of the exclusion of fringe benefits would exacerbate inequities in the treatment of employees receiving fringe benefits and those who receive income in other forms. Finally, the growing tendency to pay compensation in tax-exempt forms reduces the base for the social security taxes and thus weakens the social security system. These inequities and distortions can be reduced only if statutory fringe benefits are taxed more nearly like other income.

Fringe benefits represent perhaps the clearest instance of the second theory of the role of inquiry described in the introduction: everyone, including government, knows what needs to be done, but there is advantage in finding someone external and independent to say so.

IV. Rate Structures

This is also a subject on which the reports are almost unanimous. There is general support for tax schedules that have a small number of rate bands, each covering a wide range of incomes. Asprey stops short of proposing a specific rate schedule, but urges strongly that a revision should provide fewer and wider steps. "Blueprints" specifically urges that the number of marginal rates be reduced to three. Britain already has a rate structure in which the same marginal rate applies to most taxpayers. Meade notes that there are departures from this principle at the lower end of the income distribution, where the withdrawal of means-tested benefits interacts with the tax system to yield very high implicit marginal rates of tax, and also at the upper end, where higher rates are imposed on a minority. The report advocates that even these departures from proportionality should be rectified.

New Zealand had five marginal tax rates at the time the McCaw Report was written, and it urges a flatter rate structure. The Irish Commission—also confronted with five rates—suggests they be reduced to one. The U.S. Treasury Report reiterates the "Blueprints" proposal of a reduction to three marginal rates.

The universality of this theme is striking. Everyone suggests that the number of marginal tax rates be reduced. In those countries where that number is currently high, the objective is to bring it in line with countries with fewer; in those which already have few marginal rates, the proposal is to bring the number down further. If everyone who looks at this question agrees that the number of marginal rates should be reduced, why do so many countries continue to have so many? One possible explanation is that the proliferation of marginal rates is largely the product of confusion—a confusion from which committees which study the subject escape. In particular, there is very widespread popular confusion between the role of average and marginal tax rates in tax schedules.

The one exception to this general theme—which perhaps confirms this argument—is the Carter Report. Carter's recommendations for rate schedules are based on a distinction between necessary and discretionary income. Since discretionary income is an increasing proportion of total income as that income rises, tax should increase more than proportionately with income. So it should, but this does not imply increasing marginal rates. Indeed, the simplest formulation of the Carter approach would see all income up to some level as necessary, and everything above that as discretionary; an approach which would imply a linear tax schedule with a single marginal rate.

V. The Tax unit

All committees have considered the issue of how husband and wife should be taxed. There is almost no area of taxation, however, in which the diversity of existing practice around the world is so great. Canada had, when the Carter Committee reported, a system in which the individual was the basis of taxation, although with the inclusion of some dependency allowances (it still does). Carter recommended that this be replaced by a unit basis of assessment; there would be distinct rate schedules for single individuals and for couples, with bands less than twice as wide for couples (thus implying that marriage might increase liabilities for those with two similar incomes, but would reduce tax due if the whole of the household income was derived from one partner).

Australia also had (and has) a predominantly individual system. The Irish Commission contrasts the approaches of two committees to illustrate the possible range of disagreement. Carter writes: "We believe firmly that the family is today, as it has been for many centuries, the basic economic unit in society." Asprey asserts that "the adoption of a compulsory family unit basis must be rejected on the grounds of general social principle. The right to be taxed as an individual has always been accorded in Australia." The same quotations are reproduced simultaneously in the McCaw Report. This divergence of opinion is not, however, altogether reflected in divergence of recommendation, and Asprey proposes the institution of an optional unit basis.

The United States has a system close to that which Carter recommended for Canada. There are separate rate schedules for singles and couples, but the couple rate schedule is somewhat less generous than, for example, the French quotient system, which splits household income between household members. "Blueprints" favors retention of this method, and so does the Treasury Report.

Britain has a structure in which the income of a married woman is aggregated with that of her husband and he obtains enhanced allowances in recognition of the burden involved. There is an option for separate assessment of the wife's earnings, but this is an option which it is not normally profitable to exercise. Meade proposes that this be replaced by procedures which are symmetrical between the two partners and, although canvassing a variety of proposals, tends to support the individual taxation of earnings and the unit taxation of investment income.

The deliberations of the Irish Commission were complicated by the Murphy case, in which the Supreme Court ruled that any provisions of the tax code which might have the effect of giving a married couple a liability in excess of that which they would have as two separate individuals violated constitutional provisions requiring the state to safeguard the institution of marriage. In consequence, Ireland moved from a system close to that of the United Kingdom to one close to that of France. In the light of these developments, the commission recommended a unit basis, but with the option for the couple to be taxed as two separate individuals if preferred. Its proposal for a single general basic rate of tax makes application of this principle relatively simple.

New Zealand shares an individual basis for taxation with Canada and Australia. The McCaw Report opposes this; it gives the issue a very protracted discussion, ending with a strong recommendation for a unit basis with a quotient system with divisor in the range 1.3–1.8; i.e., with bands for the aggregate income of a couple which are that multiple of the bands for a single household.

Given the diversity of existing practice and general opinion on this subject, the extent to which these reports reach common conclusions is remarkable. There is general support for a move to a unit basis. Countries which are already there wish to stay there: countries which are not wish to move toward it. Still more remarkable is the fact that this common conclusion is entirely at variance with a widespread popular feeling that an individual basis for taxation is the most appropriate direction of change. Such a feeling is reflected, for example, in the recent EEC memorandum.

VI. Different Arguments and Common Conclusions

The seven reports considered here were prepared in very different economic circumstances; one in the 1960s, three in the 1970s, three in the 1980s. The chairmen and membership provided a range of different backgrounds, in professional expertise and in the interest groups they represented. There were considerable differences in the social and political background, and in the approach which they brought to their task.

Yet overall, the similarities in their recommendations are far more striking than the differences. We have examined proposals in four main areas: the choice of the tax base, fringe benefits, rate structures, and the tax unit. In three of these four there is a very obvious consensus in the conclusions which have been reached. As far as fringe benefits go, this is perhaps not surprising. I suspect most students of public finance, or political economy, could predict that any independent review of the tax system would favor a drive against the erosion of the tax base through fringe benefits. This is archetypally an area where individual taxpayers succeed in lobbying for concessions for themselves which run counter to the interests of taxpayers at large. Taxpayers at large are a poorly represented interest group, and acting on their behalf is one role which committees of inquiry can fill.

The two other areas of consensus are more surprising. There are relatively clear conclusions to be drawn on both rate structure and tax unit; reduction of the number of different marginal rates, and a household unit basis of assessment. Both these recommendations run counter to very widespread perceptions that an elaborately graduated rate structure is desirable to achieve progressivity and that taxpayers should be taxed as individuals. There are, perhaps, important differences here between the opinions of people who have thought about the problems and the opinions of people who have not. Many of the reasons that they have for wanting complex rate structures are confused; purely individual taxation has considerable superficial appeal. But in a world in which most households do, in reality, treat the resources of the household as a common pool, individual taxation may often give rise to more anomalies than it removes.

The fourth area—the choice of the tax base—has generated more disagreement. Carter, McCaw, and Treasury I follow broadly a comprehensive income tax approach, Asprey and McCaw favor moves toward indirect taxation, with less revenue derived from a more comprehensive income tax. Meade, "Blueprints" and the Irish Commission also wish income tax to be more comprehensive, but seek substantially to displace it by direct expenditure taxation. Although there are substantial differences of view here, they are smaller than at first sight appears. Three recurrent elements are (1) more comprehensiveness in income tax; (2) extension or retention of generous relief for life-cycle savings within that; (3) more emphasis on expenditure relative to income taxation.

I noted at the beginning of this paper that the results of these reports in terms of immediate direct implementation were disappointing—at least to their authors. But they have established a consensus of appropriate directions of reform. To what extent has that consensus influenced actual developments? Some of the trends evident in these reports have emerged clearly: the tendency to reduce the number of bands in the rate schedule, to increase the range and scope of concessions to savings, and the widespread consideration and adoption of broadly based sales taxes. Changes in the tax treatment of capital gains have been less certain in direction. The problem is evident from Asprey's discussion of the issue. Although Asprey is generally in favor of a capital gains tax, the report urges that the government (which had in any event put forward proposals to introduce such a tax) should defer these for further consideration so long as inflation remained at current levels. Attitudes to capital gains tax in the last decade have been much influenced by the knowledge that a high proportion of such gains were illusory inflationary gains, and it remains to be seen how policy in this area will develop once prices are again more stable. With that exception, however, the common elements in the choice of tax bases have been widely reflected in the development of tax policy.

To what extent did these reports reflect that climate, and to what extent influence it? It is almost impossible to tell; the various reports are obviously influenced by each other, and this is particularly true for the most innovative of them—Carter and Meade. But it is probable that the reports have been more effective than an emerging academic consensus would have been in creating a common international climate of informed opinion.

It will be seen that the reports discussed have contributed a good deal to a climate of thought about tax policy, and relatively little to immediate implementation. Their influence, though real, is long term. One recent commentator on the Asprey Report stated:

> The year of publication of the Report, 1975, was a tumultuous one politically in Australia and this may be one explanation for the commonly held view that the Report had little immediate impact on the policies of Government. In this respect the Asprey Report is often compared unfavourably with the Mathews Report [Report of the Committee of Inquiry into Inflation and Taxation, May, 1975] which was adopted by the Coalition parties in Opposition and implemented as regards two of its three major recommendations after the change of Government in 1975.

A decade later, however, it is clear that of the two Reports the Asprey Report has had by far the largest long term impact. The Trading Stock Valuation Adjustment and Indexation of the personal income tax rate scales which were adopted from the Mathews Report were abandoned in 1979 and 1981 respectively. On the other hand, an increasing number of the Asprey Report recommendations have been implemented over the years and now appear to be permanent features of the tax system (R. J. Vann, Australian Tax Foundation *Newsletter*, March 1985).

The members of the Asprey Committee were well aware that this was the choice they were making. They observed that they could approach their task either by reviewing existing legislation line by line, or by setting out blueprints for change and suggesting initial steps toward it. The rightness of their choice is demonstrated by the British Royal Commission of 1955, where the majority chose the first route and the minority the second; the long-term influence of the minority report greatly exceeded the short-term effect of the majority's conclusions.

If this is the role that blueprints are to serve, it ought to influence the approach adopted in future studies of this kind. In particular, much of the detail contained in, say, Carter or Meade may be redundant. If governments are unlikely to implement packages wholesale, but will be pushed in the right directions, it is unnecessary—and perhaps unwise—to over-detail the directions. It also follows that the emphasis on treating reform packages as a whole—stressed, for example, by the Irish Commission—is hard to reconcile with the reality of implementation, or the lack of it. "Blueprints for Basic Tax Reform" chose a title which describes the role of such studies almost exactly. They should serve to tax systems the role which corporate strategy fulfills to efficient businesses. All change must be made incrementally: the purpose of a blueprint, or a strategy, is not to dictate every incremental change but to provide a framework within which these will be seen as moves in right, or wrong, directions.

References

Carter Commission, *Report of the Royal Commission on Taxation*, Canadian Government Printer, Ottawa, 1966.

Asprey, Taxation Review Committee, *Full Report*, Australian Government Publishing Service, Canberra, 1975.

Blueprints, *Blueprints for Basic Tax Reform*, U.S. Government Printing Office, Washington, D.C., 1977.

Meade, *The Structure and Reform of Direct Taxation*, Allen and Unwin, for the Institute of Fiscal Studies, London, 1978.

McCaw, *Report of the Task Force on Tax Reform*, Government Printer, Wellington, 1982.

Irish Commission, *Reports of the Commission on Taxation*, principally, *First Report, Direct Taxation*, The Stationery Office, Dublin, 1982.

U.S. Treasury, *Tax Reform for Fairness, Simplicity, and Economic Growth*, Department of the Treasury, Washington, D.C., 1984.

Résumé

Ce rapport soulève la question de savoir pourquoi les gouvernements nomment si souvent des commissions pour examiner les politiques fiscales, contrairement à ce qui se passe dans de nombreux autres domaines de politique. Une bonne raison de se poser la question est que, ainsi que ce rapport le montre, le degré de mise en oeuvre directe des recommandations énoncées dans ces enquêtes est très bas. Par ailleurs, on avance que ces enquêtes ont eu un très important effet sur les attitudes générales à l'égard de la fiscalité et, de ce fait, peuvent influencer la politique menée ultérieurement. La vérification de ces hypothèses, sous forme de comparaisons entre le contenu et le résultat de plusieurs grandes enquêtes fiscales dans différents pays, est ensuite présentée et elle fait ressortir de remarquables ressemblances entre les options de politique recommandées dans les divers rapports.

Social Security: Problems of Maturity

Henry J. Aaron*

Policy makers in many developed countries are reexamining their social security systems. Programs that once were regarded as ornaments of welfare capitalism now seem burdensome obligations. In this paper I shall suggest that this change in attitudes is rooted in objective economic events and shall examine possible responses to them. I shall focus on retirement and survivors benefits and shall pay scant attention to disability and unemployment benefits and to family allowances.

I. Real Economic Events

The underlying economic events that have increased the cost of social insurance for currently active workers are increased life expectancy, decreased birth rates, reduced economic growth, and decreased labor force participation among certain groups.

Demography

The demographic facts are simple. In the years following World War II birth rates in most developed countries jumped well above those necessary to sustain population, but, for a variety of reasons, have fallen sharply since then. Birth rates in most of those countries currently are at or below replacement rates. At the same time, mortality rates have continued to decline as the salubrious effects of higher living standards and public health measures have been reinforced by a broad range of medical and surgical advances.

The results of these demographic trends is a decrease in the ratio of

*The author is Senior Fellow at the Brookings Institution and Professor of Economics at the University of Maryland.

The Relevance of Public Finance for Policy-Making. Proceedings of the 41st Congress of the International Institute of Public Finance. Madrid, 1985, pp. 83–95. He wishes to thank Lori Grunin for research assistance. The views expressed in this paper are those of the author and not necessarily those of the staff or trustees of the Brookings Institution or of the University of Maryland.

active workers to retirees (see Table 1). While this ratio has been falling for many years, sharp additional decreases will occur in the next two decades within most developed countries. The proportion of total population over age 65 is rising in most advanced nations and will exceed 15 to 20 percent in many by 2020 (see Table 2). If birth and mortality rates remain near current rates, the proportion of the population that is elderly could go even higher.

The ratio of the employed to the prime-aged population is subject to offsetting trends in many nations. Female labor force participation has risen (see Table 3). But so have unemployment, disability,, and voluntary male withdrawal from the labor force. Which of these forces will predominate is unclear and, to a degree, is subject to influence by tax and transfer policy.

Economics

All advanced nations finance retirement benefits by variations on pay-as-you-go methods, in which accumulated reserves equal only a small proportion of outstanding benefit obligations to current and future retirees and rarely exceed benefits payable over one or two years.[1] If benefits are not reduced when the ratio for the retired to the active population increases, current outlays rise as a fraction of current earnings and active workers must pay increased taxes or contributions.

Economic factors reinforce the demographically based tendency toward increasing social insurance costs. The most important is the slowdown in the growth of output per worker since the first oil shock. The tax or contribution rate active workers must pay to support a given "replacement rate" (ratio of retirement benefits to previous earnings) for retired workers is a diminishing function of the speed with which total earnings are growing. Earnings growth is simply the sum of the growth in the number of workers and of earnings per worker.

The following admittedly oversimplified example illustrates the impact of earnings growth on the cost of social insurance. Suppose that the adult population always consists of sixty cohorts of equal size. Forty-five cohorts are working and fifteen are retired. This assumption closely approximates work patterns in many developed countries. If pensions equal 60 percent of disposable income net of taxes to support pensions, the tax rate on active workers under a pay-as-you-go system must be 16.66 percent if there is no earnings growth; 12.8 percent if earnings grow at the equivalent of 1 percent per year; 9.6 percent if earnings grow at the equivalent of 2 percent per year; and 5.1 percent if earnings grow at the equivalent of 4 percent per year. Earlier retirement boosts these costs sharply because it causes both an increase in the number of transfer recipients and a decrease in the number

Table 1

Ratio of Retirees to Active Workers in Selected Countries, 1950–2030

Year	France	Germany	Great Britain	Japan	United States
1950	4.62	—	3.37[a]	—	—
1980	2.82[b]	2.19	2.76[c]	8.2	5.13
2000 (proj.)	2.49[d]	1.83[e]	2.99[d,f]	2.70[g]	4.10[h]
2030 (proj.)	1.64[d]	1.12[e]	2.09[d,i]	1.6[g,j]	2.10[h]

Source: *The World Crisis in Social Security*, ed. Jean-Jacques Rosa (San Francisco Institute for Contemporary Studies, 1982).
   a. 1951.
   b. 1985.
   c. 1981.
   d. Assumed fertility rate = 1.8.
   e. Assumed fertility rate not reported.
   f. 2001.
   g. Assumed fertility rate = 2.1.
   h. Assumed fertility rate = 1.8.
   i. 2032.
   j. 2025.

Table 2

Percentage of the Population Aged 65 and Older in Selected Countries, 1950–2020

Year	Canada	Germany	Japan	Netherlands	Sweden	United Kingdom	United States
1950	7.7	9.4	4.9	7.7	10.3	10.7	8.1
1980	8.9	15.0	9.0	11.5	16.2	14.8	11.3
2000 (proj.)	11.8	16.5	14.9	14.1	17.2	14.9	11.7
2020 (proj.)	16.1	21.2	21.0	20.8	21.9	17.4	15.4

Source: *World Population Prospects: Estimates and Projections as Assessed in 1982* (New York: United Nations Publications, 1985).

of taxpayers. If the duration of retirement rises by one year, causing a 6.7 percent increase in the number of retirees, the steady-state tax rate rises about 8.3 percent.

The marked deceleration in the growth of earnings over the last decade means that current and future workers must pay a much higher percentage of income as taxes to meet obligations to retirees than would have been necessary had previous growth rates been sustained.

That political concern about burdens of retirement and other social

Table 3

Labor Force Participation of Women Aged 15 to 64 in Selected OECD Nations

Country	1960	1970	1982
Australia	34.1%	46.1%	52.0%
Canada	33.7	43.2	58.9
France	45.4	47.5	52.9
Netherlands	26.2	28.0	38.8
Sweden	50.1	59.4	75.9
United States	42.6	48.9	61.4
West Germany	49.2	48.1	49.8
All OECD	45.7	47.2	54.1

Source: OECD Historical Statistics: 1960–1982 Paris: OECD, 1984.

insurance benefits greatly intensified after the first OPEC oil shock and the collapse of productivity growth that followed it is not coincidental. The increase in unemployment over the last decade directly and immediately increased the burden of social insurance, and the decline in the growth of earnings per worker had an even sharper effect on the expected future cost of social insurance. This increase in the cost of an established social program came at the same time active workers were having to adjust to the prospect of much slower prospective growth in before-tax earnings. The demographic trends that had long been apparent combined with a sharp change in income expectations to create the objective circumstances in which the examination of prior commitments was all but inevitable. The debate over whether the move to conservatism in many Western nations merely reflects the worsened terms of trade between social insurance and current consumption or represents a change in underlying political preferences will probably continue for many years. However that debate is resolved, the terms of trade *did* worsen. The next section explores the possible responses to this fact.

II. Options for Response

What options do industrial nations face in dealing with their social insurance systems? Practical options consist of variations and combinations of the following policies.

Cutbacks

The simplest response to the increase in the cost of social insurance is to curtail benefit levels or eligibility. Benefits can be reduced by overt decreases in social security benefits or by subjecting benefits to personal income tax.[2] Reductions in eligibility typically entail increases in the age at which benefits are paid. Both approaches would reduce required taxes below rates that would be necessary if all current obligations are met. If such legislative actions caused no changes in behavior, the result would be reduced incomes for retirees and for their dependents. But at least one of the following three responses is likely.

First, older workers might postpone retirement. Theory strongly suggests such a response, as the income effect would discourage consumption of leisure and the substitution effect, at best, would be neutral. But theory does not generate predictions about the magnitude of this response. Empirical work in this area is quite difficult, because the rules of social insurance programs are complex, rendering simple models and estimation techniques inappropriate. Recent estimates suggest that in the United States even sizable reductions in retirement benefits would cause only brief deferral of retirement; most of the savings would show up as reduced income for retirees [3]. These estimates take private wealth as given, a reasonable assumption for the short run, and hence a reasonable basis for estimating the effects on retirement of cohorts nearing retirement who do not have time to alter private accumulations of wealth very much by changing savings behavior.

In the short run, but especially in the long, workers may respond in a second way—by increasing saving to compensate for the reductions in social insurance wealth that a cut in benefits would cause. Although this response would take some years to have a major effect on private wealth accumulations at given ages, it is the logical response if workers do not elect, even in the long run, to adjust fully to cuts in benefits by deferring retirement. In fact, if workers behave according to the life-cycle model, the effect of social insurance on retirement and saving is intertwined, as Feldstein and others have argued [5]. The smaller the effect of changes in social insurance on labor supply, the larger the effect on saving predicted by the life-cycle model. Unfortunately for life-cycle theory, evidence is growing that the behavior of at least a significant minority of households is not even approximated by the life-cycle model (see, e.g. [4]).

The third possible response to cutbacks in social insurance is the collective decision to put some form of alternative government program or incentive for private saving in place of social insurance. Proposals along these lines typically call for some form of mandatory saving, with larger reserves than social insurance programs customarily accumulate. Succeeding sections examine these responses.

Moving to Funded Systems

No social insurance system in the developed nations holds reserves sufficient to cover most outstanding obligations. All operate more or less on the pay-as-you-go principle. One reason is that whenever legislators recognized the desirability of instituting or expanding social insurance, they were unwilling to wait the forty or so years to make those changes completely effective that would have been necessary if full reserve funding had been employed. Full reserve funding requires each cohort of workers to receive benefits equal only to the discounted value of the taxes or contributions it paid or that were paid on its behalf. Few legislators are willing to impose taxes to support benefits that will not take full effect for three or four decades. Furthermore, social insurance systems of some countries attained their current levels of generosity at a time when Keynesian fears of excess saving and attendant concern about chronically inadequate demand were widespread. In such countries, not only was pay-as-you-go financing politically attractive, it also seemed economically prudent.

Nevertheless, moving to full reserve financing now, when benefits are no longer increasing, has considerable abstract appeal because it could significantly increase national capital formation. This objective could be achieved in either of two ways. First, each worker could be given a personal retirement account into which his or her taxes would be deposited. As the worker's balance grew, so would future entitlements to retirement benefits. In effect, the government would run a set of mandatory defined-contribution retirement plans. As a variation on this theme, the government could authorize voluntary savings in tax-sheltered accounts; if a sufficient number of people took advantage of these accounts, the result would be similar to the mandatory system. Alternatively, each cohort could be given a defined-benefit retirement plan, typical of most graduated social insurance benefits, with entitlements growing as contributions accumulated. If the actuarial value of accumulating benefits equals current taxes, a reserve similar in size to that generated by a defined contribution plan will result.

The first of these approaches would preclude any interpersonal income redistribution through social insurance, except perhaps for some redistribution associated with actuarial risks such as life expectancy past retirement age. The second approach would permit interpersonal redistribution within cohorts, but would preclude redistributional schemes that transferred more income to a cohort than it had paid in social insurance taxes. Both approaches would lead to the accumulation of large reserves and potentially could add significantly to national saving.

The case for replacing current pay-as-you-go retirement programs with full reserve programs, even over periods as long as twenty or thirty years, suffers from a fundamental flaw. Moving to a full reserve system would force the transitional generation to pay for two sets of retirement benefits—its own (through the funded system) and that of previous retirees (under the preexisting pay-as-you-go system). The result would be a one-time drop in consumption for the transitional generation, a drop equal to the build-up in reserves. Although future generations might, in some sense, gain more than the transitional generation lost, the social desirability of such a shift is problematic. If there is any growth in productivity, such a course would be equivalent to taxing a relatively poor group (current workers) to pay for a project that would provide benefits only to relatively rich groups (future workers). Even if the rate of return is attractive (as would be the case if savings actually increase and if the capital stock is smaller than the "golden rule" level), such a "project" might well be rejected. This example exactly parallels a public works project financed by taxes on the poor to provide services to the rich. Even if the benefit-cost ratio exceeds unity, distributional considerations may well lead to its rejection. If an increase in the national capital stock is regarded as desirable, it is unclear why it should take the form of a capital levy on the transitional generation.[3]

On the assumption that an increase in national saving is deemed desirable, several additional questions arise. First, will the approach be effective? Quite apart from the question of whether individuals will offset the effects of building up mandatory reserves by altering their own saving, there is the added question of whether the government will offset retirement saving by altering its other fiscal operations. In particular, deficits on operations other than social insurance must be unaffected by reserve policies in the social insurance system. This assumption is crucial, as nothing would be added to national saving if social insurance reserves were wholly absorbed in buying up increased amounts of debt issued by other government agencies.

If building up social insurance reserves is an effective way to increase national saving, a second question arises: is it fair? The answer to that question depends entirely on one's judgment of the fairness of social insurance taxes. It also depends on what alternative tax instruments are available for increasing public or private saving. In short, what is the alternative to payroll taxes? Since wage taxes and simple consumption-type value-added taxes have similar lifetime incidence, there is little difference between payroll taxes and value-added taxes of the type commonly used in most nations.[4] The incidence of progressive income taxes differs significantly from that of payroll taxes. It seems clear that the incidence of voluntary private saving differs greatly from that of earnings.[5]

Third, are the side effects of a move to a fully funded system desirable or objectionable? For many supporters of a move to a fully funded system, this is the central, if seldom acknowledged, issue. A social insurance system fully funded on an individual basis precludes any interpersonal income redistribution through the social insurance system. A social insurance system fully funded on a cohort basis precludes any intergenerational income redistribution through the social insurance system. Fully funded systems have great appeal to those whose real objective is to end redistribution by government.

Is it desirable to abstain from any interpersonal or intercohort income redistribution throughout the social insurance system? This question is clearly one of values, politics, and sociology more than it is a problem of economics. My view is that unless all redistribution by government is to be ruled off limits, it is unclear why the prohibition of redistribution through social insurance implied by full funding is desirable. Social insurance has proven to be a generally accepted, stigma-free device for assisting in retirement or disability those whose lifetime earnings have been below average for personal reasons or because of war or depression. Thus, many social insurance systems provide proportionally larger benefits to retirees with low wage histories, and most social insurance systems have provided larger benefits to those who retired in the decades following the Great Depression and World War II than would be justified by social insurance taxes paid on their behalf during their working lives. For example, France bases benefits on earnings in the highest ten years.

Similar redistribution can be achieved through other means. For example, supplemental grants can be added to a fully funded social insurance system. This approach makes all redistribution explicit, an advantage within some models of rational political decision-making; but explicit redistribution often seems to carry a greater risk of stigma than does implicit redistribution. Australian experience with a public retirement system based substantially on means-tested benefits for the mass of retirees suggests that stigma may diminish if the means test is set so high that most people pass it [1]. But if such a system is envisaged, the reasons for the shift become obscure.

My own view of the replacement of pay-as-you-go social insurance with fully funded systems is summarized by the supposed advice given by a farmer to a person trying to get to a certain town: you can't get there from here, and you wouldn't want to go there if you could.

Suppolementary Funded Benefits

A stronger case can be made for adding a full funded system of retirement benefits to an existing pay-as-you-go system. Every nation must decide what level of benefits to provide through its basic social insurance system. As political sentiments and economic realities change, this judgment is likely to evolve. Most social insurance systems provide for benefits that rise proportionately with real wages. The logic behind such a policy is far from clear, however. If support for social insurance rests in part on the belief that retirees and survivors should not face the risk of large drops in their standards of living, the case for government abridgment of individual choice about the timing of consumption becomes progressively weaker as benefits rise beyond those sufficient to provide a "basic" standard of living. Since what is "basic" is subjective and evolves as living standards change, it is natural to expect benefits in the core retirement system also to increase with real wages; but there is no reason to think that all nations will or should choose to increase them *at the same rate* as wages.

For a number of reasons the addition of a fully funded government-sponsored *supplemental* system may prove attractive. These reasons include a putative insufficiency of saving, the bias of income taxes (i.e., taxes that fall not only on earnings but also on capital income) against future consumption, and the desirability of increasing the range of individual choice. Such fully funded systems may be mandatory (which does little for individual choice) or voluntary.

Although the addition of a supplemental fully funded system may be supported by those who would like to scuttle the basic pay-as-you-go system, it is important to recognize that such systems can be supported for quite different reasons and to acknowledge that such systems may be opposed by people who fully understand their advantages but who fear that once the fully funded system is in place, it will crowd out or drive out the pay-as-you-go system.

Building Up Reserves

The rising number of retirees and the reduced growth of wages, which will require increases in social insurance taxes to support given replacement rates, suggest another option. Should not the current working generation pay higher taxes than are necessary to support the benefits of current retirees? If the excess were used to build up reserves, future generations could be taxed more lightly than would otherwise be necessary. The objective is to reduce the size of the increase in taxes that would otherwise be necessary to meet the growing burden of retirement benefits. Furthermore, to the extent that reserve accumulation adds to the capital stock, *before-tax* wages would also tend to increase, further reducing the current burden on future cohorts of workers.

This policy does not call for a fully funded system of benefits either to replace the existing pay-as-you-go system or to supplement it. The current retirement benefit system would be affirmed, not replaced or cut. This option would, however, require the current active generation to pay higher taxes than necessary to support current benefits. The objective is a kind of intergenerational equity. Each generation receives a benefit that bears the same relation to its earnings as that received by every other generation; in return, each generation is asked to pay taxes that bear the same relation to its earnings. This seemingly just outcome cannot occur under a strictly pay-as-you-go system with unchanging replacement rates unless the sum of the growth of the employed population and earnings per worker is constant. Building up reserves during perids when retirement cohorts are small or wage growth is higher than normal can approximate this outcome.

The practical problems with this approach include some of the short-comings of the full-funding options. First, it requires that reserves accumulated through the social security system not be offset by deficits in other government operations. Second, it presumes an ability to forecast future growth of both population and earnings per worker. Although past success with such forecasts is not heartening, the lags between changes in birth rates and the time they affect social insurance systems is sufficient to permit some success with "fine tuning."

Raising Taxes

The final option, of course, is to meet all benefit obligations on a pay-as-you-go basis. This course requires active workers to pay increasingly heavy taxes to meet social insurance benefits. If other taxes cover other government spending, this course requires either an increase in taxes or curtailment in the scope of non-social-insurance government activity. To some degree governmental expenditures on the nonaged, most notably on children, would tend to fall with declining numbers. But the support of young adults falls more heavily on private budgets than does support for the aged. As the population ages, therefore, public spending will tend to grow.

The taxation of social security benefits raises other questions, the answers to which hinge on the nature of personal taxation. The key issue is whether the personal tax is designed to fall only on labor income (or equivalently on consumption) or on both labor and capital outcome. Naturally, the rate of tax on labor (t_l) can differ from that on capital (t_k). If $t_l = t_k$, labor and capital income are taxed equally, as under the classic income tax.

If $t_l > 0$ and $t_k = 0$, the result is a labor income tax, which is equivalent at the household level to a consumption tax; of course, labor income and capital income may be taxed at positive but unequal rates.

Under the labor income or consumption tax norm, two approaches to taxing social security are available that are equal in present value terms. First, under a labor income tax, the tax would be imposed on total labor compensation, including *all* social security taxes and general revenue contributions to the social security fund on the worker's behalf. This step would require that individuals *not* be allowed to take income tax deductions for payroll taxes they pay and that their incomes should be *grossed up* by the amount of payroll or other taxes employers paid to the social security system on their behalf and by the amount of general revenue contribution to the social security system on their behalf; the worker would pay tax also on these grossed-up amounts. No further tax would be due under the labor income tax approach.

Under the consumption tax, no tax should be paid by the worker on payroll taxes; hence, payroll taxes should be deductible. No account would be taken in the consumption taxes of active workers or employers' social security taxes or of general revenue contributions. All benefits received by pensioners, however, would be fully taxable.

Assuming a single and constant interest rate (a) for the implicit rate of return to tax payments through the social security system, and (b) for the personal rate of discount, the tax payments under the two approaches have the same discounted present value. The principles of income taxation require a different approach. An income tax falls not only on earnings, but also on interest income. Thus, income includes earnings gross of taxes (the worker's, the employer's, and general revenue contributions, if any) paid into the social security system in the year when they are made, exactly as under a wage tax. In addition, an income tax would fall on implicit interest earnings earned during each succeeding year on this initial amount. Thus, each year active workers would have to pay income tax on all payments made into the social security system on their behalf plus interest earnings on their "account."

No nation follows either of these approaches and none seems likely to do so, illustrating again the difficulty of applying any tax principle consistently. Some nations follow tax rules more generous than either approach. Italy exempts all social security benefits from tax and West Germany excludes some.[6] Thus, the United States imposes income tax on the half of social security taxes paid by workers, but it does not tax the other half of payroll taxes paid by employers (as the labor income tax approach would require), half of social security benefits (as the consumption tax approach would require), or the nearly 90 percent of benefits that the annual income tax approach would require.

What all of this means is that most nations could help defray the costs of social security or of other public spending by personal reforms in the tax treatment of social security that would simultaneously raise revenues and reform tax structure.

III. Conclusion

Real economic events have boosted the price of social insurance retirement programs. Those events—the decline of birth and mortality rates and of growth of earnings per worker—force nations to respond in some fashion. They can sustain the ratio of benefits to earnings and raise taxes, or they can maintain taxes and cut the ratio of benefits to earnings. They can force the full burden of adjustment on the current working generation, or they can spread the effects over several generations. They can maintain collective institutions for achieving some redistribution through social insurance, or they can dismantle those institutions. The attentive reader will recognize that this last issue is independent of the demographic and economic events causing the increase in the price of social insurance. Nonetheless, events aid those who wish to reopen debate on this question.

Each nation can respond to the demographic and economic events in its own way. But no nation can avoid the effects of these events. The need for new social insurance benefit or tax policy is not a matter of ideology but of mathematical necessity.

Notes

1. For a summary of current programs, see *Social Security Programs throughout the World*, 1983, Social Security Administration, Office of Policy, Office of Research and Statistics, Research Report No. 58, G.P.O., 1984.

2. The tax policy issues in taxing social security benefits are examined below.

3. If the multigeneration Ricardo-Barro model accurately characterizes behavior, no capital levy would even occur. The transitional generation would respond to the increase in social insurance taxes by curtailing other saving, leaving its lifetime consumption unchanged. But then the whole rationale for the move—that the switch to full reserve financing would boost national saving—collapses.

4. The most significant difference is that value-added taxes typically have differentiated rates, with "necessities" taxed at lower rates than luxuries. At the price of some increase in administrative complexity and the need for arbitrary distinctions, this feature changes the annual incidence of value added taxes from regressive to proportional. Henry J. Aaron, editor, *Value Added Taxes: Lessons from Europe*, Brookings, 1981. Whether differentiated rates have a similar effect on lifetime incidence is less clear. James Davies, et al., "Some Calculations of Lifetime Incidence," *American Economic Review*, vol. 74 (September 1984), pp. 633–649.

5. Since some of this difference is attributable, no doubt, to the existence of social insurance systems themselves, it is not clear how much significance should be attached to this difference.

6. See [2, p. 5]. Nine other countries tax benefits in full (Austria, Canada, Denmark, France, Japan, the Netherlands, Sweden, Switzerland and the United Kingdom.

References

[1] Aaron, Henry, "Social Welfare in Australia," in *The Australian Economy: A View from the North*, ed. Richard E. Caves and Lawrence B. Krause, Washington, D.C., Brookings Institution, 1984.

[2] Aldrich, Jonathan, "The Earnings Replacement Rate of Old-Age Benefits in 12 Countries, 1969–1980," *Social Security Bulletin*, 45; November 1982.

[3] Burtless, Gary, and Moffitt, Robert A., "The Effect of Social Security Benefits on the Labor Supply of the Aged," in *Retirement and Economic Behavior*, ed. Henry J. Aaron and Gary Burtless, Washington, D.C. Brookings Institution, 1984.

[4] Diamond, Peter A., and Hausman, Jerry A., "The Retirement and Unemployment Behavior of Older Men," in *Retirement and Economic Behavior*, ed. Henry J. Aaron and Gary Burtless, Washington, D.C., Brookings Institution, 1984.

[5] Feldstein, Martin, "Social Security, Induced Retirement, and Aggregate Capital Formation," *Journal of Political Economy*, 82, September-October 1974: 905–25.

Résumé

Après des décennies d'expansion, les programmes de Sécurité sociale ont été soumis, au cours des dernières années, à un examen minutieux dans les pays développés. Ce rapport montre que les facteurs économiques et démographiques actuels—productivité, taux réduit de naissance et de décès—ainsi que la modification des consensus idéologiques obligent tous les pays développés à revoir leurs systèmes d'assurance sociale. L'accroissement des prélèvements nécessaires pour faire face à un niveau donné d'avantages pousse à envisager des réformes. Ces réformes comprennent de simples coupes dans les avantages, un mouvement pour la constitution d'importantes réserves, l'accent davantage mis sur les plans non-gouvernementaux d'épargne-retraite et une augmentation des prélèvements suffisante pour maintenir les avantages. Bien que les différents pays puissent faire des choix différents dans ce menu, la conclusion centrale est que le ralentissement du taux de croissance de la productivité et la réduction des taux de naissance et de mortalité obligent les pays à faire des choix.

Reflections on Recent Proposals to Rationalize the U.S. Income Tax

Charles E. McLure, Jr.*

I. Introduction

Since its inception more than seventy years ago, the U.S. income tax has accorded preferential treatment to certain sources and uses of income. The biggest gaps in the definition of taxable income are among the oldest; they include the failure to tax most employee fringe benefits and net imputed income on owner-occupied housing, the deduction for mortgage interest, the exclusion of interest on debt issued by state and local governments, and the deduction for state and local taxes. Some of these provisions probably were not initially enacted with a clear-cut policy objective in mind; some may reflect archaic beliefs about the proper constitutional and economic contours of fiscal federalism; others simply may have seemed a good idea at the time. In any event, they are now defended vigorously as sound public policy, and recently the explicit use of the tax system to implement social and economic policies has grown widespread. As a result, the tax system has become more complicated, less neutral, and less fair; perhaps as important, it has come to be widely perceived as unfair.

The political perception of taxpayer discontent culminated in a mandate, delivered by President Ronald Reagan in his January 1984 State of the Union Address, for the U.S. Treasury Department to undertake a comprehensive examination of the federal income tax system and to recommend fundamental reforms by December of that year. Ten months later, in late November, Treasury Secretary Donald T. Regan submitted to President

* The author is a Senior Fellow at the Hoover Institution at Stanford University, Stanford, California. From October 1983 through July 1985 he was Deputy Assistant Secretary for Tax Analysis of the United States Department of the Treasury. In that position he had primary responsibility for development of the tax reform proposals the Treasury Department submitted to President Ronald Reagan in November 1984 and was instrumental in the conversion of those proposals into the tax reform plan Reagan submitted to the Congress in May 1985. The views expressed here are those of the author; they should not be attributed to the Hoover Institution or to the U.S. Treasury Department.

The Relevance of Public Finance for Policy-Making. Proceedings of the 41st Congress of the International Institute of Public Finance. Madrid, 1985, pp. 97–112.

Reagan the department's three-volume report, *Tax Reform for Fairness, Simplicity, and Economic Growth* [3]. Because the report adhered so closely to the objective of taxing all real income uniformly and consistently, it was commonly thought to be politically unrealistic and was informally dubbed Treasury-I, to indicate that it would probably be substantially revised before being submitted to the Congress; that designation is used in what follows. Another six months elapsed before the submission of *The President's Proposals to the Congress for Fairness, Growth, and Simplicity* [4], hereafter called the President's Proposals.

This paper provides some reflections on these two sets of proposals, the process that led to them, and the role of the formal study of public finance in that process. Section II describes the goals underlying the proposals and discusses the mutual compatibility and conflicts of those goals. Section III provides a thumbnail sketch of some of the most important proposals in Treasury-I and the President's Proposals. The process by which Treasury-I was formulated and revised is the subject of Section IV. Section V is a brief discussion of a few aspects of the interaction between scholarly research in public finance and the tax reform proposals. Section VI, a postscript added in January 1986, updates the discussion to the end of 1985.

II. Goals of Tax Reform

Advocates of tax reform in the United States have traditionally focused on vertical aspects of the fairness issue, emphasizing the inequity of loopholes and preferences that are of benefit primarily to the more affluent. Generally implicit in this approach, if not explicit, is the objective of increasing the progressivity of the tax system by closing such loopholes. Horizontal inequities and distortions of resource allocation created by nonuniform taxation of income and problems of tax administration and compliance have commonly received much less attention.

The focus of Treasury-I was quite different. The overriding objective was the uniform and consistent taxation of all real economic income, regardless of its source or use. This approach was espoused because it is unfair—and is widely perceived to be unfair—that families with the same income do not pay roughly the same tax (the horizontal fairness goal), because differential taxation of various sources and uses of income distorts resource allocation (the neutrality goal), and because the existence of opportunities to avoid taxes through tax planning complicates economic decision-making (part of the simplification objective). Moreover, a more comprehensive definition of taxable income would allow lower marginal tax rates and increased economic incentives—incentives to work, to save and invest, and to innovate.

A further objective of Treasury-I was to eliminate tax liability on families with incomes below the poverty level. Beyond that, issues of vertical equity were largely avoided; the goal was to leave the distribution of individual tax burdens among income classes above the poverty level approximately unchanged. It is true that taxable income would be expanded relatively more for upper-income families than for others, because they make relatively greater use of preferential tax treatment that would be curtailed; but that only meant that the reduction in tax rates could be greater at high-income levels than at low ones.

In general, the goals of horizontal fairness, economic neutrality, and simplification through the reduction of tax-avoidance planning are mutually consistent, because all require uniform and consistent taxation of all real economic income. Perhaps as important, uniform and consistent taxation of all income is essential to achieving the important objective of reducing the perception that the tax system is unfair. On the other hand, certain aspects of uniform and consistent taxation of income, such as inflation adjustment, the taxation of employee fringe benefits, and the tax treatment of multiperiod production, are not conducive to the simplification of recordkeeping and filing of tax returns (the taxpayer compliance objective). Nor would uniform and consistent taxation of *income* necessarily be as favorable to economic growth as a well-designed tax system based on taxation of *consumption,* or even an income tax with substantial ad hoc preferences for saving, investment, risk-taking, innovation, etc.

Faced with the need to choose between these conflicting objectives, Treasury-I adopted income, rather than consumption, as the tax base and came down squarely on the side of fairness, neutrality, and the reduction of opportunities for tax planning. The President's Proposals, by comparison, while retaining the income tax model, emphasized the need to foster economic growth, at some cost in terms of horizontal and vertical equity, neutrality, and elimination of tax planning. Taxpayer compliance—but not economic decision-making—may also be somewhat simpler under the President's Proposals.

Treasury-I and the President's Proposals also differed in another important respect, reflecting the process that produced them. In the formulation of Treasury-I, the tax base was designed to be as comprehensive as possible, subject to the desire to eliminate tax on poverty-level income, and then the rate structure was chosen to assure revenue neutrality and distributional neutrality. By comparison, in the creation of the President's Proposals, the personal exemptions and rate structure (with only minor variations in exemption levels and bracket limits) and the continuation of many tax preferences were "locked in" by political considerations, and the design of the remaining elements of the tax base became the residual to be manipulated to assure revenue and distributional neutrality. It is hardly surprising that the President's Proposals lack the economic integrity of Treasury-I.

Early in the development of Treasury-I, President Reagan announced that the home mortgage deduction would not be eliminated. This constraint was ultimately interpreted as meaning that the inflation adjustment of interest expense would not be applied to interest on mortgage debt on the taxpayer's principal residence. This artificial (if politically inevitable) constraint meant that imputed income from owner-occupied housing would continue to benefit from a negative effective rate of income tax (and only moderate taxation, even if state and local property taxes are included in the analysis). Thus, uniform and consistent taxation of all income from other forms of capital at effective rates approximating statutory rates might actually increase the misallocation of investment toward such housing. (See Hendershott [1]. McLure [2] describes the sanctity of the home mortgage deduction as the Achilles' heel of tax reform.) Moreover, the asymmetric treatment of interest expense on mortgage debt and of interest income and expense on other debt would create obvious, important, and unfair opportunities for arbitrage. (It would also be difficult to argue accurately that the preferential treatment of mortgage interest is fair, but politically that is probably no great liability.)

III. The Proposals

Space constraints preclude an exhaustive description of the two sets of tax reform proposals. The following is a partial listing of the major provisions of Treasury-I that are most likely to interest an international audience. The president's modifications of the Treasury-I proposals are indicated in parentheses. (Amounts marked with asterisks are indexed for inflation under current law, as well as in both sets of proposals, and refer to estimates for 1985 reported in the President's Proposals.)

Rate Reduction

| Individuals: | 14 rates of 11 to 50 percent are reduced to 15, 25, and 35 percent (same). |
| Corporations: | Graduated rates, with 46 percent on income above $100,000, are reduced to a flat 33 percent (same, but graduated rates are retained). |

Tax Threshold, etc.

Personal exemption raised from $1,080* to $2,000 (same).
Zero-bracket amount (a form of standard deduction):

	Current Law	Treasury-I	President's Proposals
Single Taxpayer	$2,480	$2,800	$2,900
Joint Return	$3,670	3,800	4,000
Head of Household	2,480	3,500	3,600

Earned Income Tax Credit: Indexed (credit increased and indexed).

Two-Earner Deduction: Repealed (same).

Fringe Benefits

Health Insurance: Include excess over $175 per month for family and $70 per month for single taxpayer. (Include first $25 per month for family and $10 per month for single taxpayer.)

Others: Repeal most (retain current exclusion for most).

Itemized Deductions

State and Local Taxes: Repeal (same).

Charitable Contributions: Allow only for itemizers and only for excess over 2 percent of income; limit deduction to indexed basis in case of gifts of appreciated assets (retain current law for itemized deductions).

Further Simplication

Nonfiling System: Introduce (same).

Minimum Taxes: Eliminate as unnecessary (retain and strengthen).

Taxing Real Economic Income

Depreciation: Index basis for inflation and allow only economic depreciation (index, but allow accelerated depreciation).

Investment Tax Credit: Repeal (same).

Capital Gains: Index basis for inflation and tax as ordinary income (postpone introduction of indexing until 1991; meanwhile exclude 50 percent of long-term capital gains, except on depreciable property).

Inventories: Allow use of LIFO or indexed FIFO, without conformity of financial statements (same).

Interest Income and Interest Expense in Excess of Mortgage Interest Plus $5,000: Exclude fraction, based on inflation (retain current law).

Neutrality toward Business Form

Dividend-Paid Deduction: 50 percent (10 percent).

Large Limited Partnerships: Tax as corporations (retain taxation of income to partners only).

Income Measurement

Cash Accounting: Restrict (same).

Multiperiod Production: Match income and expenses more closely (same).

Retirement Saving

Individual Retirement Accounts: Raise limits to $2,500 (retain present $2,000 limit) and make available to spouse working at home (same).

Benefit Limits: Made simpler, more consistent, and less generous (generally similar).

Energy

Intangible Drilling Costs: Replace expensing with cost depletion (retain current law, but toughen minimum tax).

Percentage Depletion: Repeal (repeal, except for stripper wells).

Life Insurance

Tax investment income (i.e., inside build-up) on policies (same).

Treat policyholder loans as coming first from tax-exempt inside build-up (retain current law).

Tax-Exempt Bonds

Repeal exemption of interest on bonds issued for nongovernmental purposes (same).

Curtailment of Tax Shelters

Disallow most nonbusiness interest deductions (including interest attributable to limited partnerships and passive interests in S corporations, those taxed as partnerships) in excess of the sum of investment income, income from limited partnerships and S corporations, mortgage on the taxpayer's principal residence, and $5,000 (same).

Extend at-risk rule (limitation of deductible losses to investor's equity and recourse debt) to real estate (same).

International Provisions

Foreign Tax Credit: Convert overall limitation to per country limitation (same).

Replace possessions tax credit with wage credit to be phased out (replace with more generous permanent wage credit).

Windfall Recapture

The President's Proposals (but not Treasury-I) contained a novel provision to recapture the benefits that would otherwise result from the combination of proposed rate reduction and the current law postponment of income via acceleration of depreciation allowances.

IV. Formulating the Tax Reform Proposals

The path from academic research to public policy is generally long and uncertain in a democracy. Seldom are the results of scholarship quickly seized and turned into law. Nevertheless, academic research can exert an important influence on policy discussions. The process by which Treasury-I was formulated may be instructive in this regard, though there is no presumption that the process is typical or replicable.

Several important characteristics of Treasury-I and its formulation—some of which it shares with the President's Proposals—distinguish it from many tax reform "proposals." First, Treasury-I was not intended merely to provide general guidance for public debate or the formulation of more specific tax policy. Rather, it was intended to be sufficiently specific to form the basis for detailed congressional consideration of tax reform and to provide guidance for legislative draftsmen. As a result, Treasury-I contains—in addition to a 262-page overview document that describes the basic objectives and general thrust of the proposals, discusses alternatives not chosen, lists transition rules for each proposal, and provides detailed revenue estimates—a 408-page volume of "general explanations," detailed descriptions of the proposed changes in U.S. tax law. (In the President's Proposals the general explanations require 431 pages.) Because these detailed general explanations were intended to provide guidance for legislative drafting, they were actually written primarily by staff attorneys, but with substantial input from economists.

Second, being intended to set the terms of reference for a legislative debate on tax reform, both Treasury-I and the President's Proposals carry important endorsements, by the Secretary of the Treasury and the President of the United States, respectively. As a result, they have vastly more visibility and influence than tax reform proposals that carry no such endorsement. Such documents are almost inevitably more "political" than the typical academic proposal for tax reform. Interestingly enough, however, Treasury-I made few concessions to the generally accepted "political realities."

Treasury-I was developed under difficult circumstances. First, a period of only ten months was allowed for the entire project. Even worse, the report on tax reform was only one of several major assignments that the Office of Tax Policy was given during 1984. In particular, the Deficit Reduction Act of 1984 was not passed until July 18, a bare four and one-half months before the due date of the report on tax reform. Until then—and even beyond, due to the crush of regulatory projects with short deadlines growing out of the 1984 Act—few members of the legal staff were able to devote significant attention to the tax reform project.

Moreover, the project was carried out during an election year in which tax policy figured prominently in debates between the presidential candidates. Any public hint of the contents of the Treasury Department's proposals for tax reform would have led to enormous pressure to have various items declared "off limits," as happened in the case of the home mortgage deduction, even without such hints. Because of the fear of news leaks, the work could not be discussed outside the Treasury Department—and, indeed, only a few high-level officials in the department outside the Office of Tax Policy knew what was being proposed. This need for confidentiality precluded access to outside experts, except for a small number hired as consultants. The very short time before the due date prevented extensive use of outside experts because of the inevitable lags in determining research needs, identifying consultants, and contracting with them.

The process that produced Treasury-I began with formulation of proposals by the technical staff and lower-level policymakers. Proposals were then funneled upward, for discussion and approval, redirection, or rejection, first to the Assistant Secretary for Tax Policy and then to the Secretary of the Treasury. Not only did each provision take considerable staff input at all levels; it was necessary to be sure that various provisions were mutually consistent. (For example, proposals for the indexing of capital gains, of depreciation, and of interest income and expense had to be consistent; moreover, they had to mesh with other proposals, for example, the proposed changes in the tax treatment of corporations and partnerships.) The process of considering alternatives, assuring consistency among proposals, and fleshing out proposals took enormous amounts of time on the part of both staff economists and lawyers, who frequently participated in long meetings to resolve various controversial points. Given these demands on the severely limited staff time and the difficulty of utilizing outside consultants, there was little opportunity for the development of new economic analysis; distillation of the conventional wisdom, as embodied in the public finance literature, was the order of the day. While there has been little evidence that the proposals were not appropriate, the relative lack of economic analysis developed specifically to undergird the proposals was costly in political terms.

The need for confidentiality had partially offsetting benefits. In the absence of leaks—which did not occur until very near the due date of the report—special-interest groups could only speculate what would be proposed, and they could not easily mobilize opposition to potential provisions that would adversely affect them. Even the opposition that was expressed could only be conveyed to the Treasury Department, where it could be considered and weighed objectively and in confidence in finalizing the proposals. Since almost no one expected the Treasury Department's proposals to the president to be so far-reaching, lobbyists and the interests they represent were caught largely flat-footed by Treasury-I.

The situation was quite different in the process of revision that produced the President's Proposals. Treasury-I was on the table for all to see and attack. While Secretary Regan and other high-level Treasury Department officials attempted to rally public opinion for the tax reforms proposed in Treasury-I, the White House understandably took a "hands-off" approach, leaving no doubt that Treasury-I was not a presidential document. The public admission that political compromises would be made (for example, when Regan noted that Treasury-I had been written on a word processor) gave representatives of special interests a clear signal to try to save their own pet preferences. Besides meeting with political and technical personnel at the Treasury Department, they could use every means at their disposal to mobilize public opinion, and they could work through members of Congress or other influential persons to make their views known in the White House, if they could not reach the president or his advisers directly. The press reported daily—and with substantial accuracy—on the tentative revisions being made. Whereas the Treasury Department has had little opportunity to develop detailed analyses of the many provisions it was proposing to change, those who would be adversely affected could—and did—spend enormous amounts on "economic analysis" purporting to show the damage various proposals would cause the nation. Refuting the numerous claims made on behalf of special interests would be an endless task, and ultimately impossible. Of course, the presentation of analysis intended to document the adverse effects of tax reform continued as action moved to the halls of Congress.

There were only two viable candidates at the beginning of the Treasury-I process, a traditional tax on annual income and a personal tax on annual consumption. Either of these would presumably be levied at graduated rates; a pure "flat tax" (levied on either base) was viewed as politically infeasible because the implied shift in tax burdens from the affluent to those with lower incomes would be too great. Introducing a value-added tax, retail sales tax, or other form of general sales tax would make sense only if substantial additional revenue was needed—something the president had ruled out explicitly during the 1984 presidential campaign. (See also [3, vol. 3].)

Of course, whether an income or consumption tax was chosen as the basic model, literally hundreds of additional decisions on details would need to be made in formulating a comprehensive tax reform package. While some issues might be the same under either basic approach (e.g., the taxation of fringe benefits and the deduction for charitable contributions and state and local taxes), many others would be quite different (or even nonexistent under the consumption option). This meant that, given limitations of time and staff resources, it would not be possible to proceed very long on a dual track; rather, it would be necessary to eliminate one option relatively soon, in order to assure that the surviving option could be adequately analyzed.

Given this constraint, the tax on consumed income was somewhat at a disadvantage, relative to the income tax, despite the considerable weight of recent academic opinion favoring it. After all, experience shows that the income tax "works," if not well. In contrast, there is no comparable experience to vouch for the feasibility of a tax on consumed income. None of the advanced countries that have recently considered adopting a personal consumption tax has yet done so. The fear of fundamental problems for which no satisfactory solution could be found created reluctance to devote all staff resources to developing details of such a tax, to the neglect of the development of the alternative comprehensive income tax. (See [3, vol. 2, chap. 9].)

V. Tax Analysis and Tax Reform

As noted above, the Treasury Department drew on a vast storehouse of economic analysis in formulating its proposals for tax reform. And yet there were many areas in which the available literature was inadequate. Of course, the tax reform proposals themselves have raised new issues that call for analysis. Perhaps as important, the release of Treasury-I inspired public debate of questions of tax policy that are generally ignored except by tax experts. The public was confronted, for example, with the decision concerning whether or not the tax system should be employed to implement social or industrial policy. The level of that debate has shown the need for increased public education about the case for tax reform. This section comments briefly on a few of the areas of interaction between the public finance literature and public policy covered in the proposals.

For the most part the tax reform proposals of Treasury-I were not new; they fell squarely in a tradition that extends back at least to Schanz, Haig, and Simons and are reminiscent of those of the Carter Commission in Canada. As noted earlier, however, the emphasis was less on vertical equity than was true in prior discussion, and more on economic neutrality and horizontal equity. Moreover, the authors of Treasury-I were gravely concerned about the dangers of an unindexed tax system, especially one that allowed unlimited deductions for nominal interest expense, something that seems to have worried their predecessors in developed countries relatively little.

The concern with tax neutrality—and with the distortions inherent in the present system—was heavily influenced by the literature of the past quarter century that emphasizes the excess burdens created by differential taxation, especially in the framework of general equilibrium models. The lesson of that analysis is that substantial economic value is sacrificed if taxes vary widely across economic activities and therefore distort resource allocation. Academic economists have documented the substantial gains in the efficiency of resource allocation that could result from fundamental tax reform.

Economists have traditionally focused on the effects of high tax rates on incentives for the efficiency of business operation. Emphasis has shifted in recent years to the analysis of ex ante marginal effective tax rates and the effects of taxes on the cost of capital. Investment incentives may, of course, reduce the cost of capital and the ex ante marginal tax rate on income from investment. Moreover, whereas high statutory tax rates have traditionally been thought to have adverse economic effects (except on risk-taking, in a world of complete loss offset), they may actually appear to be favorable to investment—particularly debt-financed investment—if depreciation allowances for tax purposes are accelerated. The Treasury-I proposals to substitute explicit rate reduction for investment incentives were thus decried by some academic economists, as well as by representatives of industries that would be most adversely affected by such a change. Further research into the relative importance of investment incentives and incentives for efficient operation is badly needed.

One important outgrowth of the tax reform project was a large new data base for the analysis of individual tax burdens. Treasury Department analysis has traditionally been based on adjusted gross income (AGI), the tax law concept of income after "adjustments" (e.g., deductions for retirement saving and moving expenses), but before itemized deductions (e.g., for state and local taxes, mortgage interest, charitable contributions, etc.). For many taxpayers this concept reasonably approximates economic income, but for many more it does not. First, it treats accounting losses resulting from tax shelter activities as though they are real economic losses. Second, it completely ignores tax-exempt sources of income, including interest on state and local securities, transfer payments, and most fringe benefits. Millions of (primarily low-income) families with only tax-exempt income are not even covered by data sets based solely on tax return data. Third, it does not allow for the effects of inflation as it erodes the value of assets and liabilities fixed in nominal terms. The use of an alternative concept, "expanded income," really does not overcome these problems, because it is also based entirely in figures appearing on the tax return. Moreover, information on AGI and expanded income is reported for tax-filing units, rather than for households or families, more useful economic units for most tax analysis.

In the data base constructed for the tax reform project, the basic measure of income was real "economic income" of families. Where "hard" data on economic income could not be obtained, income, including that from sources that are currently exempt, was statistically imputed to families. Similarly, expenditure patterns were imputed, in order to allow analysis of alternative deduction patterns and of sales taxes.

In the process of constructing this data base, substantial conceptual, methodological, theoretical, and statistical problems were encountered. They should be the subject of continued professional analysis and debate. Even when they can be answered to the satisfaction of experts, noneconomists may have difficulty in comprehending the answers. The tax reform debate has revealed clearly that the public's view of what constitutes income frequently differs substantially from the economist's definition of income.

Experience of the 1970s showed dramatically what can happen to an otherwise acceptable income tax if inflation reaches high levels. Fictitious capital gains are taxed, business firms cannot recover their investments in depreciable assets tax-free, costs of goods sold from inventory are understated, savers who are taxed on nominal interest income can easily earn negative after-tax real rates of return, borrowing becomes virtually costless, and arbitrage opportunities abound. Both equity and efficiency suffer, and real productive investment is discouraged and borrowing encouraged.

The changes in tax law enacted in 1981 did not provide a satisfactory solution to this problem. Accelerated depreciation allowances, especially on equipment, are overly generous at current rates of inflation; the effective marginal tax rates on income from various types of investment vary widely and depend on the rate of inflation, and those on income from equipment are now negative. Moreover, interest income and expense continue to be treated improperly.

Treasury-I would allow explictly for the effects of inflation in calculating capital gains, depreciation allowances, interest income and expense, and the cost of goods sold from inventories. With that done, there would be far less need for preferential taxation of capital gains or acceleration of depreciation allowances. With taxes based more nearly on real economic income, resource allocation would be more rational, and the equity of the tax system would be enhanced.

Over the past decade most tax economists seem to have come to accept the view that if the income tax is to be retained, the personal and corporate income taxes should be integrated, if only for dividends. This view is reflected in the proposal of Treasury-I to allow corporations a deduction for half of dividends paid. It is worth noting that serious attention was devoted to the possibility of allowing relief from double taxation only for dividends paid on new issues of stock, as suggested by the "new view" of the corporate income tax. Also, in the process of revising Treasury-I, consideration was given to the possibility of allowing preferential treatment only for capital gains on new shares, in order to encourage entrepreneurship and venture capital investment; such a proposal was ultimately deemed not to be administratively feasible.

It appears that the Treasury Department analysts were somewhat ahead of their academic counterparts in several areas. First, despite substantial efforts to understand the problems created by a tax system that is vulnerable to inflation, relatively little attention has been devoted to devising workable ways of dealing with the need for inflation adjustment in the measurement of taxable income. Given the apparent problems of the ad hoc approach to interest indexing proposed in Treasury-I, this is an area where there is an urgent need for research. Moreover, experience has revealed that the general public—and even many in the business community—do not comprehend the need for inflation adjustment, even at high rates of inflation.

Academic economists have also had relatively little to say about problems of matching the timing of income and expenses—the general issue of multiyear production and the time value of money—despite the enormous amounts of potential tax revenues, inequities and distortions riding, for example, on the tax treatment of defense contractors, the timber industry, the costs of "decommissioning" nuclear power plants and restoring strip mines, etc. Nor has enough been written by economists about the cause, nature, effects, and prevention of tax shelters and their adverse effects on the public perception of the fairness of taxation.

Many of the issues addressed in Treasury-I—inflation adjustment, integration of the corporate and personal income tax, multiyear production and the time value of money, and tax shelters, for example—point to the need for close cooperation between tax economists and tax lawyers in developing proposals for tax reform. (Other clear examples are the "windfall recapture tax" and the failed attempt in the formulation of the President's Proposals to develop a reasonably watertight way to provide capital gains treatment only for shares in "new ventures.") Economists may best be able to understand fully the economic effects of a particular provision or package of provisions. But lawyers are likely to understand better how the provisions work in practice, and their input is certainly essential to any effort to find workable solutions to problems such as these.

A final brief comment has to do with the basic political economy of tax reform. Virtually every provision for preferential treatment in the tax code, viewed in isolation, may seem like a good idea. But to consider any single provision by itself is to ignore a basic principle of economics—that the provision has opportunity costs, in terms of forgone revenues, higher tax rates, and resources misallocated from more productive uses. Moreover, leaving one preference intact opens wide the floodgate to requests for favorable treatment of other activities. A fundamental objective of those interested in comprehensive tax reform must be to hammer home the realization that in tax policy as elsewhere, there is no free lunch. The general interest in the benefits of tax reform—greater equity, a more productive allocation of resources, a simpler system, and lower tax rates—can be achieved in no other way.

VI. Postscript

In December of 1985 the House of Representatives passed tax reform legislation and sent it to the Senate for consideration during 1986. Though bearing a superficial resemblance to the proposals President Reagan sent to the Congress in May of 1985, the legislative provisions differed from them in important ways. Because the new proposals were much less favorable to business and were more generous to individuals, Republican members of the House voted for them only after being assured by Reagan that the defects could be remedied in the Senate and that he would veto any bill that retained the defects.

As this is being written, the prospects for tax reform in the Senate are uncertain. But it seems highly likely that Reagan, a pragmatic president who has made tax reform the top item on the domestic agenda for his second term, will sign any bill presented to him. Rather than speculate further about just where between the President's Proposals and the House bill such legislation might be, it may be useful to note briefly how different the House bill is from the proposals of Treasury-I.

Much attention has focused on the addition of a 38 percent rate to the three-bracket system of Treasury-I, but more important is the fact that the 25 and 35 percent brackets start at much lower income levels in the House bill. Thus the positive incentive effects sought in Treasury-I have largely disappeared, except for those with very high incomes. Fringe benefits remain almost totally exempt, state and local taxes remain fully deductible, and the deduction for charitable contributions is changed significantly only for those subject to the minimum tax. Efforts to fine tune in various areas add to the complexity of the tax system; in almost no ways is complexity reduced. In short, the reform of the individual income tax passed by the House is not "fundamental," as Treasury-I would have been.

None of the provisions for inflation adjustment, the most fundamental reforms proposed in Treasury-I, survived in the House bill. Thus all capital gains cannot sensibly be fully taxed, and depreciation allowances are accelerated, though not as much as in the President's Proposals. Most of the more notorious tax preferences of current law, including those for oil and gas, would be only slightly affected by the House bill. Though reduced somewhat, opportunities for tax shelters—which are constructed of deferral of the recognition of income, deductions for nominal interest expense, and preferential tax treatments of capital gains—abound. Whereas Treasury-I would have eliminated the minimum tax on preference income as unnecessary, the House bill retains and strengthens it. This testifies to the failure of the House to adopt fundamental tax reform.

In January 1984 President Ronald Reagan instructed the Treasury Department to prepare a plan to simplify the tax system and make it fair for all taxpayers. Though it had some defects, Treasury-I was such a plan. The bill passed recently by the House of Representatives is not.

References

[1] Hendershott, Patric H., "Tax Reform, Interest Rates and Capital Allocation", Ohio State University, August 1985.
[2] McLure, Charles E., Jr., "The Tax Treatment of Housing: The Achilles' Heel of Tax Reform?," presented at a conference, "The Impact of Proposed Tax Reforms on Investments in Real Estate and the Future of the Real Estate Industry," University of Illinois, Urbana, Illinois, October 4–5, 1985. Published in James R. Follain, ed., *Tax Reform and Real Estate*, Washington, D.C., Urban Institute Press, 1986.
[3] U.S. Department of the Treasury, *Tax Reform for Fairness, Simplicity, and Economic Growth*, Washington, D.C., November 1984.
[4] *The President's Tax Proposals to the Congress for Fairness, Growth, and Simplicity*, Washington, D.C., May 1985.

Résumé

Ce rapport discute les propositions de réforme fiscale contenues dans le rapport du Département du Trésor des Etats-Unis, en date de novembre 1984, adressé au Président Ronald Reagan et intitulé "Tax reform for fairness, simplicity and economic growth", communément appelé Treasury-I, ainsi que les propositions que Reagan a soumises au Congrès des Etats-Unis, en mai 1985. Outre la description des buts qui sous-tendent les propositions de Treasury-I, le rapport discute le processus qui a conduit à ces propositions et le rôle des recherches de finances publiques dans ce processus.

Les buts de Treasury-I sont : l'équité horizontale, la neutralité économique et la simplicité. Ces buts sont mutuellement compatibles et également compatibles avec le renforcement de la conviction que le système fiscal est bon. Dans une certaine mesure, les propositions du Président, qui reflètent un important compromis politique, ont sacrifié ces buts en vue de stimuler la croissance économique.

Un postscriptum, ajouté en janvier 1986, note que, de toute façon, la législation qu'adoptera en fin de compte le Congrès ne sera pas une réforme fiscale fondamentale, comme l'était Treasury-I. Elle ne sera probablement pas bonne, neutre, et simple.

Equity Principles in Public Finance

Richard A. Musgrave*

My assignment is to consider what has happened to equity principles in public finance. The implication, I take it, is that equity has been lost in the brave new world with its quest for efficiency and growth. Perhaps so, but I wonder. Measured by the number of relevant journal pages, efficiency has indeed supplanted equity as the prime concern, but given the earlier emphasis on equity, this may be only time's way of averaging out. Nor has the equity issue become dormant in recent years. The debate on distributive justice which emerged in the late 1960s and 1970s (Rawls [21], Nozick [18], and so forth) has had its bearing on matters of tax equity, as has the emergence of optimal taxation theory [6]. I am not prepared, therefore, to make this the occasion for a requiem to tax equity. The very nature of taxation, be it in theory or practice, is such that equity cannot be disregarded for long.

I. Ability to Pay: 1. Horizontal Equity in De Novo Design

As we look back at the history of equity theory, two strands—ability to pay and benefit taxation—may be distinguished. They both have their role and will be considered in turn. A convenient feature of the ability to pay doctrine, and also its greatest weakness, is that it deals with the tax side of the fiscal process only. Equity in taxation is viewed as if public expenditures did not exist or are wholly wasteful, a strange premise from which to discuss justice in taxation. But let me begin by taking the ability to pay doctrine on its own terms.

A given amount of revenue is to be raised, imposing a burden on society, and this burden is to be distributed in an equitable fashion. J. S. Mill held that this should be done so as to treat all taxpayers equally, "for the reason," as he put it, "that it should be so in all affairs of government"

* The author is H. H. Burbank Professor of Political Economy, Emeritus, Harvard University, and Adjunct Professor of Economics, University of California at Santa Cruz.

The Relevance of Public Finance for Policy-Making. Proceedings of the 41st Congress of the International Institute of Public Finance. Madrid, 1985, pp. 113–123.

[14, p. 804]. Later, this was divided into two propositions. One was given in Sedgwick's rule that people in equal positions should carry the same burden, a rule of fairness that commands general acceptance [22, p. 562]; but fairness as applied to the treatment of unequals was more difficult to interpret. The issue thus divided into two parts: horizontal equity, or the treatment of equals, and vertical equity, or the treatment of unequals. The distinction, clearly drawn by Pigou [20, pp. 8, 60], is of long standing, only the terminology is of relatively recent data [15, p. 160]. So is the proposition, shared by the respectable wing of the profession, that horizontal aspects of equity (or, at least, certain parts thereof) can be dealt with, while the vertical phase had better be left to the softer field of social ethics. Later on, I shall confess to some doubt about this dichotomy, but let me begin with the simpler or horizontal aspect.

Horizontal equity requires that taxpayers in equal pretax positions be treated equally. Or, which is essentially the same, it requires that they be left in equal posttax positions [10]. This raises two problems. First there is the necessity to define equal position. Clearly, the size and composition of "equal" taxable units should be similar. This is already a complex problem—as shown by the use of different allowances and rate schedules for various types of households—and one which has received insufficient attention by fiscal economists. Also, the units should possess equal resources by which to meet their needs. This raises the question of how resources should be defined, posing the need for a comprehensive definition of the tax base, such as accretion. Note also that the viewing of similar units with similar resources as being "equals" implies the use of a social welfare function which disregards the possibility that "sensitive" people (such as we) might derive more utility from given resources than do dullards (such as others). Such may or may not be the case, but it really does not matter. What matters is an implicit agreement that tax equity in a decent society *should* be viewed as if such differences did not exist.

Having established a group of equals, the next task is to determine what constitutes equal treatment. Matters are simple if we are prepared to assume that people have similar tastes, i.e., choose the same mix out of an equally available bundle of options. If this were the case, any tax, be it on peanuts or on income, would meet the test of equal treatment. The same pretax volume of peanuts is consumed by all equals, the same tax is paid, and the same welfare loss is suffered. The choice of tax base can then be left to efficiency considerations only, choosing that base which minimizes deadweight loss. This, essentially, is the approach taken in the theory of optimal taxation, beginning with Pigou's query to Ramsay [20], resumed in Diamond and Mirrlees' path-breaking work [7], and much discussed since [3]. As long as utility functions are assumed to be the same across individuals, the problem of horizontal equity conveniently disappears, or largely so [2].

In that context, Feldstein could conclude that the case for horizontal equity simply follows from utilitarian logic and does not require a distinct principle [9]. But this is hardly a permissible assumption. Individual preferences, as is evident from varying budget patterns, differ; and once this is allowed for, such differences will give rise to unequal treatment. Not even a broad-based tax will *do*, since goods-leisure preferences differ, and leisure, while included in the bundle of endowments, cannot effectively be included in the tax base. Even a uniformly applied base and rate thus impose differential welfare losses on pretax equals and hence leave them in unequal posttax positions. Once the assumption of identical preferences is dropped, horizontal equity is reinstated as a distinct issue in tax structure design [16].

A mighty finance minister or secretary of the treasury, disposing over a well-paid and omniscient staff of Ph.D.'s, might resolve the difficulty by treating each taxpayer individually so as to draw his or her revenue contribution at the least welfare loss; and total revenue to be drawn from a group of taxpayers of equal endowment might then be divided between them so as to equate their welfare losses, though not necessarily the amount of revenue which they contribute. The outcome would then be both horizontally equitable and efficient. But such a solution, tailored to individual taxpayers, is not practicable. Any feasible system must be second-best and apply the same base and rates to all members of the group. Unfortunately, however, there is no reason to expect that the product, the taxation of which is superior as a matter of efficiency (i.e. causes minimum deadweight loss), should also offer a superior tax base in terms of horizontal equity (i.e., involve similar shares of outlays across the budgets of similar households). A way out of this dilemma might then involve two steps. First, various bases might be evaluated with regard to horizontal equity, as measured by, say, the standard deviation of resulting liabilities across taxpayers [24]. Second, these bases might be ranked by their deadweight loss per dollar of revenue. The opportunity cost of horizontal equity might then be measured by the resulting efficiency loss, or vice versa. Thus a utility frontier is established and the best feasible solution might be chosen by how society views the two.

But even this may be too ambitious a procedure, so that the problem has to be dealt with in still more practicable terms. From this perspective it appears that horizontal equity can be achieved more readily in terms of a broad-based personal tax than by a bundle of in rem taxes. As the theory of optimal commodity taxation shows, this would not be so if tax structures were designed by wise counselors [7], but they are not. Taxes come about in the rough and tumble of tax politics, and here a more equitable (and, for that matter, more efficient) solution is more likely to result from a broad-based and single tax than from a partial tax or set thereof. Omissions from the base, as introduced by powerful pressure groups, will hardly be those which horizontal equity can tolerate or which optimal tax theory would call for. Most of the tax expenditures or loopholes which permeate the modern income tax tend to be harmful on efficiency as well as on horizontal equity grounds.

There remains the question of how the broad base should be defined. Viewing horizontal equity not in annual but in longer (ideally lifetime) terms, the income base penalizes consumers, thus offending both horizontal equity and efficiency considerations. This suggests that a consumption base is superior [10, 11, 19]. Perhaps so, but certain qualifications need be added. For one thing, the conclusion that the consumption base is preferable may not hold once allowance is made for the fact that neither base includes leisure. For another, the consumption base fails to allow for utility derived from wealth holding, and should thus be supplemented by a wealth tax [5, p. 267; 6]. Finally, the consumption base results in equal treatment only on the assumption that all income is consumed during the recipient's life. This is not the case. If horizontal equity is to be viewed in terms of single lives rather than across generations, gifts and bequests should also be included in the consumption base. Only then will people with equal options (present consumption, future consumption, and bequests) be given equal treatment [17].

II. Ability to Pay: 2. Horizontal Equity in Tax Reform

While preceding considerations dealt with the optimal design of a new tax system, this is not the typical problem. Rather, the typical problem is one of reforming (improving) an existing and defective system. Here a further problem arises, which may preclude correction of past inequity.

Suppose first that short people enjoy a 50 percent reduction in income tax, while tall people pay the full amount. People with equal pretax capacity are treated unequally and are left in unequal posttax positions. Introduction of this differentiation created a horizontal inequity which is terminated by its disallowance. The reform is a clear improvement on horizontal equity grounds and can be implemented readily. Next, suppose that brand A cigarettes are exempted from a tax applicable to brand B. This creates a horizontal inequity in the treatment of X, who prefers A, and of Y, who prefers B. Once more, tax reform, which imposes equal rates, restores horizontal equity as well as efficiency in brand choice. As before, the improvement can be implemented without difficulty.

But now consider a situation where a tax is imposed on profits from investment in industry A, but not from B. As the market adjusts thereto, the value of A falls while that of B rises, so that after-tax yields are equalized. Investor X, who held shares in A, suffers a loss while Y, who held shares in B, enjoys a gain. Next let X sell his shares to X′, while Y sells hers to Y′. Since the tax differential has been capitalized, X′ pays less and Y′ more, so that the tax affects both equally. Now let tax reform remove the exemption of B, with the result that X′ gains while Y′ loses. This does not remove the old inequity relating to the initial owners X an Y, but creates a new inequity relating to X′ and Y′. While the reform yields an efficiency gain by removing distorting effects on future investment, it also imposes a new horizontal inequity. This dampens the case for reform, but by no means destroys it. For one thing, inequity may be avoided, as Feldstein notes, by paying compensation [10]; more important, old inequities are outgrown by a dynamic economy, and a grandfather clause may be attached so as to apply the rate change to future investment only.

II. Ability to Pay: 3. Issues in Vertical Equity

I now turn to considerations of vertical equity, i.e., how to treat people in unequal pretax positions. The argument, in the tradition of Mill, Edgeworth, and Pigou, has been viewed in terms of income taxation. It begins with the assumption of a declining marginal income utility schedule, a schedule which is taken to be the same for all individuals. Against this background, three principles of burden distribution are considered, including equal absolute, equal proportional, and equal marginal sacrifice. Given declining income utility, all three rules let the tax bill rise with income, with equal marginal sacrifice most progressive, and equal absolute sacrifice progressive, proportional, or regressive, depending on whether the elasticity of the marginal income utility schedule with respect to income exceeds, equals, or falls below unity.

The first problem, then, is to choose among the three rules. Mill favored equal sacrifice, and thought (erroneously) that this would also minimize total sacrifice [14, p. 804]. Edgeworth [8] and Pigou [20] accepted equal marginal sacrifice as the correct solution. "In my view," so argued Pigou, "there can be no question at all that least aggregate sacrifice is an ultimate principle of taxation—its validity appears to me to be given directly by intuition—the claim that equal sacrifice is an ultimate principle of taxation is more controversial. Equal sacrifice, otherwise than between similarly situated persons, is not an ultimate principle of taxation" [20, p. 61]. By choosing least aggregate sacrifice, or its counterpoint of total maximum welfare, as the supreme rule, the scope of the equity issue was greatly broadened. If taxes needed to finance public services are to be distributed in line with least total sacrifice, the same reasoning also suggests that income after tax should be distributed so as to yield maximum total welfare. Given this broadened focus, and the assumption of equal declining marginal income utility schedules (and assuming total income fixed), there follows the case for income equalization.

The equal sacrifice doctrine, characteristic of the "old welfare economics," came to be rejected in the 1930s, when it was argued that welfare judgments in economic analysis should be limited to Pareto optimal improvements. Interpersonal welfare comparisons were to be ruled out, thus collapsing the very premise of the Pigouvian approach and with it a judgment on matters of vertical equity. Some of my best friends still believe this to be the case, but not all. Time has its way of returning to basic issues, and vertical equity has slowly crept back onto the scene. First, there came the construct of the Bergson-Samuelson type of social welfare function which, though involving interpersonal comparisons, did so as seen from the point of view of the particular individual whose views the function reflects [5]. But individuals, with their own personal view of the social welfare function, come to interact in the political process. From this there emerges the search for a social welfare function which provides the base for social policy. As Arrow [1] showed, there might be troubles in arriving at a representative and consistent function, but experience shows that the task of social choice is not a hopeless one, at least not in a reasonably cohesive society in which conflicts can be settled by voting rules.

This new concept of the social welfare function, or for that matter of the socially postulated marginal income utility function, however, differs from the older concept: it is not to be understood as a laboratory-derived physiological mapping of satisfaction levels which a representative individual may derive from successive units of income. Rather, it is to be taken as a reflection of how society views distributive justice. This view may change over time, and such a change is now in process. Different models may be advanced to rationalize the various approaches. These range from the entitlement theory of the Locke-Nozick type, which prohibits all but voluntary redistribution, over the utilitarian model to the Rawlsian version, which legitimizes inequality only where needed to raise the level of the lowest. The implications of these and other norms of distributive justice can be examined and clarified, but in the end the issue cannot be reduced to showing one to be "correct" and another "fallacious." People differ in their view of what constitutes a good society, differences which individuals joined in a social compact must resolve.

Attitudes toward vertical (no less than horizontal) equity have also played a major role in the choice between tax bases. Proponents of progressive taxation have favored the income tax, and opponents have favored indirect taxation. While selective excise taxes may be progressive or regressive depending on what products are taxed, items of mass consumption tend to fall in the latter group. Moreover, a general sales tax tends to be regressive, at least on an annual (though not necessarily a lifetime) basis, as the average propensity to consume falls when moving up the income scale. But though this difference between the taxation of income and consumption has played a major historical role, its logic was broken with the proposal, first advanced by Irving Fisher [10] and then by Kaldor [12], for a personalized expenditure tax with progressive rates [4, 19]. The choice between the consumption and income base can thus be separated from considerations of vertical equity and be made in efficiency and horizontal equity terms.

But whatever the base, the desirable degree of progression must still be determined, and here equity (now vertical) and efficiency considerations must again be weighed against each other. A more progressive burden distribution calls for higher marginal rates, and these result in higher deadweight losses. Noted already in Pigou's discussion of sacrifice theory [20], the discussion of this conflict has been resumed and extended in the recent theory of optimal income taxation. Based on certain assumptions regarding income-leisure preferences and the slope of the social welfare function, the optimal marginal rate of tax is shown to be relatively modest [3, 7].

The case for a broad-based tax, made previously in the context of horizontal equity, reappears even more clearly with regard to the vertical problem. To implement vertical equity, it is crucial that comparison among individuals in unequal positions be based on a comprehensive definition of what constitutes their potential, and that their tax rate relate to this global base. If the base is in terms of income, all forms of accretion need be allowed for; if it is in terms of consumption, all consumption need be included. Progressive rates, as related to parts of the income or consumption base, are meaningless. By the same token, considerations of vertical equity must be related to a person's total tax liability rather than to liabilities under a particular tax only. Once more, a global view has to be taken if equity considerations are to be applied in a meaningful form.

IV. Benefit Taxation and Tax Equity

My discussion of tax equity, so far, has been without reference to expenditure benefits, the implicit assumption being that taxation imposes a net burden (equal to revenue plus deadweight loss) on the community. To complete the picture, benefits from public services could be added back into the potential resources available to individuals, and this could then be allowed for in measuring their ability to pay. In this fashion, expenditures could be brought back into the picture, but such a procedure would not meet the spirit of the benefit doctrine, the second major strand of tax theory to which I now turn.

As is well known, both the ability to pay and benefit strands were included in Adam Smith's canons of taxation. In perhaps the most famous sentence in tax theory, he required that "the subject of every state ought to contribute towards the support of the government as nearly as possible in proportion to their respective abilities; that is, in proportion to the revenue which they respectively enjoy under the protection of the state" [23, p. 310]. If taxes are viewed as a payment for benefits received, an initial question is how these benefits should be priced. With social goods available in equal amount to all, Lindahl pricing [13] calls for differential prices, with each consumer paying in terms of his or her marginal evaluation. Smith's canon, which seems to embrace both ability to pay and benefit aspects, might indeed be interpreted as implementing the benefit rule in this way. There might be other efficient pricing rules, such as pricing which absorbs the entire consumer surplus, in which case the analogy to market pricing would not apply.

Assuming preferences to be known, any of these rules could be applied, but the crucial point is that preferences are not known. As Wicksell showed [25], a political process, combining tax and expenditure voting, is needed to reveal preferences (to overcome the free-rider problem) and thus to permit an efficient solution. At this more realistic level of analysis, the idea of benefit taxation serves not only as an equity rule but also as a mechanism by which to gather information about how consumer-taxpayers evaluate public services and hence what services should be provided. This establishes a strong presumption in favor of financing public services by benefit taxes and—to parallel private good pricing—by the use of benefit taxes which equate (for each consumer) price and benefit at the margin. Benefit taxation may then be said to remain distributionally neutral, although gains in consumer surplus may well differ. But if one accepts this neutrality of benefit taxation, what then happens to the role of taxation in relation to equity in the prebenefit tax distribution of welfare, i.e., the very aspect of the equity problem which Pigou thought of central importance?

Once more, the answer was provided by Wicksell's observation that such benefit taxes will also be just, provided that there already exists an equitable distribution of income. "It is clear," so he argued, "that justice in taxation presupposes justice in the existing distribution of property and income" [25, p. 143]. This suggests the separation of the fiscal problem into two parts, in line with the allocation-distribution branch distinction of my earlier work [15, p. 5], with the allocation branch providing benefit-tax finance for services and a distribution branch which (combining positive and negative taxes or transfers) establishes what is considered an equitable distribution. As I have noted before, views will differ as to what constitutes such a distribution, with the political process and its specific design (e.g., voting rules) once more playing a key role in implementation. Indeed, the equity problems of the distribution branch are precisely those of ability to pay taxation, subject only to the addition of a transfer side to the problem.

Various qualifications need be added to this grand design. For one thing, not all services provided by government are strictly in the nature of social goods. Their benefit may not be available equally to all individuals. For another, views of distributive justice qua Pareto-optimal giving [11] may permit donors to prescribe the uses of income by the recipient—i.e., transfers are made in kind, such as hospital services, rather than in cash. Moreover, even if distributional adjustments are based on a politically set social welfare function, the function may involve specific assignments in kind, such as distribution-based merit goods. Problems such as these—and there are others—cut across the simple allocation-distribution branch division, and this complicates a neat arrangement of fiscal affairs.

But even though only a second- or third-best solution can be hoped for in practice, this still leaves considerable scope for improvement. One such possibility relates to combining a tax-transfer system designed to address problems of distribution with the use of specific service taxes levied in the spirit of benefit taxation. Fiscal theorists, to be sure, have rejected arbitrary earmarking, by which a particular level of public services is made to depend on whatever revenue a particular tax happens to bring in. Available revenue should be allocated among alternative uses so as to maximize benefits. This, however, assumes benefits to be known. Since they are not, a linking of particular taxes to particular outlays—e.g., a defense tax, a road construction tax, an education tax—might well help the voter (or his or her representatives in Congress) to decide how much should be spent on what, thus serving efficiency in the allocation of resources to public services as well as a benefit-based distribution of their costs.

V. Conclusion

Not all aspects of fiscal equity have been covered here, the major omission being debt finance and intergenerational equity. However, the major issues in the equity of taxation have, I hope, been addressed and put into perspective. We have seen that horizontal and vertical equity are not as readily separable as frequently assumed; and that both ability to pay and benefit considerations have their place. As I see it, the doctrine of ability to pay belongs to the sphere of income distribution, while benefit taxation addresses that of public service provision. Such at least is the case if we view fiscal theory as a design for operating public affairs in a real-world setting where not all preferences are known, and where the social welfare function itself is on the agenda. Interactions and trade-offs between equity (both horizontal and vertical) and efficiency considerations are then at the heart of the matter. This, to be sure, adds to its interest, though not to one's peace of mind.

References

[1] Arrow, K., *Social Choice and Individual Values*, New York, John Wiley, 1951.
[2] Atkinson, A. B., "Horizontal Equity and the Distribution of Tax Burden", in *The Economics of Taxation*, ed. H. Aaron and M. Boskin, Washington, D.C., Brookings Institution, 1980.
[3] Atkinson, A., and Stiglitz, J. E., *Lectures in Public Economics*, New York, McGraw-Hill, 1980.
[4] Bergson, D., "A Reformulation of Certain Aspects of Welfare Economics", *Quarterly Journal of Economics*, 52, 1938:310–34
[5] Bradford, D., *Blueprints for Basic Tax Reform*, Arlington, Va., Tax Analysts, 1984.
[6] Brennan, G., and Nellor, D., 1982, "Wealth, Consumption and Tax Neutrality", *National Tax Journal*, 35, 1982.
[7] Diamond, P., and Mirrlees, J., "Optimal Taxation and Public Production", *American Economic Review*, 61, 1971:8–27.
[8] Edgeworth, F. Y., "The Pure Theory of Taxation", *Economic Journal*, 7, 1897; for excerpts, see R. Musgrave and A. Peacock, *Issues in the Theory of Public Finance*, London, Macmillan, 1948.
[9] Feldstein, M., "On the Theory of Tax Reform", *Journal of Public Economics*, 6, 1976:77–104.
[10] Fisher, I., and Fisher, H., *Constructive Income Taxation: A Proposal for Reform*, New York, Harper, 1942.
[11] Hochman, H. H., and Roger, J. D., "Pareto Optimal Redistribution", *American Economic Review*, 59, 1969: 542–57.
[12] Kaldor, N., *An Expenditure Tax*, London, Allen & Unwin, 1955.
[13] Lindahl, E., *Die Gerechtigkeit in der Besteuerung*, Lund, 1919.
[14] Mill, J.S., *Principles of Political Economy*, ed. E. Ashley, London, Longman, 1849.
[15] Musgrave, R. A., *The Theory of Public Finance*, New York, McGraw-Hill, 1959.
[16] Musgrave, R. A., "ET, OT and SBT", *Journal of Public Economics*, 6, 1976:3–16.
[17] Musgrave, R. A., "The Nature of Horizontal Equity and the Principle of Broad-Based Taxation," in *Taxation Issues of the 1980s*, ed J. Head, Melbourne, Australian Tax Research Foundation, 1983.
[18] Nozick, R., *Anarchy, State and Utopia*, New York, Basic Books, 1974.
[19] Pechman, J., ed., *What Should Be Taxed: Income or Expenditures?*, Washington, D.C., Brookings Institution, 1980.
[20] Pigou, A., *A Study in Public Finance*, London, Macmillan, 1928
[21] Rawls, J., *A Theory of Justice*, Cambridge, Mass., Harvard University Press, 1971.
[22] Sedgwick, H., *Principles of Political Economy*, London, Macmillan, 1883.
[23] Smith, A., *The Wealth of Nations* (1776), ed. E. Cannan, New York, G. P. Putnam.
[24] White M., and White, A., "Horizontal Inequality in the Federal Tax Treatment of Homeowners and Tenants", *National Tax Journal*, 18, 1965:225–39.
[25] Wicksell, K., *Finanztheoretische Untersuchungen und das Steuerwesen Schwedens*, Jena: Fischer, 1896; for excerpts, see Musgrave and Peacock, cited in [8].

Résumé

Ce rapport examine les principes d'équité fiscale dans le contexte des deux approches de la capacité contributive et de la contrepartie. Dans le contexte de la capacité, on étudie tout d'abord les questions d'équité horizontale, puis verticale. Le problème de l'équité horizontale a été esquivé dans la littérature récente grâce à l'hypothèse que les individus avaient des préférences identiques; mais c'est une hypothèse erronée. Nous mettons donc l'accent sur les complications qui surgissent quand on écarte l'hypothèse des fonctions d'utilité égale. Ceci implique de savoir comment définir des égaux et leur traitement égal; et nous suggérons une procédure qui permette de concilier les objectifs conflictuels de l'efficacité et de l'équité horizontale. Le problème de l'équité verticale est examiné en regard de la perspective des diverses approches de l'économie du bien-être et l'on étudie ses conséquences sur le choix de la matière imposable (revenu ou consommation). Dans le contexte de la contrepartie, on examine les conséquences sur l'équité de la détermination de la contrepartie ainsi que le rôle d'une fiscalité fondée sur la contrepartie, assurant des avantages ou des charges nettes équitables. Finalement, on considère le rôle des deux approches dans un système coordonné.

Part II

Empirical Evidence

Taxes, Transfers, and Labor Supply:
The Evolving Views of U.S. Economists

*Gary Burtless and Robert Haveman**

I. Introduction

Economists have long known that taxes and public transfers distort economic decision-making. The purpose of this paper is to provide a brief survey of recent research findings on the size and importance of the labor supply distortions arising from U.S. income taxes and transfers. We focus on the United States for two reasons: we are more familiar with American than with Asian and European research on this subject; and the views of many U.S. economists have undergone a significant change in the last decade and a half. It can be argued that this change in viewpoint has affected U.S. tax law and the provisions of income transfer programs, with important consequences for American economic policy.

In this introduction we briefly review the standard model of labor supply responses to income taxes and transfers. The next two sections contain a description of some of the recent theoretical and empirical developments in the U.S. literature on taxes, transfers, and work effort. The second of those sections concentrates on summarizing the recent research developments that have caused U.S. economists and policymakers to raise their estimates of the size of the labor supply distortions resulting from taxes. We refer to these new, very high estimates as the "alarmist view." In the fourth section, we provide an evaluation of this new view of the impacts of taxes and transfers. We argue that the claims of some economists and political critics of the U.S. tax-transfer system spring from a selective read-

* The authors are, respectively, Senior Fellow, the Brookings Institution, Washington, D.C., U.S.A.; and John Bascom Professor of Economics, University of Wisconsin-Madison, U.S.A. We gratefully acknowledge the helpful comments of Henry Aaron, Martin N. Baily, Barry Bosworth, Jerry Hausman, Hans van de Kar, Robert Moffitt, Alice Rivlin, Eugene Smolensky, and Barbara Wolfe. The comments of the discussants of our paper at the Congress, Marcia de Wachten and Richard Bird, are also gratefully acknowledged. Remaining errors are of course our sole responsibility. The views expressed are the authors' own and do not represent those of the Brookings Institution or the University of Wisconsin.

The Relevance of Public Finance for Policy-Making. Proceedings of the 41st Congress of the International Institute of Public Finance. Madrid, 1985, pp. 127–145.

ing of the available evidence about its effects, and occasionally from a
confusion over marginal versus average effects of the tax-transfer system.
We conclude with a brief discussion of the current state of the empirical
literature on the labor supply effects of taxes and transfers. While numerous
empirical problems need to be solved before there is a significant narrowing
of the existing range of estimates of effects, it seems likely that the current
pessimistic view will itself be superseded.

Why is labor supply affected at all by taxes and transfers? Neoclassical
economic theory provides the most straightforward basis for answering this
question. For our purposes it is convenient to describe this theory by
reference to a simple diagram. Figure 1 represents the trade-off between
hours of work (on the horizontal axis) and net income (on the vertical) under
a stylized tax and transfer system. The straight line from the origin,
OBCG, represents the trade-off between work and income in the *absence* of
taxes and transfers; its slope is the worker's gross wage rate. The solid
kinked line ABCDE represents the worker's *net* income possibilities at each
level of work effort in the presence of taxes and transfers. Along the segment AB the worker is eligible to receive a transfer which declines at a
constant rate for every one-dollar rise in gross wages; along the segment BC
the worker receives no transfers and pays no income tax; along the segments
CD and DE the worker's wages are subject to an income tax with progressively higher rates at higher income levels. In the usual model, income, or
Y, is considered a "good" and hours of work, H, is considered a "bad."
Each worker has well-defined, convex preferences across all potential combinations of Y and H. Workers choose their level of work and income by
maximizing utility over their attainable budget set, here represented by the
combinations of H and Y below and to the right of ABCDE.[1]

Figure 1 shows the economic distortion arising from this stylized tax-
transfer system. The curved line JJ represents the indifference curve of a
worker who is maximizing utility in the absence of taxes and transfers. This
worker chooses the combination of H and Y lying at the tangency of JJ and
the budget constraint OBCG. The curved line II represents the indifference
curve of the same worker as he maximizes utility in the presence of the
tax-transfer system. The selected level of H is below that chosen when
taxes and transfers are absent, though in theory H could be either higher or
lower depending on the work-income preferences of the affected worker.
Only along the segment AB does economic theory provide an unambiguous
prediction about the effect of the tax-transfer system on labor supply, and
even there the prediction depends on the assumption that leisure (which is
the complement of work) is a normal good. If leisure is normal—that is, a
good which workers consume more of as their resources rise—the tax-transfer system must unambiguously reduce labor supply of workers who would
otherwise locate along the segment OB.

Figure 1: *Work–Income Trade-off under a Stylized Tax-Transfer System*

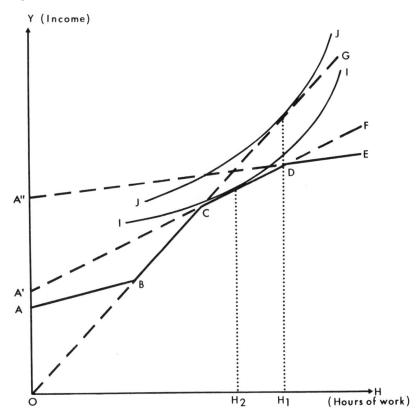

The analysis has thus far concentrated on the trade-off between work and income in a single period, say, a week or a year. The analysis can be extended in a straightforward way to take account of work responses to taxes and transfers over several periods, including the period before and after retirement. It can also be extended, though less easily, to reflect the impact of taxes and transfers on education, training, and other human capital investment decisions. These extensions are necessary to infer the theoretical effects of taxes and transfers over the lifetime, which are especially important for programs such as social security retirement and disability benefits, which have an important lifetime aspect. The lifetime effects of these programs are often theoretically indeterminate, just as are the effects of the stylized tax and transfer system just considered. The crucial question about the effects of taxes and transfers on behavior requires an empirical assessment of the magnitudes involved. We next consider the changing views of U.S. economists on this question.

II. Evolution of Research on the Labor Supply Effects of Taxes and Transfers

The Pre-1970 Consensus

Before 1970 the potential effects of taxation and transfers were widely recognized, but empirical estimates of their effects were rare. The earliest U.S. studies of the work response to taxes were essentially void of theory. Often the studies were based on survey responses to questions on the oppressiveness of high marginal taxes. This type of research was summarized by Pechman [38] as follows: "The evidence suggests that income taxation does not reduce the amount of labor supply by workers and managers. . . . Nearly all people who are asked about income taxation grumble about it, but relatively few state that they work fewer hours or exert less than their best efforts to avoid being taxed." Somewhat more effort had been devoted to estimating the labor supply response to actual and proposed income transfers, but even in this area the state of knowledge was quite primitive in 1970.

Early Econometric Studies: 1970 to the Mid-1970s

Starting around 1970, U.S. economists and statisticians began investigating labor supply behavior using the large-scale microeconomic data sets that were just becoming available. The research usually focused on the low-income population. Studies were generally based on multiple regression analysis, with annual hours of work as the dependent variable and the observed gross wage rate and non-work-related income as the relevant independent variables. Cain and Watts [15] summarized this early research, and expressed frustration with the wide variability of the estimated magnitudes of income and gross wage effects. The largest estimates of response suggested that the potential effects of existing and proposed transfer programs should be of substantial public concern, but the smaller estimates implied an opposite conclusion.

Many of the early studies were motivated by political interest in reform of the complex U.S. welfare system, which provides minimal incomes to otherwise destitute adults who have children. This system has attracted academic attention on a scale wholly disproportionate to its modest cost and size. Proposals to reform the system led the federal government to undertake four negative income tax (NIT) experiments, which represent some of the largest and most costly economic research projects ever undertaken. The experiments used controlled random assignment to test a variety of programmatic alternatives to the existing U.S. welfare system. The experiments essentially varied the slope and intercept of the first budget segment in Figure 1, that is, the location of the budget segment AB. Economists measured the responses of individual workers to these variations in marginal tax rate and basic income support levels and from those responses inferred the aggregate labor supply function of low-income workers.

The findings of the NIT experiments have been summarized in Moffitt and Kehrer [35], U.S. Department of Health and Human Services [44], and Stafford [40]. There is little doubt that the NIT experiments reduced the amount of uncertainty about the responsiveness of low-wage workers to taxes and transfers. The results from the largest and most sophisticated of the experiments showed that tested NIT plans caused substantial reductions in labor market activity, particularly for those workers enrolled in longer duration (five-year) plans and for youths and women. Prime-aged men reduced their annual hours of work by 9 or 10 percent; their spouses reduced annual hours by 17 to 20 percent; and single women heading families reduced annual hours by more than 20 percent—by as much as 28 to 32 percent in the longer duration plans. Much of the work reduction occurred in the form of withdrawals from employment rather than marginal reductions in weekly work effort. In the case of women, most of the reduction was caused by withdrawal from active labor force participation. The NIT experiments provided convincing evidence of the potential magnitude of work reductions arising out of generous income transfers and sharply higher marginal tax rates on earnings. Critics of income assistance seized upon these results to argue against increases in the income support provided to the U.S. poor or even to urge abolition of programs that presently aid the needy (see Murray [36]).

Research Findings after the Mid-1970s

Partly as a result of the resources invested in the NIT experiments, U.S. research on labor supply has grown rapidly in depth, breadth, and technical sophistication over the past decade. The NIT experiments, as well as a number of large-scale, highly detailed, longitudinal surveys, permitted economists to examine for the first time the pattern of individual labor supply over the life cycle and to measure the impacts of wages, taxes, transfers, and other sources of unearned income. The rapid development of theory and estimation technique has been described in detail by Killingsworth [31]. Three of the most significant developments have been in accounting for sample self-selection, life-cycle decision-making, and the nonlinearity of the work-income budget constraint (i.e., of the constraint ABCDE in Figure 1). The last two issues have been particularly important in analyzing the effects of social security retirement benefits and the progressive income tax on labor supply behavior.

In his exhaustive survey, Killingsworth [31] noted several highlights of the most recent generation of labor supply studies. As in the earlier generation of studies, male labor supply has consistently been found to be less sensitive to wage-rate and unearned income variations than has women's labor supply. The more recent studies have found larger female labor supply elasticities than the earlier studies. The later research, perhaps because it is based on more elaborate specifications of response, has found important discontinuities in the labor supply schedule, indicating a significant reservation level in desired hours. Killingsworth reports only small progress in the nonexperimental studies in narrowing the range of estimated responsiveness. While these results contain no direct evidence on the actual labor supply effects of taxes and transfers, they are suggestive. The high wage responsiveness of women indicates that changes in marginal rates will elicit sizable effects in their labor supply, and the findings of the NIT experiments tend to confirm this result. In fact, the recent estimates of response could easily be used to simulate the effect of changes in the tax and transfer system, and in several studies the results have been used in exactly this way. But the simulated effects will naturally reflect the same wide variance of aggregate response—and the same potential biases—as the parameter estimates themselves.

III. The "Alarmist View" and Its Origins

As the technical and statistical sophistication of the empirical studies has grown and as the new results have been used in national simulation studies using microdata from household surveys, some economists have become persuaded that the adverse effects of taxes and transfers are large. This is the alarmist view alluded to in the introduction. The findings of the NIT experiments of course attracted wide attention, and many viewed the labor supply responses reported there as serious threats to a productive economy, and as encouraging the growth of a dependent class (see Anderson [1] and Murray [36]). The experimental results showed that the earnings of a typical low-income family could fall by $0.25 to $0.50 for every $1.00 rise in income transfer support provided by the government, a finding that lent some support to the alarmist view.

Some studies of the U.S. social security system also found very large effects of retirement benefits on labor supply behavior. The labor force participation of older U.S. men has fallen substantially in recent years. In the 30 years after 1950, the participation rate of men over 65 fell by more than half, from 46 percent to 20 percent. In the same period, the rate for men aged 55 to 64 fell from 87 percent to 73 percent. Over the same 30-year interval real social security benefits were rising rapidly and eligibility for benefits was extended to a much wider population. Some economists inferred causality and asserted that the rise in social security was the main factor behind the trend toward earlier retirement (see for example Boskin [6]). It has also been claimed that increasingly generous social security disability benefits have caused the decline in older male labor force participation, particularly among blacks (see Parsons [37]) and that welfare benefits for single parents with children have led to a low labor force participation rate and reduced hours of work among single women. Unemployment insurance has been the subject of a large number of statistical studies, with most of them concluding that the U.S. system contributes significantly to raising reported unemployment or reducing employment (see Danziger, Haveman, and Plotnick [16]). Two U.S. economists have even claimed that generous unemployment benefits were the main cause of high and persistent British unemployment during the Great Depression (Benjamin and Kochin [3]). Finally, a group of U.S. and Dutch economists studied the effect on labor supply of the growth of the entire transfer system over the decade of the 1970s. The reported impacts were large for the United States; its transfer system growth was estimated to have reduced aggregate desired labor supply by 0.8 percent per year over the decade of the 1970s (Wolfe et al. [45]).

One of the most significant developments in recent years has been the rise in the estimate of the labor supply reductions caused by the income tax system. In 1981 Jerry Hausman published a landmark study of the effect of U.S. income taxes on the labor supply behavior of American adults. The new estimation methodology was based on the theory and statistical techniques developed to analyze the NIT experiments (in particular, Hall [23] and Burtless and Hausman [13]). Before the early 1970s, the income tax was simply viewed as driving a wedge between the market value of a person's work and the net wage the worker could take home. A 40 percent marginal tax, for example, was thought to reduce the after-tax value of marginal work by 40 percent. Since adult men were believed to have low responsiveness to variations in marginal wage rates—i.e., low uncompensated wage elasticities—it was widely thought that they were comparatively unaffected by income taxes.

However, careful examination of Figure 1 reveals that this analysis is an oversimplification. A progressive income tax not only drives a wedge between market wages and marginal take-home pay, it also provides an implicit "lump-sum transfer" to workers who pay progressive income taxes on marginal earnings. For example, the worker in Figure 1 who maximizes utility along the third budget segment, CD, can be viewed as responding to a tax system that implicitly pays a lump-sum transfer equal to A' and then, for every one-dollar rise in gross wage income, taxes this amount away at a constant marginal rate equal to the rate charged along the budget segment CD. The worker's labor supply is affected by the amounts of both the marginal tax wedge and the implicit lump-sum transfer.

Hausman found that the disincentive effects of these implicit lump-sum transfers were quite large, for men as well as for women. U.S. prime-aged husbands were estimated to reduce their work effort in response to the U.S. income tax by about 8 percent in comparison to their behavior in a no-tax world. Married and single women were estimated to have even larger labor supply responses than men. The Hausman study also provided an estimate of the welfare, or deadweight, loss associated with the U.S. income tax system. "Deadweight loss" is an estimate of the monetary compensation that would be required in order to make a taxpayer indifferent between the current tax system and a lump-sum system that raised the same revenue from each taxpayer.[2] For men, the welfare loss associated with Hausman's estimate of the labor supply response is about 5 percent of pretax earnings. Stated another way, the deadweight loss arising from the existing progressive income tax system on U.S. men amounts to more than 20 percent of the value of the taxes raised. For women, who have larger labor supply responses than men, the welfare loss of the tax system is an even greater share of the collected revenue.

These very large estimates of the labor supply reductions—and associated welfare losses—arising from U.S. taxes have caused many economists to reconsider their assessment of the costs of taxes. In addition, other research projects have contributed to the impression that income taxes greatly distort labor supply decisions. Studies of the effect of the Swedish tax system by Stuart [41], of the U.S. tax system by Stuart [42], Ballard, Shoven, and Whalley [2], and Browning [7], and of the tax and transfer system by Browning and Johnson [8] have substantially raised previous estimates of efficiency losses caused by taxes. Using a range of recent estimates of labor supply responsiveness, Browning [7] concludes that the welfare loss from the existing tax system lies between 8 and 28 percent of the revenues collected, with his preferred estimate being 16 percent.

Of greater interest to these authors is the *marginal* welfare loss associated with taxes in the United States. The marginal loss is the amount of added distortion that would result if taxes in their current form were raised by a small amount, say, one dollar. The recent studies conclude that, at the margin, the welfare loss from the U.S. tax system is in the range of at least 15 to 50 percent of added revenues collected. Browning's [7] preferred estimate is in the upper half of that range. Stuart [42] estimates that the marginal welfare loss from an added dollar of tax revenue is $0.20 to $0.24, based upon pre-1976 estimates of labor supply responsiveness. But he argues that this estimate of marginal loss must be more than doubled—to between $0.57 and $0.72—if the most recent estimates of labor supply elasticity are taken into account.

In another development reinforcing the alarmist view, some U.S. economists now deny there is any theoretical ambiguity about the effect of taxes on aggregate labor supply. According to the earlier view, tax increases have a theoretically indeterminate effect on labor supply. Because the net price of work is reduced, workers will want to reduce their work effort (this is the substitution effect), but because they have less after-tax income they may wish to work longer hours to make up the lost income (the income effect). The two effects may partly or wholly offset one another. According to the new view, the two effects do not offset one another in the aggregate, because what some people lose in net income is returned to others (or to themselves) in the form of increased transfers or government goods and services. Only the substitution effect matters. Hence, the effect of a tax increase must be an unambiguous reduction in aggregate work effort.

One example to illustrate the new view is an increase in the positive income tax used to finance an increase in transfers. (In terms of Figure 1, the budget segments CD and DE are moved down and to the right in order to pay for an upward movement in segment AB.) If the increases in transfers received by low-income workers are exactly equal to increases in taxes paid by high-income workers, the new theorists claim there is no income effect in the aggregate. The income effects experienced by workers who lose net income are exactly offset by those experienced by workers who receive additional transfer benefits (see Gwartney and Stroup [22]).

IV. The Basis for the "Alarmist View": Some Cautions

The labor supply research of the past fifteen years has illuminated a wide variety of subjects that were previously little understood. If the views of U.S. economists have changed, at least part of the reason is that there is now far more knowledge about the subject than existed in the 1960s. However, contrary to the alarmist U.S. view that taxes and transfers impose intolerably high work effort and efficiency losses, we believe that much of the evidence points to a far less pessimistic conclusion. While it is not our intention to give either a detailed critique of all the underpinnings of the alarmist view or a review of the contrary evidence, we will briefly consider a few of the most basic points and present a catalogue of the major issues that remain. The effect of this review is to erode one's confidence that aggregate U.S. labor supply has been dramatically reduced by the combined impacts of government taxes and transfers.

First, not even the statistical evidence in the studies showing the largest labor supply responses supports the most extreme claims about the disincentive effects of taxes on work behavior—namely, that a reduction in present U.S. rates would result in an increase in tax revenues from labor income. While Arthur B. Laffer is almost certainly correct in his belief that, at a sufficiently high marginal tax rate, further increases in the rate would depress government revenue by discouraging economic activity, he and his followers are incorrect in arguing that U.S. taxes are sufficiently high for that prediction to be true at current rates (see Fullerton [20], Hausman [25], and Browning and Johnson [8]).

Second, contrary to the recent claim that income effects are irrelevant in computing the aggregate response to taxes, it turns out that the size and distribution of income effects are critical in evaluating the sign of the aggregate response.[3] For example, referring again to an increase in positive income taxes used to finance an increase in transfer payments, it is usually the case that additional taxes will be levied on workers with high earnings while additional transfer benefits will be distributed to people with very low earnings (or possibly no earnings at all). The additional income received by people with very low earnings will induce them to reduce their hours of work, but the amount of hours reduction will be limited to the amount they already work—no one can work less than zero hours. By contrast, higher income earners, who suffer an after-tax income loss, will be induced by the income effect to work additional hours, and there is no relevant limit to the amount of extra hours they can work. For that reason, the hours gains induced by the income effect on high-earnings workers may easily exceed the hours reductions experienced by low-earnings workers. If work disincentives of taxes and transfers are concentrated on the fraction of the population that is unable to make substantial work-effort reductions, and if work-incentive effects are concentrated on those who can substantially raise work effort, a tax rise that is used to finance a transfer increase may theoretically boost aggregate labor supply.[4] Hence, the sign as well as the size of the aggregate response is indeterminate *a priori*.

Third, a careful evaluation of the aggregate labor supply responses to taxes and transfers should rest on the full body of available evidence, and not only on the estimates from a few polar studies. When economists have attempted to provide an assessment of the labor supply responses to taxes and transfers from the published studies of such effects, they have arrived at far more modest numbers than those cited by advocates of the alarmist view. In the most frequently cited review of the effects of transfers, Danziger, Haveman, and Plotnick [16] summarize the evidence on the labor supply effects of social security, unemployment insurance, and welfare:

> [It] suggests that because of labor supply reductions by transfer recipients, total [desired] work effort in the economy was 3.3 percent lower than it would have been. Adding the reductions due to the other [transfer] programs . . . gives a total reduction of 4.8 percent. In an economy with involuntary unem-

ployment, however, not all of this supply would be employed. If the unemployment rate were 7.0 percent, and if the increased labor supply of transfer recipients would find employment at a rate equal to that of other workers, the net loss of employment time would be about 4.5 percent. Because those receiving transfer benefits tend to have below average wage rates, the loss of total earnings is probably about 3.5 percent. (pp. 998–999)

Using a different approach to the evidence, Lampman [32] attempted to estimate the aggregate labor supply impact since 1950 of the *growth* in income transfers and the taxes required to finance them. Based on his survey of the empirical labor supply literature, he concluded that the increase in American social welfare benefits from 9 percent of GNP in 1950 to 21 percent of GNP in 1976 caused the quantity of labor supplied to be 7 percent less than it would otherwise have been. Browning and Johnson [8], whose study found very large welfare effects of marginal changes in taxes and transfers, estimate the total effect of a stylized version of the U.S. tax-transfer system to be a reduction in aggregate supply of about 5.2 percent. This appears roughly comparable to the estimates of Danziger, Haveman, and Plotnick and of Lampman.

Fourth, although the NIT experiments carry heavy weight in any overall evaluation of labor supply effects because of the random assignment of observations and the controlled and systematic variation of treatment, we must use caution in inferring the actual effects of the tax-transfer system from them. The experiments offered extremely generous basic payment levels, far more generous than those available to low-wage U.S. workers under the existing transfer system. Hence, the large recorded average effect was a response to a large average stimulus. Moreover, the NIT experiment benefits were awarded to all low-income workers in the treatment group, irrespective of their family situation, work capacity, and experience. The current U.S. transfer system targets its benefits on categories of individuals not able or expected to work—women with small children, the retired, and the disabled. In spite of the apparently large *average* responses observed in some of the experiments, scholarly summaries of the results have usually reached the following conclusions: (1) the observed income and substitution elasticities fall well within the range that would have been predicted prior to the experiments; (2) the responses probably fall in the lower part of that range; and (3) the range of responses across the different NIT experiments was far narrower than the range of predictions of response that existed prior to the experiments (see Moffitt and Kehrer [35] and Stafford [40]). Thus, the experimentally estimated elasticities fall within a significantly narrower range than nonexperimentally estimated elasticities, and they suggest smaller responses than would have been predicted from the average of nonexperimentally obtained estimates.

Some of the alarmist interpreters of the NIT experiments (e.g., Anderson [1] and Murray [36]) have argued that the estimated responses must understate the true long-run effects of the tested NIT programs, because the programs were limited in duration. They suggest, for example, that individuals need time to understand and respond to a new set of work incentives. In addition, a temporary experiment provides a much smaller change in lifetime income than would a permanent program of equivalent generosity, so the response must logically be greatly understated. However, systematic analysis of some of these biases has not confirmed the alarmists' assertions. In the relevant range of program generosity, there is another bias that partly or wholly offsets the biases just mentioned. Since the experiments were temporary, they essentially offered a "sale" on leisure, which participants were forced to take advantage of within a concentrated period. This encouraged greater responsiveness than would have been observed in a permanent program (see Burtless and Greenberg [12]). This conclusion is at least weakly supported by the finding that families enrolled in the longest of the experiments, who were guaranteed NIT payments for 20 years, reduced their labor supply less than did control-group families enrolled in the 3- or 5-year programs (Robins [39]).

Fifth, the underpinnings of both the theory and empirical work on labor supply response are a source of much greater controversy than is generally recognized, and this may be especially true of those studies on which the alarmists most heavily rely. In the following summary, we shall briefly mention some of the major unsettled issues, giving special emphasis to problems relevant to those studies showing the largest labor supply responsiveness.

- While the study by Hausman [24] is justly regarded as the most careful and innovative examination of tax effects on U.S. labor supply, it has not yet received the systematic scrutiny that is merited by its importance. Burtless [10] and Heckman [30] have called attention to technical features of Hausman's model that require especially careful sensitivity analysis; several of these features might lead to an overestimate of responsiveness. Until this kind of analysis is performed, Hausman's findings will be regarded as provisional by most quantitative labor economists.[5]
- Actual estimates of labor supply parameters (income and substitution effects) typically rely on untested assumptions about the attributes of work life: that the work day and the work week are flexible; that the wage rate is exogenous to the choice of work effort; that there are no time and money costs associated with working; that the budget line is continuous, though perhaps nonlinear; and that disequilibrium and rationing are absent from labor markets. While individual studies have attempted to accommodate one or even a few

modifications in these assumptions, there is little evidence on how estimated parameters would change if realistic economic conditions were better reflected in the empirical models.

- There exist a variety of technical issues in the econometric estimation of structural labor supply parameters that remain unresolved and on which little consensus exists. These include the modeling of labor supply decisions taken in the context of a household with interdependent members, the specification of the accounting period for measuring labor supply and tax and transfer incentives (and, related to this, the specification of a dynamic labor supply framework), and the accurate measurement of the marginal tax rate, exogenous unearned income, and *desired*—as opposed to observed— work effort in existing microeconomic data bases.

- A number of additional estimation issues concern the modeling of responses to taxes and transfers. In the presence of tax evasion and welfare fraud, how can the "true" marginal wage rate be measured? How can the actual availability of public transfers be imputed? How can a budget line be accurately specified when particular tax and transfer programs are associated with a variety of tied benefits or characteristics which are difficult to measure, e.g., stigma, implicit subsidies for training and education, and guarantees or generous subsidies of medical care?

- Furthermore, a complete assessment of the aggregate response to taxes must rest upon an accurate estimate of the work effort effects of the government goods and services that are provided through taxes. These effects may be either positive or negative; at present their direction and size is a complete mystery.

In sum, the state of empirical work in this area remains unsettled, in spite of important advances both in theory and empirical estimation over the past decade. When we consider, in addition, the wide variation in existing structural estimates of labor supply responses to taxes and transfers, a temperate position would be a great deal more cautious than the calls for wholesale government retrenchment implicit in the writings of some alarmists.[6]

Sixth, while it may not be widely recognized, many of the alarmist findings about U.S. work response to taxes and transfers have not been confirmed upon subsequent reanalysis. For example, the majority of recent studies has found that social security retirement benefits contributed only modestly to the trend toward earlier retirement among U.S. men. This finding has been replicated in recent cross-sectional and time-series studies, most of which have been far more technically sophisticated than the earlier research on this subject.[7] While alarmists are quick to note the sharp decline in older male labor force participation since World War II, they seldom if ever mention that participation of men over 65 fell by over one-third between 1900 and 1940—well before social security could have affected labor supply. The alarmist view of the effects of disability insurance on labor force participation has also been called into serious question by Haveman and Wolfe [28] and Haveman, Wolfe, and Warlick [29]. These studies of the behavioral effect of social security retirement and disability programs, like all empirical studies, have shortcomings. It is nonetheless the case that alarmist results have generally been found in only a minority of studies, and those findings have not stood up well to careful reanalysis designed to improve on the earlier models or data.

Seventh, it should be stressed that the wage rates of low-income workers who are eligible for most transfers are quite low. Their low wage rates reflect the market's valuation of their marginal product. Hence, the aggregate earnings loss and loss in GNP associated with program-induced reductions in hours worked will be smaller than is implied by their percentage hours reduction. If the earnings and GNP effects of recipient response are small, the welfare cost of such transfers to recipients is probably small as well.

Eighth, an important point overlooked by some readers of recent studies is that the elimination or drastic reduction of existing taxes or the substitution of a lump-sum system are probably not appropriate alternatives with which to compare the existing system. Indeed, the authors of a few of the studies had quite a different conterfactual in mind—usually, a tax system raising equal revenue but with less progressivity, a broader base, and lower marginal tax rates. Hausman [24] was explicit in this, and found that a proportional tax system with a $4,000 initial exemption would cause about half the deadweight loss caused by the present system. That is, in comparison to a relatively feasible alternative tax system that raises the same amount of revenue, the present tax system induces economic distortion. But the amount of distortion is far smaller when the present system is compared to a feasible system than when it is compared to an "ideal" lump-sum system. Browning's intermediate estimates suggest that if the existing tax system is replaced by an equal-revenue proportional tax system, the total welfare loss would fall from about 16 percent of revenues to less than 11 percent of revenues, and the marginal welfare loss would fall from 35–45 percent of revenues to 20–25 percent of revenues. Once again, this implies that the current system can be modified in order to improve its efficiency. But the efficiency gains are much smaller when moving to feasible alternative systems than when moving to a totally nondistorting system (or no system at all).

Finally, we will mention one important kind of evidence that is often ignored. The historical trends in U.S. labor supply do not appear to conform especially well to the predictions of the alarmist view. This seems to us a fundamental problem with the new view. It is well known that American tax levels and transfer benefits have grown rapidly over the past three decades. While it is true that the labor force participation of men, especially older men, has fallen over that period, this decline has been more than offset by a sharp rise in the labor force participation rate of American women. From 1948 to 1984, the participation rate of adult men fell by 10 percentage points, mostly due to a sharp decline at older ages, but the rate for adult women *rose* by 22 percentage points. The overall employment rate rose by 3 percentage points, and the participation rate by 5.5 points. This growth in paid employment and labor force participation hardly seems consistent with the view that the growing burden of taxes and rising disincentives from transfers have markedly depressed labor supply. The length of the average work week has fallen slightly, and the number of work days per year has probably fallen fairly substantially since World War II, thus offsetting the rise in aggregate labor force participation. But the length of the work year was falling long before taxes and transfers became an important part of U.S. economic life. In fact the average work year fell faster during the 40 years leading up to World War II than it has in the years since (see Lebergott [33] and U.S. Census Bureau [43]).

V. Conclusion

From our survey of the recent literature we conclude that the amount of aggregate work reduction attributable to the U.S. tax and transfer system is uncertain but probably comparatively modest. Our conclusion does not lead us to dismiss out of hand the prudent concerns of some observers that taxes and transfers have depressed total labor supply. Nor do we quarrel with the proposition that specific reforms in the tax-transfer system could encourage added work effort (see Haveman [27]). Current tax and transfer policy may also distort behavior involving human capital accumulation and family structure, in addition to the labor supply decisions considered in this paper (see [18]). But these reductions in labor supply and the distortions in other behavior may be partly or wholly offset by the effects of the government goods, services, and regulation that are purchased by taxes. (For example, tax-induced reductions in labor supply and human capital accumulation may be directly offset by government programs that subsidize investment in training and general education.) On the basis of our reading of the evidence, we judge that a reduction in labor supply of perhaps 5 percent and no more than 12 percent can be attributed to the existing combination of government taxes and transfers. Hence, we reject the claims of those interpreters of the evidence who conclude that American work habits and initiative have been grossly undermined by the present level of taxes and transfers. Of course, opinions differ as to what constitutes a large reduction of work effort attributable to taxes and transfers. Some observers clearly regard any reduction at all as intolerable. In our view, the benefits attributable to government taxes and transfers—reduced uncertainty, reduced poverty and inequality, increases in human capital investment, increases in economic stability, and the facilitation of technological change— exceed the probable losses, at least in the United States. Nonetheless, the present debate over the labor supply effects of taxes and transfers should remind us that the *marginal* trade-off between benefits and costs is likely to be far less favorable than the average trade-off.

Notes

1. We emphasize that Figure 1 provides a highly stylized version of the existing tax and transfer system. There are multiple tax schemes (federal, state, and local income tax programs, plus the social security payroll tax) and a number of complicated transfer programs for low-income families. It is unlikely that workers completely respond to or even understand the highly complex constraint they actually face; they probably respond to some simplified and smoothed version of that constraint.

2. A lump-sum tax is one that is levied on workers independently of their current or past earnings or any other measure of their ability to pay. Lump-sum taxes are used as a comparison because they are nondistortionary. A poll tax is a common form of lump-sum tax.

3. Strictly speaking, we are referring to the partial equilibrium effect on aggregate *desired* labor supply.

4. David Betson and David Greenberg [4] have recently performed population simulations for the U.S. using labor supply estimates from the NIT experiments. Their simulations demonstrate that there are many tax-financed transfer increases which raise aggregate labor supply, contrary to the claim of Gwartney and Stroup (1983).

5. Among the technical points raised are the following: (a) the estimated income effect for males is larger than estimates obtained by others using the same or similar data sets; (b) the technique of permitting a truncated normal distribution of work effort preferences may permit a limited number of observations with extremely high responsiveness to substantially affect the estimate of mean response; (c) the estimate of responsiveness may be biased upward by the truncation of response estimates to avoid the possibility that leisure is an "inferior good" for any observation in the sample; and (d) tax evasion and welfare fraud imply that the nonlinear budget constraint cannot be accurately specified (see below). We should emphasize, however, that studies by Blomquist [5] and Hausman and Ruud [26] indicate that Hausman's nonstandard specification of the taste distribution probably does *not* account for the large estimates of response.

6. With respect to the post-1975 research on labor supply, Killingsworth [31] summarizes what we have learned: "Second generation research indicates that . . . income and substitution effects are considerably greater for women than for men, but this simply confirms first generation findings. If first generation results provide a dauntingly wide range of estimates of such responses, however, the same is pretty much true of second generation work" (p. 205). The wide variation in the estimates of labor supply responses to transfer programs was also noted by Danziger, Haveman, and Plotnick [16].

7. The cross-sectional studies include Burkhauser and Quinn [9], Burtless and Moffitt [14], Diamond and Hausman [17], Fields and Mitchell [19], Gustman and Steinmeier [21], and Burtless [11]. The time-series study is by Moffitt [34].

References

[1] Anderson, Martin, *Welfare*, Stanford, Calif., Hoover Institution Press, 1978.

[2] Ballard, Charles L., Shoven, John B., and Whalley, John, "General Equilibrium Computations of the Marginal Welfare Costs of Taxes in the U.S.", *American Economic Review*, 75, March 1985: 128–38.

[3] Benjamin, D.K., and Kochin, L.A., "Searching for an Explanation of Unemployment in Interwar Britain", *Journal of Political Economy*, 87, June 1979: 441–78.

[4] Betson, David, and Greenberg, David, "Labor Supply and Tax Rates: A Correction of a Correction of the Record", *American Economic Review*, forthcoming.

[5] Blomquist, N. Soren, "The Effect of Income Taxation on the Labor Supply of Married Men in Sweden", *Journal of Public Economics*, 22, November 1983: 169–87.

[6] Boskin, Michael J., "Social Security and Retirement Decisions", *Economic Inquiry*, 15, January 1977: 1–25.

[7] Browning, Edgar K., "On the Marginal Welfare Cost of Taxation", College Station, Texas A&M University (mimeo.), 1985.

[8] Browning, Edgar K., and Johnson, William R., "The Trade-Off between Equality and Efficiency", *Journal of Political Economy*, 92, April 1984: 175–203.

[9] Burkhauser, Richard V., and Quinn, Joseph, "Is Mandatory Retirement Overrated? Evidence from the 1970s", *Journal of Human Resources*, 18, Summer 1983: 337–58.

[10] Burtless, Gary, "Comment", in H. Aaron and J. Pechman, eds., *How Taxes Affect Economic Behavior*, Washington, D.C., The Brookings Institution, 1981.

[11] Burtless, Gary, "Social Security, Unanticipated Benefit Increases, and the Timing of Retirement", *Review of Economic Studies*, forthcoming.

[12] Burtless, Gary, and Greenberg, David, "Inferences Concerning Labor Supply Behavior Based on Limited-Duration Experiments", *American Economic Review*, 72, June 1982: 488–97.

[13] Burtless, Gary, and Hausman, Jerry A., "The Effect of Taxation on Labor Supply: Evaluating the Gary NIT Experiment", *Journal of Political Economy*, 86, December 1978: 1103–30.

[14] Burtless, Gary, and Moffitt, Robert A., "The Joint Choice of Retirement Age and Post-Retirement Hours of Work", *Journal of Labor Economics*, 3, April 1985: 209–36.

[15] Cain, G.G., and Watts, H.W., eds., *Income Maintenance and Labor Supply*, New York, Academic Press, 1973.

[16] Danziger, Sheldon; Haveman, Robert; and Plotnick, Robert, "How Income Transfers Affect Work, Savings and the Income Distribution: A Critical Review", *Journal of Economic Literature*, 19, September 1981: 975–1028.

[17] Diamond, P.A., and Hausman, J.A., "The Retirement and Unemployment Behavior of Older Men", in H. Aaron and G. Burtless, eds., *Retirement and Economic Behavior*, Washington, D.C., The Brookings Institution, 1984.

[18] Driffill, E. John, and Rosen, Harvey S., "Taxation and Excess Burden: A Life Cycle Perspective", Cambridge, Mass., National Bureau of Economic Research, Working Paper No. 698, 1981.

[19] Fields, Gary S., and Mitchell, Olivia S., "Economic Determinants of the Optimal Retirement Age: An Empirical Investigation", *Journal of Human Resources*, 19, Spring 1984: 245–62.

[20] Fullerton, Don, "On the Possibility of an Inverse Relationship between Tax Rates and Government Revenues", *Journal of Public Economics*, 19, October 1982: 3–22.

[21] Gustman, Alan, and Steinmeier, Thomas, "A Structural Retirement Model", Hanover, N.H., Dartmouth College (mimeo.), 1983.

[22] Gwartney, James, and Stroup, Richard, "Labor Supply and Taxes: A Correction of the Record", *American Economic Review*, 73, June 1981: 446–51.

[23] Hall, Robert E., "Effects of the Experimental NIT on Labor Supply", in J. Pechman and P.M. Timpane, eds., *Work Incentives and Income Guarantees: The New Jersey NIT Experiment*, Washington, D.C., The Brookings Institution, 1975.

[24] Hausman, Jerry A., "Labor Supply", in H. Aaron and J. Pechman, eds., *How Taxes Affect Economic Behavior*, Washington, D.C., The Brookings Institution, 1981.

[25] Hausman, Jerry A., "Stochastic Problems in the Simulation of Labor Supply", in M. Feldstein, ed., *Behavioral Simulation Methods in Tax Policy Analysis*, Chicago, University of Chicago Press, 1983.

[26] Hausman, Jerry A., and Ruud, Paul, "Family Labor Supply with Taxes", *American Economic Review*, 74, May 1984: 242–48.

[27] Haveman, Robert, "How Much Have the Reagan Administration's Tax and Spending Policies Increased Work Effort?", in C.R. Hulten and I.V. Sawhill, eds., *The Legacy of Reaganomics*, Washington, D.C., Urban Institute Press, 1984.

[28] Haveman, Robert, and Wolfe, Barbara, "The Decline in Male Labor Force Participation: Comment", *Journal of Political Economy*, 92, June 1984: 532–41.

[29] Haveman, Robert; Wolfe, Barbara; and Warlick, Jennifer, "Disability Transfers, Early Retirement, and Retrenchment", in H. Aaron and G. Burtless, eds., *Retirement and Economic Behavior*, Washington, D.C., The Brookings Institution, 1984.

[30] Heckman, James J., "Comment", in M. Feldstein, ed., *Behavioral Simulation Methods in Tax Policy Analysis*, Chicago, University of Chicago Press, 1983.

[31] Killingsworth, Mark R., *Labor Supply*, Cambridge, Cambridge University Press, 1984.

[32] Lampman, Robert, *Social Welfare Spending: Accounting for Changes from 1950 to 1978*, New York, Academic Press, 1984.

[33] Lebergott, Stanley, *Manpower in Economic Growth*, New York, McGraw-Hill, 1964.

[34] Moffitt, Robert A., "Life Cycle Labor Supply and the Effect of the Social Security System: A Time-Series Analysis", Providence, R.I., Brown University (mimeo.), 1985.

[35] Moffitt, Robert A., and Kehrer, Kenneth C., "The Effect of Tax and Transfer Programs on Labor Supply: The Evidence from the Income Maintenance Experiments", in R. Ehrenburg, ed., *Research in Labor Economics*, Vol. 4, Greenwich, Conn., JAI Press, 1981.

[36] Murray, Charles, *Losing Ground: American Social Policy, 1950–1980*, New York, Basic Books, 1984.

[37] Parsons, Donald, "Racial Trends in Male Labor Force Participation", *American Economic Review*, 70, December 1980: 911–20.

[38] Pechman, Joseph A., *Federal Tax Policy*, 2nd ed., Washington, D.C., The Brookings Institution, 1971.

[39] Robins, Philip K., "The Labor Supply Response of Twenty-Year Families in the Denver Income Maintenance Experiment", *Review of Economics and Statistics*, 66, August 1984: 491–95.

[40] Stafford, Frank P., "Income Maintenance Policy and Work Effort: Learning from Experiments and Labor Market Studies", in J. Hausman and D. Wise, eds., *Social Experimentation*, Chicago, University of Chicago Press, 1985.

[41] Stuart, Charles E., "Swedish Tax Rates, Labor Supply, and Tax Revenues", *Journal of Political Economy*, 89, October 1981: 1020–38.

[42] Stuart, Charles E., "Welfare Costs per Dollar of Additional Tax Revenue in the U.S.", *American Economic Review*, 74, June 1984: 352–61.

[43] U.S. Census Bureau, *Historical Statistics of the United States, Colonial Times to 1970*, Bicentennial Edition, Part 1, Washington, D.C., Government Printing Office, 1975.

[44] U.S. Department of Health and Human Services, *Final Report of the Seattle-Denver Income Maintenance Experiment*, Volume 1, Washington, D.C., Government Printing Office, 1983.

[45] Wolfe, Barbara; de Long, Philip; Haveman, Robert; Halberstadt, Victor; and Goudswaard, Kees, "Income Transfers and Work Effort: The Netherlands and the United States in the 1970s", *Kyklos* 37 (4), 1984: 609–67.

Résumé

Ce rapport passe en revue les récentes recherches sur l'offre de travail et les coûts en bien-être liés au système fiscal des Etats-Unis. Ces recherches emploient des méthodes économétriques avancées pour estimer les effets des impôts et des transferts sur l'offre de travail et les techniques Hicksiennes habituelles pour déterminer les coûts en bien-être. Les estimations obtenues sont importantes et suggèrent que, à la marge, les coûts en bien-être d'un dollar additionnel d'impôt prélevé en sus de ce qui existe peuvent s'élever à 40% des ressources fournies. Notre critique suggère un certain nombre de raisons pour traiter avec prudence ces estimations. Nous concluons que la réduction totale de travail imputable à la combinaison actuelle d'impôts et de transferts aux Etats-Unis est relativement modeste—entre 5 et 12%.

Effects of Capital Taxation on Capital Formation, Distribution, and Efficiency

*Ingemar Hansson**

Introduction

In most OECD countries, the relative importance of taxes on consumption and labor has increased over time. This means that capital is now a moderately important source of tax revenue. Examples include the introduction of and increase in value-added taxes and other indirect consumption taxes, increases in payroll taxes, and integration of the corporate and the personal income tax. In Sweden and Denmark tax reforms have been implemented that reduce effective personal income tax rates on positive and negative capital income below those that apply for labor income. In some countries, major tax reforms are being considered that would amplify this shift from capital to other taxes. For example, a shift from a personal income tax to an expenditure tax, currently in vogue among economists, would in effect eliminate a substantial part of the remaining taxation of capital.

The purpose of this paper is to evaluate the economic effects of this trend toward lessening the importance of capital taxes. This evaluation may be relevant for future tax policy. Specifically, we examine how a shift from capital to labor or consumption taxes affects (1) capital formation, (2) the distribution of income, and (3) the overall welfare cost of taxation (excess burden).

The relevant capital taxes include personal and corporate taxes on capital income as well as different types of taxes on wealth, property, and estates. All potentially distort the intertemporal allocation of consumption. A consumption tax involves, however, no such distortion when the tax rate is constant over time. Instead, it is well-known that an anticipated propor-

*The author is a member of the Department of Economics, University of Lund, Sweden. Thanks are due to Richard Bird, Lars Bovenberg, Charles Stuart, and several other participants of the I.I.P.F. congress for helpful comments and suggestions. The financial support of the Bank of Sweden Tercentenary Foundation is gratefully acknowledged.

The Relevance of Public Finance for Policy-Making. Proceedings of the 41st Congress of the International Institute of Public Finance. Madrid, 1985, pp. 147–164.

tional consumption tax is equivalent to a proportional tax on labor income in the absence of bequests; see [1]. Consequently, the capital taxes examined here do not include anticipated consumption taxes.

As a pedagogical device, the basic effects of a capital tax in a stationary state or long-run equilibrium are illustrated in Figure 1. This illustration applies for a one-good closed economy, with overlapping identical generations and competitive firms, which uses capital and labor as inputs under a constant-returns-to-scale technology; see [25]. If total capital taxes per unit of capital are denoted t, the original stationary state involves capital K_0, a gross rate of return of r_0, and a net rate of return of $r_0 - t$. If all capital taxes are eliminated, the new stationary state involves aggregate capital K_1 and a gross and net rate of return of r_1.[1]

Given the slopes of the curves in Figure 1, it is obvious that a decrease in the overall capital tax increases capital, decreases the gross rate of return, and increases the net rate of return relative to the original stationary state. The first problem examined here is the magnitude of this long-run shift in capital resulting from a decrease in capital taxation. The crucial distributional question concerns the gain for capital-owners when the net rate of return shifts from $r_0 - t$ to r_1 in the long run, and the associated effect on the net real wage after a compensatory increase in labor or equivalent taxes. Since capital adjusts slowly, the short- and intermediate-run effects of decreased capital taxation on capital, net interest rate, and net wage are also important.

A basic policy question concerns the performance of capital taxes as compared to other taxes. Therefore, the third question deals with the welfare costs, or excess burden, of capital taxes as compared to labor and consumption taxes. Some important results for distribution and efficiency can readily be demonstrated by means of Figure 1. For the case of a single representative household with an infinite time horizon, i.e., perfect intergenerational altruism, and a fixed rate of time preference, the curve denoted K^S in Figure 1 is horizontal. This implies a fixed long-run net rate of return. For the case of constant returns to scale this means that a capital tax is fully shifted into a lower gross wage in the long run. Consequently, a decrease in the capital tax and a revenue-preserving increase in the labor tax involves an unchanged net wage but increases capital and hence welfare in the long run, given that the marginal product of capital is positive; see [8]. This means that stationary state consumption, and hence welfare, is maximized for a slightly negative capital tax (Golden Rule with zero growth).[2]

This analysis also involves the full set of arguments for a capital tax as compared to a labor or a consumption tax from an efficiency and a distributional point of view. First, the transition between stationary states may be important, especially if a tax on capital includes a lump-sum tax on initial capital. Second, altruism between generations may be imperfect, which

Figure 1. *Determination of stationary state capital and rates of return with and without capital taxes in a closed economy*

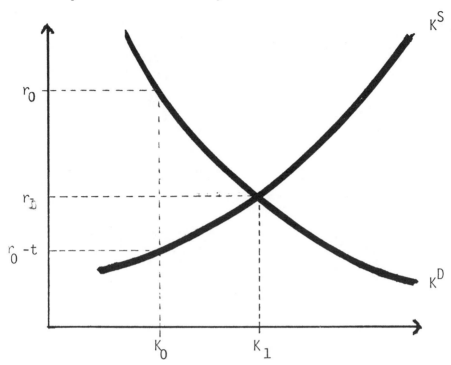

means that the tax is only partially shifted to labor. Finally, the model may not be applicable; i.e., the economy may be open, capital may be heterogeneous, taxes may be nonproportional, households may be heterogeneous, etc. The discussion below shows that the treatment of these factors is of crucial importance for the conclusions reached concerning the effects of capital taxes as compared to labor and consumption taxes.

Elasticity of Savings in Partial Equilibrium Models

According to Denison's law, the savings rate is independent of the interest rate; i.e., the curve denoted K^S in Figure 1 is vertical. Under this assumption, capital taxes have no effect on aggregate capital. The main rationale for this law is the continued constancy of the gross private savings rate in the United States; see [9] and [10]. In [5] Boskin shows, however, that even though gross private saving has been relatively constant as a share of GNP, net private saving as a share of disposable income exhibits substantial variations. This weakens the empirical support for Denison's law. The more systematic econometric studies of [27] and [4] estimate an interest elasticity of savings of 0.2, and 0.0 respectively.

All of these estimates do, however, suffer from various types of important theoretical or statistical shortcomings. While neoclassical theory predicts that savings are related to the ex ante net real rate of return, some studies instead apply gross or even nominal rates of return. Furthermore, the rate of return and savings are both determined as a part of some type of macroeconomic equilibrium, implying that single-equation partial equilibrium models are likely to give simultaneous equation bias for the estimated interest elasticity. These methodological problems are at least partly avoided by Boskin, who estimates an elasticity of savings of 0.4. Boskin also examines the effect of eliminating a 50 percent tax on capital income and finds that capital would increase quite substantially in the long run. Replacement of this tax with a lump-sum tax is estimated to yield an annual welfare gain of 3.5 percent of GNP in the long run.

The interpretation of the estimated savings elasticity and the use of the result in this type of calculation are, however, beset with problems. The observed ex post net real interest rate is likely to be a poor approximation for the relevant ex ante expected long-run net real interest rate. A more fundamental problem is that the estimated effect of a change in the real interest rate on savings *during the same year* might reveal the short-run effect of such a change, corresponding to the first-year adjustment of wealth, but provides no reliable information on the long-run effect on wealth.

Impact of Taxation on Investment in Partial Equilibrium Models

Another portion of the literature empirically examines the determination of the demand for capital in partial equilibrium models; see [11] and [18] for surveys. In the standard model, desired capital is determined by output, the wage rate, and the rental price of capital. Investment is then determined as a partial adjustment of actual capital toward this desired capital. Jorgenson [18] concludes that the cost of external funds including tax considerations is an important determinant of investment, while the availability of internal funds appears to play a minor role. This suggests that a policy that aims to promote investment should try to reduce the cost of external capital by, for example, tax changes rather than to boost profits or to "lock-in" capital in firms by means of a high tax on dividends.

This type of model is, however, also subject to several serious shortcomings. The partial equilibrium approach means that the interest rate, the price of capital goods, and the wage rate are treated as exogenous. This may be reasonable for a single firm, but not on the aggregate level. Output is also treated as exogenous, which is questionable even for the single firm.

A Simple Long-Run General Equilibrium Model

More recent models of aggregate capital formation typically treat demand and supply of capital simultaneously in a general equilibrium model, owing to the limitations, described above, of partial equilibrium models. In a simple model with overlapping generations, Summers [25] determines the stationary state savings rate from aggregate labor income as a function of the net interest rate, the elasticity of marginal utility of consumption, the pure rate of time discount, and the growth rates of population and productivity. This gives an interest elasticity of aggregate stationary state savings of 0.7–3.7, which is substantially greater than most econometrically estimated savings elasticities. These two sets of estimates are, however, not directly comparable. Summers' simulation results involve a comparison between steady states, while most empirical estimates at best reveal the short-run effect of a change in the interest rate. To fully reconcile these two types of estimates requires a full model of wealth adjustment.

Summers' high elasticities of savings have been challenged from a different perspective. In [24] Starrett shows that the result is quite sensitive to the choice of the functional form for the one-period utility function; a generalization to the Stone-Geary form by introduction of a "consumption floor" changes the results substantially. Furthermore, alternative assumptions of the pure rate of time discount and of the growth rates of population and productivity can give much lower savings elasticities; see [12].

Summers' model of savings supplemented by a production function yields the simple one-good general equilibrium model in Figure 1. Summers uses this model to examine the long-run effects in the United States of eliminating a 50 percent overall tax on capital income and preserving revenues by an increase in labor or consumption taxes, when all taxes are proportional. In the preferred case the simulations show that a shift to a labor tax would yield a 67 percent increase in steady state capital. Consumption would increase by 13 percent, yielding a welfare gain of 4.9 percent of lifetime income. Owing to an implied 14 percent increase in the gross wage, the increased labor tax causes the net wage to fall only by 2 percent in the long run.

A shift to a consumption tax yields a still larger increase in long-run capital and welfare under the crucial assumption of unchanged tax revenue in each period. This occurs because the consumption tax involves postponed tax payments, yielding larger savings and, due to population growth, a lower lifetime tax burden for each generation. These additional effects can be obtained also from the labor tax through changes in government debt and are, therefore, less relevant to an analysis of capital taxation.

Extensions of the Basic General Equilibrium Model

The simple general equilibrium model has been extended to incorporate, inter alia, an explicit analysis of the transition between steady states, endogenous labor supply, and heterogeneous capital. In [7] Chamley finds that the difference between actual and steady state capital decreases at an annual rate of 10.1 percent. This suggests that capital may adjust quite slowly to changes in capital taxes, implying that the period of transition is important in terms of distribution and efficiency. Accordingly, Chamley estimates that eliminating a 50 percent capital tax would increase consumption in the long run by 8.4 percent, while the welfare gain is equivalent to only a 3.2 percent permanent increase in consumption, owing to consumption foregone during the transition.

Chamley reports an excess burden of capital taxation as compared to lump sum taxation of 0.52 for the last (or marginal) unit of tax revenue from capital taxation. This means that an additional unit of lump-sum transfers financed by an increase in capital taxes must be worth at least 1.52 in order to compensate for the direct *and* the indirect costs of taxation. The concept of marginal excess burden thus provides a convenient and useful summary statistic for characterizing the marginal welfare cost of different taxes. This can be interpreted as a price list for political decisions concerning tax-financed government expenditure.

To simplify the comparisons, these and other results are summarized in Table 1. The upper part of the table reports results when capital taxes are replaced by lump-sum taxes (including labor or consumption taxes when labor is exogenous). The lower part of the table reports results for the more "realistic" case, when distortionary capital taxes are replaced by distortionary labor or consumption taxes.

Column (1) reports the estimated welfare gain of eliminating all capital taxation, expressed as a share of the sum of discounted future GNP. Column (2) reports the marginal excess burden resulting i.e., the additional excess burden when the revenue from capital taxes is increased by one unit (and other taxes are decreased accordingly). In many cases the calculation of these statistics requires additional, somewhat arbitrary, assumptions, which are reported in the notes. Unfortunately, most of the available evidence on capital taxation is based on data for the United States. The relevance of the results for other countries is discussed below.

Chamley examines the least distortionary *constant* taxes on capital and labor for a given level of tax revenue, finding them to be 3.6 percent for capital and 20.0 percent for labor income. The stickiness of capital during the period of transition and the temporary sacrifice of consumption call for a small positive capital tax in contrast to the earlier discussed result that the optimal capital tax is slightly negative when only stationary states are considered. The optimal capital tax is, however, still considerably lower than the labor tax. A shift from a uniform 20 percent income tax to these optimal rates is estimated to involve a welfare gain of 0.4 percent of lifetime consumption. This is much lower than most results in Table 1, partly owing to a low assumed value for the initial capital tax—20 percent instead of the typical 50 percent.

For initial tax rates of 50 percent on capital and 30 percent on labor, Judd [20] estimates a marginal excess burden of 0.99–1.47 for capital taxes and 0–0.34 for labor taxes, for a compensated wage elasticity of labor supply of 0–1. Consequently, a marginal shift from capital to labor taxes is predicted to give a welfare gain of 0.99–1.13 units per unit of tax revenue, as is reported in the lower part of Table 1.

Auerbach, Kotlikoff, and Skinner [2] find that a shift from an income to a labor (consumption) tax would increase the long-run capital-output ratio by 13 percent (44 percent) and increase the net real rate of return by 26 percent (0 percent). Since an unanticipated consumption tax corresponds to a labor tax plus a lump-sum tax on existing wealth, a consumption tax is more attractive from a welfare point of view; the implicit capital levy simply raises tax revenue without an increase in the distortionary wedges between gross and net factor prices for those factors that can adjust. Accordingly, a shift from a uniform income tax to a labor tax involves a welfare *loss* of 9.3 percent of lifetime earnings, while a shift to a consumption tax involves a welfare gain of 6.9 percent.

Ballard [3] includes bequests in the utility functions. An important implication is that all cohorts then gain from a shift from an income tax to a consumption tax. The capital/labor ratio is estimated to increase by 13.5 percent in the long run, while the welfare gain is estimated to be 0.4 percent of total lifetime wealth, including the value of leisure. If bequests are excluded, the welfare gain is about 0.8 percent. This illustrates the sensitivity of the results in these types of models.

General Equilibrium Models with Intersectoral Distortions

The above models cover only a single sector of production, implying that distortions in the allocation between different sectors of the economy are excluded a priori. In contrast, King and Fullerton [21] examine the effective marginal tax rates on corporate tangible investments for three types of physical investment, three industries, three sources of finance, and three ownership categories. This yields 81 different tax rates that exhibit huge variations. For example, the effective marginal tax rate varies between −312 and +130% for the United Kingdom and between −116 and +144 percent for Sweden. The spread of the tax rates is lower in the United

Table 1
Comparative Results of Different Studies

			Welfare gain as a share of the sum of discounted GNP (1)	Marginal Excess Burden (2)
Shift from capital taxes to a lump-sum tax				
Boskin	[5]		3.5%[a]	0.56[b]
Summers	[25],	consumption tax	11.7%	1.32[c]
Summers	[25],	labor tax	4.9%	0.54[c]
Chamley	[7]		3.2%	0.52
Chamley	[8]		—	0.68
Judd	[20]		—	0.99–1.47
Hansson and Stuart	[15],	closed economy[d]	—	0.93
Hansson	[14],	closed economy	—	0.70
Hansson	[14],	open economy, t^{used} (t^{owned})	—	0.58 (0.00)
Shift from capital taxes to specific distortionary taxes				
Chamley	[7],	labor tax[e]	0.4%	0.38
Judd	[20],	labor tax	—	0.99–1.13
Auerbach, Kotlikoff, and Skinner	[2],	labor tax	−9.3%[f]	—
Auerbach, Kotlikoff, and Skinner	[2],	consumption tax	6.9%[f]	—
Fullerton, Shoven, and Whalley	[13],	consumption tax	2.0%[g]	—
Fullerton, Shoven, and Whalley	[13],	consumption tax and integration	3.7%[g]	—
Jorgenson and Yun	[19],	no intersectoral differences	0.7%[h]	—
Jorgenson and Yun	[19],	consumption tax equivalent	1.8%[h]	—
Ballard	[3],	consumption tax	0.4% × multiple[i]	—
Hansson	[14],	labor tax, closed	—	−0.66
Hansson	[14],	open economy, t^{used} (t^{owned})	—	−0.15 (−0.73)

[a] Calculated as the reported annual gain of U.S. $60 billion as a share of 1976 GNP of $1718 billion.

[b] Calculated as the reported welfare gain in column (2) divided by the revenue of capital taxes as a share of GNP, 0.5 × 0.25, where 0.5 is Boskin's tax rate and 0.25 is the share of capital income, multiplied by two in order to translate this average excess burden into a marginal excess burden; cf. [7].

[c] Calculated as the reported annual welfare cost of U.S. $200 and $80 billion, respectively, as a share of revenue from capital taxes two years prior to the publication, 0.5 × 0.2 × 2418, multiplied by two (see footnote b).

[d] Calculated for an increase in capital taxes that are used to finance a marginal increase in government consumption.

[e] Gain when a uniform tax on capital and labor is replaced by optimal rates of 3.6 and 20.0 percent, respectively.

[f] Calculated as the reported effect a a share of lifetime resources times the reported ratio, 4, between this wealth and the discounted value of future labor earnings.

[g] The value of total resources include a labor endowment equal to 7/4 of actual labor supply. Accordingly, for a labor share of 0.75 the ratio between total resources and total discounted GNP was calculated as (0.75 × 7/4 + 0.25).

[h] Calculated as the reported gains of U.S. $679 and $1724 billion in 1980 times the applied net rate of return, 0.027, as a share of GNP in 1980.

[i] The reported gain of 0.4 percent of total lifetime resources should be multiplied by the ratio between this measure of total wealth and the sum of discounted GNP to be comparable with the other results. In other papers the analogous multiple was in the range 1.5–4.0.

States and West Germany, but is still striking. The average marginal tax rate on tangible corporate investments is calculated as 4 percent for the United Kingdom, 36 percent for Sweden, 37 percent for the United States, and 48 percent for West Germany. These results indeed indicate that the commonly applied capital tax rate of 50 percent may be too high for most countries, especially since, for example, intangibles, owner-occupied housing, and consumer durables often receive a much more favorable tax treatment than tangible corporate investment. Many of the estimates in Table 1 may, therefore, have an upward bias in the estimated welfare costs for overall capital taxation. These results also sugest that the intratemporal distortions in the allocation of capital may be substantial. Such distortions occur not only in the allocation of capital between different sectors but also for the choice between different sources of finance. For example, debt finance through a low-taxed intermediary is subject to a much lower effective tax rate than equity finance raised through an issue of new shares sold directly to households.

While King and Fullerton limit their attention to corporate tangible capital, which typically constitutes only a small part of total capital, Harberger [17] and Shoven [23] examine distortions in the allocation of capital between the noncorporate and corporate sectors that result from the corporate tax. The allocation of capital between low-taxed or even net subsidized sectors, such as housing and consumer durables on the one hand and the rest of the economy on the other hand is examined by Piggott and Whalley [22] and Hansson [14]. The former study concludes that subsidies to local housing are a significant source of the welfare cost of taxation in the United Kingdom.

While some taxation of capital might be rationalized by, for example, distributional considerations, these intratemporal distortions in the allocation of capital appear to be hard to rationalize from a social welfare point of view. In a long-run equilibrium the differential tax rates are associated with neutralizing differences in the gross rates of return. This suggests that significant efficiency gains can be obtained by replacing all existing capital taxes with a yield-preserving neutral tax, such as a uniform wealth tax that encompasses all types of wealth. The major obstacle to such a reform is probably the windfall gains that would occur, primarily for owners of corporate equity, and the windfall losses that would occur, especially for owner-occupied housing; see [26]. Advance announcement of the tax reform and gradual implementation of it over an extended period of time might limit windfall gains and losses; see [20].

Several recent papers examine the welfare cost of both intersectoral and intertemporal distortions in the allocation of capital, although they do not consider distortions between different sources of finance. As shown in Table 1, Fullerton, Shoven, and Whalley [13] find that integrating corporate and personal taxation would involve a welfare gain of 1.7 percent of total discounted GNP due to elimination of sectoral distortions, while Jorgenson and Yun [19] find a welfare gain of 0.7 percent in a similar experiment.

Open Economy Considerations

The models discussed consider the impact of taxation on capital formation in a closed economy. Little attention has been devoted to the effects of capital taxation in an economy that is open to international capital flows. In such an economy, it is important to distinguish between capital taxes applying to the use of capital (t^{used}) and taxes that apply to *ownership* of capital (t^{owned}). In most countries the corporate tax applies to capital that is used in the country, while personal income and wealth taxes apply to capital that is owned by citizens in the country.

Figure 2 illustrates the long-run effect of different types of capital taxes in a general equilibrium model of a small, open, one-good economy in a simple case where all cross effects are excluded.[4]

In a small open economy the required rate of return net of t^{used} taxes, r, is assumed to be given by international financial markets. The required gross rate of return on capital used in this country is consequently $r+t^{used}$. Combined with the production function, this determines the level of capital that is used in the country, K^{used}, as illustrated in Figure 2. Similarly, the net rate of return to savers is equal to $r-t^{owned}$. This determines the stationary state capital that is owned in the country, K^{owned}. The difference between K^{used} and K^{owned} is, of course, net foreign-owned capital.

An important implication is that t^{used} affects K^{used} only, and the magnitude of the effect depends only on conditions of demand in this simple long-run model. Analogously, t^{owned} affects K^{owned} only, and the magnitude of the effect depends only on conditions of supply. In contrast, these two taxes are equivalent in an equilibrium model of a closed economy.

This raises the question of the effects of these two types of capital taxes in an open economy. From a distributional point of view, note that an increase in t^{used} yields a fully compensating increase in the gross rate of return; i.e., such taxes are fully borne by labor in the long run. In contrast, an increase in t^{owned} decreases the net rate of return and leaves the wage rate unchanged; i.e., no shifting occurs (see Figure 2).

Bovenberg [6] finds that the welfare costs of t^{used} are similar in an open and a closed economy in the absence of foreign-owned capital and terms-of-trade effects. If part of K^{used} is foreign-owned and if terms-of-trade effects occur, this tends to decrease the welfare cost in an open economy. Intuitively, domestic welfare cost is lower if it is possible to tax (or confiscate)

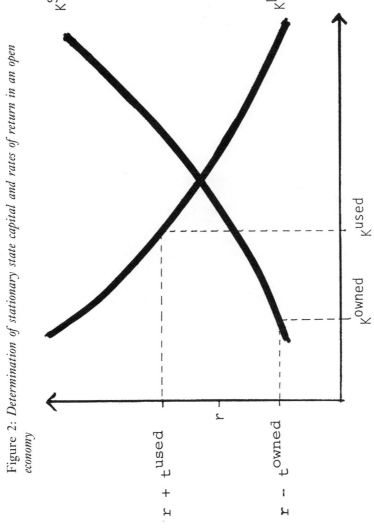

Figure 2: *Determination of stationary state capital and rates of return in an open economy*

short-run, sticky, foreign-owned capital and if the country can act as a monopolist and gain terms-of-trade improvements by decreasing output.

When the United States is treated as a closed economy, Hansson and Stuart [15] estimate the marginal excess burden for t^{used} as 0.93. In the preferred case, when the United States is treated as a large open economy, an increase in t^{used} *decreases* the present value of tax revenue. This corresponds to a negative marginal excess burden for funds that are raised when the tax rate decreases. For Sweden, t^{used} and t^{owned} are estimated to involve marginal excess burdens of 0.58 and 0.00, respectively, in the case of a small open economy, while the marginal excess burden is estimated at 0.70 for both taxes if the economy is closed. These differences in results for open and closed economies suggest that closed economy models may exclude important international interdependences that affect open economies.

Summary Evaluation of Available Evidence

A general finding of the studies is that a decrease in capital taxes increases capital formation. In a small open economy this result applies to t^{used} only. The estimated magnitude of the short- and long-run increase in aggregate capital after all capital taxes are eliminated differs according to different assumptions concerning the type of tax, technology, household behavior, and initial tax rates. The range of results is fairly wide. For instance, Summers estimates that a shift to a payroll or consumption tax increases capital in the long run by 67–72 percent, while Ballard predicts only a 13.5 percent increase in the long-run capital/labor ratio.

An increase in capital decreases the gross rate of return, and thus shifts a part of the gain from the tax decrease from capital to labor. In a small open economy, or in an economy where households have an infinite time horizon, this shift is exhaustive in the long run for t^{used} taxes. The net effect of a shift from capital taxes to labor taxes, evaluated in terms of present value, is typically a decrease in the net wage and an increase in the net rate of return. If each group of households owns at least a modest amount of capital during some period of the life cycle—say, in pension funds—then each group may gain from such a reform.

The most important result in Table 1 is that a total or marginal shift from capital to other types of taxation would, according to all but two estimates, involve significant welfare gains. Most of the estimated welfare gains from a total elimination of capital taxes (column 1) lie in the range 0.7–3.7 percent of total discounted future GNP. As expected, a shift to a lump-sum tax, as shown in the upper part of the table, tends to involve larger welfare gains than more "realistic" shifts to some other non-lump-sum tax, shown in the lower part of the table.

An interesting result is that a shift to a consumption tax typically involves a larger welfare gain than a shift to a labor tax, in spite of the equivalence between these two taxes in the standard stationary state models. This result is especially striking in [2] but is also apparent in [25] and [20]. In addition to the earlier discussed difference in the timing of tax revenue, an unanticipated increase in a consumption tax corresponds to an increase in a labor tax supplemented by an unanticipated capital levy on existing wealth. The relative attractiveness of the consumption tax thus essentially reflects the low (sometimes negative) excess burden of an unanticipated capital levy; this lump-sum tax increases tax revenue while no additional distortionary wedges are created between gross and net factor prices for factors that can adjust.[5]

This raises doubts, however, concerning the relevance of unanticipated tax increases. If a capital levy is instead anticipated, the tax is not a lump sum. In the extreme case of perfect foresight and time-consistent taxation, such taxes may indeed involve considerable distortions and low or even zero tax revenue; see [16]. Accordingly, optimal time-consistent taxation may require an explicit or implicit constitutional rule or norm that limits the use of capital levies. In this case, the attractiveness of a consumption tax as compared to a labor tax is more dubious; if the capital levy is considered to be inconsistent with explicit or implicit constitutional rules of taxation, the distortionary effects due to changed expectations may outweigh the short-run attractiveness of the capital levy.

The estimates in the upper part of column 2 of Table 1 indicate that capital taxes are associated with a marginal excess burden of 0.5–1.5 in a closed economy. For an open economy the few available estimates indicate a relatively large marginal excess burden for t^{used} and a small marginal excess burden for t^{owned}. An explanation is that t^{used}, but not t^{owned}, decreases K^{used} and thereby reduces the wage rate as shown in the simple model in Figure 2. This in turn tends to decrease in tax revenue from labor taxes. This effect is likely to be especially important in Sweden and other high-tax countries owing to high marginal taxes on labor. The lower part of column 2 shows that decreases in capital taxes and increases in labor taxes typically involve significant welfare gains.

To discuss the optimal level of capital taxes as compared to labor taxes (raised by Henry Aaron), let us take the point of view that capital taxes are fully shifted to labor in the long run under earlier specified assumptions, indicating that only labor taxes should be used. The short-run stickiness of capital, however, makes capital taxes more attractive in the short run from an efficiency, and perhaps also from a distributional, point of view. If attention is restricted to a proportional and constant-over-time tax rate in a closed economy, the optimal compromise from an efficiency point of view may involve a uniform tax on capital that is roughly one fifth of the tax on labor, as suggested by Chanley [8]. Distributional considerations may call for a higher capital tax, while the constitutional or expectational considerations, as discussed, may prompt a lower rate. For an open economy, the few available results suggest that t^{owned} are better than t^{used} from a (domestic) efficiency, and perhaps also from a distributional, point of view. If t^{used} for these reasons is set equal to zero, the most efficient portfolio of taxes includes a t^{owned} that exceeds at least one fifth of the overall tax on labor income. Again, distributional and other considerations are also important. (The actual ratio in Sweden between the average tax rate on capital and on labor is about one fourth.)

Another interesting conclusion is that elimination of intratemporal distortions through a shift to more neutral capital taxation is estimated to give welfare gains of 0.7–1.7 percent of the sum of discounted GNP. This may be an underestimate, since it ignores distortions between different means of finance.

Most of the reported results apply to the United States or "stylized" data. What then is their relevance to other OECD countries? The empirical data that are important for the numerical results in these models concern elasticities of labor supply, elasticity of savings, substitution elasticity between labor and capital in the production functions, initial income shares for labor and capital, and initial tax rates. Empirically, the first four features are likely to be fairly similar across countries. This suggests that the results for other countries may be different (given a specific model) primarily because of different initial tax rates. Available studies also show that the marginal excess burden for a given tax increases with the tax rate, especially for initial tax rates in excess of 50–60 percent. Indeed, the marginal excess burden approaches infinity when the tax rate approaches the top of the Laffer curve (typically 80–90 percent for proportional taxes on labor).

Accordingly, for a country with an overall marginal tax rate on capital income below the common assumption of 50 percent, an elimination of all capital taxes will generally exert smaller effects on capital, the net interest rate, and the net wage rate. The welfare gains from marginal and partial shifts to lump-sum taxes will hence be smaller than those reported in the upper part of Table 1. For shifts to other distortionary taxes, the initial level of labor taxes is also quite important. Generally, a higher overall marginal tax rate on labor income than the most common consumption of 20 percent yields lower welfare gains from total or marginal shifts from capital to labor or consumption taxes. This is confirmed by the results for Sweden in [14], where the 73 percent marginal tax rate on labor implies that a shift from capital to labor taxes would even cause a welfare loss.

To summarize, for lower initial capital taxes or higher initial labor taxes, a partial or complete elimination of capital taxation is likely to have a smaller effect on capital, net factor prices, and welfare than reported here for the United States. For countries that are open to international capital flows, it should be recognized that there are notable differences between the results for closed and open economies, as well as a significant difference between t^{used}- and t^{owned}-taxes.

Finally, the serious limitations of all these models should be borne in mind. First, even within the framework of the models, the results are typically quite sensitive to the explicitly or implicitly assumed elasticities of savings and labor supply, for the assumed net rate of return, and for the treatment of international interdependences. The empirical evidence on these issues is far from conclusive. Second, the results are also sensitive to the treatment of bequests. Third, the treatment of savings as pure life-cycle savings in a model with certainty, perfect foresight (also concerning the date of death), and no liquidity constraints may overestimate the savings elasticity and, thereby, yield an upward bias in the estimated welfare costs of capital taxes. Fourth, uncertainty may also be important for future tax rates. This may give rise to additional costs of tax changes, thereby providing an argument for a stable tax policy over time. Fifth, the welfare gains are typically calculated for proportional taxes with no explicit consideration of distributional effects. A tax reform that does not conflict with distributional goals may require, for example, a more progressive tax structure or a compensating increase in transfer payment that decreases the welfare gain from the tax reforms examined here. The results reported in [22] suggest that this is indeed the case for shift to a sales tax in the United Kingdom. Sixth, these equilibrium models treat prices as perfectly flexible and thereby exclude, for example, involuntary unemployment. This means that the models exclude all macroeconomic effects that may in fact arise owing to sticky prices. Seventh, the utility function is typically the discounted sum of single-period utilities for one or several representative households. The separability assumption that is involved has no convincing empirical basis. Moreover, the individualistic utility function is open to criticism.

These serious limitations suggest that the reported results should be interpreted and used with extreme care. However, the papers discussed here reflect the current state of the art and presumably provide the best available systematic evidence of the economic effects of capital taxation.

Notes

1. Note that the curves in Figure 1 differ from standard long-run demand and supply curves since different values of K involve different equilibrium wage rates.

2. For the more general case including population growth, stationary state per capita consumption is maximized for a tax on capital equal to the difference between the rate of population growth and the equilibrium net rate of return, since this means that the gross rate of return equals the rate of population growth (Golden Rule).

3. This study also estimates a total welfare loss of 6–9 percent of GDP for the U.K. tax system as compared to a lump-sum tax. A shift to a yield-preserving sales tax would, however,

involve a significant loss for the lowest-income groups, while the highest-income groups would gain.

4. If cross effects are included, an increase in a tax on capital owned in the country may influence long-run equilibrium labor supply, and thereby shift the "demand" curve for capital. Similarly, an increase in a tax on capital used in the country may decrease the wage rate, and thereby influence the "supply" of capital. This means that the figure should be interpreted as a pedagogical device only; the full equilibrium models including these cross effects are presented in the papers discussed.

5. Note that a lump-sum tax is here defined as a tax on a base that cannot adjust. Starting from a distorted equilibrium, an increase in a lump-sum tax normally alters the allocation of resources. If the equilibrium level of a taxed factor, say, increases, this involves a welfare gain and, consequently, a negative excess burden for the considered lump-sum tax. The result that a lump-sum tax has a zero excess burden holds in a nondistorted initial equilibrium only. This is an application of well-known second-best theory.

References

[1] Atkinson, A.B., and Stiglitz, J.E., *Lectures on Public Economics*, New York, McGraw-Hill, 1980.

[2] Auerbach, A.J., Kotlikoff, L.J., and Skinner, J., "The Efficiency Gains from Dynamic Tax Reform", *International Economic Review*, 24, 1983: 81–100.

[3] Ballard, C.L., "The Consumption Tax in a Computational General Equilibrium Framework", mimeo., Michigan State University, undated.

[4] Blinder, A.S., "Distribution Effects and the Aggregate Consumption Function", *Journal of Political Economy*, 73, 1965: 447–75.

[5] Boskin, M.J., "Taxation, Saving, and the Rate of Interest", *Journal of Political Economy*, 86, 1978: S3–27.

[6] Bovenberg, Lans A., "Capital Income Taxation in Growing Open Economy", mimeo., Washington, D.C., International Monetary Fund, 1984.

[7] Chamley, Christopher, "The Welfare Cost of Capital Income Taxation in a Growing Economy", *Journal of Political Economics*, 89, 1981: 468–95.

[8] ———, "Efficient Tax Reform in a Dynamic Model of General Equilibrium", *Quarterly Journal of Economics*, 100 (1985): 325–356.

[9] Denison, Edward F., "A Note on Private Saving", *Review of Economics and Statistics*, 61, 1958: 261–67.

[10] David, Paul, and Scadding, John L., "Private Saving: Ultrarationality, Aggregation, and 'Denison's Law' ", *Journal of Political Economy*, 82, 1974: 225–49.

[11] Eisner, R., and Strotz, R., "Determinants of Business Investment", in *Impacts of Monetary Policy: A Series of Research Studies Preapred for the Commission of Money and Credit*, ed. D. B. Suits et al., Englewood Cliffs, New Jersey, Prentice-Hall, 1963.

[12] Evans, O.J., "Tax Policy, the Interest Elasticity of Savings, and Capital Accumulation: Numerical Analysis of Theoretical Models", *American Economic Review*, 73, 1983: 389–97.

[13] Fullerton, D., Shoven, J., and Whalley, J., "Replacing the U.S. Income Tax with a Progressive Consumption Tax", *Journal of Public Economics*, 20, 1983: 3–23.

[14] Hansson, I., "Marginal Cost of Public Funds for Different Tax Instruments and Government Expenditures", *Scandinavian Journal of Economics*, 86, 1984: 115–30.

[15] ———, and Stuart, C., "The Welfare Cost of Deficit Finance", in press, *Economic Inquiry*, 1987.

[16] ———, "Capital Levies and Culture," mimeo., Departments of Economics, University of Lund and University of California, Santa Barbara, 1985.

[17] Harberger, Arnold C., "The Incidence of the Corporation Income Tax", *Journal of Political Economy*, 70, 1961: 215–40.

[18] Jorgenson, D.W., "Econometric Studies of Investment Behaviour: A Survey", *Journal of Economic Literature*, 9, 1971: 1111–47.

[19] Jorgenson, D.W., and Yun, K., "Tax Policy and Capital Allocation", Discussion Paper No. 1107, Harvard Institute of Economic Research, 1984.

[20] Judd, K.L., "The Welfare Cost of Factor Taxation in A Perfect Foresight Model", mimeo., Evanston, Ill., Northwestern University, 1983.

[21] King, M., and Fullerton, D., *The Taxation of Income from Capital: A Comparative Study of the United States, the United Kingdom, Sweden, and West Germany*, Chicago and London: University of Chicago Press, 1984.

[22] Piggott, John, and Whalley, John, "A Summary of Some Findings from a General Equilibrium Tax Model for the United Kingdom", in Karl Brunner and Allan K. Meltzer, eds., *Supply Shocks, Incentives and National Wealth*, Amsterdam, North-Holland, Carnegie-Rochester Conference Series on Public Policy, 1981.

[23] Shoven, John B., "The Incidence and Efficiency Effects of Taxes on Income from Capital", *Journal of Political Economy*, 84, 1976: 1261–83.

[24] Starrett, Q.A., "Long-Run Savings Elasticities in the Life Cycle Model", Research Paper No. 24, Stanford Workshop in the Macroeconomics of Factor Markets, Stanford University, 1982.

[25] Summers, Lawrence H., "Capital Taxation and Accumulation in a Life-Cycle Growth Model", *American Economic Review*, 71, 1981: 533–44.

[26] ———, "Taxation and the Size and Composition of the Capital Stock: An Asset Price Approach", mimeo., Harvard University and National Bureau of Economic Research, 1985.

[27] Wright, C., "Savings and the Rate of Interest", in *The Taxation of Income from Capital*, A. C. Harberger and M. J. Bailey, eds., Washington, D.C., Brookings Institution, 1969.

Résumé

L'importance relative de la fiscalité du capital s'est réduite dans de nombreux pays par suite de la création ou de l'accroissement de taxes sur la valeur ajoutée et de prélèvements sous forme de cotisations, ainsi que de l'intégration de la fiscalité sur le revenu des personnes physiques et des sociétés. Ce rapport essaie d'évaluer les effets d'une telle politique fiscale. Un résultat général est que le déplacement de l'imposition du capital sur le travail ou la consommation accroît la formation de capital. Quand tous les impôts sur le capital sont supprimés, l'accroissement estimé de capital dans le long terme varie entre 10 et 70%. Cet accroissement provoque une baisse du taux de rendement brut et une augmentation du salaire brut. L'effet net est sans conteste un accroissement du taux net de rendement et un faible ajustement vers le haut ou vers le bas du salaire net réel. On estime qu'un déplacement complet du capital vers d'autres impôts réduit l'excès de charge fiscale de 0,7–3,7% de la somme de la valeur actualisée de tout le PIB futur. Une diminution de l'imposition du capital qui réduit les ressources fiscales d'une unité monétaire procure un gain de bien-être estimé à 0,5–1,5 unité monétaire. L'élimination des différences entre les taux d'imposition réelle du capital dans les différents secteurs procurerait des gains de bien-être estimés au moins à 0,7–1,7% de la somme de la valeur actualisée de tout le PIB futur. Cependant, comme toutes ces estimations sont très sensibles aux hypothèses alternatives raisonnables concernant l'élasticité de l'épargne, ainsi qu' à l'exacte spécification du modèle, tous les résultats doivent être interprétés et utilisés avec une grande prudence.

A Critical Survey of Efforts to Measure Budget Incidence

Eugene Smolensky
William Hoyt
*Sheldon Danziger**

I. Introduction

A standard methodology has been developed for studying the consequences of aggregate budget incidence for the size distribution of income [27]. From the many studies in the many countries in which this methodology has been implemented, a small set of stylized conclusions has emerged. At the same time, a large body of critical literature has emerged, but it is the contention of this paper that these criticisms leave the stylized conclusions intact. Very recently, however, a new methodology—computable general equilibrium—has been developed which does have the potential to alter our perceptions of the combined effects of all taxes and transfers on the size distribution of income. This new methodology has not yet been implemented, and such implementation constitutes the academic frontier for aggregate budget incidence analysis.

The paper proceeds as follows. The next section discusses the classical accounting framework for measuring budget incidence. The third, "Technical Considerations," discusses the sensitivity of measures of the redistributive impacts of the fisc to the underlying assumptions, accounting conventions, and data. The fourth section is devoted to recent developments in and the application of computable general equilibrium models. The final section is a summary of the findings and conclusion.

We conclude that aggregate budget incidence studies have improved in recent years, but may have reached their limits. Because they do not model

*The authors are professor of economics, University of Wisconsin-Madison, Assistant Professor, University of Kentucky, and professor of social work and director of the Institute for Research on Poverty, University of Wisconsin-Madison. This research was supported by a grant from the Alfred P. Sloan Foundation to the Institute for Research on Poverty. The authors thank Ulrich Lehmann for his assistance and Robert Haveman for his comments.

The Relevance of Public Finance for Policy-Making. Proceedings of the 41st Conference of the International Institute of Public Finance, Madrid, 1985, pp. 165–179.

producer or consumer behavior, they cannot yield a true pre-fisc distribution. Computable general equilibrium models can in concept produce such a distribution [11]. While richer than the classical framework in theory, practical empirical work has just begun.

II. The Accounting Framework

The case for aggregate budget incidence studies was set down best by Dalton more than half a century ago: "Any system of public finance must be looked at as a whole, before any final judgment can be passed upon its merits or demerits. So, too, any taxes may, in some of their effects, correct and balance another" [8]. So too is it that aggregate budget incidence studies are required to evaluate the wholesale changes in the tax and transfer systems now sweeping the developed world. Nevertheless, many academic economists consider aggregate budget incidence studies to be a thoroughly disreputable branch of economics—a brute force effort to know the unknowable in a discipline that would increasingly rather be recherché than useful [4,33]. These attitudes may explain the most important fact about the aggregate budget incidence studies of the past decade: these studies are now less frequently academic exercises and increasingly are likely to be ongoing government activities (among the first was Nicholson [28]).[1] However, academics have also made considerable progress during the past ten years in integrating advances from theory into aggregate budget incidence studies. It is with these advances that this paper deals.

A simple device for summarizing and explaining the methodology of classical incidence studies is found in Reynolds and Smolensky [34]. The relationship between the post-fisc and pre-fisc income distributions is denoted by

(1) $c = m + gB - xT,$

where:

c is the row vector of post-fisc income. If the data have been aggregated over households, then element c_j is the income of the jth income class; if the data are at the household level, then c_j is the post-fisc income of the jth household.

m is the row vector of pre-fisc income. Its interpretation too depends on whether the data are aggregated or at the household level.

g is a row vector of government expenditures. Element g_i is the expenditure under program i.

x is a row vector of taxes. Element x_ℓ is the total revenue raised by tax ℓ.

B is a matrix of distributors of government expenditures. Element b_{ij} represents the share of expenditures received by income class (or household)j from program i. The rows of B each sum to unity.

T is a matrix of distributors of taxes. Element $t_{\ell j}$ represents the share of taxes borne by income class j as a consequence of tax ℓ. Each row of T also sums to unity.

Implicit in the formulation of this accounting identity are assumptions, a thorough discussion of which will reveal some of the foundations on which the classical methodology is based.

The first important assumption is that total government expenditures, $\Sigma\ g_i$, approximately equal total tax revenue, $\Sigma\ x_\ell$. This balanced budget assumption is not critical to the results and can be relaxed if debt financing plays a large role. However, the assumptions concerning the distributors, B and T, are fundamental. The elements of the B matrix are given two quite different interpretations. One is simply that b_{ij} is the share of government benefits accruing to income class j. That the rows of B sum to unity is, then, simply the requirement that all expenditures are received by some income class. Alternatively, $g_i b_{ij}$ is interpreted as the income equivalent of program i for income class j. Since $\Sigma_j\ b_{ij}\ g_i = g_i$, the total income equivalent of program i is equal to expenditures on program i. The second interpretation, the one of normative significance, is undermined by two important consequences which follow from the restrictions imposed on B. First, in-kind transfers must be valued at cost rather than at the income equivalent of the transfer. Second, consumers' surplus is not considered. The benefit of a publicly provided good is forced to equal the cost of the private goods sacrificed to produce it [31].

The tax distributors, T, represent the incidence of each tax on each income class—the cost of tax ℓ to income class j is $x_\ell\ t_{\ell j}$. This cost need not be a direct reduction in income: it also represents any loss in real income due to increased prices resulting from indirect taxes. The elements of T are derived from exogenous estimates of the incidence of each tax. That the rows of T sum to unity means that the collective cost of taxes, $\Sigma_j\ x_\ell\ t_{\ell j}$, equals the total tax revenue raised—there is no excess burden. This assumption is appropriate only when all goods, including labor, are supplied inelastically [33]. We return to this limitation below. The final implication we draw from this framework is that in it the government acts only to redistribute income, since total pre-fisc and post-fisc income are equal.

We have presented the accounting framework in detail to highlight the four practices required by classical budget incidence studies which most trouble its many critics: the annual accounting period, ignoring deadweight loss from taxation, equating the value of in-kind transfers to the cost of the transfer, and restricting the government's role to redistributing income.

The importance of these troubling practices depends on the objective. If the question addressed is "What is the post-fisc distribution of income?" these assumptions are less restrictive than when the study intends to answer the question, "What role has the government played in redistributing income?"

Conceptually, calculating post-fisc income (c) requires much less information than does pre-fisc income (m). The data required to calculate post-fisc income are reported income, direct taxes, total government spending and its distribution. To calculate pre-fisc income we also need to know the incidence of indirect taxes. While not required in theory, classical incidence studies do deduct indirect taxes from income according to the expenditures on the taxed goods by the household when deriving post-fisc income. This apparently anomalous practice is followed because there is, in fact, an interest in the effects of government on the income distribution, and therefore the effects of price changes induced by indirect taxes are of interest [6,13]. A bias will therefore be introduced in the evaluation of tax policy when comparing nations or periods of time when the mixes of direct and indirect taxation differ greatly, unless some accounting of the change is made.

This problem illustrates the frequent confounding of the two basic questions addressed by incidence studies: "What is the income distribution?" and "How much redistribution?" The bias issue arises because indirect taxes will change relative prices and the effect of these price changes affects different income classes differently. By deducting indirect taxes from income we are controlling for these differences when comparing income distributions. Since interpretation of any single post-fisc distribution will require comparison with some other post-fisc or pre-fisc distribution, it is almost always necessary to subtract indirect taxes.

The net result of the flurry of research initiated by Gillespie in 1965 [12] that implements the classical framework is a small set of stylized facts most recently summarized by Saunders [35]:

1. Despite the large differences across the developed countries in the relative size and composition of the fisc, redistributive impacts are quite similar across countries.

2. Transfers play the major role in redistribution, primarily because of old age pensions.

3. Tax systems are broadly proportional.

To this list we would add two others:

4. By any of the conventional measures, taking account of the fisc substantially reduces measured inequality in any year.

5. Consistent with point 1, substantial growth in government expenditures in a single country over time does *not* substantially increase the spread between pre- and post-fisc income inequality in later relative to earlier years [18,19,32].

These stylized facts will serve as the criteria by which we will judge the recent empirical evaluations of the classical methodology conducted during the past decade. We will then turn to the larger issues raised by equation 1.

III. Technical Considerations

Recent work indicates which of the many assumptions and accounting considerations are critical to the stylized conclusions. Note that the income unit is not explicitly specified in the accounting framework. Lydall [24] demonstrates the sensitivity of measured income inequality to differences in the income unit and offers them as a partial explanation of the differences in measured income inequality among nations. Lydall examines four recipient units: the individual, the consumer unit, the household, and the family. He is of the view that there is a reasonable and appropriate measure of income—household income adjusted for household size. Household, because it captures the vast majority of private transfers. Adjusted for size, because the material well-being of a household varies with its size, given income. Since there are some economies of scale in household production, per capita household income may not be the best adjustment [39].

Accepting that there is a conceptually appropriate unit, do the variations across studies in the income units have any empirical significance? According to Lydall, the Gini coefficient for the U.S. based on individuals is an extremely high (and misleading) .506, while for a household it is only .371—which also may be misleading, since household income was not adjusted for household size. The income unit obviously matters.

Equation 1 defined pre-fisc income as post-fisc income less the benefits of expenditures plus the cost of taxation. This identity is consistent with several concepts of pre-fisc income and the choice among them depends on the counterfactual. Gillespie [14] argues that, if the counterfactual is zero government, the appropriate pre-fisc income base is broad income. Broad income is derived from net national product (NNP) by adding factor returns unreported in the NNP and realized capital gains and subtracting indirect business taxes. Reynolds and Smolensky [34] and Meerman [26] argue that a zero-government counterfactual is not sensible and choose NNP as the income base. Our concern here is the difference in measured inequality associated with different income bases and not which income base and counterfactual are appropriate.

Normand, Hawley and Gillespie [29] find that while the choice between NNP and broad income as an income base has little effect on the difference between post-fisc and pre-fisc income inequality in any year, differences in post-fisc income inequality through time are sensitive to the income base chosen. While Reynolds and Smolensky conclude that there is little change in the post-fisc income distribution among the years of their sample, 1950, 1961, and 1970, Normand et al. conclude that there was a reduction in income inequality from 1961 to 1970 in the U.S. The income base does seem to matter.

Pfaff and Asam [31] argue that the attribution of benefits from public infrastructure investments to households has been faulty for at least three reasons:

1. These investments are not, as assumed, pure public goods.
2. Linking benefits to well-being via a constant marginal utility of income, as usually assumed, is misleading.
3. Ranking is by current rather than lifetime income.

They urge, therefore, user-based distributors and a lifetime income base. None of these proposals is likely to significantly affect our perceptions of the stylized facts. The lifetime income proposal falls into a large class of improvements which can be made in the study of a particular program, but which cannot be implemented in an aggregate budget incidence study, since such studies require a single accounting framework—one which forces all procedures that affect the entire study to the lowest common denominator. If one benefit is to be in a lifetime framework, then all other benefits, and taxes as well as income, must also be on a lifetime basis. Redoing it all in lifetime terms might indeed affect our perceptions, but such a study is not likely to be carried out soon.

Pfaff and Asam's other criticisms appear to be motivated by the work of Aaron and McGuire [1]. Whatever the merits of the Aaron and McGuire proposal [6], Gruske [18,19] has shown that its implementation is not likely to be quantitatively significant. Nor, according again to Gruske, will using simple distributors based on use, as proposed by Pfaff and Asam, have significant quantitative effects.

Gruske has pursued both strategies and their cross-section effects are now known. He classifies benefits into six categories, at least partly on their degree of publicness: e.g., pure public services like defense, limited public services like police, group benefits like education, etc. For each category, Gruske devises a set of distributors. Where consumption data are available, the distributors are relatively specific. For example, one distributor for health benefits is 67.1 percent to households with heads of family out of the labor force, 30.5 percent to households with employed heads, and the remainder to the self-employed. These percentages were derived from a utilization survey. While still a far cry from revealed willingness to pay, it must be counted an improvement over such usual practices as a distribution based on age or private health expenditures. In the end, however, when distributors are grouped into the most progressive or regressive combinations, the range of resulting Gini coefficients is well within those observed in earlier, far cruder studies. For the difference between pre- and post-fisc income, the range in the Gini is from .111 to .010 in Gruske, and between .162 and .062 in Reynolds and Smolensky.

In implementing the Aaron and McGuire framework, Gruske varies the elasticity of the marginal utility of income from 0 to −2 (a range which encompasses most estimates for the U.S. [25]) in several sensitivity tests, but maintains the same constant marginal utility for all households in any simulation. Nevertheless his results are instructive concerning the impact a variable marginal utility would likely have. The range of variation across simulations obtained in the Gini coefficient of the difference between pre- and post-fisc income is from .087 to .031, well within the range produced by variations among progressive and regressive assumptions. Varying the marginal utility of income would open the range of outcomes, but obviously not by enough to alter our perceptions. Further, these experiments probably exaggerate the impact of the Aaron-McGuire methodology. Smolensky et al. [38] examined the implications of assuming an elasticity of the marginal utility of income of −1.5. Although a substantial pro-rich tilt to the distribution of benefits follows directly, some adjustment to taxes is logically required also, since in effect the Aaron-McGuire methodology converts some of the public good to a private good, and hence some of taxes to a payment for services rendered. Most simple assignment rules to effectuate this conversion will also be pro-rich, thereby reducing the progressivity of the remaining taxes. For Smolensky et al. the exercise proved not to be quantitatively important.

The earliest incidence studies used data aggregated over households; more recent studies make use of microeconomic data. Using several simulations on a single data set, Dalrymple [9] tests the sensitivity of aggregate budget incidence results to aggregation and the choice of summary statistic. The key consequence of using data aggregated over the recipient unit into income classes and subsequently adding and subtracting various imputations is that the initial ranking cannot be altered. Any Gini coefficients calculated on the augmented income measures will be "quasi Ginis" (which range from −1 to +1) rather than true Ginis. Dalrymple finds that the quasi Ginis are always smaller than the appropriate true Ginis, but that the rankings of income concepts (pre-fisc, post-fisc, etc.) are unaffected. In moving from pre- to post-fisc income, the importance of various items added or subtracted (social security benefits, personal income taxes, etc.) are also affected by aggregation, but once again, the relative importance of the various items is largely unaltered.

The choice of an inequality index also does not seem to affect our perceptions of the stylized facts. For example, Dalrymple's result holds for the Atkinson index, although levels of the Atkinson measures are highly responsive to aggregation (whatever the aversion index chosen). On the other hand, of course, the Atkinson measures are unaffected by ranking.

One important caveat does emerge from the Dalrymple study. Our perception as to whether a tax is progressive or regressive is sensitive to the total income concept on which the original ranking is made. Thus the local property tax reduces inequality when households are ranked by broad income, but raises inequality when recipient units are ranked by factor income. Note that this important difference is due solely to the original ranking rule, not the incidence assumptions, since in both cases the property tax is assumed to be borne by owners of property in proportion to their self-reported property income. This result may explain the Normand et al. finding.[2]

If we agree on a recipient unit, say household income per equivalent adult, and use microdata so that the original ranking problem becomes irrelevant, then in all probability we have proceeded as far as we can with technical improvements in aggregate budget incidence studies.

The key issues which remain unresolved are the relevant counterfactual, the evaluation of in-kind benefits and consumers' surplus (but see [37]), deadweight losses from subsidies, and the exclusion of the excess burden. To meet these problems we need a radically new methodology—computable general equilibrium models. These models have as yet made no direct contribution to evaluating the fisc taken as a whole, but they show promise.

IV. Computable General Equilibrium

Traditional budget incidence studies account for excise taxation via incidence assumptions, but there remain two ways in which consumers and producers are taken to be unresponsive. First, since the loss of real income from a commodity tax is measured as the product of the share of the tax borne by consumers, the tax rate on the commodity, and the expenditures of the buyers on the commodity, it is underestimated. The loss from distorting the consumer's purchases is not measured. The measure of the loss borne by labor and capital from commodity taxes is also underestimated; permitting elastic factor supplies as in computable general equilibrium will yield an excess burden. These excess burdens, as we noted earlier, are set to zero in the classical accounting framework. Second, the incidence of a tax falls only on the consumers of and factors used in producing the taxed commodity. In general, cross-price elasticities are not zero, however, and the mix of factors varies among industries and across organizational forms so that the effects of tax distortions are widely dispersed.

To meet problems such as these, during the past decade a literature has developed which estimates the excess burden of taxation in a general equilibrium framework [3,7,36]. These studies are relevant for aggregate budget incidence studies for two reasons: they provide alternative tax incidence measures and, by measuring excess burden, they provide predictions of pre-fisc income more consistent with theory.

At the heart of this literature are general equilibrium models of the Harberger sort solved by computer algorithm for the effects of tax changes on incomes, prices, and outputs. In these computable general equilibrium (CGE) models, the economy is in equilibrium—all markets clear and all firms earn zero profits. The required supply and demand equations are usually derived from utility and production functions—most often variations on Constant Elasticity of Substitution (C.E.S.) functions, e.g., the Cobb-Douglas.

In addition to the parameters of the demand and supply functions, CGE studies require the underlying utility and production functions. The first step is to determine these parameters by replicating a benchmark data set for the economy in a single year. This replication, or calibration, requires data drawn from the national accounts, household income and expenditure surveys, input-output tables, tax data, trade data, and balance of payments accounts, to describe the economy-wide equilibrium with the current distribution of factor endowments—information that also must be in this data set. Rather than using the set of equations describing equilibrium to solve for equilibrium prices and outputs, parameters are chosen so that, with the current distribution of factor endowments and the current tax structure, solving the model will replicate the observed equilibrium, i.e. the benchmark data set.[3]

The parameters exogenously determined are the key parameters—elasticities of substitution in production, and the elasticities of savings and of labor supply. These key parameters are extracted from the literature or are informed guesses. Sensitivity analysis is obviously essential. Once calibrated, all parameters are determined and the model is solved for the equilibrium conditions of the economy under different tax regimes. The counterfactual equilibrium will differ from the benchmark data in prices, incomes, and outputs.

The counterfactual having been calculated, the final step is to summarize the policy implications. Since prices and incomes have changed with the change in the tax system, direct comparison of incomes in the benchmark case and under the counterfactual is inappropriate. Measures of welfare change which account for the change in prices are required—e.g., the Hicksian equivalent and compensating variations. Since utility functions were already postulated and parameterized, these measures require no additional assumptions.

General equilibrium analysis has been primarily applied to questions of efficiency. Distributional effects of tax changes are, while reported, rarely highlighted [5]. The primary purpose of including several income classes is to obtain more precise estimates of the demand and labor supply responses.

Devarajan, Fullerton, and Musgrave [10] do address the distributional consequences of taxation. Although they discuss the incidence of four separate tax changes—a progressive increase in the personal income tax, and taxes on housing, clothing and jewelry, and gasoline—we will discuss only two. Tax incidence is analyzed using both the CGE and the traditional budget incidence approaches. The results of both approaches are then compared. The tax revenue raised by each increase is treated as a transfer to taxpayers in proportion to after-tax income prior to the tax change in both approaches. Since factor supply responses are endogenous, the CGE experiments do not force a balanced budget—the counterfactual, a new tax regime, does not yield the same tax revenue as in the benchmark case. A step has been taken, then, towards comparing pre- and post-fisc income, since the analysis encompasses two tax regimes which differ in relative prices and revenues raised. The traditional approach predicts greater revenue than the CGE model except for the progressive increase in the income tax, which is to be expected since the traditional approach predicts revenue by implicitly assuming unresponsive commodity demands and supplies.

The approach used makes little difference for the change in the personal income tax, but for the tax on housing there are noticeable differences, particularly in the tails of the income distribution. In the traditional approach, the incidence of the housing tax depends on whether the tax is treated as falling on capital or as falling on consumption. As a tax on capital, the loss of income is greatest on the highest income group while all but the lowest income class actually gain income. As a tax on consumption, the results are reversed; the poorest income class suffers the greatest percentage decline in income and real income increases in the highest income class. The CGE, of course, does not assume whether the tax is a consumption or a capital tax. In general, the loss in real income in the traditional approach with the tax falling on consumption exceeds that measured using CGE, whereas with the tax on capital, the gain in real income for low-income classes is greater than that found in the CGE model, and is lower for high-income classes.

This study suggests that the CGE model offers three advantages to budget incidence studies. First, its assumptions concern individual behavior—the elasticity of labor supply, savings, and the substitution of capital and labor. In traditional studies, it is the incidences of the taxes that are assumed. However, these incidence assumptions imply further assumptions about labor supply, savings behavior, and the production process. Occam's razor, then, favors the CGE model.

Second, CGE models can measure effects which are impossible to measure within the traditional budget incidence framework: the secondary effects on the prices and quantities of goods and factors which are taxed, and excess burden. CGE studies suggest that marginal excess burden may be in the neighborhood of 50 percent of the cost of government [2], and studies which ignore it will underestimate pre-fisc income.

While CGE models are not totally flexible—in the C.E.S. framework, elasticities of substitution remain constant—they clearly are more flexible than the traditional incidence studies. Prices, the capital/labor ratio, and output all change in general equilibrium analysis; in traditional budget incidence studies all these variables remain constant—even for the move from post-fisc to pre-fisc income. In addition, within the CGE framework, the actual calculation of pre-fisc income is quite straightforward. The counterfactual is solved with taxes and government revenue set to zero. Once the new equilibrium vector of prices, outputs, and incomes are found, the pre-fisc income can be converted into an equivalent income under the prices found in the benchmark, post-fisc income. There is a sense, then, in which CGE models are more appropriate for nonmarginal analysis; e.g., computing the effects of large changes in the tax regime.

V. Conclusion

Among the four especially troublesome aspects of classical studies highlighted in Section II were these three: ignoring the deadweight loss from taxation, equating the value of in-kind transfers to their cost, and restricting the government's role to redistribution. In principle, all of these difficulties can be resolved by appropriate computable general equilibrium modeling and simulation. CGE models are also conceptually compatible with the infamous "zero government" counterfactual. Further, of all the technical and conceptual issues that have been considered, only the CGE models are at all likely to upset the stylized facts that are the primary contribution of aggregate incidence studies to public economics.[4]

Empirical work has thus far, however, been confined to taxes—just a few taxes at that. Theorists have just begun to examine fundamental ideas such as the meaning of equilibrium in such models [20]. While the conceptual issues of the classical approach are settled, as Gillespie, Lydall and Dalrymple have shown, some recalculation may be warranted. Current methodology needs to be introduced into those countries lacking prior studies [23]. Carefully controlled cross-country comparisons are also required. For academic aggregate incidence studies, however, the frontier is to find the robust stylized facts, if any, that CGE models can deliver.

Heading down the CGE road is, of course, replete with risks. A host of questions are yet to be answered. By what criteria do we judge alternative CGE models? How important is the purely competitive equilibrium assumption? How do we calibrate a competitive equilibrium when in the base data there are unemployed resources receiving transfers? Are scale economies important? Economic rents? Is it wise to return to emphasizing the relationship between the size and functional distribution of income, when we know that their relationship is extremely loose? Most relevant of all, how difficult is it going to be to put expenditures into the model? Further, irony of ironies, old settled questions will be reopened. To give just one example, for all practical purposes, CGE takes us back to aggregated data, and the initial ranking problem.

Studies of the effects of the fisc contribute to policy-making by setting the essential backdrop to the discussion of particular tax and transfer policies. The fairness of the fisc at a point in time or the justice of a package of fiscal proposals by an administration cannot be judged element-by-element and without regard to what is left unchanged. Tax systems consist of a mix of progressive and regressive components. The political debate must be forced to take the whole into account at once. Hence, the demand for studies of the aggregate incidence of the fisc will call them into existence.[5]

Notes

1. Government studies tend to be restricted to programs with clearly defined beneficiaries. For example, the incidence of defense spending is not generally studied, while that of social security taxes and spending is. This probably biases the fisc toward progressivity [30].

2. However, Wolfson [40] has argued that growth in government changes the mix of factor demands and hence the pre-fisc distribution of income. If this had occurred between 1961 and 1970, it would have had a relatively larger effect on the NNP base than on broad income, since the latter is larger.

3. Calibration typically involves a single observation, data from one year, and without some exogenously specified parameters will not yield a unique set of parameters.

4. The effect of government on inequality other than through the fisc—such as through fiscal, monetary and trade policy—can also be integrated into the CGE framework.

5. Yet more aggregative models more directly focused on the income distribution may displace both the traditional aggregate budget incidence studies and CGE models. Gottschalk and Danziger [15] propose a simulation model of the distribution itself. Lampman [21] applies a benefit-cost model to program net benefits and a simplified income distribution. Le Grand [22] takes a distinctly literary approach. A linearized early prototype model is Golladay and Haveman [16].

References

[1] Aaron, Henry, and McGuire, Martin, "Public Goods and Income Distribution", *Econometrica*, 38, November 1970: 907–20.

[2] Ballard, Charles; Fullerton, Don; Shoven, John B.; and Whalley, John, *A General Equilibrium Model for Tax Policy Evaluation*, Chicago, University of Chicago Press, 1985.

[3] Ballard, Charles; Shoven, John B.; and Whalley, John, "General Equilibrium Computations of the Marginal Welfare Costs of Taxes in the United States," *American Economic Review*, 75, 1985: 128–38.

[4] Bird, Richard M., "Income Redistribution through the Fiscal System: The Limits of Knowledge", *American Economic Review*, 70, May 1980: 77–81.

[5] Bovenberg, A. Lars, "Reflections on the Significance of the General Equilibrium Approach for the Analysis of Public Finance Instruments," in this volume.

[6] Brennan, Geoffrey, "The Distributional Implications of Public Goods", *Econometrica*, 44, March 1976: 391–407.

[7] Browning, Edgar K., "The Marginal Cost of Public Funds," *Journal of Political Economy*, 84(2), April 1976: 283–98.

[8] Dalton, Hugh, *Principles of Public Finance*, 4th ed., New York, Frederick A. Praeger, 1955.

[9] Dalrymple, Robert, "The Sensitivity of Measured Comprehensive Income Inequality to Aggregation, Re-ranking and Underreporting", unpublished doctoral dissertation, University of Wisconsin-Madison, 1980.

[10] Devarajan, Shantayanan; Fullerton, Don; and Musgrave, Richard A., "Estimating the Distribution of Tax Burdens", *Journal of Public Economics*, 13, April 1980: 155–182.

[11] Fullerton, Don; King, A. Thomas; Shoven, John B.; and Whalley, John, "Corporate Tax Integration in the United States: A General Equilibrium Approach", *American Economic Review*, 71, September 1981: 677–91.

[12] Gillespie, W. Irwin, "Effect of Public Expenditures on the Distribution of Income", in Musgrave, Richard (ed.), *Essays in Fiscal Federalism*, Washington, The Brookings Institution, 1965.

[13] Gillespie, W. Irwin, "Taxes, Expenditures and the Redistribution of Income in Canada, 1951–1977", presented at the Conference on Canadian Incomes, Winnipeg, Manitoba, May 10–12, 1979.

[14] Gillespie, W. Irwin, *The Redistribution of Income in Canada*, Ottawa, Gage Publishing, 1980.

[15] Gottschalk, Peter, and Danziger, Sheldon, "A Framework for Evaluating the Effects of Economic Growth and Transfers on Poverty", *American Economic Review*, 75, 1985: 153–61.

[16] Golladay, Frederick, and Haveman, Robert, *The Economic Impacts of Tax-Transfer Policy: Regional and Distributional Effects*, New York, Academic Press, 1977.

[17] Griliches, Zvi; Krelle, Wilhelm; Krupp, Hans-Jurgen; and Kyn, Oldrich, *Income Distribution and Economic Inequality*, New York, Halsted Press, 1978.

[18] Gruske, Karl-Dieter, *Die Personale Budgetinzidenz*, Göttingen, Vandenhoeck & Ruprecht, 1978.

[19] Gruske, Karl-Dieter, "Redistributive Effects of the Integrated Financial and Social Budgets in West Germany", in *Public Finance and Social Policy*, Proceedings of the 39th Congress of the International Institute of Public Finance, Detroit, Wayne State University Press, 1985.

[20] Kehoe, Timothy, and Levine, David K., "Comparative Statistics and Perfect Foresight in Infinite Horizon Economies", *Econometrica*, 53, March 1985: 433–54.

[21] Lampman, Robert, *Social Welfare Spending: Accounting for Changes from 1950 to 1978*, New York, Academic Press, 1984.

[22] Le Grand, Julian, *Redistribution and the Social Services*, London, George Allen and Unwin, 1982.

[23] Leu, Robert E.; Frey, René L.; and Buhmann, Brigitte, "Taxes, Expenditures and Income Distribution in Switzerland", *Journal of Social Policy*, 14, July 1985: 341–60.

[24] Lydall, Harold F., "Some Problems in Making International Comparisons of Inequality", in John R. Moroney, ed., *Income Inequality*, Lexington, Mass., Lexington Books, 1979.

[25] Maital, Shlomo, "Public Goods and Income Distribution: Some Further Results", *Econometrica*, 41, May 1973: 565–67.

[26] Meerman, Jacob, "Do Empirical Studies of Budget Incidence Make Sense?" *Public Finance: Finance Publiques*, 3(3), 1978, 295–313.

[27] Musgrave, Richard A.; Case, Karl E.; and Leonard, Herman B., "The Distribution of Fiscal Burdens and Benefits", *Public Finance Quarterly*, July 1974: 259–311.

[28] Nicholson, J. L., "Redistribution of Income in the United Kingdom in 1959, 1957, and 1953", in Colin Clark and Stuvel Geer, eds., *Income Redistribution and the Statistical Foundations of Economic Policy*, International Association for Research in Income and Wealth, Series X, London, Bowes and Bowes, 1964.

[29] Normand, Denis; Hawley, Gilbert; and Gillespie, W. Irwin, "In Search of the Changing Distribution of Income During the Post-War Period in Canada and the United States," *Public Finance*, 38, 1983: 267–81.

[30] O'Higgins, Michael, "The Distributive Effects of Public Expenditure and Taxation: An Agnostic View of the CSO Analyses", in C. T. Sandford, C. Pond, and R. Walker, eds., *Taxation and Social Policy*, London, Heinemann, 1980.

[31] Pfaff, Martin, and Asam, Wolfgang, "Distributive Effects of Real Transfers via Public Infrastructure: Conceptual Problems and Some Empirical Results", in Griliches et al. [17].

[32] Pechman, Joseph A., *Who Paid The Taxes, 1966–85?* Washington, D.C., The Brookings Institution, 1985.

[33] Prest, A., "The Budget and the Distribution of National Income", York, Proceedings of the International Institute of Public Finance, 1968.

[34] Reynolds, Morgan, and Smolensky, Eugene, *Public Expenditures, Taxes, and the Distribution of Income: The United States, 1950, 1961, 1970*, New York, Academic Press, 1977.

[35] Saunders, Peter, "Evidence on Income Redistribution by Governments", OECD Economics and Statistics Department, Working Papers, No. 11, January 1984.

[36] Shoven, John B., and Whalley, John, "Applied General-Equilibrium Models of Taxation and International Trade: An Introduction and Survey", *Journal of Economic Literature*, 22, September 1984: 1007–51.

[37] Smeeding, Timothy M., *Alternative Methods for Valuing Selected In-Kind Transfer Benefits and Measuring Their Effect on Poverty*, U.S. Bureau of the Census, Technical Paper no. 50, Washington, D.C., U.S. Government Printing Office, 1982.

[38] Smolensky, Eugene; Stiefel, Leanna; Schmundt, Maria; and Plotnick, Robert, "Adding In-Kind Transfers to the Personal Income and Outlay Account: Implications for the Size Distribution of Income", in F. Thomas Juster, ed., *The Distribution of Economic Well-Being*, Cambridge Mass., Ballinger Publishing Co., for the National Bureau of Economic Research, 1977.

[39] Van der Gaag, Jacques, and Smolensky, Eugene, "True Household Equivalence Scales and Characteristics of the Poor in the United States", *Review of Income and Wealth*, 28, 1982: 17–27.

[40] Wolfson, Dirk J., "On the Social Selectivity of Public Spending Programs", *The Netherlands Journal of Sociology*, 19, 1983: 182–97.

Résumé

Un petit ensemble de conclusions stylisées émerge des nombreuses applications dans de nombreux pays de la méthodologie habituelle pour l'étude des effets budgétaires globaux. Tandis que la méthodologie habituelle a fait l'objet d'un grand nombre de critiques, les conclusions stylisées demeurent intactes, en grande partie parce que nous ne pouvons pas savoir, dans la méthodologie habituelle, quels seraient les effets si l'on tenait compte de la perte de capacité provenant de la fiscalité, ou des transferts correctement évalués, ou du rôle du gouvernement s'étendant au-delà de la redistribution. Une simulation à l'aide de modèles d'équilibre général susceptibles de calculs est un moyen d'évaluer les conséquences du fait d'écarter ces caractéristiques fondamentales de la méthodologie classique, mais aucune simulation de ce genre n'a jusqu'alors été tentée. La frontière académique est l'élaboration de modèles d'équilibre général susceptibles de calculs dans suffisamment de pays et à suffisamment de points différents dans le temps, afin de développer un nouvel ensemble de conclusions stylisées pour comparer avec celles résultant de la méthodologie classique.

On the Efficacy of Public Finance Instruments in Protecting the Environment

Alfred Endres*

I. Introduction

A wide range of public activities are directed toward protecting the environment, and the number of instruments that can be used or advocated for this purpose have different characteristics. This paper focuses on three: effluent charges, the command and control approach, and transferable discharge permits (TDPs).[1] Two forms of TDPs are considered: those that may be auctioned off, or those that are given free of charge to the polluters according to a certain allocation scheme. In the latter case, the initial allocation of pollution permits among different sources may be related to the emission quantities tolerated by the regulation effective before the TDP policy was introduced ("grandfathering").

The following discussion assesses the efficacy of these instruments on theoretical grounds.[2] The criterion of efficacy is defined to contain three elements:

(1) the efficiency of an environmental policy instrument, i.e., its ability to attain a predetermined regional emission level at minimum abatement cost;
(2) the accuracy of an instrument, i.e., its ability to arrive at the target without cumbersome trial and error processes;
(3) the innovative direction of an instrument, i.e., its ability to induce progress in pollution abatement technology.

Some empirical evidence concerning the efficiency of the instruments is presented in section III, followed by consideration of the question of why instruments using economic incentives, such as emission taxes and transferable discharge permits, though very popular among environmental

*The author is a member of the Technical University of Berlin, Federal Republic of Germany. He is indebted to G. Muraro and B. Wolfe for their stimulating discussion of this paper during and after the conference.

The Relevance of Public Finance for Policy-Making. Proceedings of the 41st Congress of the International Institute of Public Finance, Madrid, 1985, pp. 181–192.

economists, are rarely used in practice. Section V demonstrates that these instruments, if used at all, are very different in design from their description in textbooks on environmental economics. Conclusions are presented in the final section.

Economic reasoning is used to make a rational choice among alternative environmental policy instruments serving to attain a certain target level of pollution reduction. Of course, to be complete and consistent, economic reasoning should also be employed to determine that level. The optimal amount of pollution reduction is defined by equalizing the marginal costs and the marginal benefits of pollution control (given that the mc- and mb-functions are well behaved). Economists have endeavored to identify this level. Assessing the benefits of environmental improvement has proved to be more difficult than estimates of its cost, because no market for a clean environment exists. In the "contingent evaluation" approach, particular groups affected by pollution are asked about their willingness to pay for pollution reduction. The problems of free rider and protest responses have to be taken into consideration in this approach. A different route is represented by the "hedonic approach." There, the market prices of private goods (land and housing prices in particular) are used to determine people's evaluations of environmental quality improvements.[3]

A discussion of the methods of establishing a rational environmental policy goal is beyond the scope of this paper; such issues are henceforth ignored, since the properties of the environmental policy instruments, discussed below, are independent of whether the goals to be attained by means of them are optimal or not.

II. The Economic Theory of Public Finance Instruments

Efficiency

In the literature, effluent charges are considered to be efficient instruments (see [8,18]). Reducing emissions to the point at which marginal abatement costs equal the effluent charge rate, polluters automatically meet the efficiency condition of equal marginal abatement costs across all sources.

Transferable discharge permits are equally efficient, substituting the permit price for the tax rate. In contrast, command and control regulations forcing the polluters to maintain certain emission standards are not efficient, in general. Regulators do not have sufficient information to differentiate the standards for individual sources according to their marginal abatement costs.

Accuracy

In regard to its ability to attain with precision a predetermined pollution target level, the effluent charge suffers from the fact that it acts as a "price" for discharging to which each firm is free to adjust its discharge quantity. The predetermined regional emission target will therefore be achieved only after a process of trial and error. In contrast, the advantage of transferable discharge permits is that the level of pollution is under direct control of the environmental agency through the number of permits auctioned off (or given away free). So, permits exhibit maximum accuracy.[4] This also holds true for a command and control policy that specifies absolute emission ceilings for the polluting sources.[5]

Innovative Direction

The change to a better pollution control technique makes a polluter's marginal abatement cost curve shift downward.

Under an effluent charge, there is a twofold incentive to introduce the new technique. First, the new technique attains the firm's "old" (before the technical change) abatement level in cheaper fashion than does the old one. Second, the firm benefits from increasing pollution abatement beyond its "old" level: moving from the point where the tax rate equals the "old" marginal abatement cost to the point where the tax rate equals the "new" marginal abatement cost, the firm saves on taxes (net of additional abatement cost). The dynamic thrust of auctioning off transferable discharge permits is the same as in the effluent charge case: achieving given abatement levels at lower costs saves abatement cost. Achieving higher abatement levels at lower costs than the permit price saves permit expenditure (net of additional abatement cost). Hence, the price of the permit plays the same role as the tax rate in the effluent charge case. However, as polluters substitute for better abatement technologies, demand for permits decreases and so does their equilibrium price. Therefore, as time goes by, the dynamic incentive of transferable discharge permits is automatically reduced (unless the environmental agency reduces the supply of permits).

Under a command and control approach, there is an incentive to introduce new methods by which to meet the standards at lower cost. There is no incentive, however, to introduce new methods to reduce emissions below the level tolerated by the standards.

III. Empirical Assessment of the Cost Advantages of Economic Incentive Instruments

An increasing number of interesting simulation studies compare charges and TDPs to the command and control approach, in terms of efficiency. This section reviews the results of two such studies.[6]

Atkinson and Tietenberg [1] compare the costs of achieving primary and secondary ambient air quality standards in the St. Louis Air Quality Control Region by means of a range of transferable permit and administrative rule policies. The benchmark for the comparison is the cost of maintaining current air quality in the region.[7] The cost of achieving the primary and secondary standards of 75 and 60 μg/m³ (annual geometric mean) of particulate emissions, respectively, with the emission allocation implied by the current SIP (State Implementation Plan), are estimated to exceed the benchmark regional control cost of $6,726.26/day by $798.55 (12 percent) for the primary standard and $25,026.60 (372 percent) for the secondary standard. This command and control system is compared with two alternative kinds of TDP systems: (1) an emission permit system (EPS) in which emissions are traded on a 1:1 basis, regardless of the locations of their sources; (2) an ambient permit system (APS), in which the trade ratio between emissions depends on "transfer coefficients," taking into account the dispersions of emissions from their sources to specific receptor points.

An EPS which would achieve the standard with the same amount of regional pollution reduction as in the SIP-case is simulated to cost less than the benchmark cost by $5,844.34 (or 87 percent of the benchmark) for the primary standard, and to exceed the benchmark cost by $7,728.52 (115 percent) for the secondary standard. The APS which would allow for the attainment of primary and secondary standards with the control of a smaller amount of regional emissions than the SIP is simulated to cost less than the benchmark cost by $6,643.33 (99 percent) for the primary standard, and to exceed this cost by $491.04 (7 percent) for the secondary standard.

Maloney and Yandle [14] investigate the cost of reducing the Dupont Company's hydrocarbon emissions under alternative control policies. The cost of achieving a reduction target of 85 percent of the current level is estimated to be $105,740,000 per year under a policy requiring uniform abatement standards for each technical source of pollution. The cost is reduced to $67,960,300 and $25,490,300, respectively, if uniform standards for each plant and a TDP-system are respectively used. For a reduction target of 99 percent, the costs of source standards, plant standards, and TDPs are $200,221,000, $152,446,000, $141,146,000, respectively.

These studies and others suggest that the efficiency of environmental policy can be increased considerably by switching from command and control polices to approaches using price incentives for pollution control, such as TDP systems or emission taxes. If these efficiency gains are distributed prudently between business and the environment, better environmental quality may be achieved at lower resource cost. Furthermore, these studies indicate that the relative superiority of price incentive policies over command and control policies decreases as the desired level of pollution reduction increases. This is due to the fact that the key to the higher efficiency of the price incentive policies is the possibility of having those with the lowest cost of abatement substantially reduce their pollution, while those with higher costs reduce their pollution levels much less.

IV. Why Is Environmental Policy in Practice So Different?

Among environmental economists, the economic incentive instruments of effluent charges and TDPs are the most popular policies. In actual practice, however, they are rarely used; regulation by command and control is the dominant approach. In view of the subject of this conference, the divergence appears particularly important. The reasons for it are manifold: an important handicap of effluent charges and TDPs is their lack of intuitive appeal in the political process that shapes environmental policy. The environment is seen as the heritage of mankind, to be preserved for future generations. Putting a price tag to it, or selling it to the highest bidder, just does not seem right.

It is often argued that TDPs or charges are unacceptable because they establish a "right" to pollute. Overlooked is the fact that the command and control approach also implicitly defines the right to pollute up to the level allowed by the standard. Moreover, a right to pollute can be downgraded to allow for more ambitious environmental policy goals. To do that under a TDP policy, the permits would have to be devaluated; under an effluent charge policy, the tax rate would have to be raised; and under a command and control policy, the standard would have to be tightened.

A second important reason for the rare use of economic incentives is that industry is not pushing very hard for a change of environmental policy instruments. In many countries industry has managed to keep command and control regulations at a tolerable level for them and has often avoided full implementation of environmental policy standards. The threat of accommodating the cost of meeting effluent standards by reducing employment has often proved to be effective. Moreover, direct regulation usually is lenient in the case of an established industry and more restrictive in the case of new facilities. So direct regulations are favored by established industry, since they serve as a barrier to the entry of new firms. This point is made by Maloney and McCormick [13], who argue that regulation by the Environmental Protection Agency of sulfur oxides and particulate emissions created barriers to entrance into the nonferrous ore smelting industry. The authors find that the value of some of the existing firms in this industry rose considerably after this regulation took effect. A related point is made by Buchanan and Tullock [5], who suggest that direct regulations cause firms to reduce their output, providing cartel-like gains for polluters by price increases.

Even though their argument is correct in the context of their model, its importance should not be overestimated in a policy context. The authors' assumption that output reduction is the sole means of pollution control heavily biases the model toward profit increases under regulation. Since other means for pollution control exist, the regulative agency may choose effluent reductions or the installation of some technical abatement device for implementation of its ruling. As firms adjust to these types of rulings, the importance of price increases that result solely from reduced output, and thereby the importance of a cartel-like increase in profit, decreases. Even in such cases, however, it is possible that some firms within the regulated industry gain by the regulation. Maloney and McCormick (pp. 163–164) present some conditions under which an industry may gain from an environmentally motivated input restriction, and offer some empirical evidence for the case of cotton dust standards in U.S. textile plants. In an empirical analysis of eleven industries, Yandle [20] found strong evidence in the case of one industry, and some evidence in the case of two industries, of behavior following the lines of the Buchanan and Tullock hypothesis.

In spite of these sophisticated analyses, however, a look at the genesis of environmental regulation reminds us that industry, even though it accepts the command and control approach in principle, has rarely been found to lobby for stronger regulation.

Possibly the most important reason for which the polluters consent to the command and control approach, in principle, is the fact that under this policy, the generation of emission is allowed and is costless up to the limit defined by the regulatory standards; the only cost for polluters, therefore, is that of holding emissions to the maximum level compatible with the standards specified. The burden of this action is often even lessened by subsidies for investment in pollution control devices. Unlike that, in the case of effluent charges and permit auctions, polluters pay twice: once for reducing emissions, and once for taxes or permit purchases. Thus, even though more efficient in the sense of using fewer resources for pollution control, taxes and auctions may be much more expensive to polluters than the requirement to meet standards.

Of course, the financial situation of the polluters brightens if TDPs are distributed free instead of being auctioned off. Since, in this version of the transferable discharge permit, efficiency gains can (at least in part) be appropriated by the polluters, there has been some pressure by industry toward that kind of system. So the chances for surviving the political process are much better for the TDP system with free initial distribution of rights than for its counterpart of auctioning off permits or for effluent charges. Additional support may come from environmentalists if they can be convinced by the idea that more ambitious targets of pollution control will be politically feasible if more cost-effective policies are used.

V. Elements of Economic Incentive Instruments in Mixed Environmental Policy Systems

Enviromental policy is a blend of many different types of instruments. Even though pure economic incentives do not play a very important role, as mentioned above, there are interesting economic incentive elements in the environmental policy of some countries.

Effluent Charges

In Western Europe, a large number of emission taxes are used. The most interesting ones are the waste water charges in France [2,4,9,16 (paper by Crampes, Mir and Moreaux), 15] the Netherlands [2,16 (paper by Bressers),15], and Western Germany [9,16 (paper by Ewringmann,12,15].

These charges all draw on the idea of an effluent charge as described in the preceding sections, but differ from this theoretical concept in a number of pragmatic modifications. A very important modification is that the taxes are not an alternative to direct regulation, as suggested by environmental economic theory, but are supplements. To illustrate, in West Germany permits are required to discharge effluents into water. They require the application of reasonably available control technology (allgemein anerkannte Regeln der Technik) according to the Federal Water Act (Wasserhaushaltsgesetz), or more restrictive standards imposed by regional authorities. Of course, the need to comply reduces the possibility that firms will choose between the reduction of emissions (saving the charge) and the generation of emissions (saving abatement cost).

This freedom of choice, however, is the key to efficiency of the theoretical effluent charge. Since in the West German case firms are not free to adjust their abatement levels to the effluent charge rate until the required abatement level is realized, marginal abatement costs will not be equal across firms. Moreover, it is only beyond the abatement levels required by the standards that the charge can become an incentive to reduce pollution. In many cases the rates charged turn out to be too low (compared to polluters' marginal abatement cost when complying with standards) to do so.

Another important modification is that in practice effluent generation is not measured continuously. All of the countries mentioned above use more or less crude assessment methods—e.g., in France the charges are based on the average daily emissions of the month in which a polluter's emissions are maximal. This simplification keeps administrative costs down but it weakens the incentive to reduce emissions as compared to the theoretical rate charged.

Despite these "practical compromises," effluent charges seem to have been quite effective. This is particularly well documented for the case of the Dutch waste water charges: Bressers [in 16] investigates the reasons for which Dutch industrial discharges of biologically treatable waste decreased by almost 70 percent from 1969 to 1980. His analysis takes advantage of the fact that direct regulations are quite uniform throughout the country, whereas charges vary substantially across the Dutch water boards. He finds that the level of abatement in each branch is negatively correlated with abatement cost as well as output increase, and positively correlated with the pressure put upon the industry by the effluent charge. This pressure is assessed by a "charge factor" indicating the pollution intensity of an industry's production value. This factor turns out to be the most important one of the three that accounts for 53 percent of the variation of abatement activities across different polluting industries. On the whole, Bresser's model explains 63 percent (76 percent) of the branch-to-branch differences in abatement in an analysis of 14 (12) polluting industries. There is strong evidence that the relationships are causal, suggesting that effluent charges have been an effective instrument of environmental policy in the Netherlands.

Transferable Discharge Permits

In U.S. air pollution control policy, growing disappointment with the economic and ecological effects of the traditional command and control (CAC) approach stimulated the development of a "pragmatic" TDP system, the Controlled Emission Trading Policy [3,6,19]. Its most important elements are the bubble and the offset concepts. Under the bubble concept, an emission standard does not have to be met by each source of pollution but by a group of sources (located not too far away from each other). Thus, firms operating the pollution sources may agree to restrict pollution from low-cost sources to a greater degree than a CAC standard would require, compensating for this extra abatement by a lower reduction in high-cost sources. Under the offset concept a new source of pollution is allowed to begin operation if its additional pollution is (more than) compensated by a reduction in the emissions of sources already operating in the area.

The idea that both concepts share with the theoretical TDP approach is that emission rights are not tied to individual sources (as in the CAC case) but may be traded among sources. However, differences between theory and practice also prevail here. The TDP idea, for instance, assumes a perfectly competitive permit market. In contrast, bubble and offset transactions are usually bilateral trades with considerable involvement of a regulatory agency. Moreover, the offset policy requires that new sources meet the New Source Performance Standards, a restriction not implied by the TDP idea.

The introduction of Controlled Emission Trading seems to have had economic effects: e.g., the U.S. Environmental Protection Agency estimates the cost savings of the bubbles that have been approved to average $4 million. More ambitious environmental quality goals will probably turn out to be attainable by making pollution control cheaper. There are also problems with this approach, however:

1. If a firm innovates in abatement techniques affecting a particular source, it is possible that the consequent emission reduction will not be credited, but will lead to higher performance standards (for many of the firm's sources). This creates a severe disincentive for innovation. Therefore, TDP systems might better not be combined with standards for best available control technology (or, lowest achievable emission rate) but with reasonable, available control technology. This would relax the connection between innovation and the tightening of standards, eliminating the disincentive to make progress in abatement technology.

2. Changing from a command and control to an economic incentive policy may reward the laggards (see [19]). These firms may now buy rights and save the cost of capital investments. Even though it is far from obvious that this is always a cheaper alternative, noncomplying firms are better off than those that comply, since they have a choice the others do not have. The weight of this argument is somewhat diminished, however, if economic incentives are combined with some direct regulation, as indicated above.

3. Emissions are reduced when sources are shut down, even if the closing is solely for economic reasons. If these emission reductions are credited in the context of emission trading, the life of emissions is extended in comparison with the CAC policy, where emission rights expire if the source is closed. The environmental agency should devaluate emission rights to compensate for this effect. (The devaluation should not be tied to individual closings, to avoid adverse incentive effects.)

4. There is an additional problem, that of defining the area in which emissions are transferable. Here, a compromise between efficiency (increasing with larger areas) and local environmental protection (requiring small areas) has to be worked out.

VI. Conclusion

Theoretical reasoning and empirical evidence suggest that the economy and the environment could gain from moving from a command and control policy to a system of price incentives in environmental policies. Theoretically, the economic incentive instruments of transferable discharge permits and effluent charges could play an important part in this process. In practice, however, resistance in the political arena is usually strong. Therefore, environmental economists generally recommend a step-by-step integration of price incentives into the given command and control framework instead of trying to implement a completely new environmental policy based solely on economic incentives. Presently, transferable discharge permits with free initial distribution of rights seem to be the most promising instrument. As for effluent charges, very effective policies are currently in practice, particularly in the area of water pollution control. These policies could be improved by more closely tying the level of charges to the amount and noxiousness of pollution generated. Progress in measurement techniques will substantially facilitate this task.

Notes

1. Space limitations confine the analysis to these three instruments. In the working paper version of this article, two additional forms of subsidies for pollution abatement were discussed. See A. Endres, "On the Efficacy of Public Finance Instruments with Regard to the Environment," Technische Universität Berlin, Wirtschaftswissenschaftliche Dokumentation, Discussion Paper No. 97, 1985.

2. A more extensive discussion appears in the working paper version of this article, cited in footnote 1.

3. For these and other approaches, see, e.g., Endres [7]; Freeman [10], [11]; and Schulze, d'Arge, and Brookshire [17].

4. Of course, accuracy is reduced if some firms pollute (outside of the environmental agency's business hours) without having a permit. The issue of noncompliance, however, is a problem affecting all kinds of policy instruments.

5. If the regulation sets forth terms of emission *concentration*, the accuracy of the command and control approach is deficient.

6. The working paper version of this article reviews other studies.

7. It has been argued (see Tietenberg [19, p.20]) that the cost advantages of economic incentive approaches over direct regulation are often overestimated, because most studies analyse the cost effects of switching from a situation with no environmental policy to one with a command and control *or* an economic incentive policy. In actual policy cases, however, the choice is to continue a regulation or to switch from regulation to economic incentives. Since the regulation induced some (inefficient) capital investment, there is less saving from the switch than if incentives had been established initially. Atkinson and Tietenberg avoid these problems by using the current regulative program as a benchmark.

8. See the working paper version of this article for a more extensive treatment.

References

[1] Atkinson, S. E., Tietenberg, T. H., "Approaches for Reaching Ambient Standards in Non-Attainment Areas", *Land Economics*, 60, 1984: 148–59.

[2] Barde, J.-P., et al., "Water Pollution Control Policies are Getting Results", *Ambio*, 8, 1979: 152–59.

[3] Bonus, H., "Marktwirtschaftliche Konzepte im Umweltschutz", Ulmer Verlag, Stuttgart, 1984.

[4] Bower, B. T., et al., *Incentives in Water Quality Management*, RFF, Washington, D.C., 1981.

[5] Buchanan, J. M., and Tullock, G., "Polluters' Profits and Political Response: Direct Control Versus Taxes", *American Economic Review*, 65, 1975: 139–47.

[6] Crandall, R. W., *Controlling Industrial Pollution*, The Brookings Institution, Washington, D.C., 1983.

[7] Endres, A., "Ökonomische Grundprobleme der Messung sozialer Kosten", *List-Forum*, 11, 1982: 251–69.

[8] Endres, A., *Umwelt- und Ressourcenökonomie*, Wissenschaftliche Buchgesellschaft, Darmstadt, 1985.

[9] Ewringmann, D., and Schafhausen, F., "Abgaben als ökonomische Hebel in der Umweltpolitik", *Berichte des Umweltbundesamtes*, Nr. 8, Berlin, 1985.

[10] Freeman, M. A., *The Benefits of Environmental Improvement*, Johns Hopkins University Press, Baltimore and London, 1979.

[11] Freeman, M. A., *Air and Water Pollution Control*, John Wiley and Sons, New York, 1982.

[12] Hansmeyer, K. H., "Abgaben als Instrumente der Umweltpolitik", in H.-J. Ewers and H. Schuster, eds., *Probleme der Ordnungs- und Strukturpolitik*, Vandenhoeck & Ruprecht, Göttingen, 1984.

[13] Maloney, M. T., and McCormick, R. E., "A Positive Theory of Environmental Quality Regulation", *Journal of Law and Economics*, 25, 1982: 99–123.

[14] Maloney, M. T., and Yandle, B., "Estimating the Cost of Air Pollution Control Regulation", *Journal of Environmental Economics and Management*, 11, 1984: 244–63.

[15] OECD, International Conference on Environment and Economics, *Background Papers*, Vol. II, OECD, Paris, 1984.

[16] Schneider, G., and Sprenger, R.-U., eds., *Mehr Umweltschutz für weniger Geld*, Ifo-Institut, Munich, 1984.

[17] Schulze, W. D., R. C. d'Arge, and D. S. Brookshire, "Valuing Environmental Commodities: Some Recent Experiments", *Land Economics*, 57, 1981: 151–72.

[18] Tietenberg, T., *Environmental and Natural Resource Economics*, Scott, Foresman and Co., Glenview, Illinois, 1984.

[19] Tietenberg, T., "Regulatory Reform in Air-Pollution Control", *Resources* (RFF), No. 79, 1985: 17–20.

[20] Yandle, B., "Polluters' Profits: An Empirical Note", *Journal of Industrial Economics*, 11, 1984: 359–66.

Résumé

Le critère pour juger de l'efficacité d'un instrument d'une politique d'environnement comprend l'efficience de cet instrument, sa précision et sa force d'innovation. Les instruments de réglementation directe, de redevance et de permis de décharge transférable de droits (contre paiement ou accordé gratuitement) sont brièvement examinés en fonction de ces souscritères, sur un plan théorique. On examine ensuite des estimations empiriques de l'efficience des instruments. Ces analyses suggèrent que les objectifs en matière d'environnement sont atteints à un coût significativement plus bas par les instruments d'incitation économique (redevance ou permis de décharge transférable), comparé à l'approche de règlementation divecte. Cependant, il y a une profonde divergence entre la haute estime dans laquelle sont tenus les instruments d'incitation économique par les economistes et leur rare utilisation dans la pratique. On en examine les raisons en faisant particulièrement référence à l'influence des groupes d'intérêt dans la prise des décisions politiques. Enfin, on évalue les éléments d'incitation économique pratiqués dans les politiques mixtes d'environnement. Les redevances auxquelles on a recours en France, aux Pays-Bas et en R.F.A. sont brièvement exposées et comparées au concept théorique de perception de droits. Pour terminer, on discute du commerce d'émission contrôlé, en vigueur aux U.S.A., comme un exemple de politique pratiquant le permis de décharge transférable.

Public Sector Productivity: Recent Empirical Findings and Policy Applications

*René Goudriaan, Hans de Groot and Frank van Tulder**

1. Introduction

This paper deals with the application of public sector productivity studies to government policy. Section 2 briefly discusses the theoretical underpinnings of public sector productivity measurement and existing empirical work. Sections 3 and 4 present recent empirical evidence for the Netherlands, based on a larger study by the Social and Cultural Planning Bureau [11]. Section 3 sketches productivity trends of publicly provided services to citizens, and section 4 offers empirical results on the productivity of administrative agencies, hitherto rarely studied, in central and local governments. Section 5 discusses existing and potential policy applications, and section 6 summarizes findings and conclusions.

2. Theory and Measurement of Public Sector Productivity

2.1 Kinds of Activities

Theory and measurement of public sector productivity is a long-standing issue in public finance. This section deals briefly with the problems involved as far as relevant to policy applications.

The public sector, defined to include government-subsidized, private, nonprofit institutions, provides public goods. The term "public goods" is used here in a broad sense including impure public goods; i.e., publicly provided individual goods. Two kinds of activities of the public sector should be distinguished: those aimed at providing public goods directly consumed by citizens, so-called "final public goods", and those regulating

*Social and Cultural Planning Bureau, The Netherlands

The Relevance of Public Finance for Policy-Making. Proceedings of the 41st Congress of the International Institute of Public Finance. Madrid, 1985, pp. 193–209.

the economic and social process. The first category includes the provision of education, health care, social security, etc. The second category includes general legislative and regulating activities producing not commodities for final consumption, but "intermediate public goods", which are inputs to production of other goods either within or outside the public sector. Examples in the second category are agencies that monitor the quality of food, education, and health care, and also the administrative agencies that prepare government policy, distribute funds for public services, etc.

2.2 Measures of Output

Following Bradford, Malt, and Oates [4], it has become customary to distinguish "direct output" (D-output), the immediate physical output of the production process, from "effective output" (C-output) or the ultimate effect of the productive activity on the consumer of the service under consideration. Effective output may be measured in simple physical units, but it often requires additional elements to provide an adequate description. In the private sector the subtleties of measurement of direct or effective output are usually replaced by valuing the physical output at market price. In the public sector, prices are usually determined by administrative rules or are absent. For that reason, the national accounts of many countries value output of (parts of) the public sector as the *cost* of inputs to production. An analysis in which output, as valued in this way, is related to inputs is of course useless. This means that to measure productivity in the public sector, direct or effective output must be estimated by some form of output measured in physical units, which in turn can be related to such inputs as labor and capital.

Direct output is, depending on its definition in specific cases, related to a greater or lesser extent to effective output. Sometimes this relationship is quite weak and direct output could better be designated as "throughput" or "activities". For instance, the number of police patrols in a neighborhood is sometimes described as direct output of the police force, while the effective output is the amount of crime prevented. Obviously the latter is not a simple consequence of the former. In the same way, the number of students trained is often designated as direct output of the education process, but is not necessarily related to the number of students successfully graduated or the skills acquired by them. An extensive survey of the literature on theoretical problems of output measurement can be found in Hanusch [6] and is not repeated here.

The choice of output indicator is equally important for the interpretation of productivity measures. Productivity in terms of technical efficiency is measured when direct output is related to inputs. Productivity in terms of effectiveness is measured when effective output is related to inputs.

2.3 Empirical Research

Most empirical research on public sector productivity concentrates on calculating the cost of all inputs or the employed labor in man-years per unit of direct output. In view of the lack of robust theories concerning determinants of public sector productivity, comparisons are often made with similar producers in the private sector. These producers serve as a counterfactual in which productivity is assumed to be at an optimal level. A useful international survey of results obtained this way is that of Borcherding, Pommerehne and Schneider [3]. Most of the studies in their survey are of the United States, although a few concern selected services in West Germany, Switzerland, Canada, and Australia. A more recent survey for the United States is given by Fisk [5], who draws three important conclusions:

1. State and local governments collect considerable data on productivity, although this information is uneven regarding service area and level of government. Some services, particularly those with tangible products and involving the federal government, are well covered at the individual government level. For instance, solid waste collection, public transport, and water supply have been extensively examined. These services, however, typically involve 1 or 2 percent of the total number of state and local government employees. Services such as general management have been entirely ignored or examined only superficially.
2. Many studies cover state or local governments, prohibiting generalization at the national level. Most studies are cross-sectional; only a few examine time-series data.
3. The time-series studies, although ad hoc and restricted to a few areas, have generally concluded that state and local government productivity has remained stagnant or has decreased over the past several decades.

The survey in [3] indicates that these conclusions are valid for countries other than the United States.

2.4 Analyzing Intermediate Goods

The almost total absence of research on the production process of intermediate public goods is remarkable. In our view, the production of such goods can be analyzed within an existing framework, even when direct output measurement is difficult.

The key notion is that producers of intermediate goods, more loosely termed as "intermediate producers", within the public sector can be considered part of a chain of producers, leading to a final product directly consumed by the population. The chain of producers can be considered one aggregate producer of the final product. Labor and other inputs at the level of the intermediate producers are inputs to the aggregate production process, as are inputs at the final production level, more loosely termed "final producers". For example, a civil servant working at the Department of Education is, just like a public school teacher, an input in the production process of education. The concept of productivity can thus be extended to intermediate production levels in the public sector. Comparing output measured in the final production process with inputs at the intermediate level gives insight into the productivity of the intermediate production process, although more in terms of effectiveness than of efficiency. Of course, this approach implicitly assumes complementarity of intermediate and final producers in producing the final public good. In applied cases this complementarity must be verified. For example, the activities of the Department of Economic Affairs (in the Dutch central government) could be negatively correlated with the growth of private sector output owing to a countercyclical budgetary and economic policy of the government. Moreover, differences in the production process of intermediate and final public goods and consequently differing opportunities for cost-saving innovations (see [2]) may lead to divergent trends in inputs of a given kind (e.g., labor) at the two levels.

The direct output of the intermediate producer, for instance, the number of requests for grants handled by a civil servant in the Department of Education, plays no direct role. Of course, if data are available, which is often not the case, productivity in terms of efficiency could be analyzed at the intermediate level as well. In section 4 we compare labor inputs at the intermediate and final level in an empirical analysis of central and local government agencies.

3. Productivity of Producers of Final Public Goods in the Netherlands

3.1 Introduction

This section presents some results concerning productivity of producers of final public goods. Following the usual practice in the Netherlands, we use a broad definition of the public sector: government as well as the government-subsidized, private, nonprofit institutions that provide health care, education, social and cultural services, and public transport. The public sector so defined now accounts for 30 percent of total employment in the Netherlands. About 90 percent of the total cost of production is financed by the public budget.

Unlike most other studies, ours analyzes public sector productivity at the national level, using time-series data. Owing to data problems the period of observation is short, covering the years 1975–83. To increase the policy relevance of our results, we have tried to include a large part of the Dutch public sector in our analysis, choosing a simple but *uniform* approach. This enables us to concentrate on differences among six large subsectors: health care, education, social and cultural services, public transport, police and justice, and tax and social security administration. Except for defense and producers of intermediate public goods (see section 4), we cover all types of public sector services, at least in part. These services comprise 56 percent of total public sector employment. The analysis is based on productivity trends in 32 large, publicly provided services within the six subsectors: 10 health services, 7 types of education, 5 social and cultural services, 3 modes of public transport, 4 services of the police and justice system, and 3 executive branches of the tax and social security administration.

For these 32 services we employed the usual indicators of direct output, such as pupils trained (education), patients treated (health care), passenger miles (public transport), and so on (see Appendix). Sometimes more than one indicator is needed to describe outputs of a service. In those cases we weighted the different output indicators by cost per unit of output in the year 1975 to construct a composite output indicator. The same procedure was followed to sum the outputs of different services. Thus, changes in output so defined may be interpreted as changes in cost, assuming constant unit cost.

Like most public sector productivity studies, our approach ignores changes in quality of output and changes in environment. This is clearly a limitation, although measurement of productivity trends in the private sector has flaws too, since it largely depends on the choice of the right (i.e., hedonic) output deflator. In our analysis, all variables measured in money terms have been converted into real values by means of the household consumption deflator. So, for the sake of simplicity, all real costs may be interpreted as the purchasing power that households cannot spend on private goods. This approach eliminates the choice of a sometimes arbitrary specific deflator and simplifies the interpretation of our results. Moreover, the various potential deflators of nonwage cost show remarkably similar trends (except for the energy price index). Nevertheless, one has to keep in mind that changes in real cost as defined above should not be interpreted as changes in volume of cost (or inputs), which are required for productivity measurement in the usual sense.

3.2 Empirical Results

Table 1 presents recent trends in output and real cost per unit of output in the six subsectors.

Table 1

Trends in Output and Real Cost per Unit of Output, 1975–1983
(Index: 1975 = 100)

	Output	Real Cost per Unit of Output	Labor Input per Unit of Output	Real Wage Cost per Man-Year	Real Nonwage Cost per Unit of Output
Health care	110	114	111	98	128
Education	110	93	101	90	100
Social and cultural services	112	120	107	110	123
Public transport	110	113	102	95	140
Police and justice	123	97	101	91	117
Tax and social security administration	142	86	87	96	98
Total	112	104	105	95	119

Over the period 1975–83 aggregate output of the 32 services has risen 12 percent (1.5 percent per year). On balance, output of all six subsectors has grown. Growth in output of the tax and social security administration has been substantial. Within the subsectors large differences in some output trends can be observed: in education, for example, because of the declining birth rate, output of nursery and primary education has decreased; on the other hand, because of increasing participation in education, output of higher education has increased.

During this period the aggregate real cost per unit of output rose by 4 percent (0.5 percent per year). The table shows, however, remarkably divergent trends in real cost per unit of output. The tax and social security administration, where output has grown fastest, has experienced a large decline, 14 percent, in real unit cost, whereas real unit cost of social and cultural services has increased by 20 percent.

Within the different subsectors trends in real cost per unit of output also diverge: in nursery and primary education, where demand and output have fallen, real unit cost has risen; yet, real cost per unit of output in higher education, where demand and output have risen, has gone down sharply. Generally speaking, most declining services have faced a sharp rise in real cost per unit of output, whereas many expanding services have experienced a modest rise or even a decline in real unit cost. Economies of scale may explain only part of this phenomenon: these diverging trends in real unit cost may be attributed more to a slow adjustment of (fixed) cost to changes in the level of output, to which inertia in public decision making has contributed.

To identify some of the causes of increased real unit cost of public services, we decomposed that cost into three parts: labor input (man-years) per unit of output, real wage rate, defined as total real wage cost divided by the number of man-years employed, and real nonwage cost per unit of output. These results are also shown in Table 1.

Over the period 1975–83 the average growth of labor input per unit of output was 5 percent (0.6 percent per year). This increase is of the same magnitude as growth in real unit cost. Health care in particular shows considerable increase in labor input per unit of output, reflecting an increased supply of professional medical personnel.

Generally speaking, government policy during the second half of the seventies endeavored to expand the public sector to fight unemployment, without taking sufficient account of the allocation function of the public sector. In the eighties the government's financial position sharply deteriorated, and it abandoned the policy of expanding employment in the public sector. Moreover, serious doubts were expressed concerning the desirability of continuing to increase public sector services.

On balance, the increase of labor input per unit of output has been offset completely by a decrease in the real wage rate, which on average has fallen by 5 percent (0.6 percent per year). As a consequence of lower real wage rates in the public sector, real unit wage cost has remained constant. In view of the rising average level of education of public sector employees, the decline of real wage rates in the public sector is all the more striking. It should also be noted that the real wage rate in the private sector rose by 8 percent from 1975 to 1983. In the seventies public sector wages were closely linked to private sector wages, a practice that ended because of budget cuts in the eighties. Since *at that time* all labor markets had excess supply, it was possible to achieve these relative wage cuts in the public sector without producing understaffing. The education subsector even made additional wage cuts to maintain employment. On the other hand, because of the large increase in the average level of formal education of employees in social and cultural services, the average real wage rate in this subsector has risen substantially.

Since real unit wage cost on average has remained constant, the 19 percent rise in real nonwage cost per unit of output (2.2 percent per year) must be the major factor in explaining the growth of real unit cost. Real unit nonwage cost has risen sharply in all subsectors, with the exception of the tax and social security administration, and education. Public transport, the subsector with the largest share of nonwage cost to total cost, has experienced the largest increase in nonwage cost per unit of output. In most subsectors the cost of energy, depreciation, and interest have gone up sharply. Increase in depreciation and interest costs reflects large capital formation, partly based on optimistic expectations, in the seventies. In contrast with the private sector, the increased capital intensity of most public services did not, however, result in higher labor productivity.

4. Productivity of Producers of Intermediate Public Goods

In Section 2 we introduced the concept of producers of intermediate public goods to designate governmental activities that do not produce final public goods for consumers but which are inputs in the production process of those final goods. In this section we try to identify such producers and the relevant final producers and products in the Dutch public sector.

Our analysis dealt with ten departments of the central government, and with local government. The agencies within each department were categorized as (predominantly) final producer or intermediate producer. For each intermediate producer the relevant final producers, inside *and* outside the department, were identified. For the years 1975 and 1983 we collected data on the manpower involved, measured in man-years. Table 2 describes these final producers for each department.

Some final producers are members of the department while others are private nonprofit institutions or enterprises. In the case of the Departments of Foreign Affairs and Defense the output is typically a pure public good and the final product is not easily identified. The distinction between intermediate and final producers requires rather arbitrary assignment. For instance, in the case of defense, who should be considered the final producers? Only military personnel or also part of the civilian personnel? We decided to exclude these two departments from the analysis.

Designating agencies within each department as intermediate and final producers respectively, we can construct index figures on growth of both types of producers between 1975 and 1983, as shown in Table 3. It also shows the ratio of intermediate to final producers. Manpower employed by intermediate producers constituted 28 percent of total civilian employment in the central government in 1983.

The table indicates considerable expansion of manpower employed by intermediate producers within the central government: the annual growth rate there was 3.2 percent. The Departments of Home Affairs, Social Affairs and Employment, Economic Affairs, and Education and Science show the largest increase of manpower at the intermediate level. In comparison with manpower employed by the corresponding final producers, we observe a particularly high ratio of intermediate to final producer manpower growth for those agencies that produce intermediate goods related to the private sector: the Departments of Social Affairs and Employment, Economic Affairs, Agriculture, and Transportation. The relevant final producers experienced considerable productivity increases (inferred from pro-

Table 2

Description of Final Producers relevant for Each Department

Department	Final Producers
Justice	Courts of justice, prisons, child protection, police
Home Affairs[a]	Final producers for local government, such as police, refuse collection, social services, etc.
Education and Science	Educational institutions
Finance[a]	Tax collecting agencies
Housing[a]	Housing societies
Transportation	Transportation and communication services
Economic Affairs	Private sector
Agriculture	Agricultural sector
Social Affairs and Employment	Private sector and social security administration
Social Welfare, Health and Culture	Social work, home help services, health care, performing arts, museums, public libraries, etc.

[a]Only partly covered in this analysis.

ductivity figures not shown here), which led to a fall in private sector employment in the period 1975–83. Of course, the economic stagnation after the second oil crisis, in 1979, also played a role. Among the departments that do not produce intermediate goods for the private sector, the ratio of intermediate to final producer growth is particularly high for the Department of Home Affairs. Only one department, Justice, shows a modestly decreasing ratio of intermediate to final producers over the period 1975–83. Of course, these results are only a first indication of relative performance of the central government bureaucracy. Our findings should be supplemented by analysis of the causes of the divergent relative growth of the separate parts of the central government bureaucracy and investigation of the validity of assuming complementarity of intermediate and final producers.

We conducted a more detailed study of three departments of central government: Justice, Education and Science, and Social Welfare, Health and Culture. The various agencies of these departments were examined separately. The corresponding final producers, inside and outside the department, were identified and manpower figures were collected for the 1975–83 period. Output of the final producers was proxied by simple indicators, such as pupils trained (education), patients treated (health care), etc., which were the output proxies used in section 3. The output of each final producer is weighted with labor input per unit of output in 1975 to obtain an output estimate for the subsector involved. We present the results for the Department of Education and Science in Table 4.

Table 3

Manpower Employed by Intermediate Producers in Central Government and Relevant Final Producers in 1983 (Index: 1975 = 100)

Department	Intermediate Producers (1)	Final Producers (2)	(1)/(2) × 100
Justice	122	124	99
Home Affairs[a]	164	114	145
Education and Science	136	111	123
Finance[a]	136	117	117
Housing[a]	135	127	107
Transportation	123	101	122
Economic Affairs	140	94	149
Agriculture	119	91	130
Social Affairs and Employment	141	95	149
Social Welfare, Health and Culture	120	117	103
All departments	129	102	127

[a]Only partly covered by this analysis.

The table shows that all subsectors except secondary education register an increase of intermediate producers relative to final producers, particularly for primary education. This can perhaps be explained by the fact that during these years it was decided to integrate nursery education and compulsory primary education. At the same time the final output of this subsector, as measured by number of pupils, decreased by 16 percent owing to decline in the birth rate, without a corresponding decrease in manpower employed by the final producers, i.e., primary and nursery schools. It is also interesting to note that higher education shows a considerable productivity increase at the final production level without a similar increase at the intermediate production level.

Finally, we performed a similar analysis for local government, which in the Netherlands comprises two levels, provinces and municipalities. Nearly 60 percent of all civilian employees work in local government, 91 percent of them in municipalities. Owing to lack of data only intermediate and final producers within local government could be established with any degree of accuracy. The growth of intermediate producers in municipalities between 1975 and 1983 was slightly less than average growth among the same type of producers in central government. Again, final producers, such as police, fire brigades, and social services, tended to grow at slower rates than intermediate producers. The intermediate producers in the provinces had a growth rate almost twice that of such producers in municipalities, probably owing to increasingly decentralized planning procedures imple-

Table 4

Manpower Employed by Intermediate Producers in the Department
of Education and Science, Manpower Employed by Final Producers,
and Weighted Output in 1983 (Index: 1975 = 100)

Subsector	Intermediate Producers (1)	Final Producers (2)	(1)/(2) × 100	Weighted Output
Primary education[a]	181	103	175	84
Secondary education	120	120	100	120
Higher education	131	107	123	136
General management	158	110	144	107
Total	145	112	130	115

mented by the central government. Also on the provincial level, final producers, such as electricity and water supply services, tended to grow at much slower rates.

From our results we draw the following conclusions. Almost without exception we find an increasing ratio of administrative services in the public sector compared with the corresponding final producers, inside or outside the public sector. There is a long time lapse between the fall in demand for particular public services and the adjustment of manpower employed by the final producers, and an even longer interval before there is a corresponding decrease of personnel (if there is any decrease at all) in central or local government administrative services. The results underline the need for better monitoring of the productivity of intermediate producers in the production of public services.

5. Policy Applications

This section points out the possibilities for applying productivity studies to government policy. Lack of information on other countries restricts our discussion to the public sectors in the United States and the Netherlands. Following Fisk [5], we distinguish four possible areas of policy application: national policy formulation, federal or central government program management, state and local government policy formulation, and day-to-day operations in state and local government.

National policy formulation. Productivity estimates in the private sector are a standard ingredient of national economic planning and forecasting. They are important for forecasting national labor demand, formulating national wage policies, etc. These studies usually assume constant productivity in the public sector, which implies a substantial bias in the results. Wage policies in the public sector are usually based on the average growth rate of wages in the private sector. Ad hoc deviations, motivated by budgetary problems, do occur, however, as was the case in the Netherlands (see section 3). Productivity studies have almost never been taken into consideration, largely owing to the lack of public sector productivity estimates at the national level.

Federal or central government program management. Productivity estimates for the public sector could be helpful in guiding the budget allocations among levels of government or agencies. The performance of various agencies or government levels could thus be compared. Fisk [5] mentions the use of productivity measures by the U.S. Employment Service in its allocation of funds to the states, and the U.S. Unemployment Insurance Service uses similar figures to justify its requests for funds. Other programs could benefit from a similar approach. Apparently the use of productivity studies at this level is rare, as is true in the Netherlands.

Until the mid-seventies the budget allocation process of the Dutch central government did not incorporate any formal procedures taking into account output or productivity data and/or targets. In 1976, following the experience of foreign governments with Planned Programming Budget and similar systems, a modest attempt to improve the essentially input-oriented budget process was made by the Department of Finance. Departments are required to provide for as many expenditure programs as possible, information on direct output in relation to inputs in money terms. Since 1978 this information has been published in an appendix to the annual budget for each department. Such information does not, however, seem to play an important role in the budgetary process. A recent report of a government commission on the control of public expenditure makes no reference at all to the system of performance or output budgeting [12]. In a series of reassessments of public expenditure programs, productivity figures occur incidentally, but play a minor role [8]. Systematic use of output figures has been made by an interdepartmental commission, instituted in 1983 to incorporate the demand for services in the budget allocation process. Each year this commission compares the five-year budget projections of different departments with a normative forecast, based on projections of output indicators for more than 50 services and a simple production technology [10]. The projections are kept within budgetary limits set for all of the services together by imposing equal productivity increases upon each service. Indications are given as to what programs should be allocated increased or reduced funds [9].

The implementation of such recommendations has caused political problems. In the two years of operation of this monitoring system, there has been strong opposition from agencies designated as candidates for budget cuts. Reductions in the education budget as a consequence of the declining birth rate have not been easily accepted. Proposed budget reductions have been welcomed by the Department of Finance, adding to the pressure exerted on the spending departments. Less popular are proposed relaxations of budget reductions in areas where, for instance, the aging of the population will lead to increased demand for services. Nevertheless, a few small corrections have been made in that direction.

It is to early for a final evaluation of this monitoring system which is far less ambitious than a performance-budgeting system at all levels of the public sector. It is clear, however, that the largest impact of the system was felt right after a cabinet change in 1983, when policy proposals for the 1983–86 period had to be formulated. A major obstacle, inherent in the Dutch system, is the relatively large autonomy of the ministers of the various departments, which produces strong incentives for budget maximization, regardless of structural reallocations dictated by an optimal supply of public services. Also, internal reallocation of funds within a particular department is considered the exclusive responsibility of the minister concerned.

State and local government policy formulation. These levels of government could benefit from productivity studies concerning specific services. Budget allocation could be rationalized and productivity could be monitored to identify declining efficiency. In the United States, productivity studies seem to have been used only occasionally. For example, some cities, notably New York, have tied increases in pay to increases in productivity. The situation in the Netherlands is probably worse; there are no indications of systematic use of productivity data.

State and local government operations. Productivity measures probably find their greatest use in the day-to-day operations of state and local government, at least in the United States. Several sources indicate that a majority of medium-sized and large local governments in the United States collect productivity data in some form. Systematic information on other countries is not available.

Despite increased interest in the productivity issue, especially in the United States in the late seventies, policy applications still seem rather limited. The priority given the productivity issue by top government administrators is not as high as many scholars have assumed. Ammons and King, [1], recently reported on a survey of local government administrators in the United States, showing that productivity improvement ranked only fourth on a list of issues considered of high importance, and that familiarity with a number of relevant productivity studies was disappointingly small. The authors concluded that incentives are needed to stimulate administrators to improve productivity. Personal benefits, such as "productivity rewards" or other types of public recognition, are important. Keeves [7] mentions the success of a "productivity investment account" in the New Jersey state government. The account finances investments by departments in productivity improvements, and any savings so gained can be kept by the department after a small donation to the investment account.

6. Summary and Conclusions

The theory and measurement of public sector productivity has long been an issue in public finance. The existing empirical literature provides no definite conclusions, owing mainly to the lack of generally accepted productivity measures and the limited nature of many productivity studies. Most of the empirical findings concern "final services", such as garbage collection, public transport, and education. Research on "intermediate producers", such as the administrative services of central and local governments, is almost nonexistent, nor is there a uniform approach that covers most public services over different years. The few existing time-series studies conclude that public sector productivity has remained at the same level or has decreased over the past several decades.

In this paper we have indicated how productivity studies could be extended to cover, at least provisionally, intermediate production in the public sector, which is not easily measured. We have presented our empirical results on public sector productivity in the Netherlands concerning both intermediate and final producers over the years 1975 to 1983. The analysis covered most of the large final public services in the Netherlands and an important part of the intermediate administrative services. Relatively simple output indicators were used to obtain an overall view of the public sector.

Our most important conclusions may be summarized as follows:

— Real cost per unit of output of final producers in the public sector has on average increased at an annual rate of 0.5 percent. Economies of scale seem to have played only a minor role.
— Between and within subsectors of the public sector, striking differences in productivity trends appear. In general, those services that have experienced large growth in output have experienced a fall in real unit cost, whereas declining services have faced a rise in real unit cost.
— In spite of a 0.6 percent annual increase in unit labor input for final producers in the public sector, real wage cost per unit of output has not risen, owing to a fall in the real wage rate of public sector employees amounting to 0.6 percent annually. As a result, the rise of unit nonwage cost (at an annual rate of 2.2 percent) has been responsible for increased total unit cost.

— Almost without exception, manpower in intermediate (mostly administrative) services in the public sector has grown faster than manpower employed by final producers inside or outside the public sector.

Our brief discussion of policy applications of productivity studies in the United States and in the Netherlands indicated that use of such in the decision-making process at the central government level seems quite limited in both countries. Attempts in the Netherlands to incorporate the results of output or productivity studies in the budget allocation process are hampered by both bureaucratic and political resistance to rationalizing decision making. Ad hoc use of productivity studies is chiefly confined to the day-to-day operations of state and local governments, at least in the United States. In the Netherlands, and probably in other developed countries as well, the same situation probably holds.

We conclude that the policy relevance of productivity studies can be extended by presenting an overall picture to policy makers, using relatively simple measures. Studies should concern not only the usual final services to citizens, but also, even if provisionally, intermediate services. Bureaucratic and political resistance to rationalizing the decision-making process should not be underestimated, however. An incentive structure including productivity investment accounts, productivity rewards, etc. must be developed to assure sufficient cooperation of the government bureaucracy and related institutions.

Notes

* The authors are members of the Social and Cultural Planning Bureau, the Netherlands. The comments of Kees Goudswaard, Peggy Musgrave and Flip de Kam on an earlier version of this paper are gratefully acknowledged.

References

[1] Ammons, D.N., and King, J.C., "Productivity Improvement in Local Government: Its Place among Competing Priorities", *Public Administration Review*, 43, 1983: 113–20.

[2] Baumol, W.J., "Macroeconomics of Unbalanced Growth: The Anatomy of Urban Crisis", *American Economic Review*, 57, June 1967: 415–26.

[3] Borcherding, T.E., Pommerehne, W., and Schneider, F., "Comparing the Efficiency of Private and Public Production: The Evidence from Five Countries", *Zeitschrift für Nationalökonomie*, 42, 1982, Supplement 2: 127–56.

[4] Bradford, D.F., Malt, R.A., and Oates, W.E., "The Rising Cost of Local Public Services: Some Evidence and Reflections", *National Tax Journal*, 22, June 1969: 185–202.

[5]   Fisk, D.M., *Measuring Productivity in State and Local Government*, Washington, U.S. Government Printing Office, 1983.
[6]   Hanusch, H., "Determinants of Public Productivity", in Haveman, R.H., ed., *Public Finance and Public Employment*, Proceedings of the 36th Congress of the International Institute of Public Finance, Jerusalem, 1980, Detroit, Wayne State University Press, 1982: 275–88.
[7]   Keeves, R.F., "State Productivity Improvements: Building on Existing Strengths", *Public Administration Review*, 40, 1980: 451–58.
[8]   Ministerie van Financiën, *Miljoenennota 1985*, The Hague, Staatsuitgeverij, 1984 (in Dutch).
[9]   Ministerie van Binnenlandse Zaken, *Prioriteitenschema Planvorming Kwartaire Sector 1985–1988*, The Hague, Ministerie van Binnenlandse Zaken, 1984 (in Dutch).
[10] Sociaal en Cultureel Planbureau, *Trendrapport Kwartaire Sector 1983–1990*, Rijswijk, Sociaal en Cultureel Planbureau, 1984 (in Dutch).
[11] Sociaal en Cultureel Planbureau, *Kosten van Kwartaire Diensten, 1970–1983: Een Statistische Verkenning van Kostenstructuur en Voorzieningengebruik*, Rijswijk, Sociaal en Cultureel Planbureau, 1986 (in Dutch).
[12] Studiegroep Begrotingsruimte, *Beheersbaarheid van Collectieve Uitgaven*, The Hague, Staatsuitgeverij, 1983 (in Dutch).

Résumé

Ce rapport résume les récents résultats empiriques concernant la productivité du secteur public. On porte une attention particulière à la productivité d'organisations jusqu'ici rarement étudiées et relevant du gouvernement central, tel le Département de la Justice, ou les "biens intermédiaires". On fait des essais préliminaires chiffrés pour appliquer des mesures de production au processus d'allocation budgétaire. Ces essais suggèrent que cette approche serait utile pour améliorer l'efficacité et les décisions d'allocation budgétaire.

Appendix: Services and Output Indicators

Services	Output Indicators
Health Care	
Hospitals	Inpatient days, discharged patients, outpatient services
Mental Hospitals	Inpatient days, admitted patients, outpatient services
Nursing Homes	Patients (annual average)
Institutions for Mentally Deficient	Inpatient days
Specialists	Patients treated
General Practitioners	Consultations
Physiotherapists	Treatments (2 types)
District-nursing	Persons assisted
Maternity Ward	Persons assisted
Education	
Nursery Education	Pupils (annual average)
Primary Education	Pupils (annual average)
Special Education	
(for handicapped children)	Pupils (annual average)
Secondary General Education	Pupils (annual average)
Secondary Vocational Training	Pupils (annual average)
Vocational Colleges	Students (annual average)
Universities	Students (annual average)
Social and Cultural Services	
Homes for the Aged	Inmates (annual average)
Home Help Services	Hours of assistance
Homes for the Handicapped	Inmates (annual average)
Dayroom for the Handicapped	Visitors (annual average)
Public Libraries	Books lent
Police and Justice	
Police	Traffic accidents, cleared crimes (3 types), registered minor offenses, other cases of assistance
Courts of Justice	Lawsuits (16 types)
Prisons	Prisoners (annual average)
Institutions for Child Protection	Pupils (annual average)
Public Transport	
Public Railways	Passenger miles
Urban Public Transport	Passenger miles
Rural Public Transport	Passenger miles
Tax and Social Security Administration (executive branches)	
Tax Administration	Returns and assessments (5 types)
Executive Branches Social Security Administration:	
National Insurance (all residents)	Number of benefit payments
Employee Insurance (employees only)	Number of benefit payments

Part III

The Role and Impact
of Advice

Obstacles to Tax Reform in Developing Countries

Richard Goode*

Although progress has been made in improving many tax systems, it is easy to find fault with existing systems. Most of them fall far short of the ideals promoted by the authors of treatises and textbooks and official reports. There is a large stock of reform proposals that have neither been put into effect nor definitively rejected. Why is tax reform so difficult? In considering obstacles to reform, I shall concentrate on developing countries, though industrial countries face similar difficulties.

Shortcomings of Existing Tax Systems

The most obvious shortcoming of the tax systems of the great majority of developing countries is their inadequate yield. They do not produce enough revenue to pay for the ambitious expenditure programs that governments have undertaken. The resulting budget deficits have been financed to an excessive extent by money creation and borrowing abroad with consequent inflation and foreign debt problems. In principle, the deficit problem could be resolved by cutting expenditures and raising charges for services. But, with realistic allowances for expenditure economies and nontax revenue, it seems clear that many countries will need to increase tax revenue.

Tax reform for these countries should provide both for improvements in the tax structure and for additional revenue. Structural improvements would make it possible to raise more revenue with smaller undesirable effects than would occur if rates of existing taxes were simply increased or another tax were added to those in effect. Admittedly, there is a risk that controversies about structural revisions will unduly delay revenue increases and also a risk that the attempt to raise more revenue will solidify opposi-

*The author is Guest Scholar, the Brookings Institution, Washington, DC. Opinions and interpretations are the author's and should not be ascribed to the trustees, officers or staff members of the Brookings Institution or to the International Monetary Fund, where the author served as Director of the Fiscal Affairs Department from 1965 to 1981.

The Relevance of Public Finance to Policy-Making. Proceedings of the 41st Congress of the International Institute of Public Finance. Madrid, 1985, pp. 213–223.

tion to the whole program, including revisions that otherwise would be acceptable.

Recognition of these risks has stimulated interest in the possibility of revenue-neutral tax reform. In my opinion, however, that approach would rarely be advisable for a country that needs more revenue. Significant changes in tax structures usually are connected with revenue increases or decreases. One reason is that, with many subjects competing for attention, decisionmakers in government are unlikely to take up taxation repeatedly in any short period of time. Another reason may be that in a revenue-neutral reform the redistribution of taxes between groups and individuals is obvious and is especially likely to arouse the hostility of losers, who cannot be mollified by arguments about the dangers of the budget deficit or the harm in cutting expenditures.

Over time, revenue adequacy would be enhanced by revisions that would make tax yields more responsive to economic growth and less vulnerable to inflation. Sometimes it is argued that revenue elasticity is objectionable because it allows a tax increase without explicit legislation. I find that position unrealistic. In the great majority of countries government expenditure tends to grow faster than national income [4, pp. 53–59]. Political leaders are reluctant to propose frequent increases in tax rates or the introduction of new taxes, probably because they believe that by doing so they would use up political capital needed for other purposes. Hence, the absence of revenue elasticity is likely to be more conducive to large budget deficits than to expenditure restraint or frequent discretionary tax increases. Of course, the share of government expenditures and tax revenue in national income cannot grow without limit; at some point high income elasticitiy will cease to be a virtue.

A second set of criticisms concerns inequities in taxation in the developing countries. If judged by strict standards, horizontal inequities occur because the excises and import duties that are prominent in the revenue systems of these countries discriminate among persons on the basis of their taste for the taxed items rather than more appropriate indices of ability to pay or benefit. By less exacting standards, horizontal inequities result from unequal and incomplete application of both indirect and direct taxes. Because of the predominance of indirect taxes, the revenue systems of developing countries are often believed to be regressive. That opinion, however, was not confirmed by the incidence studies examined by De Wulf in 1975 [3]. The studies, it should be recognized, are inconclusive because of statistical and theoretical weaknesses.

Taxation is charged with creating or aggravating economic inefficiencies in developing countries. The unequal incidence of taxes—due partly to legal provisions and partly to incomplete enforcement—tends to direct activities to lightly taxed sectors, which may not be those that are most productive. Tax systems, combined with other forms of government intervention, frequently handicap exports, provide unintended and excessive protection from imports, discriminate against the employment of labor compared with capital, and distort business organizations. The interaction of taxes with inflation tends to discourage saving through financial intermediaries and to encourage borrowing and speculation.

Tax systems are unnecessarily complex. Some of them include scores or even hundreds of taxes adopted over time with little consideration of how they relate to each other or to economic objectives. A series of taxes and surcharges may be levied on the same base or, worse, on slightly dissimilar bases. Many of the measures may yield only trivial amounts of revenue.

Tax administration in many developing countries is weak and taxpayer compliance poor owing to a variety of causes. Technical divisions tend to be understaffed while more routine positions are often overstaffed. Training is generally inadequate and compensation too low. Revenue organizations, influenced by countries' colonial heritages, may disperse responsibility for different taxes among agencies, while within each agency excessive centralization of authority exists. The spirit of voluntary compliance with tax laws is weak, and modern accounting and other information sources are little developed.

Intellectual or Analytical Difficulties that Hinder Reform

The shortcomings of the tax systems of developing countries have been described in detail in numerous reports and journal articles. Proposals for their correction have been repeatedly presented. Why then has not greater progress been made in tax reform? One obstacle may be intellectual complexities and analytical problems that, though not peculiar to taxation, limit our ability to assess the consequences of existing tax systems and possible changes.

Analytical difficulties occur at both the microeconomic and macroeconomic levels. Since reliable estimates of elasticities and cross-elasticities of demand and supply of taxed and untaxed goods are seldom available for developing countries, the revenue effect and economic impact of changes in commodity taxes are problematical. Revenue estimates often appear to imply the assumption of zero elasticity of demand and either perfectly elastic supply or a special kind of oligopolistic pricing. More serious is the absence of consensus, even of a qualitative nature, about questions such as the effect of a tax on interest income on the amount saved, of a tax on wages on work done, of a corporate profits tax on prices. Hard as it is to answer such questions on the simplifying assumptions (often made but seldom emphasized) that the market is unified nationally but closed internationally, the difficulties multiply when these assumptions are relaxed. A realistic analysis has to relax the assumptions and to allow for movements of factors of production and goods between the modern sector and the traditional sector of the taxing country and between that country and other countries— movements that often are sluggish but sometimes are surprisingly quick.

Another kind of difficulty is the lack of sufficient statistical data on the yield of detailed tax provisions, consumer budgets, and the distribution of household incomes to serve as a basis for quantitative estimates of the incidence of existing and alternative taxes.

Persons who are acutely aware of the theoretical uncertainties and the statistical gaps could well be immobilized. That would be especially likely if they considered it necessary to have a planning model of the economy in order to identify even a limited set of improvements in the tax system (as has been maintained by critics of the customary pragmatic approach of tax specialists [1]). Indeed, tax revisions that appear to rectify inefficiencies and inequities may make them worse. The now widely accepted "general theory of second best" [6] leads to the conclusion that, where many separate tax provisions causing economic inefficiencies exist, the elimination of some of them can move the economy farther away from an optimum allocation of resources. Many apparent inequities have been mitigated, or eliminated, by adjustments of prices and factor rewards and particularly by tax capitalization.

The intellectual and analytical difficulties have hindered tax reform, but I do not think that they have been the main obstacle. They have not prevented tax specialists and general economists, including some of those who have elaborated on the difficulties, from confidently advancing many recommendations for tax revision. My impression is that the theoretical uncertainties are most often adduced to cast doubt on the efficacy of measures disliked for other reasons. The uncertainties do figure to some extent in the deliberations of government policymakers. The possibility of finding respectable experts on both sides of questions greatly helps those who wish to defeat a proposal or to delay action.

Political Obstacles

Political obstacles are important barriers to tax reform. Loosely defined, they include the clash of values or objectives, the influence of the desire of government leaders to remain in power, the activities of interest groups, and the efforts of bureaucratic elites to retain and enhance their power and perquisites.

Tax reform seldom has a strong and active constituency outside government. To be sure, demands for changes are common, but usually they call for specific tax reductions or tinkering rather than principled reform. In the suggestive terminology of Albert Hirschman [5], systematic tax reform generally may be classified as a "chosen" problem selected by policymakers for attention rather than a "pressing" problem forced on the policymakers by the pressure of interested or injured groups. The pressing problems are likely to be given priority.

The best way for advocates of reform to induce action on a chosen problem may be to link it to a pressing problem by asserting that the former is the root cause of the latter, or that the solution of the chosen problem must precede the solution of the pressing problem. Only rarely is such a link successfully forged for tax reform. Although government expenditures usually are required to attack pressing problems, expenditures for particular purposes are not perceived as depending on tax reform, even when the reform would raise additional revenue. Fiscal conservatives can argue that other, less essential expenditures should be cut to make room for the new or enlarged program. Or following an easier course, the government may finance the expenditures by money creation or borrowing abroad. If, as seems to be so, tolerance of inflation and opportunities for borrowing abroad have diminished, the connection between a strong tax system and the possibility of responding to expenditure demands may become clearer to political leaders and others.

In regard to taxation, real or apparent conflicts exist among economic objectives. Individual political leaders often may find it hard to choose their preferred tax package. For example, shall liberal investment incentives be offered to stimulate growth, or shall progressive taxes be applied to profits to prevent increased concentration of wealth? Shall variable export duties be used to mitigate cyclical instability, or shall exports be tax-free to promote growth? Shall import duties be applied selectively to encourage the substitution of home production for imports, thereby emphasizing self-reliance at the cost of slower growth and greater income concentration? These choices may pose intellectual or moral dilemmas for anyone. They become political issues because of the different weighting that participants in the decisionmaking process place upon the objectives.

Even in a government regarded as a dictatorship, a considerable number of persons usually are able to influence decisions on taxation, either in their official capacities or as informal advisers. Although differences in economic priorities and consequent disagreements about taxation are better publicized in open, democratic systems than in dictatorial or authoritarian regimes, they usually exist also in the latter and may inhibit tax reform. Issues may continue unresolved for a long time because the head of government finds other questions more interesting, more important, and easier to understand or because his power is less absolute than it may appear.

Closer to the popular understanding of politics are the efforts of government leaders to prolong their tenure by favoring their actual and potential supporters, or at least not alienating them. The concerns of interest groups or pressure groups in regard to taxation are acute and are particularly significant in blocking tax reform. In less developed countries, institutions for the articulation and aggregation of interests are less numerous and weaker than in politically more mature societies, but this does not mean that either idealistic leaders or technocrats can dominate the formulation of tax policy. As examples of interest groups, large landowners and representatives of multinational enterprises may come first to mind, but also influential are the military—an especially strong interest group in many developing countries—and the political and bureaucratic elites.

The emergence of a strong middle class has been considered favorable to vigorous growth and development, and that seems to be correct. But the consumption demands of the urban middle class frequently inhibit the taxation of nonessential goods, particularly durables, which if properly applied could direct resources to development purposes and constitute a progressive element in the revenue system.

The bureaucratic elite may identify more with the interests of client groups than with broad objectives as visualized by other policymakers. The close community of interests between highway departments and road and bridge builders and highway users is an example. This community of interests tends to hold down gasoline taxes and other taxes on road users and to perpetuate earmarking of the gasoline taxes that are imposed. Officials in financial agencies such as central banks, development banks, and security market commissions tend to oppose strict taxation of investment income and to support tax exemptions for interest and dividend income. The staffs of development agencies frequently advocate generous tax holidays and other tax benefits for foreign investors and oppose the curtailment of any existing privileges. In official circles, proposals for tax reform are met with statements of fear of capital flight or loss of additional investment, which are not always based on objective evidence and careful analysis.

But are the pressures of interest groups always antagonistic to tax reform? Is there no political counterpart of the invisible hand that Adam Smith believed would guide participants in the market to serve the public interest? Becker suggests that there is such a counterpart. He argues that competitive pressure groups, comprising taxpayers and recipients of government subsidies, will favor and lobby for economically efficient taxes, that is, for taxes with lower deadweight costs, because not only will taxpayers benefit but beneficiaries of government expenditures will gain because of lessened opposition to taxation [2]. I find this proposition unconvincing. Tax revisions are almost never Pareto improvements in the strict sense. They almost invariably increase taxes on some and frequently decrease taxes on others; the losers are never compensated.

A reform that eliminates tax provisions causing economic inefficiencies may result in a widely shared gain in real national income. But, unless total revenue is reduced, it will increase taxes for some. If those whose taxes would be increased by a proposed reform compose a relatively narrow group but not a petty one—for example, investors and workers in an industry—they may successfully oppose it. Narrow interest groups are easily made aware of their particular benefits or losses from legislation and can be mobilized to support or oppose changes, whereas individual members of the general public, having less at stake and being more numerous, usually are less informed, less motivated, and harder to organize and hence are less influential even in democratic countries [7].

The disparity between the influence of narrow interest groups and the broad public need not always be unfavorable to tax reform. It could facilitate adoption of a proposal to eliminate a provision that causes a misallocation of resources by applying a high tax to a narrow sector and to make up the revenue loss by a widely shared tax increase. If the general analysis is correct, this situation will be less common than the opposite one, because the efforts of influential interest groups will tend to prevent the introduction of provisions unfavorable to them or to cause the early elimination of such provisions.

Unsuitable Advice

Another reason for slow progress in tax reform in developing countries is the character of much of the advice received by policymakers. In the majority of developing countries—but by no means all of them—there is a shortage of local fiscal experts. Governments have not established official tax research and planning units. There are few if any independent research organizations concerned with public affairs, and university studies usually are not oriented toward immediate issues in taxation. Advice on tax policy has often come from national officials who lack specialized knowledge or experience of the field or busy tax administrators who may take a parochial view or from visiting foreigners acting under various auspices and with different degrees of experience and expertise. My remarks are directed particularly to the work of the visiting foreigners.

However well conceived and presented, advice may fail to be accepted. Sometimes governments request advice, not because of serious interest in it, but to please an international organization or bilateral aid donor or to quiet domestic critics. But the advisers often are partly to blame for the failures. They frequently advance proposals that seem un-realistic to political leaders and impracticable to administrators. Concepts of allocational efficiency and excess burden—not to mention the more esoteric doctrines of optimal taxation—that economists may employ with-out adequate explanation and justification are puzzling or repugnant to most politicians and officials. Economists often fail to recognize the short-ness of the time horizons of most politicians. Economists tend to emphas-ize long-run benefits of tax changes and to neglect intervening transitional costs; politicians tend to do the contrary. Foreign experts may fail because they are unfamiliar with the country's history and institutions and are insensitive to the constraints that political leaders consider binding.

Of course, all advisers are the products of their culture and personal experience, and the advice they give inevitably will be shaped by that background, sometimes obviously, often in more subtle ways. Persons who are knowledgeable and experienced in regard to the tax systems of their own countries frequently suffer from ignorance of other systems and from lack of recognition of the connection between tax provisions that they take for granted and conditions existing in their own country but absent in the developing country they are advising.

Advisers may present their findings and recommendations in a form that decisionmakers find either too general or too detailed or obscure. They may address their reports more to fellow experts or to the world at large than to the readers who must be convinced if tax reforms are to be under-taken. This obstacle is less easily surmounted than may be supposed. Many good tax experts are poor writers. A clear and jargon-free prose style is not always highly valued in either the bureaucracy or the academy. Experts have their professional standards and are understandably reluctant to omit qualifications and refinements that seem significant to them though esoteric to ministers of finance. Furthermore, it is prudent to recognize that minis-ters often seek second and third opinions and to try to present a report in a way that will guard against damaging criticism by other experts without overcomplicating it for the original readers. Not an easy task.

Another weakness often found in tax reports is the advocacy of a comprehensive set of proposals for the complete reconstruction of the tax system rather than selected urgent revisions. Only rarely is the time ripe for a sweeping reform. Those who elaborate proposals for the full reconstruc-tion of a tax system tend to underestimate the extent to which the existing system has influenced relative prices and property values and to pay too little attention to the economic costs and impairment of legitimate or quasi-legitimate vested interests when sudden, drastic changes in taxation occur. Moreover, a set of interrelated proposals that depend for their success on the enactment of the entire set is almost certain to fail because some compo-nents will be rejected or, if accepted in form, will not be effectively applied.

Administrative and Compliance Weaknesses

Many tax administrators are skeptical of innovations. They will oppose changes at the discussion stage and sometimes will withhold their best efforts to apply them if they are enacted. Policymakers may hesitate to accept recommendations because of the opposition of administrators or because of well-founded doubts about the administrative capacity of the revenue department.

Weak administration and poor compliance have made some tax legislation that seemed attractive in principle ineffective or inequitable in practice. For example, provisions for the taxation of capital gains, income from foreign sources, or personal wealth may be so sporadically applied that they become a trap for the unwary or the unlucky rather than a contribution to equity and revenue. India and Sri Lanka were unable to apply the direct taxes on personal consumption expenditures that they adopted on the recommendation of a distinguished foreign economist, Nicholas Kaldor, who put in concrete form an idea which had appealed to John Stuart Mill, Alfred Marshall, Irving Fisher, and Luigi Einaudi—and which Kaldor had unsuccessfully advocated for his own country.

Concluding Remarks

The obstacles to tax reform are formidable. But I do not wish to leave too dark a picture. Progress has been made. In most developing countries, tax revenue has grown faster than national income, as the result of the introduction of new taxes and rate increases, though revenue has lagged behind government expenditures in many cases. An important innovation has been the wide adoption and reasonably successful application of broad sales taxes. Global income taxes have replaced schedular taxes in several countries, and global complementary taxes usually supplement the schedular taxes in countries that have not adopted a unitary tax. Revenue departments have become more competent. The pressing need for revenue and the gravity of economic adjustment problems may concentrate the minds of government leaders and make them more receptive to new measures and to the elimination of unproductive and harmful provisions.

I believe that ordinarily fairer, more productive, and economically less harmful tax systems can better be achieved by a series of incremental improvements than by attempting one-time, comprehensive reforms. Because of the complexity of tax problems, competition among objectives, conflicting interests, and weak administration, ideal solutions may be difficult to state, except perhaps in highly abstract terms, and impossible to put into effect. There is no one model tax system suitable for all countries or even a few models for large groups of countries. Conditions differ too much to allow such a model or models to be acceptable. For any country, tax reform should be seen as a process of adaptation to changing conditions and priorities, informed by experience and innovations elsewhere, rather than a quick or slow movement to a fixed goal.

In most countries, desirable directions of immediate change on many points are fairly clear. While it may not be possible to demonstrate that the particular measures are optimal in any strict sense, it is possible to establish a rebuttable presumption that they are improvements. Opportunities for reform may arise when a new minister of finance or a new government takes office. Policy decisions often have to be taken to meet a specific problem or to respond to an emergency. It is important that these opportunities not be wasted by either inadequately considered ad hoc actions or in debate about stylish but impracticable ideas.

References

[1] Andic, Suphan, and Peacock, Alan, "Fiscal Surveys and Economic Development", Kyklos, 19, 1966: 626–39, reprinted in Richard M. Bird and Oliver Oldman, Readings on Taxation in Developing Countries, 3d ed., Baltimore, Johns Hopkins University Press, 1975.
[2] Becker, Gary S., "A Theory of Competition among Pressure Groups for Political Influence", Quarterly Journal of Economics, 98, August 1983: 371–400.
[3] De Wulf, Luc, "Fiscal Incidence Studies in Developing Countries: Survey and Critique," International Monetary Fund, Staff Papers, 22, March 1975: 61–131.
[4] Goode, Richard, Government Finance in Developing Countries, Washington, D.C., Brookings Institution, 1984.
[5] Hirschman, Albert O., Essays in Trespassing: Economics to Politics and Beyond, New York, Cambridge University Press, 1981.
[6] Lipsey, R. G., and Lancaster, K., "The General Theory of Second Best", Review of Economic Studies, 24, 1956: 11–32.
[7] Olson, Mancur, The Logic of Collective Action: Public Goods and the Theory of Groups, Cambridge, Mass., Harvard University Press, 1965.

Résumé

Parmi les défauts bien connus des systèmes fiscaux de la majorité des pays en voie de développement, on trouve: un rendement inadapté, dû en partie à la faible élasticité-revenu et à l'inflation; des injustices; des inefficacités économiques; la complexité; et une administration faible. Les obstacles à une réforme, qui sont spécialement sensibles dans les pays en voie de développement mais qui ne leur sont pas particuliers, comprennent: les difficultés intellectuelles et analytiques à apprécier les systèmes existant et les modifications possibles, des barrières politiques, des avis nonappropriés venant de conseillers à la fois nationaux et étrangers et, de la part de l'administration, faiblesse et complaisance. En dépit de ces obstacles, des progrès ont été réalisés dans l'amélioration des systèmes fiscaux. Des modifications progressives, dans un processus continu, sont plus prometteuses que les efforts pour mener d'un seul coup une vaste réforme.

A Review of Major Tax Policy Missions in Developing Countries

Vito Tanzi*

I. Historical Background

The provision of technical assistance for national tax reform must be a phenomenon that dates far back in history. I am sure that during the Roman or some other empire there must have been tax experts who "assisted" the newly conquered territories in reforming their tax systems. In this paper I concentrate on more recent assistance provided by outsiders, as individuals or as parts of organizations, in response to requests from independent countries.[1]

As far as I have been able to determine, the first modern example of such independent technical assistance is a report written for the government of Cuba in the 1930s by Professors Seligman and Shoup. An apocryphal story tells that the Cuban government was so incensed by the message of the report that it ordered the Spanish version of it burned. After World War II, Carl Shoup engaged in the first major postwar attempt at reforming the tax system of another country. In 1949, as director of the commission to study the tax system of Japan, Shoup recommended, inter alia, the introduction of a value-added tax. This was a pioneering and daring recommendation, since no country at that time had such a tax and little was known about it.[2] The fact that in 1985 the Japanese were actively studying the possibility of introducing that tax shows that Professor Shoup was ahead of his time. At least 35 countries have such a tax now.

Also ahead of its time was Nicholas Kaldor's recommendation of an expenditure tax, made to India and Sri Lanka. The tax was introduced in India in 1957 and in Sri Lanka in 1959. As an observer put it somewhat diplomatically, in India "the imposition of the expenditure tax was the subject of considerable public controversy and aroused strong opposition."[3] It was repealed (in India) in 1962 when the finance minister who had

*The author is Director of the Fiscal Affairs Department, International Monetary Fund.

The Relevance of Public Finance for Policy-Making. Proceedings of the 41st Congress of the International Institute of Public Finance. Madrid, 1985, pp. 225–236.

introduced it was replaced. It was reintroduced in 1964 when that same finance minister regained his post, and it was repealed for good in 1966. It had generated an insignificant amount of revenue and a significant amount of administrative and political headaches. The experience of Sri Lanka was similar: it also experimented twice with the tax. Goode reports that "in 1977, when proposing repeal of the expenditure tax—after a second trial— the Minister of Finance of Sri Lanka characterized it as 'unworkable and impractical in an economy like that of Sri Lanka'."[4] The opposition to the tax at times took a violent turn. As yet no country has introduced an expenditure tax, although various official or semiofficial studies in the United States, the United Kingdom, Sweden, and Ireland have recommended it.[5]

At about the time that Kaldor was advising India and Sri Lanka, Professor Shoup was engaged in another major attempt at reforming the tax system of a country. In 1958 he submitted his report to the government of Venezuela. Written by a working group that included some of the best-known public finance scholars of the time, the report was published as a book that came to influence much of the thinking in this area.[6] It served to educate those in Venezuela and elsewhere who were interested in tax reform.[7] What it did not do, however, was reform Venezuela's tax system, even though some of its recommendations were eventually enacted. Not until 1967 did major legislative changes take place, and it is not clear whether any of them originated from the Shoup Report.[8] Many of the report's recommendations were not followed; more important, some of the subsequent changes, especially in the area of tax administration, went against the spirit of the Shoup report. A recent IMF mission there found many areas in which regress rather than progress had taken place since 1958.

Together with Nicholas Kaldor and Carl Shoup, perhaps the best known and most influential name in tax reform of developing countries is that of Richard Musgrave. He came to be identified with major attempts at tax reform in Colombia (1969) and Bolivia (1977).[9] In both cases Musgrave directed outstanding groups of public finance specialists and in both, but especially that of Colombia, the resulting volumes became standard works in the field of taxation in developing countries. Both reports were very good, as one would have expected from the quality of authorship.[10] The concrete results, however, as measured in terms of their impact on the nations' tax systems, have so far been very different.

Caesar might have summarzied the Bolivian experience as follows: They came, they studied the tax system, they wrote a good book, they left, nothing happened. Recently a visitor to Bolivia was unable to locate anyone who had either read the report or had a copy of it. Perhaps he talked to the wrong people, or, more likely, those who had participated in the Musgrave

Commission (many Bolivians did so) were no longer in government. In Colombia, on the other hand, the Musgrave report played a large role in one of the major tax reforms of recent decades. Several factors contributed to this positive outcome; perhaps the most important was the involvement of various Colombians.[11] Some of the main actors in the 1974 Colombian tax reform had worked with the Musgrave Commission. Four of the eight-member commission were Colombians, as were the two advisors and the secretary and coordinator. Eleven of the 23 members of the technical staff were Colombians. Many of them became or remained influential in the Colombian government and were behind the 1974 reform. Some became ministers; others served as commissioners' of internal revenue. As a consequence that reform had a large domestic content. It was brilliant in conception and very innovative, although perhaps too ambitious. It has not survived the test of time well.

Shoup, Kaldor, and Musgrave have not been the only actors in the tax reform scene. Others include Oliver Oldman, Richard Bird, and Malcolm Gillis (all of whom played a large role in some of the reforms already mentioned), Milton Taylor, Gerson da Silva, Roy Bahl and Charles McLure. These experts were often, though not always, parts of teams organized by the Harvard International Tax Program, by the OAS-IDB Joint Tax Program, by the U.S. Internal Revenue Service or Agency for International Development (AID), by the United Nations, and occasionally by other groups. Milton Taylor and Gerson da Silva were associated with the OAS-IDB Joint Tax Program;[12] Oldman, Bird, and Gillis were associated with Harvard; Roy Bahl has been closely associated with AID. Chile, Egypt, Argentina, Panama, Brazil, Peru, Indonesia, Jamaica, Liberia, and a few other countries have received much attention from outside experts. Major attempts at tax reform are now under way in Jamaica and Indonesia.

The Indonesian effort represents an interesting experiment. Led by Malcolm Gillis, under the umbrella of Harvard University, with the Indonesian Government covering the costs, it has involved in one way or another most of the current leading public finance experts with some knowledge of developing countries (and even some without) as well as a large investment in money by Indonesia and in time by Professor Gillis.[13] It is a reform far more daring in scope than almost anything attempted before.[14] If successful, it will transform the Indonesian tax system and may serve as an example for other countries. Serious administrative problems have, however, developed along the way, threatening some of the policy changes. At this time it looks promising, but it is too early to tell whether it will stand the test of time well.

A similar experiment is under way in Jamaica, where another large group of leading scholars, financed by AID and led by Roy Bahl, has been formulating recommendations. Because little has happened so far in terms of reform, no conclusions can yet be drawn. In this paper I define a successful tax mission as one that results in reform of the tax system of a country along the lines proposed by the mission. Obviously such a definition suffers from two potential problems. The first is the time horizon to consider before one assesses the success of the mission, and the second lies in attribution to the work of the mission of all future changes that are consistent with its recommendations. Both problems can affect any assessments that are made.

II. Common Characteristics of Tax Reform Attempts

It is perhaps foolhardy to attempt to sort out some of the common characteristics in these many and varied attempts. I am sure that most of those engaged in these enterprises would object to any common characterization, and they would be right, since all the attempts reflect individual and sharply distinct efforts. Still, common denominators among several can be found. I will try to list a few.

Experimentation

It would seem that a developing country with few resources is the least likely place in which one would want to experiment, yet we find several examples. An extreme version was Kaldor's attempt at introducing an expenditure tax in India and Sri Lanka. Another example was Shoup's proposal for a value-added tax in Japan after World War II. These are the most visible, but not the only, examples. It takes many years to work out all the administrative implications of new taxes and to find solutions to anticipated as well as unanticipated hurdles. The value-added tax is still being modified within the European Economic Community, and many problems (as for example the taxation of financial activities) are still without a solution. One can imagine the difficulties that the Japanese administrators would have faced in 1949 if they had gone the route recommended by the Shoup mission. Most public finance experts still shudder at the administrative complications that an expenditure tax would face if introduced in an advanced country such as the United States. The problems faced by the administrators of India and Sri Lanka are well documented.

Cultural Biases

Regardless of the attempts on the part of experts to remain immune from cultural biases, such biases inevitably occur, in either technical or social form. The changes recommended to the developing countries often reflected the values (progressivity is good; the tax system *must* redistribute income, etc.) of the experts rather than of those receiving the advice. The belief that objectives are universal and that if something is good in Washington, New York, or London, it must be so in La Paz, Bogota, or Delhi, predominated. This meant that the advice given often had objectives that did not necessarily reflect those of the governments receiving it. Also it meant that the experts were not necessarily concentrating on the most important taxes. Compare, for example, the attention paid to income taxes, or even to capital gains taxes, with that paid to foreign trade taxes, which still contribute the lion's share of tax revenues in many developing countries.

Optimism about What Taxation Can Do

There were at least two sides to this characteristic. The first was an overoptimistic and, with the benefit of hindsight, perhaps naive view of the development process. Earlier attempts equated more taxes with more government saving and thus with more developmentg expenditure. This expenditure was in turn believed to promote more growth. Tax reform was therefore identified with tax increase, and was seen as a step toward accelerating the rate of growth. Fuat Andic, in reviewing the report of the Musgrave Commission for Colombia, summarizes its "general methodological approach" as follows: "Decide upon the target rate of per capita income growth. Translate the rate into the required rate of capital formation on the basis of a rough estimate of the so-called marginal capital-output ratio. Determine the share of public investment based upon developmental requirements; this will determine the requirements for public saving" [1, p. 164]. The idea that governments were also capable of wasting resources was not fashionable. Today, of course, we run the opposite risk: that of coming to believe that governments cannot do anything right. I would not be surprised if one of the main objectives of future tax reforms becomes a reduction in the tax ratio.

Second, there was often an implicit belief that many of the distortions that prevailed throughout the economy were the natural result of underdevelopment rather than of public policy. A similar belief was associated with the distribution of income; the *normal* working of the market of a developing country was believed to promote an uneven income distribution. As a consequence, taxes should be neutral in their impact on prices, and should promote a more even distribution of income. Many of the tax reformers were willing to sacrifice simplicity to achieve these objectives of neutrality and equity. During much of this period the equity that concerned the tax reformers was vertical; hence the emphasis on progressive taxation. The fact that progressive taxes could create or aggravate problems of horizontal equity has not attracted much concern until recently. None of the many tax incidence studies done for developing countries had much information about the dispersion of the tax burden *for individuals in the same income classes.* They all had information about the average burden by income classes.

Unfortunately, in many countries, the distortions in relative prices, as well as the effects on income distribution associated with taxes, paled in comparison with those brought about by other government policies. In the majority of developing countries, one finds that government policies directed toward exchange rates, capital movements, import restrictions, pricing of public services or agricultural outputs, interest rates, etc., often distort relative prices to such an extent that whatever improvement one can get from the tax system is of marginal relevance. If this improvement comes at the cost of other objectives, including that of simplicity and ease of administration, then one must wonder whether it is worth it.[15] In many of these countries the distribution of income that results may be more the product of government policies than of the private ownership of factors of production. Those who, because of political or other connections, manage to get access to scarce foreign exchange, import licenses, subsidized credit, or manage to have a quota imposed upon the importation of a product which they produce domestically, end up with huge incomes which may bear little relationship to whether they own specific factors of production.[16] Access to public favors often becomes more important in determining incomes than access to property, and the income distribution comes to reflect "who one knows" as well as "what one owns." Thus, the great preoccupation with capital gains, with wealth taxation, and with highly progressive income tax rates that characterized many of the tax reform proposals may have been based on a somewhat unrealistic view of the economies to which they were addressed.

Fashions

During certain periods, some recommendations enjoyed a greater vogue than others. Intellectual fashions have appeared and disappeared over the past three decades. For example, in the 1950s and 1960s unification of schedular income taxes became the vogue. In that period it would have been difficult to find a report that did not propose a global income tax. In the 1960s and 1970s, the OAS-IDB program actively promoted the introduction of suspense or "ring-type" sales taxes. Today, more reports recommend a value-added tax. Perhaps these changes are the result of a learning process, whereby new alternatives come to be seen as genuinely better than earlier alternatives. On the other hand, they may simply result from fads.

Comprehensiveness of Proposed Changes

Most of the tax reform attempts aimed at reforming the whole tax system rather than just parts of it. In theory this comprehensive approach is preferable to one that aims at modifying only part of the existing system, because of the interconnection of the various parts: it is difficult to reform domestic indirect taxes without reforming foreign trade taxes, and so on. In practice, however, one runs the risk that in attempting to get too much one gets nothing. Comprehensive reform is much more unsettling than partial reform. Even when a strong claim can be made that in terms of the objectives of taxation the tax system that would emerge from the reform would be clearly superior to the one that it would replace, one must pay attention to the transition costs. These costs are often ignored in the Paretian approach to policy. Option B may be better than A once we reach it. The trouble is that if the transition costs are high, we may never get to B. The more comprehensive is the reform, the more demands are likely to be made on the administrators who will have to administer the new system as well as on the politicians who will have to legislate the new tax laws. There is just so much change that the tax administration of a country or its political body can accommodate. There is also the concrete danger that the government will not go along with the whole package but will pick and choose among the comprehensive proposals. In the process it may even reduce the quality of the tax system rather than increase it. Finally, the current government may be out of power before the reform process is completed, since that process will require a long time, and the new government may wish to institute its own reform.

Excessive Emphasis on "Policy"

A final aspect, of perhaps greater importance than all the others mentioned earlier, is the emphasis in the tax reform on "policy." Administration has often been the stepsister of the tax reform process. This emphasis was inevitable when the advisers were general economists rather than tax experts. In an important Latin American report, for example, at least three of the five-man tax mission consisted of well-known economists who had practically no background in taxation and even less in taxation in developing countries.[17] But the same emphasis can be found in reports written by public finance experts.

One of the countries in which technical assistance in taxation seems to have been highly successful in Chile. This country received assistance from the United Nations, the Internal Revenue Service of the United States, Harvard, and the Organization of American States. A major part of this success can be attributed to the fact that tax reform efforts were pursued at the same time that major improvements in tax administration were being enforced vigorously. In those countries where technical assistance concentrated mainly on the reform of the tax structure, and where tax administration was considered only incidentally, the results were much less favorable.

III. Requirements for the Success of Tax Reform

In the previous section I speculated briefly on some of the shortcomings common to many, but by no means all, tax reform efforts promoted by outsiders over recent decades. That discussion also points in the direction of the requirement for a successful tax reform. I will now briefly outline some of these requirements.

As I look over the experience of this period, there are some obvious aspects to the success of tax reform in some countries and not in others. If I had to list the basic ingredients that make for a successful tax reform I would include the following:

1. Government with a Long Horizon

Genuine tax reforms require time as well as the commitment of the country's government, which will have to use up some of its political capital in order to bring about changes in the system, especially when the benefits from the tax reform are widespread, while its costs are concentrated among specific groups that can get organized and oppose it. The cost rise when these groups become politically powerful and organized. There is thus always a cost and a risk for a government in engaging in tax reform. This brings two consequences. One is that such a process will be started and will be continued only when a government has a long time horizon in front of it. The costs of the reforms are always immediate; the benefits are almost always spread over the future. The rate of discount that the government will use to make the benefit-cost evaluation of the reform will often by determined, or at least will be influenced, by how long it expects to remain in power. If a government expects to be out of power relatively soon, it will apply a very high discount rate to those benefits and will have very little interest in pursuing a genuine, as distinguished from a demagogic, tax reform.

2. Presence of a Politically Powerful Domestic Mentor

Of equally great importance is the fact that when one talks about "the government" one really should be talking about one or perhaps a few powerful figures who have the stamina, the interest, and the vision to push for the reform and to stay with it over a period that is likely to extend over years. A government that remains in power but whose members keep changing will have less chance of seeing a major reform accomplished. We have reviewed experiences, as in India with the expenditure tax, where taxes disappeared when their mentor lost his job. On the other hand, when a powerful political figure (within a government with a long time horizon) retains an interest in the reform, and adopts it as his own creation, there is a better chance of its success.

3. Recognition that Reform Is More than a Change in Policy

As previously indicated, the reforms that succeeded were those in which great importance was paid to administration. Successful tax reform requires an equilibrium between political objectives, tax policy changes, and administrative development. All of these have to move together. When political objectives overtake the other two, we often have demagoguery. In that case the government is not genuinely interested in tax reform but only in scoring political points. When policy moves alone, while the other two elements do not move, we have aborted reforms. Successful tax reform must not overemphasize the theoretical aspects (or tax policy aspects) while paying little attention to the more mundane, but perhaps more important, administrative aspects. Tax reformers must realize that making tax policy recommendations is only the first step, albeit a necessary one. These recommendations must be translated into tax laws, regulations, reorganization of tax offices, changes in administrative procedures, preparation of lists of taxpayers with relevant addresses, redesigning tax forms, modification of penalities, new audit concepts, new training of administrative personnel, taxpayer education, etc.[18]

One mistake that foreign experts have often made is to go to a country, write a report, and leave, under the assumption that once policy changes have been proposed, the government will see their wisdom and will take over and carry the torch the rest of the way. In most cases, nothing will happen. What this means is that the group of tax reformers must include more than tax policy experts. It must also include tax administrators, and especially tax administrators with an intimate knowledge of the specific country. There are areas in which a tax administrator who is good in one place can also be good in other places, but there are other areas in which this translation of skills from one place to another does not work.

4. Adaptation of Reform to Domestic Economic Conditions

There is a story about a tax expert who provided advice to several American states. After he wrote the first well-received report for a given state, he decided that its analysis and recommendations were equally applicable to other states. When he received requests for similar studies from other states, he took the old report, changed the name of the state and some of the statistical material, and sent it to the new clients. I have not heard such a story concerning technical assistance provided to countries, but the story has a message. Some experts may convince themselves that particular recommendations have merit independently of local conditions. If this happens, they may not make as great an effort as desirable at adapting their tax proposals to local conditions. Such adaptation often requires close knowledge of the country's economic, political, and social conditions. This requires the need for substantial domestic participation in the reform process; or, alternatively, the need to spend very lengthy periods of time in a country. One does not learn much by studying the existing tax laws, as actual practice may be very different from the law. And one does not learn very much by looking at the available and often questionable statistics. The limited quantity of statistics available and their often poor quality means that much of the advice provided will be based on intuition or guesses, and these will be good only when the expert really understands the country. Obviously, this understanding often requires the knowledge of the country's language and customs.[19]

5. Support from the Country's Tax Administration

Successful reforms require not only an intimate knowledge of the country's economic, political, legal, and social structure, but also the support of those who are currently administering the tax system. Reforms are unlikely to succeed when little attention is paid to those who will administer the new taxes or when the latter see the reform as something imposed by outsiders. At times good proposals may be blocked for totally unanticipated reasons. For example, in one country the recommendation to reduce the role of excise taxes and to expand that of broader taxes was blocked mainly because the head of the excise tax department would lose power as a consequence of loss of personnel assigned to these taxes. What the tax advisers had ignored was the fact that this gentleman was a special adviser to the prime minister, and thus had enough power to prevent the change.

The point is that all tax reforms bring with them not only changes in the burden of taxes on taxpayers but also changes in the relative power of the different parts of the tax administration. These shifts in power cannot be ignored by those who are recommending the reform, since the affected individuals often have the power to make or break the reform. The civil servants of the countries must become part of the act and must have input. One reason why a traditional recommendation of most experts—to use import taxes only for protection and to transfer their function of discrimination against nonessential goods to the domestic indirect taxes—has rarely if ever been followed is that it would lower the relative influence of the customs administration. In many countries customs administrators are powerful enough to be able to block such reforms.

Notes

1. By agreement with the chairman of the scientific committee in charge of the 41st Congress, no mention is made in this paper of the role of the Fiscal Affairs Department of the International Monetary Fund (IMF) in tax reform. I wish to thank Milka Casanegra, Carlos A. Aguirre, and Peter Griffith for valuable advice. The views expressed are personal, and should not be construed as official IMF views.

2. See [18]. It should be noted that the report was requested by the Supreme Commander for the Allied Powers. Since Japan was then under occupation, this technical assistance did not reflect a request from an independent government.

3. See [9], p. 360.

4. See [5].

5. See [21, 11, 10, and 3].

6. The Commission to Study the Fiscal System of Venezuela included, in addition to Carl Shoup, John Due, Lyle C. Fitch, Sir Donald MacDougall, Oliver S. Oldman, and Stanley S. Surrey. See [17].

7. Writing in 1968, Oldman referred to the fact that "the Stroup Report is still considered a principal reference work on the tax problems of less developed countries," and "the impact of the Report in other countries ought not to go unnoticed." See his Introduction to [4].

8. See [4].

9. Both reports were later published by the International Tax Program of Harvard Law School. See [13, 12].

10. For reviews of the Colombia Report, see [19, 1].

11. This tax reform is surveyed in [20] and [2].

12. Milton Taylor led OAS-IDB Joint Tax Program misions to Panama, Colombia, and Peru during the 1960s. The resulting publications are [14, 15, 16]. The OAS-IDB Joint Tax Program was very active from the early 1960s to the mid-1970s. Three conferences that it organized had much influence, especially in Latin America. See [6, 7, 8].

13. The extent of Gillis' involvement is indicated by the fact that he learned the Indonesian language over this period.

14. Inter alia, the reform has included the introduction of a value-added tax, the elimination of most incentives, and an extreme simplification of the income tax. The value-added tax has just one rate (10 percent) and the income tax just three rates (15, 25, 35).

15. The same comment applies to the policy recommendations that orginate from the optimal taxation literature.

16. There is now a growing literature on rent seeking and its impact on income distribution.

17. The report is [16]. The three economists included an internationally known macro theorist and two prominent monetary economists.

18. A recent example should suffice to show the importance of this point: after a country introduced a value-added tax it realized that it did not have an updated list with addresses of taxpayers, and when it tried to contact the taxpayers by using the old list, more than 80 percent of the letters sent came back undelivered.

19. How customs can differ is indicated by the fact that in a certain country I was told that it would be considered morally wrong for a tax inspector to report to his superiors the name of a taxpayer who has tried to bribe him; the inspector is only expected to politely decline the bribe offer.

References

[1] Andic, Fuat M., "Fiscal Reform in Colombia: A Review Article," *Finanzarchiv*, 32, 1973.

[2] CEPAL, *La Reforma Tributaria en Colombia, Revista de Hacienda*, July–September, 1977.

[3] Commission on Taxation, "First Report of the Commission on Taxation," *The Irish Banking Review*, December, 1982.

[4] Gittes, Enrique F., *Income Tax Reform, the Venezuelan Experience*, Cambridge, Mass., Harvard Student Legislative Research Bureau, 1968.

[5] Goode, Richard, *Government Finance in Developing Countries*, Washington, D.C., Brookings Institution, 1984.

[6] Joint Tax Program, OAS/IDB/ECLA, *Fiscal Policy for Economic Growth in Latin America*, Baltimore, Johns Hopkins Press, 1965.

[7] ———, *Problems of Tax Administration in Latin America*, Baltimore, Johns Hopkins Press, 1965.

[8] ———, *La Politica Tributaria Como Instrumento del Desarrollo*, OAS, 1973.

[9] Khanna, K. C., "An Expenditures Tax in India," *Bulletin for International Fiscal Documentation*, September, 1964: 353–63.

[10] Lodin, Sven-Olof, *Progressive Expenditure Tax—An Alternative?* Stockholm, Liber Förlag, 1978.

[11] Meade, J. E., *The Structure and Reform of Direct Taxation*, London, Institute of Fiscal Studies, 1978.

[12] Musgrave, Richard A., *Fiscal Reform in Bolivia*, Cambridge, Mass., Harvard Law School, International Tax Program, 1981.

[13] Musgrave, Richard, and Gillis, Malcolm, *Fiscal Reform in Colombia*, Cambridge, Mass., Harvard Law School, International Tax Program, 1971.

[14] OAS-IDB Joint Tax Program, *Fiscal Survey of Panama*, Baltimore, Johns Hopkins Press, 1964.

[15] ———, *Fiscal Survey of Colombia*, Baltimore, Johns Hopkins Press, 1965.

[16] ———, *Estudio Fiscal del Peru*, OAS, 1969.

[17] Shoup, Carl (Director), *The Fiscal System of Venezuela, A Report*, Baltimore, Johns Hopkins Press, 1959.

[18] Shoup Mission, *Report on Japanese Taxation*, 4 vols., Tokyo, General Headquarters, Supreme Commander for the Allied Powers, 1949.

[19] Tanzi, Vito, "Fiscal Reform in Colombia: The Report of the Musgrave Commission," *Inter-American Economic Affairs*, 28, 1972:71–80.

[20] ———, "The 1974 Colombian Tax Reform: Description and Evaluation," Mimeo., 1975.

[21] U.S. Treasury Department, *Blueprints for Basic Tax Reform*, Washington, D.C., 1977.

Résumé

Ce rapport passe en revue les principales missions de politique fiscale dans les pays en voie de développement. Tout d'abord, il trace un arrière-plan historique, discutant brièvement quelques uns des principaux réformateurs et réformes des trois dernières décennies. Ensuite, il tente de trouver des caractéristiques communes à ces efforts de réforme. Il discute les rôles de (a) l'expérimentation, (b) les influences culturelles, (c) l'optimisme sur ce que la fiscalité peut faire, (d) les modes, (e) l'importance excessive accordée à la politique. Dans une troisième section on dresse la liste de plusieurs conditions nécessaires au succès d'une réforme: (a) le maintien au pouvoir des gouvernements; (b) la présence d'un dirigeant national muni de pouvoirs; (c) admettre qu'une réforme est plus qu'une modification des lois fiscales; (d) adapter la réforme aux conditions économiques internes; (e) l'adhésion des administrateurs fiscaux du pays.

The Impact of the Shoup Mission

Hiromitsu Ishi

I. Introduction

It is widely acknowledged that the postwar tax system in Japan was based on the tax recommendations of the Shoup Mission in 1949. Like the Carter Report in Canada and the Meade Report in the United Kingdom, the Shoup Report has been well rated by many tax experts (see, for example, Hicks [7]), especially for its theoretical and logical consistency.

The Shoup Report was of epoch-making significance in the history of Japanese taxation. In contrast to the tax reports noted above, most of the Shoup recommendations were put into practice, although modification of them began soon after implementation. In the postwar period, the Shoup report has served as a benchmark for a well-designed tax system whenever tax reform is discussed in Japan.

The following sections provide background information, describe the basic framework of the report, and discuss the aftermath of the tax reform.

II. Background of the Shoup Mission

Headed by Carl S. Shoup, the mission visited Japan in April 1949 at the request of the Supreme Commander for Allied Power (SCAP).[1] Its members stayed in Japan for about four months, investigating the Japanese tax system as well as its economic and social contexts. After intensive study, they submitted to SCAP a paper, titled "Report on Japanese Taxation by the Shoup Mission," in August 1949. Following the Shoup recommendations, the Japanese government attempted to reorganize its entire system of national and local taxes, effective with the next supplementary budget in 1949.[2]

*The author is on the faculty of Hitotsubashi University. The editorial help of Robert Dekle is appreciated, and the comments of C. Shoup, Vito Tanzi, P. R. McDaniel are gratefully acknowledged.

The Relevance of Public Finance for Policy-Making. Proceedings of the 41st Congress of the International Institute of Public Finance. Madrid, 1985, pp. 237–249.

What were the main reasons for the visit of the Shoup Mission? The first was the chaotic condition of the postwar economy, resulting mainly from rampant inflation, which raised havoc among business accounts, tax assessments, and revenue collection. Second, there was mutual understanding between the United States and Japan concerning the necessity of overhauling the tax structure and its administration after implementation of the "Dodge Line."[3] The Shoup tax reform was not the first reform attempted in Japan during the occupation period, but earlier efforts had proved far from satisfactory.[4] A rigorous plan was required to revise the Japanese tax system in the interests of equity and efficiency, rather than as a political expedient.

In the earlier years of the occupation, the tax system had developed certain defects which the Shoup Mission was asked to remedy. The most important were the following:

1. Personal income taxes had risen and become more progressive, with few exemptions and broad coverage. Heavier tax burdens destroyed tax administration, weakening tax morale. Revenues were collected by the "goal system," with each tax office assigned a goal or quota.
2. Corporate income and excess-profits tax rates were high, and business firms, corporate or not, were not permitted to adjust depreciation allowances in the face of drastic price hikes.
3. Taxation remained concentrated in the hands of the national government, although a large number of public functions were allocated to local governments (prefectures and municipalities) in the name of strengthening "local autonomy."

In addition to trying to remedy these defects, the Japanese government negotiated with SCAP over substantial reductions in taxes (especially in the personal income tax). SCAP did not concur in the necessity for such tax cuts,[5] however. The question of tax reductions had become an issue before the Shoup Report was published.

Fortunately, economic conditions had begun to improve before the Shoup Mission arrived, for inflation had been halted following the Dodge stabilization policy of 1948. Nevertheless, a number of difficulties remained for the mission to address. Among them was that, in view of the Japanese anti-tax and anti-inflation sentiment, a goal was to provide a tax cut for every citizen without unbalancing the budget.

III. Basic Framework of the Shoup Report

The Shoup Report contained the new and advanced views long held by Shoup, Surrey, Vickrey, and other tax experts. In other words, the

Shoup Mission attempted to reconstruct the Japanese tax system along lines generally familiar to American tax experts, and a number of experimental features were designed to make the Japanese system "the best tax system in the world" (Shoup Report, Vol. 1, p. ii).

When the report was published, it called for vigorous discussion of its recommendations. The report stated:

> It will present in detail not only the recommendations, but the reasons why they were reached. It is hoped that through the publication of this report an intelligent discussion of the Japanese tax system will develop in the Press, in the national and local tax offices throughout the country, in the business circles, in the women's organizations, and in the universities and secondary schools" [18].

Three basic points characterize the report as a whole. First, the fundamental aim was to establish a permanent and stable tax system over the long run.[6] What the mission intended was establishment of a modern tax system based on direct taxation. It would have been possible to choose another form of taxation, based instead on the indirect tax, which the Japanese government preferred, mainly because the Japanese system had developed in that direction during the prewar period. The Shoup Report clearly states that it had two choices, direct or indirect taxation, the argument being that "The long-term program itself could have been either of two kinds. We could have recommended a rather primitive type of tax system, one which would depend on external signs of income and wealth and business activity, not on carefully kept records and intelligent analysis of difficult problems" (Shoup Report, Vol. 1, p. i).

The mission did not recommend the indirect tax system, for two reasons: (1) that system could raise the required revenue, but would perpetuate gross inequities among taxpayers, dull the sense of civic responsibility, keep local governmental units in uneasy financial dependence on the national government, and give rise to undesired economic effects on production and distribution; (2) the mission soon became convinced that the difficulties then being experienced in achieving fair and efficient administration of the tax laws and a high degree of compliance by the taxpayer in Japan could be overcome.

Moreover, the report was intended to form a single, integrated plan; the authors felt strongly that the whole would be destroyed if any parts were discarded. The Shoup report argued this point in strong terms:

> What we are recommending here is a tax system, not a number of isolated measures having no connection with one another. All of the major recommendations, and many of the minor ones, are interconnected. If any of the major recommendations are eliminated, some of the others will thereby become of less value, or even harmful. Consequently, we disclaim responsibility for the

results that may follow the adoption of only part of our recommendations" (Vol. 1, p. ii).

When they said "a tax system," strong emphasis was placed in the interconnections of individual taxes. For example, the personal income and net worth taxes, or the succession and the real estate tax (the land and house tax) are considered jointly. The principle of full inclusion of capital gains and losses in income taxes is closely related to the interrelationship of personal and corporate income taxes. The basic idea of the Shoup Report was that the whole income tax structure would be seriously weakened without full inclusion of capital gains and losses.

Throughout the report, great importance was placed on tax equity. In press interviews immediately after the mission arrived in Japan (May 19, 1949), Shoup himself emphasized that restoring fairness in the Japanese tax system was one of five objectives of his reform. The basic philosophy in support of tax equity is as follows:

> A tax system can be successful only if it is equitable, and the taxpayers must realize that it is equitable. We have often encountered surprise at the emphasis we place on the search for equity. But no one remains in the tax field for long without realizing that nothing he recommends will stand up unless it meets the test of fairness in the distribution of the tax burden (Shoup Report, Vol. 1, p. 16).

Several points in the recommendations are worth noting. First, a series of recommendations was designed to establish an integrated system of direct taxes, comprising a personal income tax, a corporate tax, a net worth tax, a cumulative tax on gifts and acquisitions over the lifetime, and a "local inhabitants" tax assessed on income at the level of the local government. Particular attention should be paid to the fact that the progressive and broad-based personal income tax was retained as the mainstay of the Japanese tax system. In retrospect, the personal income tax proposed by the mission was an ideal form of comprehensive tax base with a single, progressive rate system in the true sense of the term. Of course, this was the first time that anything of the kind had been attempted in Asian countries, although Japan had experienced schedular income taxes since 1887 on a smaller scale.[7]

Second, a major concern was improvement of the tax administration, which concerned mainly the income tax. Withholding taxes from wage and salary incomes and self-assessment with universal filing of returns were recommended. Use of the "blue form" for tax returns was well suited to encourage accurate keeping of accounts, particularly in the case of small businesses.[8]

Third, a general reevaluation of all assets (i.e., land and fixed capital) was recommended as a prerequisite to adoption of the Shoup plan. Since the value of the yen had depreciated on the order of two or three hundred-fold in comparison with the prewar period, such reevaluation would stimulate private capital accumulation. In addition, it was proposed that a tax of 6 percent be imposed on the written-up value, although appreciation would consist almost wholly of paper gains in terms of book value.

Fourth, great emphasis was placed on the reform of local finance as a means of educating the Japanese in democratic citizenship. Providing a fiscal framework for "local autonomy" was an important element of the Shoup proposal. Its general recommendation was that local powers and duties should be substantially increased; in particular, priority should be given to the lowest of the three levels of government, municipalities. For this purpose, local governments were given new tax resources (such as the property tax and a value-added tax) and intergovernmental transfers were overhauled in a new scheme for the equalization of local budgets called the Equalization Grant Scheme.

Finally, the Shoup tax plan proposed several fiscal experiments. The mission suggested that these efforts be tried in Japan, even though there were no large-scale experiences with them in other countries. Special attention was given to three, although they were minor in size: the net worth tax, the accession tax, and the value-added tax.

IV. Aftermath of the Shoup Tax Reform

Rarely in history has a tax reform report been put into practice. The Shoup Report was enacted almost wholly through the 1949 supplementary budget and the 1950 budget. However, upon enactment several elements of the tax plan were criticized as too theoretical to be applied, given the state of socioeconomic development in postwar Japan. The mission doubtless thought of the tax reform primarily in terms of American practice and experience, as was apparent in such matters as the treatment of capital gains and the emphasis on "local autonomy."

Accordingly, modification of the "Shoup tax system" began soon after 1950. Two tendencies were apparent in the changes that were made. One was the revival of the old system: equity was sacrificed for the convenience of administration. The other was a reduction in the tax burden on firms, especially big businesses. The goal was to give priority to restoration of the postwar economy and the promotion of capital accumulation. Tax equity, on which the Shoup Mission put utmost priority, began to be replaced by the criterion of efficiency.

The modifications were generally accepted as inevitable by the Japanese. Hanya Ito commented: "However, it is to be observed that the tax system in practice is a product of historical development depending on the

Table 1
Shoup Mission Recommendations and Subsequent Modifications
(Major items only)

Shoup Recommendation	Japanese Legislature (1949–56)	Present Tax System (1958)
I. Personal Income Tax		
(1) *Type of Tax* Single, on an aggregate basis, not schedular.	Carried out. Subsequent Japanese moves toward schedular income tax; e.g., special treatment of bank interest, dividend, retirement income, etc.	Partial schedular income tax continued.
(2) *Top bracket rate* To be lowered from 85% to 55% with eight income brackets.	Carried out. Top bracket rate raised to 65% (1953) when net worth tax was repealed.	Top rate is 70% with fifteen income brackes.
(3) *Exemption, deduction and credit* Personal exemption, dependent and earned income credit alone to be introduced.	Carried out. Social insurance and life insurance payment deduction (1953). Medical deduction (1953).	Scope is greatly expanded. Approximately twenty exemption and deductions; six credits.
(4) *Capital gains and losses* To be included or deducted fully in income, and treated as a form of fluctuating income with averaging system.	Carried out. Both gains and losses from security sales disregarded (1952), replaced by security transfer tax.	Capital gains from land and buildings alone are generally taxed as other income.
(5) *Interest Income* Source collection (separately from other income) to be abolished.	Carried out, but old system revived at 50% rate (1951); rate cut to 10% (1953); bank interest income made tax free (1955).	Separate taxation on interest income at 35% rate.
II. Corporate Income Tax (and Asset Revaluation)		
(1) *Corporate income tax rate* Not to be increased above 35%. No progression to be imposed.	Carried out. Raised to 42% (1952); lowered to 35% on first 500,000 income, 40% on the remainder (1955).	43.3% (33.3% reduced rate applicable to dividend). Both rates are further lowered for small- and medium-sized firms.

242

(2) *Excess profit tax* (To be repealed)	Carried out.	
(3) *Revaluation procedures* Land and depreciable assets to be revalued as of July 1, 1949.	Three revaluations carried out (1950, 1951. (1954); last revaluation made compulsory for corporate assets and depreciable assets. Farm land not to be revalued until sold.	No revaluation has been made since the fourth (1957).
(4) *Tax on revaluation gain* To be set at 6% of gain. Payable in installments over 3 years for depreciable assets. Payable for nondepreciable property at time of sale.	Carried out. Repealed in connection with 1954 revaluation.	

III. National Indirect Taxes

(1) *Turnover tax* To be repealed as soon as revenues permit.	Repealed as of Jan. 1, 1950.	
(2) *Textile consumption tax* To be repealed.	Carried out.	
(3) *Alcoholic beverage excises* a) Rates to be raised to May 1949 level, with further increases as local liquor taxes are repealed.	Partially carried out.	Rates system became more complicated.
b) Liquor consumption tax to be repealed.	Carried out.	
(4) *Tobacco taxes (monopoly profits)* Prices of cheapest (rationed) cigarettes and cut tobacco to be reduced.	Never carried out. Tobacco prices increased by local tobacco consumption excises (1954).	Monopoly profits changed (into national tobacco consumption excises.
(5) *Commodity taxes* Rates to be reduced.	Substantially carried out.	Rates and coverage substantially changed.
(6) *Minor excises to be repealed* Soft drinks.	Never carried out. Soft drinks included in items subject to commodity tax.	Repealed.
Travel (on 3rd trip)	Carried out.	
Registration and stamp taxes.	Never carried out.	Continue to exist.

Table 1 (continued)

Sboup Recommendation	Japanese Legislature (1949–56)	Present Tax System (1958)
IV. Local Taxes and Intergovernmental Fiscal Relations		
(1) *Value-added tax* Enterprise tax to become VAT (base to be calculated on payments to factors of production) exclusively at prefectural level.	Never carried out. Effective date postponed annually through 1953; tax repealed (1954). Enterprise tax remained in effect.	Never restored.
(2) *Resident's tax (local income tax)* a) Allocation: To be reserved for municipalities.	Carried out. Made partially prefectural (1954).	
b) Variable element: To be based on income alone, not property or social status, as formerly. Base may be (i) income tax (ii) taxable revenue, or (iii) the difference (ii)–(i).	Carried out. National income tax used as standard. Takes form of 18% surtax.	
c) Corporations to be exempted.	Carried out. Corporations made taxable (1951), tax taking form of 15% surtax on national corporate income tax. Surtax lowered to 12.5% (1952).	
(3) *Property tax* a) Allocation: To be reserved for municipalities.	Carried out. Made partially prefectural (1954).	
b) Coverage: To be extended to depreciable assets as well as real property, but not to inventories.	Carried out.	

244

c) Assessment: To be based on capital rather than on rental values of property.	Carried out, with capital values determined by selling prices and volume of business. Rate originally set a 1.6% of base, subsequently lowered twice. In 1955, 1.4%.	Present percentage is 2.1%.
(4) *Equalization grant*		
a) To be established as replacement for shared taxes and partial subsidies, but approximately double total amount of former.	Carried out. Equalization grant system abolished (1954); new tax shared program introduced.	
b) Distribution among local units to be based on algebraic formulae involving needs, for major activities.	Carried out for 90% of grants (1951–54).	Formula plan still used for distribution of shared taxes by Ministry of Home Affairs.
c) Distribution element of income taxes to be eliminated.	Carried out. 20% of personal income, corporate income, and liquor taxes distributed to local governments (1954). Percentage raised to 22% (1955).	Percent percentage is 32.0%.
(5) *National subsidy of local activities* Methods to be changed:		
a) 100% subsidies to be replaced by national government performance.	Partially carried out. (In some cases, subsidy reduced instead.)	
b) Partial subsidies to be replaced by equalization grant (except for promotional purposes).	Never carried out.	

social, economic and political conditions of time and place. It would not be wise to condemn such a course of events merely from the standpoint of abstract theory" [9. p. 382]. With the progress of time, essential features of the Shoup plan have been eroded or dismantled by subsequent tax reforms enacted by government (see Table 1). Although many points deserve attention, the most symbolic was the repeal in 1953 of full taxation on capital gains from sales of securities. It has often been noted that the Shoup Mission was well aware of the shortcomings of the American tax system regarding capital gains taxation, and it tried to introduce better treatment of capital gains as an experiment in Japan. Despite its strong recommendation, the capital gains tax since 1953 has disregarded proceeds from security sales, partly because of the difficulties in its administration and partly because the promotion of capital accumulation became a national goal.

The innovative tax devices of the Shoup Report were either never tried or were abandoned after brief trials. The net worth and accession taxes were abolished in 1953, because of inadequate revenues. The value-added tax was never put into operation; its enactment was postponed twice, and it was finally repealed in 1954.[9]

When the Japanese departed from the Shoup system, it was not in the direction of further experimentation, but toward a return to prewar traditions and practices which the Japanese government considered particularly suited to its economic situation.[10] It thus seems that the tax innovations advocated in the Shoup Report were a failure.

V. Concluding Remarks: Necessary Conditions for a Successful Tax Reform

In retrospect the reforms were only a partial success, largely because subsequent modifications gradually made the tax system more inequitable and complicated. In spite of these drawbacks, the mission's contributions to reconstructing the postwar tax system in Japan are considerable. Throughout the postwar period, the Japanese tax system has retained major features of the Shoup framework. In this sense many would support the view that the Shoup reform should be considered one of the most successful in the world.

What are the necessary conditions for a successful tax reform? Three points in particular stand out.

First, and most important, the foundations on which the Shoup Mission built the new tax structure in Japan represented a complete break with the past, owing to the events of World War II and postwar inflation. Prewar values had become irrelevant as a basis of postwar taxation, and their inequities could be disregarded amid the sweeping changes that had affected all values. Furthermore, the changes recommended by the mission were far less drastic than the overhaul of values that the Japanese experienced during the war. These circumstances facilitated the work of the mission and encouraged it to experiment with tax reform. To use Feldstein's terms, a sort of a "tax design," rather than "tax reform," could be put into effect (Feldstein [6]).

The second point, related to the first, is that conditions generally favored the work of the Shoup Mission. Seldom has any group been given the scope, or a goal as broadly defined, as in the case of this mission.[11] Its arrival coincided with the introduction of a national program for the redirection of the entire economy, after chaotic conditions had settled to a considerable extent. Thus, the mission was implicitly given scope for wide and sweeping changes in drafting the tax plan. Of utmost importance was the strong support of SCAP and General MacArthur. Because of this authority, the recommendations were given high priority by the Japanese government. These circumstances put the mission in an exceptionally favorable position. The Japanese government and Diet acted with vigor in accepting nearly all of the tax proposals.

Third, from a professional point of view, the Shoup Report itself was considered to be of the highest quality. The academic specialists of the mission first followed the basic principles of taxation as developed in the textbooks, then tried to link theoretical considerations with the institutions of Japan, although they were handicapped by unfamiliarity with the Japanese tax system. It is often pointed out that the Shoup proposals are not only logical and well-balanced in theory, but also can stand the test of practicality to some extent. When the results of tax missions to other countries generally fell short of expectations, the countries concerned often tended to refuse wholehearted enforcement of any proposals. In the case of the Shoup proposals, this tendency was minimized. The Japanese understood that they were given an opportunity to benefit from some of the best American thinking on tax issues.[12]

It is clear from this discussion that the conditions under which the mission provided a "tax design" for Japan were exceptional. They would never in the future be replicated.

Notes

1. For information on how the mission was invited, see Moss [14], MOF [1977a]. The Mission was composed of seven members: C. Shoup, S.S. Surrey, W.S. Vickrey, J.B. Cohen, H.R. Bowen, R.F. Hatfield, and W.C. Warren.

2. General MacArthur sent a private letter to Prime Minister Shigeru Yoshida (*The Asahi Shimbun*, Sept. 17, 1949) urging the Japanese government to enact the recommendations as soon as possible.

3. The "Dodge Line" was the name of the anti-inflationary program conceived by Joseph Dodge, an American Banker, who was invited by General MacArthur in 1948 to develop a formula for arresting inflation. Dodge focused on stabilizing the value of the yen by establishing a true balance in the consolidated budget and eliminating the subsidies which had been the main cause for the continuing growth of fiscal deficits. His plan was successful in halting inflation, although a severe depression ensued. See Cohen [4].

4. For a comprehensive discussion, see Shavell [16, 17].

5. For a view from the Japanese side, see E.S.B. (Economic Stabilization Board) [5]. However, Dodge completely disagreed with these requests for tax reductions. See SCAP [15].

6. The Shoup Mission envisioned that the reformed system would be maintained for more than ten years. Shoup referred to this point when he came to Japan in 1972; see MOF [11]. Furthermore, since there was at the time little immediate need for revenue, the mission could recommend a tax plan which would only bear fruit in the long run.

7. Hicks argued that the income tax was introduced in somewhat primitive conditions, commenting that "it is not the sort of economy in which one might, on a priori grounds, expect to be able to recommend a very large sphere for income and profits taxes" [7], pp. 200–201. See also Kimiura [10].

8. The mission also attached great importance to providing regular training for tax assessors and collectors, establishing training colleges, and generally to improving salaries and work conditions in the tax administration.

9. For more detailed discussion, see Ito [8], Bronfenbrenner [1].

10. See Bronfenbrenner and Kogiku [2, p. 241]. Ito [9] also argues that "judging from the development of tax reforms these last three years, Japanese taxation is showing a tendency to restore the old system which was in effect before the Shoup recommendation" (p. 358).

11. Shoup himself mentioned in retrospect that General MacArthur never intervened in the work of the mission, and that he cooperated fully with them [11].

12. For discussion of the relationship between the Shoup Mission and Japanese taxation, see Sundelson [19] and Bronfenbrenner and Kogiku [2, 3].

References

[1] Bronfenbrenner, Martin, "Japanese Value-Added Sales Tax", *National Tax Journal*, 3, Dec. 1950: 298–313.

[2] Bronfenbrenner, M., and Kogiku, K., "The Aftermath of the Shoup Tax Reforms, Part 1", *National Tax Journal*, 10, Sept. 1957: 236–54.

[3] ———, Part 2, *National Tax Journal*, 10, Dec. 1957: 345–60.

[4] Cohen, Jerome B., "Fiscal Policy in Japan", *Journal of Finance*, 5, March 1950: 110–25.

[5] E.S.B. [Economic Stabilization Board], "Reduction of Tax Burden and Slash in Expenditures", (July 21, 1949), unpublished series of documents collected by Ministry of Finance (no. Z703–6).

[6] Feldstein, Martin, "On the Theory of Tax Reform," *Journal of Public Economics*, 6, July/Aug. 1976: 77–104.

[7] Hicks, Ursula K., "The Reform of Japanese Taxation", *Public Finance*, 6, 1951: 199–217.

[8] Ito, Hanya, "The Value-Added Tax in Japan", *Annals of the Hitotsubashi Academy*, 1, Oct. 1950: 43–59.

[9] ———, "Direct Taxes in Japan and the Shoup Report", *Public Finance*, 8, 1953: 357–83.

[10] Kimura, Motokazu, "Conditions for Direct Taxation", *Annals of the Hitotsubashi Academy*, 2, April 1952: 148–71.

[11] Ministry of Finance, *Summary of Lectures of Professors Shoup and Surry* (in Japanese), unpublished material, 1972.

[12] ———, *The Fiscal History, 1945–1957*, Vol. 7 (in Japanese), 1977.

[13] ———, *The Fiscal History, 1945–1952*, Vol. 8 (in Japanese), 1977.

[14] Moss, Harold, "Memorandum to General Marquat: Subject, Proposed Radiogram Cover-

ing Tax Program", (Dec, 13, 1948), unpublished series of documents collected by Ministry of Finance (no. Z702–6).

[15] SCAP, "Teleconference between Tokyo and Washington: Subject, Taxation in Japan", *ibid.* (no. Z703–6).

[16] Shavell, Henry, "Postwar Taxation in Japan", *Journal of Political Economy*, 56, April 1948: 124–37.

[17] ———, "Taxation Reform in Occupied Japan", *National Tax Journal*, 1, June 1948: 127–43.

[18] The Shoup Taxation Mission, "Reform of Japan's Taxation System", *Contemporary Japan*, 18, July/Sept. 1949.

[19] Sundelson, J. Wilner, "Report on Japanese Taxation by the Shoup Mission", *National Tax Journal*, 3, June 1950: 104–20.

Résumé

Le système fiscal d'après-guerre au Japon a été fondé sur les recommandations émises en 1949 par la mission Shoup. Cette mission a marqué une époque dans l'histoire de la fiscalité japonaise. Contrairement à d'autres rapports fiscaux bien connus, tels les rapports Meade et Carter, la plupart des recommandations de Shoup ont été mises en pratique au Japon. Le rapport Shoup a fourni une base pour un bon modèle de système fiscal, chaque fois qu'une réforme fiscale est discutée. L'expérience de la mission Shoup donne un certain nombre de leçons pour déterminer les conditions nécessaires au succès d'une réforme fiscale.

Public Finance and Governance in a New Democracy: Opportunities and Problems

Ramón Trías Fargas
and
José Raga*

This paper is a synthesis of two papers delivered by the authors at the IIPF Madrid Congress.[1]

I. The New Role of the Public Sector

Over the past ten years both internal and external pressures have shaped development of the Spanish public sector. The transition from authoritarian regime to democracy has been accompanied by fiscal reform to rectify past mistakes and new economic policies that have thrust greater responsibilities upon the public sector. Those tasks were made more difficult because they had to be carried out while changes in the world economy were having adverse effects on many nations, including Spain.

Reform of the Tax System and Other Changes before 1975

In the last years of the Franco regime, the tax system of Spain was badly in need of reform. Several earlier attempts to improve it had not been able to cure its traditional inefficiency. As matters grew worse, politicians and theorists put together a new reform which it was hoped would create a more equitable system, scheduled to take effect in 1973.

Under the traditional system, wages were taxed more heavily than profits, indirect taxes were levied in a complicated fashion, and there was a

*The authors are, respectively, a member of the Spanish parliament and professor of public finance at the University of Barcelona; and professor of economics and public finance at the University Complutense of Madrid.

The Relevance of Public Finance for Policy-Making. Proceedings of the 41st Congress of the International Institute of Public Finance. Madrid, 1985, pp. 251–257.

proliferation of other types of taxes. This situation, combined with the general inefficiency of the machinery of tax inspection, made evasion inevitable.

The reforms of November 1973 and April 1975, while Franco was still in power, attempted to correct these defects by introducing more equity into the system and placing more emphasis on individual income taxes. This was a period of turbulence in the world economy, brought on by shortages of raw materials, imbalance in the international monetary system, the energy crisis, and, most important, rising oil prices.

In the face of the energy crisis, Spain decided that the public sector would absorb the price increase of crude oil. The public sector thus took on a new burden, expected to be short-term, but, the crisis continued. Delaying the effects of the crisis had two adverse consequences: First, society continued to live in the opulent life style of the late 1960s and early 1970s under a subsidized price system that was far removed from real production costs. Second, postponing the effects of the crisis created distortions in the economy which removed it even further from real market trends.

Even though there had been much past discussion of the need for equity in distribution of the tax burden and the need to achieve a more just distribution through direct taxes, 1975 ended with heavier taxes on production than on incomes. Direct taxes in 1975 constituted 4.4 percent of GDP, whereas the indirect taxes related to production and imports amounted to 6.7 percent. Social security contributions increased from 7.9 percent of GDP in 1970 to 10.3 percent in 1975. Public expenditures on social security increased from 7.5 percent of GDP in 1970 to 9.3 percent in 1975.

New Policies after 1975

Such was the condition of the public sector in 1975 when the democratic system was put in place. The new political system had to come to terms with certain inescapable facts. On the one hand, it was essential that the shift from an authoritarian regime to a representative one be accomplished peacefully and with the least possible upheaval. On the other hand, the new system would have to meet demands for change, which in the financial field meant fiscal reform and a new budgetary policy. And all this had to be done just as Spain was beginning to feel the effects of the world economic crisis. Trends in public expenditure appeared to be dictated by the need to maintain the democratic system just as if the economic crisis had never happened.

The public sector had to deal with attempts to introduce a redistributive policy, which caused expenditures to rise from 24.9 percent of GDP in 1975 to 37.4 percent in 1984. This policy of expansion in both private and public sectors led to inflation, which made the crisis even more acute. Most of the increase in public expenditure was due to substantial increases in the costs of the social security system. The political change meant a greater assumption of governmental responsibility for this function, which in itself meant greater public spending, and at the same time the economic crisis was creating new public needs, as demonstrated by unemployment figures. In 1975 there were 540,000 unemployed persons in Spain; at the close of 1984 there were 2,869,000, and the forecast was that before the end of 1985 the number of unemployed would surpass three million. Expenditures on unemployment rose from 9.3 percent of GDP in 1975 to 15 percent in 1983 and 14.8 percent in 1984.

As far as payments into social security were concerned, there was a notable increase in contributions, which in 1975 amounted to 10.3 percent of GDP, but rose to 13.2 percent in 1983 and 12.7 percent in 1984. On the other hand, the balance between indirect and direct taxation did not change until 1980 even though it had been an objective of fiscal reform since 1977.[2] In 1981 the balance reverted to its 1979 structure, where it remained until 1984.

The public sector, due to the economic crisis, also faced declining revenues, which had to be compensated for by greater pressure to contain the deficit, which met with little success. The deficit rose to 5.9 percent of GDP in 1983, then leveled out at 4.8 percent in 1984.

When the political change occurred, it was said that the economic community would demand fiscal reform for two purposes: first, to achieve growth in the public sector in order to meet existing social demands and, second, to provide greater equity in the fiscal system. A reform of great technical complexity was drawn up according to fiscal rationality criteria, but containing all the usual margins of error. The apocalyptic terms in which this fiscal reform was couched, rather than its actual content, has contributed to scaring off productive capital investment. A surplus of money in the hands of the public and the rigidity of the market pushed up market interest rates, making it still more difficult to provide incentives to invest, which were already dampened by lack of familiarity with the political system and fiscal uncertainty.

What role has public finance and those who are advisers played in making recommendations for and influencing the direction of taxation during this important transition period in Spain? We turn to this question now.

II. Governance in a New Democracy

Even though political nonconformity was prohibited under Franco, civil servants, because of their professional qualifications and scientific theories, were gradually able to influence politicians to follow certain courses of action. They did not directly oppose the current orthodoxy; rather, their theories were adopted by those in power and put into practice. All of us who lived in Spain during those years know well that administrators, economists, and architects imposed certain patterns on legislation and practice which lay to the left of the ideology of the politicians of the time. Technicians also acquired a force and weight in formulating policies that they do not usually exert in democratic governments.

With the advent of democracy the functions which politicians, civil servants, and technicians had exercised became less clearly defined, more diverse, and at the same time strengthened. Now not only was it possible to disagree with other opinions, but it became fashionable to do so. Even academic opinions, which had before been asserted in semiclandestine manner and with remarkable unanimity, became, under conditions of freedom of thought, multiple, divergent, and frequently clashing. These first years of democracy in Spain have seen a readjustment in responsibilities and functions. Those who govern as direct or indirect representatives of the people—do not overlook the fact that in Spain such a relationship is a new development—can be grouped into three major categories: politicians, technical experts, and civil servants. All are new to their respective functions, but a more precise definition of their separate roles is taking shape. One can also begin to detect the development of a professional hierarchy.

Politicians and Theorists

In Spain, the civil servant, or, if you wish, the administrative executive, is in charge of carrying out decisions made at the political level, with the additional assistance, on a parallel but not executive level, of a host of technicians. The senior civil servant is formally required to be a university graduate, but does not necessarily use the subject he studied—we find engineers in the ministry of economy and history graduates in the ministry of public works. Only the technician operates solely on the strength of his specialized knowledge, but his role is always the secondary one of advisor or consultant. The technician never makes decisions or carries them out, but provides information and advice on the means available for achieving certain aims. To put it in a nutshell, the politician decides, the civil servant performs, and the technical expert advises.

In practice, however, things are not quite so simple. Even the thesis that the technical expert must abstain from any discussion of the objectives to be attained in order to concentrate on analyzing means and ends is presently being questioned. Some are of the opinion that the economic adviser should make plain his basic beliefs and that, once a decision has been taken, he need not refrain from recommending the policies he prefers. Differences of opinion among economists should not be a reason for silencing them.

The truth is that politicians resent this active participation of the technicians in the adoption of political decisions. Not very long ago, during the administrations of the Union del Centro Democrático, the press reported that the head of the Spanish government was attending classes in economics to acquaint himself with the theoretical intricacies of such a complex science. Apart from the futility of undertaking such a task while carrying other responsibilities that would in themselves monopolize the attention of anyone, the news highlighted the fact that politicians in Spain were confusing technical advice with strictly political decisions. The inexperience of our politicians can be illustrated by a statement of Chancellor Helmut Schmidt, made to the press, at roughly the same time, that years before he had been an economics professor at a German university, but that he now kept his knowledge of economics in the background since his mission was to lead the nation, which meant that he did not have time to keep up with current academic trends.

In Spain under Franco, the only way of dissenting from the ruling authority, with all due caution, was to express oneself in scientific fashion. Those of us who couched subjects in scientific terms sufficiently abstruse as to be over the heads of the censors were able to put on record unorthodox opinions. Economists began to recommend policies based on theoretical concepts that were adapted to their aims and objectives. In this way, a more liberal economic policy was urged on a Spanish economy that remained largely tied to an autarchic framework. By the same token technical experts, converted into technocrats, acquired a measure of power that at times had a mollifying effect on the dictatorship and on other occasions lent it a sense of academic respectability and guided it along better-thought-out lines. The inclination of technicians to take political positions led them to put their theoretical knowledge at the service of the politician. We are afraid that in Spain, still engaged in the transition toward greater freedom, where governments are still influenced by the situations they have inherited, that politicians have not yet come to understand that they have a role separate from that of the technicians. It also seems to us that the technicians do not fully appreciate that, upon the arrival of democracy, they should take second place.

Politicians and Civil Servants

In principle the politician represents social interests. But in the modern industrial world, states are administered and run by public servants. The role of bureaucracy in modern states cannot be ignored. We have the impression that civil servants have pondered long over what Marx said about the state being at the service of the dominant class. We fear that as the state, or its functionaries—which amounts to the same thing—increased in power during the last years of the nineteenth century and throughout the twentieth century, fuctionaries became aware of that fact and decided to establish themselves in their own right and to serve their own interests, above all. And let us make it clear that we are speaking about our western democracies.

In the Spanish parliament one rarely hears flowery speeches of inflamed rhetoric and expansive imagery. Our chamber becomes heated only on exceptional issues, especially when it is discussing the salaries of quantity surveyors employed by the ministry of public works or the professional situation of engineers or architects of the finance ministry and, in general, the wages or pensions of civil servants. This is principally because many members of parliament are civil servants themselves, a group that has prestige in Spanish society and which can, as a class, exert influence on politicians.

Civil servants are on the firing line every day. Their influence is unavoidable. Democratic politics are still full of dilemmas and uncertainties for our politicians. This is not true, however, of civil servants, who know how to distinguish what affects them directly and immediately.

The technicians, however—or the economists, to be more precise—do not all hold the same theoretical convictions; there is no single voice to defend or promote a determined course of action. No single opinion seems to prevail concerning any one problem. And although this situation says much for our profession, which believes in freedom of thought, it weakens our credibility as advisers.

Clearly, however, if theory is to have any influence in politics, there must be points of agreement among the theorists, or technicians as we prefer to call them, in order to win the ear of politicians and civil servants. Recently Bruno S. Frey and others attempted to throw light on this question by conducting an opinion poll among almost three thousand economists of various countries, of whom 45 percent responded. The poll was prompted by a statement in a publication: "There is a large degree of consensus in economic doctrine, but much less unanimity in practical economic policy." Shortly after, the *Herald Tribune*, complaining about disagreement among professional economists, wrote: "Hardly anybody has a good word for economists, not even economists themselves." Yet what economists think is important because it affects economic policy.

It is therefore not surprising that Spanish politicians, still not wholly accustomed to freedom of political opinion, should find little comfort and guidance in conflicting academic advice.

They respond increasingly to public opinion—gaining favorable electoral results, but perhaps listening and gaining less from economists. On the other hand, Spanish politicians are becoming more and more adept at sounding out public opinion, which in practice means obtaining favorable electoral results. We would all probably agree, however, that the general public is not always right, nor that when it holds opinions it is for the right reason. If what Keynes said is true, that behind the opinions of a politician can always be found ideas conceived much earlier by an economist, it does not seem that public opinion is very familiar with what scientists, or even politicians, think.

In short, the advent of democracy in Spain has brought politicians to the forefront of the stage, yet neither public opinion nor the supposed experts seem to be in a position to give them much guidance.

Notes

1. The names of the lectures are "Civil Servants, Theorists and Politicians in Spain" by Ramon Trias Fargas and "The Public Sector in Spain: Current Problems" by Jose Raga.
2. Direct taxes were 6.0 of G.D.P. in 1979 and 7.0% in 1980 while indirect taxes were 6.3% and 6.5% in these same years.

Résumé

Ce rapport est la synthèse de deux conférences faites par les auteurs au congrès de l'I.I.F.P. La première partie expose les modifications dans le rôle du secteur public, avant et après le régime franquiste. On met en évidence les difficultés quand on cherche à accroître l'équité par des politiques de redistribution durant une période de faible performance économique. Dans la seconde partie du rapport, on discute du rôle des finances publiques et des conseillers en finances publiques durant la période de transition. On pose la question de savoir s'il est ou non judicieux que les praticiens de finances publiques discutent les objectifs. Enfin, on souligne la difficulté de rester neutre et de n'offrir qu'un avis technique.

The Role of Public Finance in Socialist Economies

Boris Boldyrev, Vladimir Ilyin, Nikolai Sichev

Under socialism, management of the national economy is a state function and public finance is therefore macroeconomic in character. Financial relations reflect the socialist state's active role in regulating economic relations and guiding the economic basis of society.

In the socialist economy, finance is the monetary expression of the relationships between socialist enterprises as they acquire stocks of commodities and materials and sell products and services, and as funds are redistributed between plants and organizations for capital investment and between the state and enterprises. Payments from the enterprises go into the budget, which in turn funds capital investment and spending on social programs.

Finance is also instrumental in relations between enterprises and their workers, who are paid for their work, and between the state and individual citizens, who make mandatory and voluntary payments.

Soviet finance comprises national finance, the finance of enterprises and corporations and of other economic agents.

Accordingly, financial operations involve two major, interconnected sets of relations: centrally regulated money relations to meet the financial requirements of both productive and nonproductive spheres, and relations on a profit-and-loss basis, which ensure that plants and amalgamations can be self-supporting financially.

The basis of the Soviet financial system is the finance of socialist enterprises, corporations, other economic agents and branches. With their direct participation, the national product is created and distributed.

At present, finance is playing an increasing role in planned management, owing chiefly to the following factors:

1. A considerable increase in the volume of financial assets and the need to carry out large-scale socioeconomic and scientific-technical programs requiring large one-level outlays.

2. The growing role of finance in balanced economic growth through a

The Relevance of Public Finance for Policy-Making. Proceedings of the 41st Congress of the International Institute of Public Finance. Madrid, 1985, pp. 259–263.

closer and more flexible dovetailing in the movement of the material and value proportions of socialized production.

3. Continued development of cost-accounting relations in the activities of enterprises and corporations, whose enlargement depends on enhancing the effectiveness of financial levers and instruments.

The Dynamics and Structure of Financial Resources at Present

A major issue in economic policy has been and remains that of financial assets, which are indispensable for the development of socialized production.

The large scale of the socialist economy means that there is a considerable volume of financial assets. More than 2.5 trillion rubles have been directed to implementing the programs of the Eleventh Five-Year Plan (1981–1985), an amount that is 20 percent higher than for the preceding five-year plan. The growth rates of financial assets exceed the rates of growth of national income. This trend has prevailed in past years and will continue in the future owing to higher rates of growth of net profit and of the depreciation fund, relative to overall national income.

We can characterize the financial assets of the USSR's economy by analyzing their structure and the changes taking place in their various sources. Financial assets derive from the profits of state-owned enterprises and organizations, net revenues from the turnover taxes of collective farms, depreciation charges, deductions from the social security fund, proceeds from state insurance of property and life, taxes and excises paid by the population, etc. All of these revenues are created in the process of distributing and redistributing the social product and the country's national income. Changes occur in the structure of these sources if the formation of financial assets reflects the intensification of the economy, a continuing enlargement of its scale, and a change in the size of components of socialized production.

Profit is the most important source of financial assets. During the Eleventh Five-Year Plan, profits will total 720,000 million rubles, representing a 40 percent increase in constant prices. The growth of profit results chiefly from increase in the volume of output and a reduction of the prime cost of the products.

The turnover tax is also an important source of financial assets, and will also increase by 40 percent in the Eleventh Five-Year Plan period. Changes being made in the structure of the turnover tax paid by industries mean that the share of its receipts from heavy industry are increasing.

Its size and share of the depreciation fund in financial assets is growing: in the Eleventh Five-Year Plan period, the fund will represent 17.4 percent of financial assets in 1985, as compared to 15.5 percent in 1980.

The centralized financial fund for state insurance of property and life is projected to increase by 36.2 percent over the preceding Five-Year Plan period.

State financial assets are also formed through the social insurance payments from corporations, enterprises, and other organizations. Personal taxes play a small role in the formation of financial assets. In 1985, they will represent only 5.5 percent of this asset total.

Financial assets are formed in both a centralized and decentralized manner. The size and the optimum correlation of centralized and decentralized assets are determined from plans for the country's economic and social development. Most financial assets are concentrated in the hands of the state: over the period 1980–1984, 65.3 percent of all financial assets were accumulated in the state budget of the USSR. The rest was used directly by enterprises, amalgamations, and organizations for the development of production and to provide economic incentives.

This encourages corporations and enterprises to ensure optimum use and mobilization of the material and financial resources in the economy.

Planning for the formation and use of financial assets is embodied in the consolidated balance sheet of the economy, implemented by the State Planning Committee (GOSPLAN). The balance sheet includes the financial assets of the state, collective farms, consumer cooperatives, public organizations, etc., as well as long- and short-term credit funds.

Implementation of the consolidated balance sheet increases the impact of finance on the whole process of national economic planning, improves the interconnection of all day-to-day financial balance sheets, and ensures coordination of production, economic and financial indicators.

Participation of Finance in Extended Reproduction

Both the finance of amalgamations, enterprises, and branches and national finance, composed chiefly of the state budget funds, influence the processes of production, distribution, and utilization of the social product and national income.

In the current stage of development of the Russian economy, finance is taking a larger role in the increased production of enterprises, owing to expansion of their financial rights of production, the larger volume of financial assets left at their disposal, greater economic and material incentives for their workers, and their growing responsibility for the formation and utilization of key assets.

The state budget, which is the nation's main day-to-day, coordinating finance, is closely linked to all branches of socialized production and has a decisive impact on the productive process. Most of the financial assets accruing from organizations and enterprises are concentrated in the state budget. The development of the economy is ensured to a considerable extent through budget funds.

During the Eleventh Five-Year Plan period, the contribution of finance to production has grown. More than 1.6 trillion rubles have been appropriated from all sources for economic development. In this period, the role of the budget is to expand production as a result of a more rational distribution, redistribution, and utilization of financial resources among the branches of the economy, economic regions, and republics for development of the country's productive force. The budget will play a larger role in coordinating the financial plans of the branches of the national economy, and in tapping the reserves of the economy and strengthening financial control over the activities of economic organizations and ministries.

The Role of Finance in Enhancing the Effectiveness of Socialized Production

Understandably, the growing role of finance in the socialist economy is due not only to the steady growth of financial resources themselves, although this is very important, but also to the growing impact of the financial mechanism on the development and increasing effectiveness of the socialist economy. The degree and effectiveness of the impact of finance on economic development is determined in large measure by improvement in the financial mechanism, the quality of financial plans, and the effectiveness of financial instruments and levers. The financial mechanism of the socialist economy is developing and improving as it adapts to new conditions and requirements for development of the socialist economy.

At present, the most important direction of the financial mechanism is toward increasing its impact on economic intensification, which takes place in several ways. The three most important are (1) improvement of the process of financial planning; (2) change in the relationships between state enterprises and the budget in the area of distribution and centralization of revenues; (3) greater financial incentives for better use of material, labor and financial resources.

1. Improvement in financial planning can be seen in greater emphasis on long-term planning. Today financial plans are drawn up at all levels for the entire five-year period, with targets distributed over certain years. This is a new stage in financial planning for in the past targets were restricted to yearly plans.

2. Changes have been introduced into the relationship between enterprises and the state budget. This relationship is based on the principle of "normative distribution of profit". The essence of this method is that the ministries and enterprises are assigned in advance their share of funds, to be

appropriated for their own needs, such as funds for development of production, science and technology, and creation of the necessary incentives. The remainder is allocated to the budget. In addition, to enhance the responsibility that the ministries and enterprises bear for the budget, they must guarantee a certain contribution to it.

This method on the one hand creates conditions for greater independence of the ministries and enterprises in utilizing financial assets, and on the other enhances their responsibility to the state in regard to fulfillment of their financial obligations.

3. The third trend consists of broader development of those financial instruments and incentives that have direct impact on better utilization of the productive, labor, material, and financial resources at the disposal of enterprises. This is evident in the payments that the enterprises make to the budget, whose size depends on the resources they have at their disposal. These payments are constructed in such a way as to stimulate better utilization of production and water resources and thus ensure their rational use.

Restructuring of management and planning provides a stronger scientific basis for current and long-term plans and more balance among them; greater orientation of indicators toward final economic results and the interests of the consumer; more skillful utilization of financial incentives and credit instruments, cost accounting, the system of payment for work, prices and other economic incentives; the introduction of a stable (five-year) payment standard for the funds, a standard method for redistribution of profit and formation of the wage and material incentives funds; and improvement of the organizational structure of management in all branches of the economy. The financial mechanism will be perfected according to and on the basis of these measures.

Résumé

Les ressources financières jouent un rôle important dans la réalisation des objectifs économiques et sociaux de l'Etat soviétique. La plus importante partie des ressources financières est constituée par le revenu net, sous forme de bénéfices et d'impôt sur le chiffre d'affaires, ainsi que par les prélèvements pour dépréciation.

Pendant la période de l'actuel Plan de cinq ans, les finances entrent pour une grande part dans la croissance de la production, son intensification et les demandes de planification, d'administration et de méthodes de gestion.

Some Gratuitous Advice to Fiscal Advisers

Alan Peacock*

1. Introduction

1.1   In the early days of this century a Cambridge don, F. M. Cornford, wrote a splendid tract called *Microcosmographia Academica*, designed as a guide to the young academic who sought to understand the politics of academe. Though it is based wholly on Cambridge life, which is really a *rara avis* in the world of universities, the work has an immediate appeal to anyone interested in politics in general. The work is still in print. Let me give you a quote from it which is germane to this lecture:

> You think . . . . that you have only to state a reasonable case, and people must listen to reason and act on it as well? It is just this conviction that makes you so unpleasant . . . . If you want to move people you must address your arguments to prejudice and the political motive . . . . You would rather batter away at the Shield of Faith than spy out the joints in the harness.

1.2   This lecture does not seek to emulate Cornford's profundity and wit, but is written in the belief that it may be useful to say something about the "barriers to entry" into the advice business which beset those of us who have been attracted by the prospect of applying the science of public finance to the problems of government. Nor does it assume in a gathering of this kind that I am speaking only to novitiates. To those who have not had the opportunity to test out their ideas, perhaps my warning signals will be useful. To those who have had the opportunity and have grasped it, I hope to recall to you some of your own experiences which are worth retailing. To those who have rejected the opportunity to have anything to do with government, I suspect that I offer some reasons why you may have made a wise decision. Though I use the binding force of economic analysis to bring my ideas together, I am all too aware that my experience, like Cornford's, is peculiar, and I would not presume to believe that any universal propositions can be drawn from it.

*The author is Research Professor in Public Finance, The Esmee Fairbairn Research Centre, Heriot-Watt University, Edinburgh and Executive Director of the David Hume Institute, Edinburgh.

The Relevance of Public Finance for Policy-Making. Proceedings of the 41st Congress of the International Institute of Public Finance. Madrid, 1985, pp. 265–276.

2. Proposition 1: "Beware the Optimization Paradigm"

2.1   A typical policy model employed by economists in attempting to justify their own role in policy-making assumes:
(i) Governments have objectives in which trade-offs are clear and which can be translated into some quantitative form, i.e., appear as terms in a set of equations.
(ii) Governments maximize these objectives subject to constraints, which are known and accepted. Problems arise in defining the extent of constraints, including admission of "feedback" (see, for example, Alt and Chrystal [1]).
(iii) Governments have an interest in choosing instruments which minimize the "cost" of implementing policies, including feed-back effects.

2.2   If the economic and political system were subject to conditions which would exercise skills similar to that of a control engineer, then the role of advisers would be clear. They would have a clearly scientific role designed to improve the *predictive* capacity of economic and political models so that the precise relations between the dependent variables—the policy aims—and the independent variables—the instruments—would be known as far as possible. Research effort would undergo constant adaptation as the government welfare function changed or as new instruments needed to be devised as old ones "wore out." Politicians would choose policies, and economic and political advisers—heavily influenced by research input—would choose the instruments. Some economists, notably Ragnar Frisch, the Nobel Laureate in Economics, have claimed that in fulfilling their professional role in government as advisers backed by first-class research effort, the economists would create a political consensus in respect of economic policies (see Bergh [2]).

2.3   In a general sort of way the type of macro-economic policy models used by those responsible for economic planning performs the kinds of coordinating function suggested by our paradigm. It forces policy makers to specify targets which can be translated into dependent variables for which values can be found, for example inflation measured by a consumers' price index or numbers unemployed. It allows economic advisers to specify the quantifiable links between movements in these target variables and the "mix" of policy instruments (taxes, borrowing and expenditure variables) in the "right" direction. It gives direction to the research effort necessary to establish these links in a fully articulated macro-economic model and to the properties of the computation system which has to be able to offer sensible and speedy simulations of policy scenarios.

At the same time, it must be realised that such models can only embody a strictly limited range of objectives, primarily short-term ones, which can be given quantitative expression. Their usefulness depends on much more than econometric skill but on the judgment which enters into the choice of the values of certain important independent variables, notably concerning the anticipated behavior of trading partners which has to be reflected in forecasts of the volume of world trade. Furthermore, their influence on policy depends on their credibility with politicians in power who are not necessarily impressed by the technical skill of the model builders. In short, the macro-economic policy models convey a very restricted view of the skills required in advising governments on fiscal matters as well as a false impression of the kind of situation in which the fiscal adviser may find himself.

2.4 It is paradoxical that it has been certain branches of economic research which have led some economists to question the relevance of the paradigm itself, which would be a convenient myth to perpetuate if one wanted to create the most congenial conditions for advisers and their research staffs. Let me elaborate this point. The development of public choice theory and the associated economic theory of bureaucracy has led professional economists to look closely at the motivation of politicians and bureaucrats, to build models of their behavior and to devise testable predictions of the consequences of their attempts to maximize their utility. This is not the place to evaluate the contribution to our understanding of government of the economics of politics. I would only remark that its value in this context lies in the attention drawn to certain facets of political and administrative behavior which are relevant to the understanding of the forces governing the "supply" and "demand' for policy advice in government.

2.5 If it is broadly true, following Downs, that political parties in power endeavor to maximize their length of life in office, then it may not be in the interests of a government to specify too exactly its economic and social targets for fear of political "backlash." If targets such as the rate of unemployment and inflation matter, there may be a temptation to operate a "political business cycle" in order to win elections. Individual politicians as members of a government may trade off their political ambitions within their party against the need for collective responsibility for decision-making. They will differ in their degree of commitment to government objectives and also to the choice of instruments which, as department heads, they have under their immediate control. The monitoring of the actions of public officials, we are told, is so difficult because they have discretionary power which enables them to promote policies of their own as well as to pursue their personal ambitions, material and otherwise. As the objectives of all these various parts of government and those whose actions they seek to control—industry and consumers—conflict, and as each group has weapons as its disposal to influence if not to deny the "supply" of services upon which the other depends, then the "control system paradigm" is inapplicable and needs to be replaced by one which highlights the importance of multisector bargaining (see Peacock, [5]).

2.6 This view of the process of government presents a very different picture of the problems facing the adviser within and outside government and working for government deparments and agencies. The choice of advisers, their terms of reference and the purpose of their advice, as well as the use made of it, will be conditioned by very different forces than those that would obtain if the monolithic view of coordinated and "objective" policy making implicit in the original paradigm is considered relevant.

3. Proposition 2: "There is no 'Welcome' Mat Spread before You"

3.1   You are an economist with a good training and a good research and publication record behind you and you are asked to join a department of government concerned with economic affairs—it might be industrial matters—to give general economic advice. You are excited at the prospect and are bubbling over with ideas for immediate execution. Hold yourself in check. As a wise predecessor of mine in government advised me: do not announce your arrival except to those who pay you. Do not look for work. Let everyone else find out for themselves that you exist—even ministers. Only respond, do not initiate. This gives you six months to find out what is going on, and who will take you seriously and who will not. Why did he say this? Let me explain.

3.2   Take first of all your system of values. You may be tempted to say that your values are irrelevant and that you are there to demonstrate the virtues of fiscal economics as a positive science. The first thing that will happen is that you will find an administrator with a training in philosophy who proves that your Paretian or your Neo-Utilitarian axioms which "demonstrate" the desirability of certain types of taxes and tax schedules in preference to others are nothing more than political nostrums in disguise. If you adopt the other tack and say that you are content to accept the value judgments of others and to examine their implications for the design of tax systems, incredulity will be written over the faces of your audience, and at least one unkind member of it will say that you are the kind of person who would be willing to do a cost-benefit study of the design of torture chambers. In this Catch-22 situation, particularly if you are young or young-ish, it is better to admit some political bias. To say that you have Social Democratic leanings will probably make you sound respectable and relatively harmless.

3.3   Second, your professional competence will be subject to ordeal by skepticism. Practically every senior administrator believes that he is at least as good a fiscal economist as you are and that only the doctrine of comparative advantage prevents him arguing for the abolition of your post. You will be put to the test through the obvious device of showing that the government macro-economic model performs worse than those of outsiders and that all such models contain margins of error which are greater than the GDP changes which you wish to see brought about by budgetary means. You have to admit this and a possible reply is to claim that such models perform at least marginally better than "back of the envelope" calculations and, if you are brave, ask your questioner to give particular reasons why he thinks the model performs badly so that you can help to rectify it. Nine times out of ten you can point out to him, tactfully of course, that his "model" embodies much stronger assumptions than that of the economists. There will usually be one senior administrator who positively welcomes your presence. Avoid him or her if you can. Unsullied by an economics education, he has probably been working away for years on an economic theory of his own which will save the economy—it is usually a crude variant of single-tax theory. He will want to spend hours with you, his kindred spirit, and if you tell him he is a crank you may have made an enemy for life. The general line to take with your colleagues can be summed up in a paraphrase of the wise words of Alice Rivlin, that distinguished public financier and ex-director of the U.S. Congressional Budget Office: "The main problem with economists is that we make decisions harder for you, but you can't do without us" (see Rivlin [6], for the original statement).

3.4 It must follow that any "original" views you may have about the use of policy instruments are not likely to be greeted with cries of approval. All forms of tax reform, you will discover, have been proposed before. Of those, as in the Gospel of St. Matthew, Chapter 22 verse 14, "many are called but few are chosen." Those that get through are probably the legacy of some quite catastrophic event, such as the survival of the income tax after the Napoleonic Wars and the system of Pay as You Earn taxation, its great-grandson, after the Second World War. From time to time, intelligent but inexperienced ministers who consult outside advisers may insist on the "working-up" of schemes which have some passing intellectual attraction strong enough to require administrators to respond. I went through an elaborate exercise in which I had to produce at very short notice a scheme for preventing wage inflation in which employers were to be taxed if they allowed wage claims which exceeded some policy "norm." Various "placebos" were built into the variants of the scheme, including the compulsory investment of the tax in shares in the offending company which would ultimately become the property of employees. Senior administrators watched with amused tolerance as the scheme went through the various hurdles which they had erected to prevent it reaching the status of a Cabinet paper. They slept easily in their beds for they knew that even having reached that stage it would be rejected, as indeed it was, without discussion. You begin to realise that the inventor of the Value Added Tax, Maurice Laure, must have been a genius in salesmanship as well as an accomplished expert in fiscal matters. In short your "triumphs" will be measured in terms of the fresh arguments that you can produce in order to impede rather than to promote change, always making it clear to your political boss that you are anxious to prevent him or her from contracting that fatal disease of the politically ambitious—ridicule.

4. Proposition 3: "The Part Is Greater than the Whole"

4.1 A few years ago two of my young colleagues at York were invited to write a report on some aspects of the economics of income taxation in a South American country. They were very shocked at their reception and possibly even more shocked when I told them I was not surprised at their experience. As they stepped off the plane, they were met by a charming young official from the Ministry of Economic Planning who gave them a list of the conclusions which his ministry expected them to reach about tax reform. This attack on their professional virtue was renewed by the Revenue Service, which informed them through an equally charming official that full cooperation was assured, provided that they would feel able to reach the conclusion that no changes in the structure of the income tax were necessary! One cannot blame my colleagues for not having been brought face to face with my proposition 3: "The part is greater than the whole." But our friend Cornford knew this, as I shall now explain.

4.2 Cornford spent some time in government and noted with regret that academic life was one genus of a larger species. "College feeling" was a kind of parochial loyalty corresponding to "departmental feeling" in government, which "like other species of patriotism, consists in a sincere belief that the institution to which you belong is better than the institution to which other people belong." It is certainly my experience that departmental loyalties are extremely important in government and are reinforced in the United Kingdom by the placing of cabinet ministers in administrative charge of a department. This offers them the strong temptation to employ the policy instruments that they control in order to dramatize their policy role, subject to the overall constraint of having to accept some collective political strategy at cabinet level if only in the interests of preserving political credibility with the electorate. Just as nations or indeed football teams have "anthems" which prescribe the nature and bounds of this patriotic feeling, departments have crude symbols of their aims. Therefore, the purpose of the Inland Revenue in the United Kingdom is summed up in the phrase "protect the revenue at all costs," whereas the Treasury is there to "protect the expenditure estimates." Ministries of Agriculture and Industry are somewhat cynically regarded as "captives" of farmers and industrialists respectively, whereas in the United Kingdom, at least, the famous Board of

Trade (now incorporated in the Department of Trade and Industry) has long been in the business of trying to stop ministers from erecting tariff barriers.

4.3 It is easy to see that as governments took on more and more direction of the economy, economic coordination, blissfully assumed to be already in being the policy paradigm of economists, becomes more and more essential—and more and more difficult to achieve. Even if there is lipservice to such coordination, there will be strong competition between departments, spurred on by the natural ambitions of ministers and senior officials, to be "in the lead" in economic policy matters. At the very least—and this is where the adviser has an important role—such ambitions cannot be realized without the minister and his senior officials being manifestly well informed on economic matters, and, if possible, better informed than "rival" ministries.

4.4 Let me quote an example from experience. The perceived task of the Department of Trade and Industry in the United Kingdom is to protect the interests of industry (if not of industrialists) whether or not these interests coincide with the interests of other groups "sponsored" by other departments. In 1974, in the shadow of the famous Oil Crisis, a long-drawn-out battle took place against the Treasury and the Inland Revenue in order to obtain relief for industry from profits taxation through a change in the method of valuing their stocks, which would have offended against the doctrine of "protect the revenue at all costs." One of the main factors in achieving "victory" (as the DTI saw it) was the fact that the department controlled the main sources of financial information and the speed of their general release within government. Officials were thoroughly primed in the ways in which this information could be used to support their case.

4.5 This points towards a dilemma for the professional adviser on fiscal matters. On the one hand, his professional influence in a department may be a function of his willingness to be one of a team promoting departmental interests, acting as a kind of expert witness or, put more crudely, as a "hired gun." On the other hand, repeatedly advising on professional grounds against a course of action to which senior officials and ministers are committed hardly helps one to win friends and influence people.

4.6 Nobody can resolve this dilemma for the adviser, though I am convinced that sticking to one's professional guns is not only a morally unassailable but also an expedient position to take. One is not necessarily without allies if one takes an uncomprising professional line and provided one does not claim that fiscal analysis is the revealed truth. It may not always be possible for a "departmental line" to be clearly drawn, in which case one may find allies from within. If the decision to be taken involves interdepartmental negotiation, as is often the case in fiscal matters, then a "coalition of economists" across departments can be quite a formidable pressure group. At the very least, if one is maximizing long-run utility and is not wedded to working in government forever, it hardly does one's professional reputation any good if one becomes known as a "trimmer"— and such news travels very fast.

5. Proposition 4: "Put Not Thy Trust in Princes"

5.1   I have concentrated so far on advisers on fiscal matters who are employed by government, but have not considered the position of advisers who may be brought in to make recommendations *ad hoc*, as with specially appointed commissions or committees on matters of national importance such as a major tax reform. Although I have these kinds of adviser in mind, this is not to say that my views are not necessarily applicable to "internal" advice-giving situations. I choose the more "open" situation because it is perhaps more familiar to members of the IIPF, many of whom must have served on such bodies.

5.2   No homily on advice-giving would be complete without a reference to Machiavelli, and it is all set out for us in his *Discourses* (see Machiavelli, Modern Library Edition, 1950)—Book III, Chapter XXXV is ominously entitled: "Of the Danger of Being Prominent in Counselling Any Enterprise, and How that Danger Increases with the Importance of Such Enterprise." Machiavelli asks the question, what is the fate of the advice-giver if his advice is taken/not taken and if it is accepted/not accepted? We can construct a "pay-off" matrix representing the marginal utility *to the advice-giver* of alternative outcomes:

	Advice Right	Advice Wrong
Advice Taken	?	?
Advice Not Taken	?	?

Our Italian political philosopher is quite explicit about the signs in the elements! If your advice is taken by the prince or republic and is wrong, then your enemies destroy you. If it is taken and it is right, then "glory is not assured," particularly if your advice contravenes that of others. If your advice is not taken and is wrong you will be ignored, and if it is not taken and you are right, then you may be in credit and be listened to more carefully in future. You would have thought that Machiavelli would have advised his readers to keep out of the advice game, but, thinking of prominent people, he claims that for them to withhold counsel would be to risk the charge of disloyalty. (For them, unfortunately, it is the only game in town!) He concludes that if you are forced willy-nilly into the position of giving advice, then do not advocate any enterprise "with too much zeal" but "give one's advice calmly and modestly." Amen to that!

5.3   As with many creative minds, what interests us in their speculations is the methodology rather than the results and this example from Machiavelli is no exception. I would make two points about it of relevance to advice-giving. The first is that whereas Machiavelli'a game players are forced to play and for high stakes, we consider a situation where no one is forced either to give or to take advice and where the consequences of being wrong or right are fortunately nothing like so severe. In consequence we find that the supply of advice is very inelastic with respect to money price and the position of the supply curve is such that a very large quantity of it will be supplied free. Economists are falling over themselves to tell governments what to do about fiscal matters and the main ingredient of positive utility is more likely to the the prospect of a respectable professional audience in a refereed journal than of being taken seriously by government. (I have known economists say that the moment when governments like their ideas is the moment to reconsider them very carefully!) It is an added bonus if one gets paid by anyone for expounding one's views on what the government budgetary policy ought to be. In practice, one finds that a large segment of government demand for fiscal advice consists of requests to internal fiscal advisers to provide a running commentary on the relevance of the countless proposals emanating from a whole range of sources. Only very occasionally will this commentary lead to the stage where it will be followed up, perhaps by hiring the originator of the idea as a consultant.

5.4   The second point concerns the position of the *ad hoc* adviser who presumably has taken on the job of heading up a commission or a committee or joining one of these bodies because he or she will derive positive utility from giving right advice and having it taken, otherwise he or she would not be in the game. Anyone in this position should think very carefully about *assigning probabilities to the outcomes*. As my previous exposition indicates, it is far from certain that there will be agreement within government as to what would constitute good advice, given the shifting power structure and conflicts of interests within government. Even if you satisfy the "prince" (i.e., the minister) who has hired you, the politics of government may force him to make bargains with his colleagues who have different interests and the cost to him may be the sacrifice of your proposals. So when I quote the Psalms: "put not your trust in princes." I am not saying that princes are untrustworthy but that they may not be able to deliver.

5.5   Let me give an example. In late 1983 the Conservative government decided to review the state pension scheme. Index-linked, earnings-related, and with a growing proportion of pensioners per head of population, the scheme, as with many others in Western Europe, threatens to become a formidable fiscal burden. I was taken on as adviser to the Government Inquiry into Retirement Provision along with two others. Although the chairman was the Secretary of State for Health and Social Security, he was surrounded by ministers representing employment, trade, tax, and budgetary matters, all being briefed by departmental officials. My own proposal was to scrap the earnings-related element in the state scheme, though to retain some fiscal advantages for voluntary saving for retirement and to raise the basic flat-rate pension to protect the poor. The net result in budgetary terms would have been a rise in pensions expenditure in the short run compensated by a much greater fall in such expenditure in the longer run. The Treasury strongly opposed *any* immediate increase in expenditure as contrary to their "rule" (see 4.2 above), implying that any future savings should be subject to an infinite rate of discount. The "protection of the revenue" meant implacable opposition to anything smelling of a tax concession to savers, even though this might increase the rate of private saving as an offset to a fall in public saving. Neither of these bodies would allow the discussion to be extended to the case which could be made for cutting other kinds of spending or raising other taxes elsewhere in order both to meet their rigid rules and also to implement the pension scheme, even though they had no *locus standi* in the question of expenditure decisions which are a cabinet matter. The final proposals embody a series of compromises (see Secretary of State for Social Services [7]) and it is not at all certain that these proposals will be implemented. I have to be satisfied with the fact that my proposals got a "run for their money!"

6. Conclusion

6.1   Anyone who gives fiscal advice on a continuing basis within government will be expected not only to provide it but to "package" and "sell" it to his colleagues and superiors. This is not a job for the sensitive and nervous. It is also one which purists regard as at least potentially corrupting, for it tempts one to make compromises with one's analysis. For some this adds interest to the challenge of obtaining credibility for one's views but without losing one's professional virtue. For others, the burden may become too great to bear.

6.2   On the other hand, there are attractive professional as well as material rewards. The very nature of fiscal advice entails contact with a wide range of government activities and therefore the acquisition of considerable knowledge of the process of government. This knowledge, coupled with professional insight, is essential material for the formulation and testing of hypotheses associated with public choice theory and for the application of such hypotheses to the design of useful methods for controlling the size of government.

6.3 Even if your advice, continuous or *ad hoc*, is rarely taken, you can sing with Florestan in Beethoven's "Fidelio": "Süsser Trost in meinem Herzen, meine Pflicht hab' ich getan" ("The sweet consolation in my heart is that I have done my duty").

I am well aware that poor Florestan had to witness the digging of his own grave and was nearly murdered by his worst enemy, but he did triumph in the end! May you do the same without undergoing his vicissitudes.

References

[1] Alt, James E., and Chrystal, K. Alec, *Political Economics*, Part III, Harvester Press, Brighton, 1983.
[2] Bergh, Trond, "Norway: The Powerful Servants", in *Economists in Government: An International Economic Survey*, ed. A.W. Coats, Duke University Press, Durham, N.C., 1981.
[3] Cornford, F. M., *Microcosmographia Academica*, Bowes and Bowes, Cambridge, 1908.
[4] Machiavelli, Niccola, *The Prince and the Discourses*, Modern Library Edition, New York, 1950.
[5] Peacock, Alan, *Economic Analysis of Government*, Chap. 1, Martin Robertson, Oxford, 1979.
[6] Rivlin, Alice M. "An Intelligent Politician's Guide to Dealing with Experts", in *The Rand Graduate Institute: Commencement Address 1974–83*, Rand Graduate Institute, June 1983.
[7] Secretary of State for Social Services, *Reform of Social Security: Programme for Change*, Her Majesty's Stationary Office, London, June 1985.

Résumé

L'analyse économique peut servir à démontrer l'existence de "barrières à l'entrée", à l'encontre des économistes qui souhaitent donner des avis au gouvernement. L'auteur présente quatre propositions pour illustrer sa thèse:
1. "Méfions-nous du paradigme de l'optimisation". Les modèles économiques de macro-politique donnent une vue très restreinte des aptitudes des économistes à gouverner et une vue erronée sur la manière dont l'analyse économique est perçue en tant qu'instrument de gouvernement.
2. "Il n'y a pas de tapis de bienvenue déroulé devant vous". Les administrateurs opposent de vigoureuses résistances à la demande d'avis économiques, car ils pensent généralement qu'ils en connaissent autant, sinon plus, en matière de politique économique et financière, que les économistes.

3. "La partie est plus grande que le tout". Les départements ministériels sont rivaux dans l'offre de conseils politiques aux hommes politiques et placent leurs donneurs professionnels d'avis économiques et financiers dans la position d'échanger leur loyauté à l'égard du département ministériel contre leur probité professionnelle.

4. "Ne place pas ta confiance dans les princes". Même si l'avis économique et financier est respecté, il n'y a aucune garantie qu'il sera pris.

Le rapport conclut avec l'observation que le problème de "vendre" comme de "produire" un avis financier n'est évidemment pas pour les coeurs sensibles ou faibles.

De la "Théorie" au "Conseil" et à la "Politique": l'experience Française du Conseil des impôts*

*Pierre Llau**
et
*Guy Gilbert***

1—De l'analyse économique de la fiscalité au conseil

L'analyse des liens qui unissent la théorie économique aux conseils et avis en matière fiscale implique dans un premier temps une réflexion sur la nature de ces relations. Un second point précise les différentes dimensions de cette liaison du point de vue de l'analyse économique.

1.1. La nature des relations théorie-avis

Cette nature apparaît clairement si l'on considère l'avis comme un service susceptible d'être échangé sur un marché spécifique dont il convient de préciser les caractéristiques du point de vue de l'offre, de la demande ainsi que de leurs mécanismes de confrontation (A.Peacock-1981).

Du côté de l'offre, quatre groupes de "donneurs d'avis" peuvent être distingués : les "conseils fiscaux", qui exercent cette profession à titre principal et dont la formation est presque exclusivement juridique; un second groupe rassemble des donneurs d'avis plus occasionnels, universitaires de formation juridique ou économique, qui envisagent une activité secondaire de conseil fiscal comme champ d'application des hypothèses ou de résultats issus de l'analyse théorique. Les membres des administrations publiques fiscales ou non constituent une troisième catégorie de donneurs d'avis notamment lorsqu'ils appartiennent à un corps dont c'est la vocation explicite. Une dernière catégorie rassemble des membres d'assemblées ou de commissions parlementaires et d'une façon générale les spécialistes en fiscalité des partis politiques (1).

*Professeur à l'Université de Paris X-Nanterre, Membre du Conseil des Impôts 1983–84.
**Professeur à l'Université de Rennes I.

The Relevance of Public Finance for Policy-Making. Proceedings of the 41st Congress of the International Institute of Public Finance. Madrid, 1985, pp. 277–292.

La demande d'avis émane en général soit de l'administration, du gouvernement en place et des partis politiques, soit des groupes d'intérêts fiscaux à titre principal ou non (2). De même que pour l'offre d'avis mais plus nettement encore, la demande d'avis peut être interprétée comme le résultat d'un comportement de maximisation d'une fonction d'intérêt plus ou moins local ou catégoriel. Mais la demande d'avis résulte également des obligations faites par la loi de requérir en des circonstances précises des avis (discussions parlementaires, rapports du Conseil des Impôts, avis de ministères. . .); elle est donc en large partie administrée.

Peut-on au total parler d'un "marché" de l'avis? Cet échange est largement dominé par la demande dont les caractéristiques conditionnent les paramètres de l'offre. D'autre part, on ne peut guère observer sur ce "marché" les mouvements de prix et de quantités qui permettraient de le régler en permanence à l'équilibre. On peut s'interroger enfin sur l'unicité ou la multiplicité de marchés différents, ceux-ci correspondant aux aspects spécifiques de l'avis (juridique, administratif, politique et économique).

Ces brèves remarques relatives à la nature des relations qui président à l'échange d'avis sur la fiscalité n'ont d'autre but que de préciser le champ dans lequel s'insèrent les conclusions de l'analyse économique. *L'analyse économique apparaît ainsi sous le triple aspect d'un facteur inducteur de l'offre d'avis, d'un instrument d'expertise des effets supposés des mesures de politique fiscale, d'un élément de discours justificatif enfin.*

Les dimensions analytiques de l'instrument d'expertise seront développées au point suivant. La place de l'analyse économique en tant qu'élément de discours justificatif apparaît clairement si l'on considère les attendus des rapports majeurs qui ont marqué l'histoire de la fiscalité contemporaine (Commission Carter au Canada, Rapport Meade en Grande Bretagne, ou plus récemment aux USA le rapport relatif à la "Tax Reform for fairness, simplicity and economic growth", 1984) (3).

1.2 Les dimensions analytiques de la relation théorie économique-avis.

L'influence prédominante de la demande publique d'avis, *les canaux de transmission* qu'ils empruntent expliquent pour une large part la théorie économique sur laquelle ils se fondent.

Pour se limiter au cas de la France, les travaux demandés par le Conseil des Impôts, par les différents ministères, par le gouvernement et les cabinets ministériels, le sont pour l'essentiel à des services internes (4). Si tous ne sont pas des donneurs d'avis à titre principal, ils en sont souvent à l'origine (5); les instruments qu'ils utilisent leur permettent par ailleurs d'apprécier l'impact voire dans certains cas l'opportunité des mesures fiscales à l'étude. Si les avis sont requis par le demandeur, on conçoit d'abord qu'ils concernent à titre principal les *effets* des mesures à l'étude et non leur opportunité qui reste du domaine du décideur ; il s'agit là d'aspects exclusivement *positifs* de la discipline.

Ces instruments sont également typés du point de vue *paradigmatique*. L'usage est très généralisé dans l'administration économique de grands modèles macroéconométriques dont la référence à la macroéconomie keynésienne est le plus souvent revendiquée. Les comportements y sont plus sensibles en général aux effets-revenu des mesures du système fiscal qu'à des effets de substitution limités voire inexistants. Ainsi, aucun modèle d'équilibre général calculable ne permet aujourd'hui d'apporter une vision alternative des effets sur l'efficacité économique de la politique fiscale. Dans ces conditions, il est aisé d'expliquer l'absence en France de toute référence de quelque importance à l'approche des Choix Publics à l'appui de tout avis fiscal. Outre les réticences de divers ordres que suscitent les hypothèses et les conclusions propres à ce courant, on voit mal par ailleurs comment pourrait se répandre un mode d'analyse visant à endogénéiser l'action fiscale de l'Etat dans un contexte politique et institutionnel marqué de longue date par l'interventionisme public.

Enfin et en dépit de leur grande taille, les modèles macroéconométriques agrégés sont le plus souvent d'une précision insuffisante pour fournir une mesure fiable des effets de mesures fiscales ponctuelles. On recourt alors à des modèles de simulation (6) dont la vocation est de chiffrer précisément cet impact mais en général sans bouclage macroéconomique explicite.

Afin de préciser l'impact de l'analyse économique sur la production d'avis, l'on s'attachera maintenant à l'echo qu'ont pu rencontrer en France les débats et les progrès de la théorie au niveau des avis fiscaux.

Trois domaines seront brièvement examinés ; le problème du choix de la *base d'imposition optimale*, la nature graduelle ou non de la *réforme fiscale*, le traitement des *dépenses fiscales*.

Si l'on considére les acquis récents de la littérature relative à l'*impôt optimal*, la prétendue supériorité de l'impôt direct sur le revenu, ou de la base-dépense apparaissent aujourd'hui dépourvues de toute généralité. C'est notamment le cas lorsque l'on se situe dans un cadre d'équilibre général, lorsque l'on prend en compte les coûts d'information et d'administration (7). De même, aucune régle générale d'affectation d'un instrument fiscal à un objectif spécifique ne semble émerger : l'impôt progressif sur le revenu n'apparaît pas plus apte que l'impôt sur la dépense à atteindre des objectifs de redistribution. La littérature relative à l'impôt optimal en est au mieux à explorer "la grammaire des arguments" selon l'expression d'A. Atkinson et J. Stiglitz. Le regain d'intérêt dont bénéficie aujourd'hui l'impôt sur le revenu dépensé se fonde plus sur la loi de considérations de nature empirique, d'arguments de faisabilité ou de coûts d'assujettissement que sur la base de leurs propriétés en matière d'équité ou d'efficacité (8). L'absence de toute référence à la littérature relative à l'impôt optimal dans les textes des avis des Commissions du Plan, des Rapports du Conseil des Impôts, ou de la majeure partie des travaux de l'INSEE ou de la DP doit-elle être interprétée alors comme le signe d'une méconnaissance de la littérature ou comme la sanction de son impertinence par rapport aux sujets étudiés? Comme nous l'avons montré plus haut, la formation des donneurs d'avis ne les prédispose pas toujours à étayer leurs argumentations sur ce type d'analyse. On peut considérer ensuite que l'absence de conclusion tranchée de la théorie sur nombre de points cruciaux de la politique fiscale constitue pour ceux qui ne l'ignorent pas une incitation supplémentaire à ne pas y faire référence, à se tourner vers des paradigmes concurrents ou vers des études empiriques plus ou moins déconnectées de tout fondement théorique explicite. L'on peut supposer enfin que ce sont les faiblesses inhérentes à ce type d'approche qui empêchent qu'elle soit retenue par les donneurs d'avis (comme l'irréalisme de la norme parétienne de référence, la quasi-vacuité empirique du concept d'"impôt forfaitaire", le mode d'introduction des coûts d'information, d'assujetissement, l'existence d'une illusion fiscale).

Lorsque l'on considère la *base d'imposition-revenu*, une argumentation du même type conduit à remettre en cause les mérites de la règle du revenu global de Haigs-Simons. Cette règle ne vaut que par référence au principe de l'équité horizontale qui enjoint de traiter fiscalement tous les revenus de façon identique, quels qu'en soient l'origine, la nature ou les titulaires. Or, la littérature récente montre qu'en général le respect de cette règle ne con- duit ni à l'efficacité ni surtout à l'équité maximales (9). En somme qu'il s'agisse de l'impôt sur le revenu ou de l'impôt sur la dépense "les arguments théoriques sont, au mieux, inconclusifs et la décision en faveur de l'impôt sur la dépense repose sur des considérations essentiellement pratiques" (J.Kay) (10).

Un second résultat achève de semer le doute. D'une part, sous des conditions très générales il apparaît que l'ensemble des équilibres compor- tant une fiscalité sur les ménages n'est pas connexe, donc que toute réforme fiscale est susceptible d'engendrer des inefficacités temporaires au sein du système productif. Une réforme fiscale, fût-elle possible et orientée dans la bonne direction, ne garantit pas que l'on se rapproche du but à atteindre c'est-à-dire l'optimum de premier rang qui requiert pour sa part la mise en place exclusive d'impôts forfaitaires. L'on comprend que, dans ces condi- tions, la théorie de la *réforme fiscale graduelle*, proposée par M. Feldstein (1974) et R. Guesnerie (1977) n'ait pas trouvé un écho substantiel au sein des "donneurs d'avis".

L'apport de la théorie économique récente aux avis en matière de base d'imposition apparaît donc beaucoup plus comme la fin des "idées reçues" que sous la forme d'un soutien articulé à l'usage de telle base, de tel barème ou au type de réforme graduelle à mettre en place.

La fortune relative du concept de *Dépense Fiscale* corrobore les re-marques précédentes. Malgré les difficultés conceptuelles qu'elle suscite (G.Gilbert - 1980), le succès de la notion tient en définitive au fait qu'elle peut rassembler les tenants de l'analyse traditionnelle de l'économie pu-blique, ceux du "Public Choice" et des spécialistes des sciences juridique et administrative peu déroutés par le caractère principalement juridico-institu-tionnel de la norme de référence finalement retenue (11).

Si donc l'influence de la théorie économique sur le contenu des avis apparaît indubitable, elle est cependant limitée par des facteurs tenant à l'organisation des échanges d'information entre protagonistes, à la com-pétence économique des acteurs, à la nature multi-dimensionnelle de l'impôt. La modestie de l'influence tient, aussi et plus paradoxalement, aux progrès mêmes de l'analyse économique, relativisant les "idées reçues" antérieures mais ne proposant pas en retour de résultats aisément in-tégrables dans les avis.

2—Du conseil à la politique: l'exemple francais du Conseil des Impôts

La détermination finale de la politique fiscale française relève, comme dans toutes les démocraties occidentales, du Parlement i.e. de la représen-tation nationale (12).

Comment des avis, liés à des degrés divers aux enseignements de la théorie économique de l'impôt, peuvent-ils inspirer ou influencer cette prise de décision de politique fiscale? C'est ce que l'on s'efforcera de montrer ci-après en centrant l'analyse sur l'expérience française du Conseil des Impôts. Après avoir précisé la place de ce Conseil au sein des donneurs d'avis et des acteurs de la politique fiscale, on montrera quel a pu être l'apport de cet organisme à l'évolution de cette politique, notamment en matière d'imposition du revenu.

2.1. Le conseil des Impôts au sein des donneurs d'avis et acteurs de la politique fiscale.

Le Conseil des Impôts est un organisme associé à la Cour des Comptes (13), que l'on présentera brièvement avant de faire apparararître son rôle dans le processus de préparation des décisions de politique fiscale.

2.1.1. L'organisation et le fonctionnement du Conseil des Impôts. Le Conseil des Impôts a été créé en 1971 avec pour mission originelle de dresser un cons-tat, de "dire le vrai", en matière de situation des agents économiques au regard de l'imposition du revenu. Cette mission a été élargie en 1977 à l'ensemble des Impôts (14).

Le Conseil des Impôts comprend aujourd'hui onze membres : le Premier Président de la Cour des Comptes (qui préside de droit le Conseil) et dix autres personnalités choisies pour leur compétence et leur indépendance (15).

Le Conseil des Impôts est, de facto, un organisme sans service administratif spécifique (16). C'est qu'en effet le Conseil n'a pas à être une administration nouvelle. Il collecte les études et données disponibles dans les divers services administratifs, il impulse des enquêtes, études et recherches nouvelles et élabore en vue du constat dont il est chargé, une synthèse exhaustive et impartiale -autant que faire se peut- de l'ensemble des informations disponibles. Sur la base du plan de travail arrêté par le Conseil, un rapporteur général prépare le projet de rapport, point de départ de la discussion des membres du Conseil et de l'élaboration du rapport final. Ce projet (ainsi que les documents annexes afférents) sont communiqués aux administrations concernées. Des représentants de ces dernières participent aux séances, au cours desquelles les rapports les concernant sont examinés, de sorte que le Conseil des Impôts peut arrêter les éléments de son constat en disposant de l'ensemble de l'information disponible.

2.1.2. Le Conseil des Impôts et la préparation des décisions de politique fiscale. Le Conseil des Impôts n'est pas *directement* associé au processus de préparation de la décision fiscale. Il est un donneur d'avis dont l'influence sur cette préparation s'opère par une double voie : élaboration de rapports informatifs à l'intention des pouvoirs publics et de l'ensemble des contribuables ; relations directes avec les administrations économiques et financières et notamment l'administration fiscale chargée de la préparation des projets de loi en la matière.

Les rapports du Conseil des Impôts
Le Conseil des Impôts élabore deux séries de rapports :

— La première série, la plus importante, correspond aux sept *rapports publics au Président de la République*. Ces rapports, dont les thèmes particuliers sont précisés en bibliographie, ont été essentiellement consacrés à l'analyse de l'imposition sur le revenu (à l'exception du sixième rapport consacré à la taxe sur la valeur ajoutée) (17).

— La deuxième série, moins nombreuse, correspond à des *rapports spéciaux (non publiés) élaborés à la demande du Ministre des Finances* : on citera à titre d'exemple en ce sens, un récent rapport dit "rapport sur la simplification", axé prioritairement sur la fiscalité du revenu (juillet 1983).

Le Conseil des Impôts, les Administrations et les Pouvoirs Publics

Le Conseil des Impôts bénéficie, tant vis à vis des administrations que des pouvoirs publics, d'une parfaite indépendance, condition basique de fiabilité de la mission qui lui est impartie. Mais bien entendu, l'élaboration du constat auquel se livre le Conseil implique -via l'action des rapporteurs précités- un contact étroit avec les administrations, notamment fiscales et financières. De même, la remise des rapports aux pouvoirs publics permet une articulation entre organisme donneur d'avis et décideur politique.

Les relations entre le Conseil des Impôts et les Administrations s'opèrent à l'occasion de la collecte des informations et de la mise en place des études et enquêtes propres au Conseil.

Les administrations impliquées sont essentiellement : la Direction Générale des Impôts et le Service de Législation Fiscale (transmission des données statistiques, traitement particulier de données, enquêtes spéci-fiques. . .) ; la Direction de la Prévision (modélisation et simulations via les modèles périphériques fiscaux. . .) l'Institut National de la Statistique et des Etudes Economiques (enquêtes périodiques sur les revenus fiscaux des ména-ges avec notamment ventilation par catégories socio-professionnelles. . .) ; l'Inspection Générale des Finances (enquêtes particulières. . .)

Bien entendu, les relations entre Conseil des Impôts et Administrations ne sont pas des relations à sens unique (18), les travaux du Conseil étant une occasion pour l'administration de repenser sa démarche d'approche des problèmes fiscaux : cela a été le cas notamment à la suite des travaux du Conseil sur les dépenses fiscales (IVème rapport), sur les conditions d'imposition des bénéfices agricoles (Vème rapport). Il y a ainsi en quelque sorte une "fertilisation croisée" des apports réciproques, indépendamment de la prise en compte des avis du Conseil dans le cadre de la préparation des textes fiscaux législatifs ou réglementaires.

Les relations entre le Conseil des Impôts et les pouvoirs publics s'opèrent sur la base des rapports remis à ces derniers. Ces rapports, par leur dimension "constat", éclairent la situation des redevables au regard de la fiscalité et constituent autant *d'avis susceptibles d'influencer ou d'inspirer tant le pouvoir exécutif* au niveau de la préparation de la loi fiscale, que *le pouvoir législatif* au niveau de l'amendement et du vote de cette loi (19).

2.2. *Le Conseil des Impôts et l'évolution de la politique fiscale.*

L'insertion du Conseil des Impôts au sein des donneurs d'avis et des acteurs de la politique fiscale, permet-elle de mettre en évidence les *processus de passage de l'avis à la politique* sur cet exemple privilégié? A s'en tenir à l'imposition sur le revenu, on peut noter l'existence de ces processus dans quelques domaines fondamentaux, avant de s'interroger sur la portée de ce même processus.

2.2.1. L'impact des avis du Conseil des Impôts sur la décision de politique fiscale. Une étude de l'impact des avis du Conseil des Impôts sur la politique fiscale française fait apparaître, en matière d'impôt sur le revenu, quatre séries d'influences essentielles que l'on peut articuler autour des thèmes suivants : dépenses fiscales, élargissement des bases d'imposition, harmonisation des conditions d'imposition des diverses catégories de contribuables, simplification (20).

Les dépenses fiscales.

Le concept de "tax expenditure" cher à S. Surrey a fait l'objet, sous le vocable de dépense fiscale, d'une étude quantifiée systématique pour la France, dans le quatrième rapport du Conseil des Impôts en 1979 (21). Ce rapport propose une définition, un plan d'approche, et un essai de quantification du phénomène. Les dépenses fiscales sont définies comme "les pertes de recettes . . . (découlant) . . . de dispositions fiscales particulières prises notamment dans un souci de simplification et ayant pour effet d'accorder un avantage fiscal assimilable à une aide aux bénéficiaires de certaines catégories de revenus" (22). Le plan d'approche du phénomène est décomposé en quatre étapes : "identifier par rapport à un système de référence les mesures dérogatoires et en faire un recensement aussi exhaustif que possible ; chiffrer, pour les mesures étudiées, leur coût et leur évolution dans le temps ; déterminer les bénéficiaires des mesures, par secteur d'activité et par catégorie de redevables ; confronter aux objectifs des diverses mesures examinées, le coût des allégements et les résultats obtenus" (23). Analysant ces dépenses fiscales, le Conseil des Impôts a recensé 87 mesures de cette nature (sans compter celles concernant les bénéfices industriels et commerciaux) ; il a par ailleurs quantifié le coût de 41 dépenses fiscales. Estimant qu'une étude systématique et approfondie de ce concept devrait permettre une meilleure rationalisation des choix budgétaires (centrée cette fois-ci sur le côté recettes du budget), le Conseil a proposé que l'étude en soit faite pour l'ensemble de la fiscalité et qu'un rapport périodique puisse permettre d'en apprécier le coût et la portée.

Cet avis du Conseil des Impôts a été suivi par le législateur, l'article 32 de la loi des finances pour 1980 ayant prévu que désormais la liste et le coût des dépenses fiscales seront publiés dans le fascicule "Voies et moyens" qui constitue une des annexes essentielles du projet de loi de finances. Cette disposition nouvelle appliquée lors de la présentation du projet de loi de finances 1981 et poursuivie annuellement depuis lors, *est un exemple privilégié d'impact d'un avis du Conseil des Impôts sur la décision* de politique fiscale.

L'élargissement des bases d'imposition.

L'élargissement de l'assiette de l'impôt sur le revenu par prise en compte de revenus dont la non-imposition n'apparaît plus justifiée, est une préoccupation de long terme des avis du Conseil des Impôts, ce qui va d'ailleurs tout à fait dans le sens d'une remise en ordre d'un encadrement des dépenses fiscales. On citera en ce sens simplement trois séries d'avis du Conseil ayant conduit à une évolution de la législation fiscale : la suppression de l'exonération attachée aux allocations forfaitaires pour frais, allouées aux dirigeants de sociétés, préconisée dans le premier rapport du Conseil, a été réalisée par l'article 15 de la loi de finances pour 1973 ; un réexamen de l'ensemble de la fiscalité des revenus de transfert (préconisé par le deuxième rapport du Conseil en 1974) (24), a inspiré diverses modifications législatives (notamment l'article 76 de la loi de finances pour 1979 qui soumet à l'impôt sur le revenu, sauf cas particulier, les indemnités journalières pour maladie versées à compter du 1/1/1979) ; un réaménagement du régime des plus-values a de même été mis en place (loi du 19 juillet 1976 sur les plus-values immobilières allant dans le sens de l'avis du premier rapport du Conseil des Impôts ; lois du 19 juillet 1976 et du 5 juillet 1978 faisant suite aux propositions du second rapport du Conseil des Impôts : ces lois prévoient en matière de gains nets en capital nés de la cession de valeurs mobilières, un système particulier de taxation de ces gains au titre des bénéfices non-commerciaux, allant dans le sens des régimes de plus-values existant à l'étranger) (25).

L'harmonisation des conditions d'imposition des diverses catégories de contribuables.

Le rapprochement des conditions d'imposition des différentes catégories de contribuables s'inscrit dans un effort "classique" d'équité horizontale. Deux séries d'avis du Conseil des Impôts ont été en ce sens suivies d'une évolution de la législation fiscale.

Des propositions de rapprochement ont été faites pour les régimes d'imposition des bénéfices industriels et commerciaux, des bénéfices non commerciaux et des bénéfices agricoles. Cela a conduit notamment à un non-relèvement des plafonds de chiffres d'affaires ou de recettes limitant l'application de plein droit des régimes du forfait et de l'évaluation administrative, ainsi qu'à l'institution d'un régime simplifié en matière agricole (article 3 de la loi de finances pour 1977) inspiré d'un avis du Conseil des Impôts dans son premier rapport.

Des propositions de rapprochement ont été faites entre l'imposition des salariés et non salariés. Le rapport spécial du Conseil des Impôts de mai 1972 avait proposé ce rapprochement dans le cas de professions non salariées dont les recettes sont déclarées par des tiers : diverses dispositions législatives ont été prises en ce sens (agents d'assurance en 1972 et auteurs-compositeurs en 1973). D'une manière plus générale, le Conseil des Impôts a toujours lié l'unification des conditions d'imposition à une amélioration

des connaissances des revenus nets déclarés. Cette préoccupation a conduit
à la mise en place des centres et associations de gestion agréés dont les
membres peuvent bénéficier (sous certaines conditions) d'un abattement sur
le bénéfice imposable du type de celui consenti aux salariés. Les dispositions législatives prises en ce sens ont bien été conformes aux avis du
Conseil des Impôts ; on notera cependant dans le dernier rapport de ce
Conseil (1985), les interrogations suscitées par ce rapprochement à la suite
de l'enquête approfondie menée par le Conseil sur la pratique effective de
ces centres et associations de gestion agréés (26).

La simplification.
La simplification des conditions d'imposition sur le revenu est un exemple typique des possibilités de passage de l'avis à la décision de politique
fiscale, dans la mesure même où un rapport spécial sur ce thème a été établi
en 1983 par le Conseil des Impôts.

Ce rapport spécial a présenté tout d'abord les facteurs de complication
de la loi fiscale : absence d'homogénéité de la notion de revenu imposable ;
diversification excessive des régimes d'imposition de l'activité professionnelle, extension incontrôlée des mécanismes de dépense fiscale. Il a ensuite
insisté sur les limites inhérentes à tout effort de simplification : multiplicité
des aspirations des redevables, préoccupations diversifiées des administrations. Il a enfin mis l'accent sur les conflits possibles entre la simplification
et les autres objectifs de la politique fiscale, notamment en matière
d'impératif budgétaire, d'équité, de réalisme et de contrôle fiscal. Le rapport spécial a proposé trente huit mesures techniques de simplification artic-
ulables autour de trois thèmes : unification des modalités d'imposition des
revenus, allègement des procédures, limitation et encadrement du recours
aux dépenses fiscales.

Quatre séries de mesures proposées par le Conseil des Impôts ont été
retenues dans la loi de finances pour 1984. Ces mesures s'inscrivent :soit
dans le sens d'une limitation d'un recours aux dépenses fiscales ; soit dans
l'optique d'une harmonisation des régimes d'imposition des non-salariés ;
soit dans la perspective d'un allègement des obligations déclaratives des
contribuables (27). Le passage de l'avis à la décision de politique fiscale, en
matière de simplification, est bien l'expression de convergences communes
du conseiller et du législateur. A l'évidence les propositions non retenues ne
s'inscrivaient pas dans la perspective . . . ou l'opportunité politique du
moment.

2.2.2. Portée et limites du passage de l'avis à la décision de politique fiscale.
L'activité du Conseil des Impôts est, en France, un bon exemple de passage
de l'analyse économique de la fiscalité au conseil, et du conseil à la décision

de politique fiscale : c'est un exemple qu'il convient de focaliser avant d'en montrer les limites.

Le Conseil des Impôts est un "donneur d'avis". Situé du *côté de l'offre*, il comprend des membres des administrations publiques dont un universitaire, correspondant à deux des catégories de donneurs d'avis précisées antérieurement. A l'évidence, l'étendue des connaissances de l'état de la science fiscale par ces donneurs d'avis témoigne d'un effort d'expertise certain des effets supposés de la politique fiscale. La *demande d'avis* adressée au Conseil émane essentiellement des pouvoirs publics ; mais cette demande est aussi une demande latente ou implicite des citoyens-contribuables dans la mesure où les rapports publics remis au Président de la République, chargés de "dire le vrai" en matière fiscale, font l'objet d'importants compte-rendus attendus par les "médias", ainsi que d'une diffusion nationale non négligeable (28). Les mécanismes de *confrontation entre offreurs et demandeurs d'avis traduisent*, ainsi que montré plus haut à propos de l'imposition du revenu, l'existence d'une convergence certaine de préoccupations et donc de possibilités de passage de l'avis à la décision. Il n'est pas néanmoins interdit de penser que la perspective ou l'opportunité politique jouent un rôle central dans ce passage : si l'analyse économique peut ainsi apparaître comme un élément inducteur d'avis, elle peut aussi parfois se révéler ex-post comme un élément de discours justificatif. Au total, est-il en un certain sens possible de parler d'un marché de l'avis? Une réponse positive est loin d'être évidente, et ce pour deux raisons. L'offre d'avis est d'une part largement dominée par la demande, qui répond pour l'essentiel à des préoccupations internes à l'Administration lato-sensu. Les mécanismes de confrontation de l'offre et de la demande sont d'autre part essentiellement internalisés au sein du Conseil. Ils s'expriment plus ou moins explicitement à propos du choix des thèmes d'étude, de la personnalité des membres composant le Conseil, voire de la nature des conclusions remises au terme des travaux. Le choix des thèmes de réflexion, quoique déterminé par le Conseil, est sensiblement influencé par les demandeurs d'avis : en effet, la composition du conseil, le rôle effectif joué par ses membres ainsi que les avis "secondaires" qu'ils sollicitent, témoignent de l'omnipotence des principaux acteurs du jeu fiscal internes à l'Administration, et donc du rôle directeur des demandeurs d'avis potentiels. Ainsi, les prises de position des représentants de ces acteurs au cours des séances de travail du Conseil sont-elles interprétées comme la position quasi-officielle de celle-ci pour chaque problème en débat. Sans remettre en cause l'indépendance réelle du Conseil des Impôts, les contraintes qui pèsent sur le choix de ses thèmes, sur sa composition et sa procédure d'investigation, témoignent cependant de la prééminence des effets directs et indirects des demandeurs d'avis sur la nature des conclusions émises par l'offreur. Tout ceci tend à confirmer le fait que les mécanismes de confrontation de l'offre et de la demande d'avis en oeuvre au sein du

Conseil des Impôts ne peuvent en aucun cas être assimilés à ceux qui prévaudraient sur un marché "externe" ; il s'agit plutôt d'*un "marché interne" fortement segmenté* où les ajustements se manifestent simultanément sur les règles, le champ d'investigation et la nature des conclusions.

Les limites du passage de l'avis à la décision conduisent à s'interroger, au delà de l'acceptation ou du refus des avis, sur la "faisabilité" d'une réforme fiscale, en l'espèce d'une réforme fiscale "graduelle" puisque les propositions du Conseil des Impôts se situent de facto dans ce registre.

La prégnance des contraintes économiques permet une compréhension partielle du "paradoxe de faisabilité" d'une réforme fiscale dans une économie en crise. Dans une économie en croissance, l'hétérogénéité du processus de croissance favorise les mutations structurelles de l'imposition (introduction de la T.V.A. en 1954, extension de cet impôt en 1968, mise en place d'un véritable impôt général sur le revenu au cours des années 60 . . . dans le cas de la France). Dans une économie en crise, la demande de réforme fiscale est sans doute plus importante alors qu'apparaît un frein à la mutation des structures fiscales (en France, depuis 1981, la création de l'imposition sur les grandes fortunes est de fait la seule réforme fiscale importante . . . dont l'impact demeure somme toute limité à une centaine de milliers de foyers fiscaux (29)).

La permanence des contraintes spécifiques de politique fiscale explique, pour sa part, les limites du passage des avis des conseillers à la décision de politique fiscale. *Les contraintes politiques* sont à l'évidence essentielles sur ce point : l'absence d'arbitrages clairs entre objectifs poursuivis par les "décideurs" fiscaux (que l'on songe par exemple aux contradictions éventuelles de toute politique fiscale interventionniste à base d'innovation fiscale) conduit souvent à une propension à l'immobilisme global masquée par de nombreuses modifications ponctuelles. *Les contraintes administratives ne peuvent pour leur part être négligées.* L'absence d'un mécanisme général de retenue à la source en matière d'imposition sur les revenus dans la législation française (dans l'hypothèse où une telle mesure trouverait matière à application), au delà des difficultés techniques et économiques bien connues de mise en place, ne s'explique-t-elle pas par une répugnance fondamentale de l'Administration à l'égard de ce mode de recouvrement fiscal ? (30). *Les contraintes* sociales voire "*sociétales*" ne peuvent être ignorées : tout avis sur la fiscalité et a fortiori tout passage d'un avis à une décision de politique fiscale est un révélateur de choix social et entre donc, ipso facto, dans le champ du politique où il rencontre inévitablement, tant les stratégies et les tactiques des mouvements politiques, que le jeu des groupes de pression et notamment ceux des groupes d'intérêt fiscaux.

Conclusion

L'analyse des activités menées ên France par le Conseil des Impôts fait apparaître l'existence d'un quasi-marché interne de l'avis. Dans cette optique, le passage de la théorie à l'avis traduit bien une triple dimension de la théorie fiscale : facteur inducteur de l'offre d'avis, instrument d'expertise et élément de discours justificatif ; le passage de l'avis à la décision est pour sa part marqué, tant par les contraintes socio-institutionnelles propres du Conseil des Impôts, que par les contraintes plus générales de la politique fiscale. Lazare Carnot notait à la fin du XVIIIème siècle qu'en France, "toutes les agitations du peuple, quelles qu'en soient les causes apparentes ou immédiates, n'ont jamais au fond qu'un seul but, celui de se délivrer du fardeau des impositions" (31). Malgré son caractère exagéré, la part de vérité que contient ce propos n'explique-t-elle pas pour partie à la fois la timidité relative des avis des conseillers et les difficultés du passage de l'avis à la décision?

Notes

1. On négligera ici les donneurs d'avis très occasionnels ainsi que les fiscalistes d'entreprise.
2. Une typologie des groupes d'intérêt fiscaux est proposée par A.Peacock et F. Forte (1981) Tableau 1.1.
3. Notamment dans les 400 pages d'annexes du second volume du rapport.
4. Par exemple à la Direction de la Prévision du Ministère de l'Economie et des Finances, à l'Institut National de la Statistique et des Etudes Economiques (I.N.S.E.E.), à la Direction Générale des Impôts (D.G.I.) du même ministère.
5. A se borner au cas du Conseil des Impôts, sa compétence se limite au domaine qui lui est fixé par les décrets constitutifs. Le choix du champ d'investigation est "libre" à l'intérieur de ce domaine. Dans la réalité cependant, la solidarité interne aux grands corps de l'Etat présents simultanément au Conseil, dans les cabinets ministériels et à la DGI, rend le choix des thèmes moins exogène qu'il pourrait paraître de prime abord.
6. Les grands modèles sont articulés à des modéles périphériques (RECFISC par exemple, les Modèles d'Impôts sur le revenu (MIR 4 et MIR 5) de la Direction de la Prévision). (B.Bobe et P.Llau (1978) 2ème partie).
7. Une remarquable synthèse de la littérature est proposée notamment par A. Atkinson et J. Stiglitz (1980) et une critique stimulante par M. Ricketts (1981).
8. Telle est finalement l'argumentation décisive du rapport Meade ou des propositions de J.Kay et M. King (1980) pour le Royaume-Uni. Pour une synthèse des argumentaires utilisés dans divers ouvrages contemporains de fiscalité à propos de la réforme fiscale, voir G. Gilbert (1982).
9. Cette même littérature conduit par exemple à recommander une imposition allégée sur les revenus de l'épouse dont l'élasticité de l'offre de travail à l'impôt est en général supérieure à celle du mari, ce qui viole le principe d'équité horizontale.
10. Cité par A. Atkinson et J. Stiglitz (1980) p. 963.

11. Voir sur ce point les travaux du Congrés de Jérusalem de l'I.F.A. et les remarques de J.Stiglitz - M. Boskin (1977).

12. On ne saurait omettre à l'évidence : l'existence du contrôle de la constitutionnalité des lois (Conseil Constitutionnel) ; le rôle joué par la jurisprudence (juridictions administratives, civiles, voire pénales) dans le réglement du contentieux fiscal opposant les contribuables à l'Administration fiscale.

13. La notion "d'organisme associé" à la Cour des Comptes traduit le fait que le Conseil des Impôts prolonge l'action de la Cour, en élargit de facto la composition, et utilise en les adaptant les procédures de la Cour (Cf. sur ces points l'analyse de B. Beck "La notion d'organisme associé" in Cour des Comptes - Université de Paris II, (1984).

14. Le Conseil est en effet désormais chargé de "constater la répartition de la charge fiscale et d'en mesurer l'évolution, compte tenu notamment des caractéristiques économiques et sociales des catégories de redevables concernés" (art. 2, décret du 21/11/1977).

15. Ces dix personnalités sont des hauts fonctionnaires membres des grands corps de l'Etat (dont un universitaire).

16. A l'exception d'un secrétariat général dont un conseiller-maître à la Cour des Comptes assume la responsabilité.

17. Le huitième rapport, actuellement en préparation, sera consacré à l'imposition du patrimoine.

18. Il faut noter en effet que les membres du Conseil ainsi que les rapporteurs spécialisés de cet organisme demeurent en contact étroit avec leurs Corps et Administrations d'origine : ils sont ainsi à même de transmettre directement les informations disponibles nécessaires à la bonne marche du Conseil. On notera qu'une liaison institutionnelle directe n'apparaît pas entre le Commissariat Général du Plan et le Conseil des Impôts (phénomène hautement regrettable). La présence de membres ou de rapporteurs communs aux deux organismes permet cependant une liaison de fait entre les travaux impulsés par le Service du Financement du Plan et le Conseil des Impôts.

19. On notera par ailleurs, que les rapports publics jouent un rôle non négligeable d'amélioration de l'information fiscale des redevables : les rapports bénéficient d'une certaine "aura" d'impartialité ; ils nourrissent le débat fiscal en l'objectivant . . . et en combattant nombre d'idées reçues.

20. On ne saurait prétendre à une étude exhaustive, il s'agit d'un simple balisage de points fondamentaux.

21. Le thème avait déjà été abordé par le Conseil des Impôts dans son premier rapport de 1972, et a fait l'objet à la même époque de divers autres travaux français, notamment : P. Dumas, (1979) p.586 et suivantes, G. Gilbert (1980).

22. Conseil des Impôts, quatrième rapport . . . , p. 109.

23. Conseil des Impôts, quatrième rapport . . . , p. 110.

24. Le thème se retrouve dans le rapport spécial sur la simplification de 1983.

25. Cet élargissement des bases d'imposition est aussi allé de pair avec une modulation des règles de détermination du revenu imposable dans le sens de l'équité (cf. les exemples donnés en ce sens par J.Delmas-Marsalet in Cour des Comptes-Univ. de PARIS II, (1984), p. 168)

26. Conseil des Impôts, septième rapport . . . , Chap. III, p. 175 à 193.

27. Les mesures retenues correspondent aux articles 3, 72 à 80 et 93 de la loi de finances pour 1984. L'article 3 est relatif à la déductibilité de certaines charges afférentes à l'habitation principale qui ont été transformées en réductions d'impôt. Les articles 72 à 80 ont conduit en matière de bénéfice agricole, tant à un aménagement du régime simplifié d'imposition, qu'à une simplification des mécanismes d'ajustement au régime réel. L'article 86 a conduit à un regroupement sur un document unique (établi tous les ans par les établissements financiers et transmis tant à l'Administration qu'au client), de l'ensemble des opérations sur valeurs mobilières relatives à un contribuable. L'article 93 a conduit à un aménagement du délai de dépôt des déclarations en cas de cession ou de cessation d'activité des entreprises : on distingue désormais le dépôt de la déclaration de cession ou cessation d'activité stricto sensu, du dépôt de la déclaration de résultats y afférents (qui nécessite un plus long délai).

28. Les rapports sont diffusés à une dizaine de milliers d'exemplaires.

29. Il ne faut pas omettre cependant, notamment pour les revenus les plus élevés, les

effets de conjonction de cette imposition avec l'alourdissement de la progressivité de cette imposition (notamment tranche à 65%, majorations "temporaires" d'impôt . . .)

30. On notera que, dans son rapport précité sur la simplification, le Conseil des Impôts s'est prononcé majoritairement contre l'instauration d'une retenue à la source ; le Conseil propose une simplification du recouvrement par un développement de la procédure de mensualisation du paiement de l'impôt sur le revenu.

31. La citation est placée en exergue de la communication de G. Dominjon in Cour des Comptes - Université de Paris II, (1984), p. 13.

Bibliographie

Atkinson, A.B. et Stiglitz, J. (1980), *Lectures on Public Economics*, Maidenhead, Mac Graw Hill.

Bobe, B. et Llau, P. (1978), *Fiscalité et choix économiques*, Paris, Calmann-Levy.

Conseil Des Impôts:

—Premier Rapport au Président de la République (relatif à l'impôt sur le revenu), Paris, Imprimerie des Journaux Officiels, août 1972.

—Deuxième Rapport au Président de la République (relatif à l'impôt sur le revenu), Paris, Imprimerie des Journaux Officiels, août 1974.

—Troisième Rapport au Président de la République (relatif aux bénéfices industriels et commerciaux), Paris, Imprimerie des Journaux Officiels août 1977.

—Quatrième Rapport au Président de la République (relatif à l'impôt sur le revenu), Paris, Imprimerie des Journaux Officiels, octobre 1979.

—Cinquième Rapport au Président de la République (relatif aux bénéfices agricoles), Paris, Imprimerie des Journaux Officiels, juillet 1980.

—Sixième Rapport au Président de la République (relatif à la taxe sur la valeur ajoutée), Paris, Imprimerie des Journaux Officiels, février 1983.

—Septième Rapport au Président de la République (relatif à l'impôt sur le revenu), Paris, Imprimerie des Journaux Officiels, mars 1985.

Cour des Comptes - Universite de Paris II (1984), (éd.)*Le Conseil des Impôts et le Comité central d'enquête, organismes associés à la Cour des Comptes*, Paris, P.U.F.

Dumas, Ph. (1979), "Le concept de dépenses fiscales", *Banque*, mai, pp. 586–592.

Feldstein, M.S. (1976), "On the theory of tax reform", *Journal of Public Economics*, 6, pp. 77–104.

Gilbert, G. (1980) "La norme de référence associée à la dépense fiscale", G.R.E.F.I. Université de Paris X-Nanterre, ronéoté.

Gilbert, G. (1982), "Economie de la réforme fiscale et systèmes fiscaux comparés: une revue de la littérature", *Revue Economique*, 33,4, pp. 750–768.

Guesnerie, R. (1977), "On the direction of tax reform", *Journal of Public Economics*, 7, pp. 179–202.

Kay, J.A. et King, M.A., (1980) *The British Tax System*, 2ème édition, Oxford, Oxford University Press.

Peacock, A.T. (1981), "Fiscal theory and the markets for tax reform" in K.W. Roskamp et F. Forte (éds.), *Reforms of Tax Systems*, Actes du 35ème Congrès de l'I.I.F.P., Taormina, 1979, Detroit, Wayne State University Press.

Peacock, A.T. et Forte, F. (1981), "Tax planning, tax analysis and tax policy", in A.T. Peacock et F. Forte (éds.), *The Political Economy of Taxation*, Oxford, Basil Blackwell, pp. 3–28.

Ricketts, M. (1981), "Tax theory and tax policy", in A.T. Peacock et F. Forte (éds.), *The Political Economy of Taxation*, Oxford, Basil Blackwell, pp. 29–46.

Treasury (Department of the) (1984) *"Tax Reform for Fairness, Simplicity, and Economic Growth"* Report to the President, Office of the secretary, Department of the Treasury, nov., 2 vol.

Stiglitz, J.E. et Boskin, M.J. (1977), "Some lessions from the new public finance", *American Economic Review*, 67, pp. 295–301.

Summary

Are there any relationships between economic analysis and the fiscal policy measures adopted by governments? What place has the counsel and advice occasionally or otherwise furnished by fiscal economists? If it is in fact true that fiscal measures derive rarely from an explicit analytical argument, this is not necessarily the case for the counsel which accompanies the action decision. Doesn't the latter therefore not transmit an influence of analytical economies onto fiscal policy? In this paper an effort is made to state explicitly some aspects of the relationship between theory and policy measures. At first the relation between economic analysis and advice and then the relationship between advice and fiscal policy is explored. After the totality of this complex of problems is investigated, several transmission channels between theory and advice are identified. The method of analysis is applied to the activity of the Conseil des Impôts in France since 1971.

Regulation and Deregulation: An Economic Viewpoint

Paul Mentré*

I. The Form and the Economic Costs of Regulation

The economics of regulation is a relatively new concept. The seminal work of George Stigler (1) has received public attention only in the last ten years. But economic regulation as such has a long history. It began in the second half of the nineteenth century with control of monopolies, and gradually extended to promote fair competition in general—in itself a dual activity as represented by such antitrust laws as the Sherman Act, adopted by the U.S. Congress in 1890—as well as protection of technical monopolies against unfair pricing. In many countries tariff and market regulations were imposed at the beginning of the twentieth century on such industries as railways, telecommunications, and electricity. The market crash of 1929 led in the 1930s to extension of those regulations, broadening transportation regulations to cover road, air, and maritime transportation; creating organized markets for agricultural products in the United States and Europe; increasing particular regulations on financial activities, especially banking. At the same time, labor regulations were involved in the major social and political debates which dominated Europe and, to a lesser degree, the United States earlier in this century.

The 1960s and 1970s saw the emergence of new objectives: a desire to better protect consumers in the marketplace, workers in their activities, and environmental values in industrial development. These aspirations led to the implementation of new regulations, broader and more diversified.

Typology

These historical patterns suggest a systematic distinction among the forms of regulation. The typology can be viewed from various perspectives.

*Inspecteur Général des Finances
Ministère des Finances, Paris

The Relevance of Public Finance for Policy-Making. Proceedings of the 41st Congress of the International Institute of Public Finance. Madrid, 1985, pp. 293–305.

Mitnick (2) proposed a very broad one, according to the nature of the regulator and the nature of the "regulatee": a private regulator and a private regulatee (private "self-regulation"); a private regulator and a public regulatee ("capture"); a public regulator and a public regulatee (government "self-regulation"); a public regulator and a private regulatee (traditional regulation). A distinction can also be made between social regulation (activities with direct effect on individuals, such as safety regulations) and economic regulation (instrumental market activities, such as rate regulation or entry controls), or between intraorganizational and interorganizational levels of regulation. Since the thrust of this paper concerns public regulation and deregulation and their economic effects, a less ambitious typology is adopted, distinguishing sectoral regulations from general regulations. The former consists of regulations applicable to all enterprises in a given economic sector; the latter concern regulations applicable to all enterprises regardless of sector. The boundary between the two is of course not always distinct: environmental regulations, which are general, have a specific content and effect for such industries as paper pulp or chemicals. But the distinction of these two types is helpful in describing current regulations throughout the world.

Sectoral Regulations

These may be found within all sectors—agriculture, industry, and services, with particularly strict rules applicable to such professionals as physicians, lawyers, or accountants. The most important, in economic terms, are those applied to sectors on which all other sectors rely—basic ones, whose outputs represent a signficant part of the inputs of other sectors. In major industrial countries, the situation among such sectors was as follows at the end of the 1970s, when the current trend toward deregulation started (3,4):

Energy. The United Kingdom, France, and Japan had relatively strict regulations, in contrast with Germany, which had a free-market approach. With the imposition of price controls on oil products in 1971, the United States during the 1970s joined the first category.

Transportation. In all countries, including the United States, air and land transportation and maritime commerce were subject to strict regulations concerning entry, capacity, and tariffs.

Telecommunications. State monopolies, derived from the old postal monopolies, were operative in all major countries, but beginning in the 1960s some degree of competition had been introduced in the United States.

Financial services. In the wake of the financial crisis of 1929, all countries imposed detailed regulations on the activities of banks, insurance companies, and other financial intermediaries. In many countries, interest rates charged to customers were also regulated.

Clearly, these sectors showed a large potential for deregulation.

General Regulations

The level and composition of general regulations at the end of the 1970s reflected the legacy of history, diverse social values, and economic priorities. In global terms, general regulations fell broadly into the following categories.

Labor. Unionized activities and negotiations were in all countries subject to detailed regulations consisting of legal requirements or binding collective agreements concerning the hiring and the dismissal of workers and their protection in the workplace.

Wage and price determination. In countries such as Germany and, except during some periods, the United States, wage and price determination resulted from the operation of the market, but countries such as France had a tradition of price controls and strong interference by the state in wage determination, especially through imposition of minimum wages.

Competition. There has always been a sharp contrast between the United States, with its strict and binding antitrust regulations, and countries such as France and the United Kingdom, where competition is not strongly protected. In all countries, however, policies aiming at consumer protection developed over time.

Environmental policy. As a legacy of the new social and individual values that emerged in the 1960s and 1970s, regulation aimed at reducing industrial pollution gradually spread throughout the world, notably in the United States and Japan.

Foreign relations. Finally, through trade restrictions and exchange controls, and in spite of the institutional international framework promoting freedom in trade and monetary relations, foreign dealings in most industrial countries are subject to regulation, either broadly defined, as in Germany, or under more detailed terms, in countries such as Japan, France, and Italy.

Economic Effects of Regulation

The first oil shock and its constriction of the rate of growth throughout the world drew attention to the economic effects of an added external burden ("the oil bill") as well as to the economic effects of existing internal burdens, e.g. taxes and regulations.

Renewed interest was given to studies measuring the economic costs of regulation, which had been conducted in the 1960s and the beginning of the 1970s in sectors as diverse as land transportation, air transportation, telecommunications, agriculture, and industrial products protected by trade restrictions (see (3,4) for a detailed description and sectoral estimates). According to Murray Weidenbaum (5,6), the total cost of regulation amounts to about 3 percent of GNP owing to three cumulative effects: paperwork; global regulation, notably to protect the consumer and the environment; sectoral regulations.

In a separate study, Denison (7) measures the development of productivity in the United States from 1948 to 1979, as follows: 1948–55, −3.4 percent; 1955–65, +3.1 percent; 1956–73, +2.3 percent; 1973–77, +1 percent; 1977–79, +0.2 percent.

The decline in growth between the 1948–65 period and the 1974–79 period amounts to 2.5 percent a year, of which 0.3 percent was induced by reduced growth, meaning a structural decline of 2.2 percent a year. Denison and Kendrick attribute this decrease to the following factors: decline in the investment rate (0.3 percent); less qualified manpower (0.1 percent); increase in energy prices (0.2 percent); increased regulations (0.2 percent); a higher rate of growth in the tertiary sector, which has low productivity, than in industry (0.3 percent); residual factors (0.1 percent). The relative weights of energy and regulation are comparable, which is consistent with other estimates of the economic cost of regulation.

In Europe, analyses of this kind have been less frequent, but documents such as the Rueff-Armand report in France (8) or OECD studies (9) show that a similar development has occured there also.

II. Sectoral and Global Trends

Sectoral Deregulation

The move toward sectoral deregulation began in 1976–78, with U.S. deregulation of the airlines, amid considerable publicity. It spread rapidly to other sectors—transportation, energy, telecommunications and financial services—and to other countries, notably Japan and the United Kingdom.

Air Transportation. Ending a process that started in 1978, on January 1, 1985, the Civil Aeronautics Board was abolished. Having controlled air transportation in the United States since 1938, the CAB was a victim of the first oil shock. Rising fuel costs had led United States airlines to increase their fares sharply, causing a revolt among consumers and their representatives in Congress. A Senate inquiry demonstrated that the regulation of air transportation was no longer justified and had become largely detrimental to the consumer.

In October 1978, Congress approved an act abolishing the power of the CAB to authorize new lines and air fares, and phasing out the CAB itself. Competition now rules the market. The second oil shock increased air transportation costs by 35 percent in two years; fare increases were limited to 8 percent. From 1973 to 1977, a cost increase of 56 percent led to a fare increase of 32 percent (10). Deregulation has induced greater productivity gains and offered new services to passengers. Even though competition led to reduction in services to smaller communities and cuts in wages, few in the United States have suggested returning to the previous situation.

The trend toward deregulation is now spreading in Southeast Asia and in Europe, particularly in the United Kingdom, among domestic and international lines, and in the Netherlands.

Land transportation. The success of airline deregulation was followed by a move in the United States to do the same for surface transportation. Highway freight carriers had in the past been subjected to load restrictions and tariff authorizations. Starting in 1980, many restrictions and limitations were abolished, with the intent of ultimately abandoning all individual authorizations and dismantling the regulatory agency, the Interstate Commerce Commission. During the first eighteen months of this new policy, 5000 new companies entered the market. It has been calculated that deregulation resulted in a decline in fares of 10 percent to 20 percent (10).

Concurrently, some amount of deregulation was introduced in rail transportation, resulting in mergers within the industry and fare reductions.

The United Kingdom followed the same path by granting complete freedom to road transportation and privatizing some activities of the national railways. Other European countries, notably France and Germany, have been reluctant to follow suit, which may explain present EEC difficulties in defining and implementing a common transportation policy.

Energy. Deregulation of the oil market in the United States in 1980–81 proved to be a major international event. Beginning in 1971, oil price controls had kept domestic prices considerably lower than international prices, which resulted in a complex system of taxes and rebates between refiners and importers. The system discouraged domestic production, which had been cut from 450 million tons in 1973 to 350 million in 1980, and was subsidizing oil imports. After the second oil shock these effects were enhanced: the world price level was double that of domestic prices; regional shortages appeared.

At the Bonn summit in 1979, President Carter decided to decontrol oil prices. His timetable was accelerated by President Reagan, who removed all controls in April 1981. Simultaneously, natural gas and electricity were also deregulated to some extent. The results were spectacular. The decline in domestic oil production was curbed, drilling activities were resumed, and the strong elasticity of oil consumption to GNP growth was reduced. Internationally, together with an increase in non-OPEC production, the U.S. decontrol proved to be a major and lasting factor in a better balance within the oil market, a lessening of the role of OPEC countries, and a decline of prices. The oil shocks of the 1970s induced a world crisis; the decline of oil prices in the 1980s fueled the economic recovery that started in 1982.

This example was in part followed in Europe. Germany and the Netherlands had long relied on free oil markets and free oil imports. The United Kingdom in 1985 dismantled the British national oil company and abolished its role in the commercialization of oil. In France, where detailed regulations had been imposed in 1928, some import controls and some prices were liberalized. But the basic components of a system which, according to a study by the French administration, causes an additional cost of 10 percent for the consumer of oil products, were retained (3).

Telecommunications. The United States had long relied on a private telephone monopoly, AT&T, although during the 1970s the Federal Communications Commission permitted exceptions in the case of telephone equipment suppliers, long-distance transmission, and radio telephones. In 1982 two major antitrust decisions accelerated deregulation. The first was an agreement with AT&T to split the company into (a) regional companies, offering services to all long-distance carriers, (b) an equipment company, and (c) a long-distance transmission and dataprocessing company, competing with other computer companies. One of these competitors was IBM, who had all antitrust actions that had been taken because of the enlargement of its original industry, computers, to a broader one covering computers, telecommunications, and data processing dismissed in 1982.

These decisions speeded the growth of a new industrial sector, dominated by competition and encompassing data processing, data transmission, telecommunications, and the new information media. It brought diversification of choices offered to consumers, and costs were reduced through competition among long-distance carriers, while local call fares increased.

The world of telecommunications is internationally integrated, and under pressure from consumers, the U.S. deregulation pattern soon spread to other countries. In Japan, Nippon Telegraph and Telephone is to be privatized, competing with other long-distance carriers and opening itself to foreign firms. In the United Kingdom a parallel move occurred with the privatization of British Telecom, the biggest single privatization in the world (about $4 billion), and the launching of another private competitor, Mercury, operating internationally.

Other countries, especially Germany and France, have been more conservative. According to a study in the *Annales des Telecommunications*, in December 1984 the additional costs to French firms resulting from the state monopoly and its tariff structure amounted to FF 5 billion. Consequently, pressure is growing from consumers to move toward deregulation. This move will be accelerated if sectors that are large customers of the telecommunication industry, such as banks and insurance companies, are also deregulated, giving them more incentive to cut their costs.

Deregulation seems to spread in waves: when a sector is deregulated, it advocates deregulation of its suppliers in order to reduce its costs through competition.

Financial services. As a reaction to abuses that contributed to the 1929 crisis, detailed regulation of financial activities was introduced by the United States in the 1930s. It distinguished various categories of banks, controlled interest rates on deposits, and required prior authorization of many operations by regulatory agencies. The trend toward deregulation was launched by the consumers themselves, in particular by big corporations, through development of the commercial paper market, use of the deregulated Eurodollar market, and repurchase agreements ensuring free remuneration of deposits. Progressively, individual customers also benefited from such financial innovations as variable interest rate loans and money market funds.

The U.S. authorities continued this evolution. The act of 1980 deregulated financial institutions, blurring the distinction between various categories of banks while maintaining limitations on interstate activities. The result is a move toward a flexible financial system, in which all institutions offer a wide variety of financial products under free competition. Obviously, deregulation has increased volatility of interest rates and the vulnerability of some banks, particularly those too heavily engaged in financing the energy sector or developing countries. But, contrary to some pessimistic assumptions, no major crisis in the banking sector has developed.

Financial deregulation in the United States spreads throughout the world, first through extension of the $3,000 billion Eurodollar market; second by the deregulation of other financial centers, aimed at maintaining their competitive position with U.S. financial markets. In London, increased competition in rates and banking conditions has taken place and a "financial futures" market has started. In Tokyo, as a result of the desire of U.S. authorities to ensure greater internationalization of the yen, a broadly based deregulation trend is also under way. Continental Europe is traditionally more cautious, but in a country like France, new instruments such as futures, commercial paper, and money market funds were developed and the scope of competition increased.

General Deregulation

In most countries, sectoral deregulation is accompanied by abandonment of structural rigidities which also impede economic growth.

Prices, wages, and employment. The comparison between growth of employment in the United States and job stagnation in Europe has often been made. In the last ten years, under comparable GNP growth of about 2.2 percent a year, employment increased at an annual rate of 2 percent a year in the United States and was nearly stagnant—the annual rate of increase was 0.2 percent—in EEC countries. The contrast results largely from the differing evolution of wages and productivity, shown in Table 1.

Labor costs rose more in Europe, as did productivity, while employment stagnated; labor costs were stable in the United States and employment increased by 25 percent over this period. Deregulation contributed to wage restraint in the United States. For many years a dominant school in the United States has stressed the need for parallel wage growth in various sectors. For instance, President Kennedy's wage and price guidelines, as proposed by Walter Heller, were aimed at uniform wage gains and price differentiation among sectors according to relative productivity growth. In recent years there has been a shift toward greater adaptability of wages to

Table 1

Employment and Labor Costs
(Base 100 in 1973)

	1975	*1980*	*1985*
United States			
Production	100	115	135
Employment	100	115	125
Labor costs	98	100	105
Productivity	98	102	105
European OECD Countries			
Production	102	117	125
Employment	99	101	100
Labor costs	105	120	125
Productivity	102	115	125

Source: OECD, June 1985.

sectoral productivity changes. In deregulated sectors, there were wage agreements implying a marked slowdown in real wage increase, as in the road transportation industry, and even in some cases, such as the airlines, there were agreements to cut real wages. In all sectors there has been a closer adjustment to the circumstances of individual firms.

This tendency toward wage deregulation is also apparent in Europe— abandonment of wage indexation in France; in Belgium and Italy, added flexibility in rules concerning the hiring and dismissal of workers. According to the June 1985 OECD *Economic Survey*, a strict correlation exists between wage rigidity (measured as the ratio between elasticity of wages to prices and the elasticity of wages to unemployment) and unemployment (9). This added flexibility throughout Europe may well pave the way to some resumption of job creation, a major challenge for many countries.

Competition. In general regulations, such as those concerning the environment, there has been a tendency in the United States and Japan to restore the proper functioning of markets and competition to ensure greater flexibility by means of tax incentives, the marketing of rights, or a trade-off between compensating actions under a global ceiling (3,10).

There were some setbacks in consumer protection as a result of increased external trade restrictions. According to an OECD study (9), the share of imports subject to restrictions in total imports of manufactured goods increased over the 1981–83 period from 6 percent to 13 percent in the United States and from 11 percent to 13 percent in the EEC. And the same

Table 2

Mergers and Acquisitions in the United States

	1975	1976	1977	1978	1979	1980	1981	1982	1983	1984 (9 months)
Number of operations	2,997	2,276	2,224	2,106	2,128	1,889	2,395	2,346	2,533	1,899
Amount (billion US $)	12	20	22	34	43	44	83	54	73	103
Amount (billion 1983 US $)	20	32	34	49	57	53	91	56	73	100

Source: (10).

302

Table 3

Distribution of Mergers and Acquisitions

More than 5% of Total		25% to 5% of Total		Other	
Oil and gas	21.1%	Food	3.8%	Commerce	2.5%
Banking	11.2	Conglomerates	3.6	Securities	2.4
Insurance	7.9	Transportation	3.3	Others	34.8
Mining	6.8	Television-radio	2.7		
	46.9%		13.4%		39.7%

study quotes a British analysis indicating an estimated 20 percent additional cost to consumers of textile products as a result of quantitative restrictions imposed by the multifiber agreement. This is undoubtedly an area where deregulation should be resumed by means of a new round of multilateral trade negotiations.

Finally, regulations concerning competition have been by and large maintained, although there is a tendency in the United States to relax some of the constraints imposed on U.S. companies by antitrust legislation. In addition, according to the Council of Economic Advisers, there has been a sharp increase in mergers and acquisitions (10), shown in Table 2.

These mergers and acquisitions were concentrated in a small number of sectors, four of them (oil, banks, insurance, mining) representing one half of such operations and accounting for less than 10 percent of total production. See Table 3.

This concentration illustrates the effects of deregulation and economies of scale offered in sectors recently deregulated, such as insurance, transportation, financial services, oil and gas. Together these deregulated industries account for 50 percent of all mergers, which means that deregulation has a major impact on the restructuring of large economic sectors.

Capital markets. The trend toward deregulation of financial activities had induced a worldwide movement toward rapid development of new financial instruments. For the U.S. market the Bank for International Settlements (11) gives the figures shown in Table 4.

In the international market, following the debt crisis of 1982 there has been a trend toward desintermediation and securitization of loans. In 1984 traditional syndicated loans represented 40 percent of international financial operations (compared to 60 percent in 1981); bonds represented 20 percent and new instruments (note-issuance facilities and floating rate notes) 20 percent. As underlined by the Bank for International Settlements, this

Table 4

Financial Instruments in the United States

	Rate of Increase	
	1962–1982	*1980–1982*
Nominal GNP	78%	16%
Total financial liabilities	153	27
Money market funds	822	201
"Futures"	—	109
Banking acceptances	243	41
Commercial paper	214	37

Source: (11).

evolution offers a new challenge for central banks in their conduct of monetary policy and bank supervision. This will probably be one of the most important problems during coming years in terms of effectiveness of economic policy. It means that deregulation requires adaptation not only by private agents in the marketplace but also by policymakers.

The economic impact of these deregulation trends remains to be assessed, especially for global deregulation with less direct consequences; but the regulatory burden has clearly been eased. At a time when the external burden is also easing for industrial countries, new opportunities are thus offered for a resumption of employment and income increase.

Conclusion

All western developed countries in recent years have moved in the direction of deregulation, greater flexibility, and adaptability. Beneficial effects in terms of consumer savings and employment have been observed in sectors as diverse as energy, transportation, and telecommunications. Conversely, some workers and some consumers have been affected in terms of wage levels, quality of services, or costs. There have been major consequences in fields as diverse as wage determination, merger activities, and the structure of financial assets and liabilities.

References

[1] Stigler, George, "The Theory of Economic Regulation", *Journal of Economics*, 1971; and *The Citizen and the State*, Chicago, University of Chicago Press, 1975.

[2] Mitnick, B., *The Political Economy of Regulation*, New York, Columbia University Press, 1980.

[3] Mentré, Paul, *Gulliver Enchaîné*, Paris, La Table Ronde, 1982.

[4] U.S. Senate, *The Regulatory Reform Act*, Report of the Committee on the Judiciary, Washington, D.C., GPO, 1981.

[5] Weidenbaum, Murray, and Defina, *The Cost of Federal Regulation of Economic Activity*, Washington, D.C., American Enterprise Institute, 1976.

[6] Weidenbaum, Murray, *The Future of Business Regulation*, New York, Amacom, 1979.

[7] Denison, E., "Accounting for Slower Economic Growth: An Update," in Kendrick, J., ed., *International Comparisons of Productivity and Causes of the Slowdown*, Washington, D.C., American Enterprise Institute, 1984.

[8] Rueff, Jacques, and Armand, Louis, *Rapport sur les Obstacles à l'expansion économique*, Paris, Imprimerie Nationale, 1960.

[9] OECD, *Competition Policy in Regulated Sectors*, Paris, 1979; *Coûts et Avantages des Mesures de Protection*, May 1978; *Perspectives Economiques*, June 1985.

[10] *Economic Report of the President*, Washington, D.C., GPO, 1980, 1981, 1982; "Regulatory Reform Highlights", 1980; "Program of Regulatory Relief", 1981.

[11] Banque des Règlements Internationaux, *Rapport Annuel, 1984*, June 1985; *Les Innovations Financières et Leurs Implications*, December 1985.

Résumé

Dans tous les pays, l'Etat intervient dans les transactions du marché. Pour atteindre ses objectifs, l'Etat peut utiliser les dépenses publiques, les mesures fiscales d'incitation ou de dissuasion, les mesures d'intervention directe et la réglementation directe. Les dépenses publiques et les impôts sont soumis à un contrôle parlementaire détaillé et à des débats publics, mais le contrôle sur les instruments de réglementation est plus diffus. Au cours des dernières années, nous avons acquis une meilleure connaissance des coûts économiques de la réglementation. Un vaste mouvement de déréglementation , qui a commencé aux Etats-Unis, est en train de s'étendre à travers le monde. Ce rapport retrace les progrès de la réglementation et de la déréglementation dans deux domaines : les catégories et les coûts économiques de la réglementation et les tendances globales et sectorielles.

From Expansion to Restraint: Recent Developments in Budgeting

Daniel Tarschys*

Budgeting is at the core of the political process. In their annual decisions on taxation and public expenditure, economic policymakers strike a
balance among many conflicting claims. What they deal with, however, is
neither the bulk of the fiscal system nor the bulk of public commitments,
but merely the margins of each conglomerate. Without the freezing of most
government revenues and expenditures from one year to another, the volume of controversy would be entirely unmanageable. As a procedure for
handling marginal conflicts, the budget process performs an important
function in maintaining social peace and political stability.

The marginal character of budgetary decisions goes a long way toward
explaining variations in the pulse and rhythm of the process. Under conditions of stable growth, i.e., when economic resources grow faster than
expectations for public and private consumption, disagreement over the
distribution of benefits and burdens tends to remain within reasonable
limits. Nor is it too difficult to cope with stagnation and economic decline if
pretensions have been adjusted to the actual capacity of production. The
real challenge for the budgetary system emerges when claims and expectations expand far beyond the economy's ability to deliver. Nonincremental
adaptations are required when major political changes occur or when the
general economic situation sharply deteriorates. If the resulting disequilib-
ria cannot be handled within the framework of the budgetary process, they
are easily translated into inflationary pressures, growing public deficits, and
rising social tensions.

Recent efforts to strengthen the budgetary capacity are closely linked
to such trends in the economies of the OECD countries. While low growth
rates have aggravated the problem of budgeting, the most decisive factor
behind recent difficulties in the budget process appears to have been the
onset of economic decleration after an unprecedented buildup of expecta-

*This paper was prepared for the OECD's group of Senior Budget Officials. All views
expressed are the author's own.

The Relevance of Public Finance for Policy-Making. Proceedings of the 41st Congress of the
International Institute of Public Finance. Madrid, 1985, pp. 307–320.

tions for sustained growth. Remarkable and unique for this period of expansion was also the extent to which such expectations were institutionalized in statutory entitlements and more or less irreversible investments. The past period of exploitation has left us with a successive cumulation of largely inflexible costs.

In the same period, the organizational environment of budgeting has developed to the extent that an ever-growing number of particular interests are now defended with increasing vigor and sophistication. Political scientists have noted an emerging pattern of "corporatist" intervention in the policymaking of industrialized nations[12]. Economists have argued that the progressive mobilization of group interests has put a brake on the pace of economic expansion and have found evidence of "social limits to growth" in that an increasing number of individual aspirations are becoming mutually exclusive[3,10,15]. Sociologists have traced the declining ability of the state to reconcile separate interests to a loss of system legitimacy[1,2,9]. From the perspective of the budget office, such trends complicate the formulation of authoritative decisions as they imply more persistent demands for public outlays and more forceful and intelligent resistance to cutbacks and new obligations. Simultaneously, the budget process has become more transparent. What could previously be settled behind closed doors must now often be transacted in the open and with a wider participation of affected interests. In many countries, public sector trade unions and professional organizations have been able to strengthen their standing through the adoption of procedures for codetermination. The growing vigilance and activity of various political interests has widened the arena of budgeting and increased the number of actors involved in economic decisionmaking.

Recent developments in the organization of budgeting reflect the resolution of OECD governments to come to grips with this new situation. Successive attempts to apply entirely new "systems" to economic policymaking—such as the planning and program budgeting system (PPBS), management by objectives (MBO), zero-base budgeting (ZBB), rationalization des choix budgétaires (RCB)—have been abandoned after shorter or longer test periods but have nevertheless left their mark on budgetary thinking and behavior. A common denominator in such approaches and in a wide array of piecemeal innovations has been the intent to strengthen the elements of foresight, coherence, and rational choice in budgetary policymaking. In the following analysis of these efforts, I distinguish three main directions of institutional reform in the budgetary process: (1) investments in consensus, (2) investments in analysis, and (3) investments in authority.

Investments in Consensus

The classical division of labor in budgeting assigns different roles to three classes of actors. *Spending agencies and program managers* have first-hand experience in various policy areas and will often become sensors and detectors of new social needs. In their requests for appropriations, there are a great many suggestions about the need for additional government funding. *Sectoral ministries* fulfill the double function of conveying such demands to the center and at the same time seeking to restrain them and to keep the spending needs in line with general government policy. In this way, sectoral ministries are brokers working in two directions. The *budget office*, finally, seeks to assert the interest of the whole by keeping revenue up and expenditure down. In the budgetary dialogue, its officers frequently earn a reputation for cold hearts and tight lips. To a thousand good arguments in favor of as many worthy causes, they have but one reply. In the short version, it is "no." In the long version it is "sorry, we have no money."

While the right to say "no" may suffice under economic expansion, because spending agencies may always expect a "yes" somewhere in the future, the budget office needs additional good ideas and suggestions in a period of restraint and austerity. In this situation, a wealth of constructive ideas about feasible savings and potential for rationalization are required, but such proposals seldom emerge spontaneously from the implementing agencies. Nor does it seem possible to gain respect for ever more stringent budget circulars unless the recipients of these instructions have adapted their expectations to the new economic outlook. To manage its difficult tasks, the budget office therefore finds it increasingly imperative to reduce the normal difficulty of the budgetary process and to gain acceptance for its own diagnosis of the economic situation among a wider sphere of actors. At this stage, consensus-building becomes an important strategy for mitigating budgetary conflicts and achieving some measure of cooperation with programs and agencies affected by cutbacks.

Presenting "the treasury view" to a wider audience and promoting a greater degree of agreement on the need for patience and restraint is done in many different ways. A noticeable tendency has been to dispel some of the mystique surrounding the budgetary process. "Sunshine rules" and other practices intended to eliminate policy secrecy have been adopted in several countries. Budget offices and ministries of finance have engaged more extensively in publishing popular brochures on government decisions and their economic background. Contacts with mass media are carefully cultivated, and public relations departments are built up or expanded. There is clearly a strong feeling that more transparence is needed in order to foster public understanding of budgetary decisions. Even from Japan, where the budget process has traditionally been quite open, it is reported that education of the public on the impact of budgetary policy has assumed particular importance in connection with the fiscal stress experienced in recent years. Many other governments have followed suit.

Besides attending to their public relations, budget offices have also sought to develop their more private relations with other parts of the central government. Reminding the cabinet of economic realities is one of their chief functions. Special cabinet meetings are frequently employed to discharge this mission. There are also particular techniques for involving a larger number of ministers in the scrutiny of particular claims.

In some countries key priorities are decided by "inner cabinets." Cabinet committees for different policy areas play an important role in preparing budgetary decisions and are in some systems responsible for handling particular "envelopes" of government policy. This mechanism of reinforcing consensus within particular program areas has received its most elaborate implementation in Canada, but recent efforts in the same direction are reported also from Australia.

Below the cabinet level, an important target for information is the upper echelon of the staff in sectoral ministries. Under a policy of austerity, these civil servants will often suffer from their double loyalties. Most ministers are sensitive to the ubiquitous tendency to rate cabinet ministers by their ability to withstand pressure from the minister of finance. A "weak" minister is unable to protect his sector from fatal cutbacks; a "strong" minister does not merely prevent such assaults but can also conquer new resources in the midst of austerity. To reduce the impact of such pressures of opinion on ministers and their immediate collaborators, the budget office must offer a different standard for measuring ministerial failure and success. The natural ally in this pursuit is normally the head of the government. Unless the prime minister can provide strong leadership and instill a certain team spirit into the cabinet and the senior officials of the sectoral ministries, the budget office stands little chance of broadening its constituency within the central government.

Consensus-building at lower levels of the government hierarchy is also necessary. Cutbacks can damage both efficiency and morale, particularly if those affected by the reductions are left uninformed or misinformed about the reasoning behind the new policy. Many governments have felt a need to contravene such risks by expanding internal education and establishing new forms of contact and communication within the public sector. Ventures with this purpose are sometimes combined with the dissemination of new knowledge on management techniques, organizational development, and labor relations. Thus, the Swedish government has embarked on an ambitious program of "leadership education" involving all heads of government agencies and, in separate courses, the various strata of "middle management" in the public sector. The Dutch government has endeavored to increase the sense of economic responsibility by introducing the concept of "budgetholder."

In some cases, an "information package" has been integrated into the budget cycle. In preparing for the second budget of the Carter Administration, for example, the OMB conducted a major campaign to convince agencies of the need for economy. The usual budget guidance was accompanied by visits to the larger agencies to explain the dire budget outlook and to emphasize the need for holding budgets to the ceilings. Conformance to those ceilings was reported to have been unusually high that year. Beyond a general agreement on the economic situation and the perspectives for the immediate future, decremental budgeting also requires consensus on certain technical fundamentals. An issue that easily becomes controversial when ministries are required to produce a certain volume of savings is the definition of a "saving." A Dutch consultant observes that there has been much confusion on this point in the Netherlands. When the magnitude of a cutback is established, the reference point can be either a present expenditure level or a calculated future level. In some cases, incidental windfalls have been advertised as structural savings. In the United States, federal expenditure cuts are typically calculated for a "current services" baseline, but this baseline has been subject to several changes. The requirement established by the ministry of finance in Sweden is that, to qualify as cuts, measures must result in a direct quantity reduction as compared with current regulations.

When material interests are at stake, persuasion alone may not be a very powerful tool for building consensus. In their effort to gain a positive response from the recipients of public appropriations, budgetary policymakers have also developed procedures for making more or less formal agreements with spending ministries and agencies. A German observer refers to this as "the cooperative style of retrenchment;" a concept used in the United States is "the collaborative budget." This style is characterized in particular by waiving control over details in exchange for better control over totals. Budget officers refrain from issuing very specific conditions about the ways in which appropriations may be used, and in return the spenders agree to refrain from excessive claims.

Under austerity, the essence of the trade-off is frequently greater freedom under lower ceilings: appropriations are reduced, but the recipients are allowed to use their best judgment in deciding about the use of shrinking resources. From the perspective of the budget office, this means that difficult choices are decentralized to a level that knows more about the merits of various policy ends and policy instruments. Consensus is bought by concessions; control is sacrificed for cooperation.

The Canadian "envelope approach" and the Australian "parcel approach," or "offsets arrangement," exemplify efforts to practice the cooperative style of budgeting at the national level, but there are also many cases in which choices are delegated to a lower level of government. In the financial relations between national and subnational governments, there appears to have been a general trend towards the consolidation of specific grants into block grants. This is partly the result of the considerable expansion of equalization measures purporting to bridge the growing gaps between rich and poor regions. This development has been accompanied by more intensive consultation between the financial organs of the different levels, extending to such matters as deregulation and formula modification in connection with various grants. Several countries (e.g., Germany and the Netherlands) have set up formal institutions for such consultations.

Another facet of the cooperative style of budgeting is the increasing tendency to involve in consultations and negotiations with trade unions and other interest groups affected by policy changes. Codetermination reforms affecting the public sector have introduced new requirements into the policymaking process in some countries. But there has also been a tendency to involve other groups in budgetary decisions, such as trade unions, business, and pensioner organizations.

An important instrument for consensus-building in budgetary decisions is, finally, the cross-partisan commission. The considerable political costs already incurred in the search for cutbacks have led many governments to the conviction that responsibility for such measures ought to be shared with the opposition. Hence, it has been quite common to set up "search commissions" with the objective not only of locating suitable reductions but also of establishing the necessary consensus for getting such proposals accepted. The threatening character of such commissions is frequently reflected in the popular names they acquire: the Danes have had an "excavation committee" and a "vacuum-cleaner gang," the Lynch committee on privatization in Australia was called "the razor gang," and a Swedish defense committee charged with finding army regiments to dissolve was soon known colloquially as "the death squad." In numerous cases, the unanimity of such commissions is to no avail, as the parties and organizations involved disavow their own representatives when the going gets rough. Yet there are also many examples of reductions carried out on the basis of such cross-partisan proposals. The 1983 social security reform in the United States was to a large extent based on the report of the Bipartisan Commission (see [8]).

Investments in Analysis

A second line of reform has been to develop the capacity for analyzing budgetary problems. Dissatisfied with its old role as a mere recipient and examiner of information from a vast array of program managers and policy advocates, the budget office has sought to extend its own resources for reflection and research. To enhance the rationality of policymaking, the budget office has taken steps to expand government's planning horizon, to provide more useful data for the review and analysis of statutory entitlements and other established programs, and to ensure that short-term and long-term consequences of different policy options are identified.

An emphasis on the analytical dimension was an important ingredient in the various "rationalist" concepts of budgeting propagated and tested in the 1960s and early 1970s. In this period, governments generally introduced some form of multi-annual budget or forecast and also made certain forays into the area of impact analysis (cost-benefit studies, cost-effectiveness studies, effectiveness auditing, establishment of structural budget margins, etc.). Policy evaluation was introduced on a grand scale in the United States and to a lesser degree in other countries. Considerable efforts were made to formulate public budgets in program terms and to assess the output or impact of various programs on more relevant dimensions than outlays expended.

There were early signs that PPBS and related concepts of budgeting required larger armies of analysts than governments could marshal. From the mid-seventies, it also became increasingly clear that, for all their logic and intellectual rigor, the systems did not meet the pressing need of governments to embark on retrenchment. As a Dutch observer puts it: "Planning did not turn out to be recession-proof." With the turn to austerity, there was a general tendency to employ fiscal and expenditure analysis in a more selective manner. It was recognized that while interest groups and spending agencies could be relied upon to continue furnishing governments with expansive suggestions, the budget office had to assume a much more active role in securing the informational basis for cutbacks and rationalizations. After a few initial budget cycles in which savings were achieved largely by deferment, improvisation, and across-the-board measures, many budgetary decisionmakers came to the conclusion that more trenchant analysis was required to eschew the pitfalls of expenditure cuts that were either economically unsound or politically fatal, or both. And in many cases, institutional innovations were undertaken to secure this additional supply of information for decremental budgeting.

The role of legislatures in inflating the demand for budgetary analysis requires particular attention in this report. While parliaments generally continue to play second fiddle in the budget process and seldom manage to revise the proposals of the government (which they are even formally forbidden to do in some countries), there has been a noticeable revival of parliamentary interest in scrutinizing policy proposals and monitoring the effects of ongoing programs. The 1974 Budget Reform Act in the United States has afforded the Congress new opportunities for influencing fiscal and expenditure decisions, particularly through the so-called reconciliation procedure in which both houses agree to certain block totals for different policy areas. The federal legislature's own capacity for economic analysis has been vastly expanded by creation of the Congressional Budget Office. In the United Kingdom, select committees have been established with the mandate to examine the budgets of various departments. The Comptroller and Auditor General who provides Parliament with information for its scrutiny has recently been given more far-reaching powers of audit and investigation.

In several countries, there have been specific demands for more information on the costs connected with various programs at different stages of the legislative cycle. Such requirements tend to investigate the legislative process with the budget process and make decisionmakers more aware of the economic repercussions of seemingly inexpensive proposals. In Australia, there is now a formal requirement that all new legislation laid before Parliament must be accompanied by a statement indicating its financial impact on government receipts and outlays. The Swedish constitution has recently been amended to oblige the government to present similar information in connection with "plans for governmental activities" that the parliament is asked to adopt. The Danish government discusses "the fiscalization of the legislative agenda and debate." Thus, there are now far more stringent demands for long-term cost estimates than used to be the case when most welfare-state programs were elaborated and adopted.

While inquisitive parliaments may complicate the life of governments, they seem to bother the budget office far less than the spending departments. In many cases, parliamentary requests tend to facilitate the task of restraining risky new ventures and are therefore more than willingly invoked in circulars emitted by the budget office. Such circulars have tended to become more exacting in their demands for full costing. In the first place, spending agencies and program managers are now normally required to present multi-annual estimates of expenditure needs. Second, there is increasing interest in the meaningful measurement of output and impact. Third, there is the problem of cost incidence. A standard sequence in the macroeconomic dialogue is that the government, in its pursuit of economic stability, urges the major organized interests to contribute to the struggle against inflation, only to encounter the rejoinder that higher spending (by subnational governments), higher prices (by enterprises), and higher wage demands (by trade unions) are the inevitable effects of cost increases caused by the government through new taxes, new charges, new regulations, or new expenditure cuts. To meet this rebuttal, it is customary for governments to impose limitations on its own machinery (e.g., by withdrawing regulatory authority) and to issue commands that all new policy proposals must contain a full analysis not only of budgetary effects but also of secondary costs inflicted on others.

The experience with such exhortations, however, is less than encouraging. In many countries, the needs of analysis seem to have brought about a reverse dependency of the budget office on spending agencies for detailed information. Yet in spite of instructions conveyed in one budget directive after another, spending agencies and program managers are hard put to supply the required information. Different reasons for this can be imagined—methodological difficulties, problems of expressing soft data in quantitative terms, little motivation to provide uncomfortable facts, and the lesson of past experience that in the budget dialogue compliance is often punished more severely than disobedience. Yet whatever the motives, the result is discomforting for the budget office and compels it to consider alternative strategies for gathering information. Besides the "consensual" arragements already dealt with—where the cooperation of spending agencies is achieved at the price of certain concessions—the first obvious option is to make better use of existing instruments for control and oversight, such as auditing.

In several countries the auditing bodies are increasingly mobilized to support retrenchment operations. The old emphasis on legality and book-keeping accuracy is giving way to effectiveness studies and value-for-money audits. The search for better alternatives to established policy solutions has become a legitimate sphere of inquiry. "Parliaments have 'rediscovered' the Auditor's Offices and expect from them monitoring results useful for the parliaments," writes a German observer. In Finland, a government committee has recently reviewed the whole auditing system and proposed an extension of its mandate to cover state aids and state joint-stock companies. A similar expansion is under way in Sweden, where the state auditing agency and related bodies are now being tied more closely to the ministry of finance and auditing projects are integrated into the budgetary process. In the United Kingdom the successful passage of a private member's bill has led to the establishment of a National Audit Office, which is to perform value-for-money audits in central government departments and many of their associated bodies. An Audit Commission has been established for local authorities, and a similar body has been suggested to scrutinize the National Health Service.

While auditing institutions now tend to focus on the specific problems of making government work with shrinking resources, a great many other independent and semi-independent organizations have also entered the arena of "austerity analysis." In the United Kingdom one can see a number of new specialized institutes for the study of taxation, public expenditures, public finance accountancy, and public sector management. Australia has set up a number of semi-autonomous government organizations to carry out evaluation of programs in different sector, including a social welfare policy secretariat, a bureau of labor market economics, a bureau of transport economics, and a bureau of agricultural economics. Similar sectoral research bodies exist in many countries and have proven their ability to contribute to the budgetary process in recent years. In Sweden, the ministry of finance has set up a semi-independent research body of its own to promote studies in public economics.

In addition to these more or less permanent institutions, governments employ a vast number of temporary task forces and committees to examine particular areas. As the emphasis has shifted from policy analysis to policy review and reconsideration, some cabinets have opted for a more comprehensive approach by appointing commissions mandated to scan the whole gamut of government expenditures for rationalization opportunities and potential cutbacks. Notable examples are the Pliatzky commission on quangos (quasi nongovernmental organizations) and the Rayner project in the United Kingdom, the Lynch commission in Australia, the rounds of reexamination initiated by the Dutch cabinet, and the President's Private Sector Survey on Cost Control (the Grace Commission) in the United States. In mapping the options for decremental budgeting, the reports of these commissions have raised fundamental questions about the proper boundaries of the public sphere. A general tendency has been to move from considerations of administrative expediency towards what the Germans call *Aufgabenkritik*, i.e., a fundamental discussion of state functions and public objectives.

Investments in analytical capacity have also been made within ministries. Several governments have introduced management information systems and financial planning systems within their sectoral departments. While some of the more advanced undertakings were perhaps overambitious—the early euphoria with computerized political planning in the Federal Republic may be cited as an example—many such systems are still in operation. A white paper presented by the government of the United Kingdom in 1982 outlined a method for financial management in ministries by which departmental work would be divided into blocks and cost centers would be identified. The expected effect was to enhance accountability and initiative. Similar ideas were set forth in the diagnostic study published by the Financial Management Improvement Program in Australia in 1984. A problem in implementing schemes of this kind appears to be the partly conflicting expectations of different participants in the budgetary process. While it is normally predicted that more elaborate systems for financial planning in ministries will increase cost consciousness and economic responsibility, they may also reinforce the position of ministries as bulwarks of policy advocacy.

Finally, there is the budget office itself. Over the last decade, many ministries of finance appear to have developed their resources for in-house analysis in several directions. Considerable work has been done in the area of off-budget expenditures.

Tax expenditures have been thoroughly mapped in the United States, Canada, and Ireland, and other governments are well along way toward analyzing the budgetary effects of various concessions[11]. The analysis of government subsidies is particularly well developed in the Federal Republic, where a comprehensive report is regularly presented to parliament. The

Dutch government has devoted special attention to the problem of distinguishing between "productive" vs. "non-productive" outlays in an effort to reconsider the structure of public expenditure. It has also tried to assess the various hidden costs of government decisionmaking. In the new budgetary vocabulary there are frequent references to such concepts as "indirect costs, "bureaucracy costs," "workload costs," "transaction costs," "deadweight loss," "excess burden," etc. In sum, the modern budget office has become increasingly versed in a variety of methods of analyzing the wider implications of government receipts and expenditures.[13,14].

Investments in Authority

Investigating required increments has always been the legitimate function of the budget office. Is challenging established programs and benefits quite another matter? As recent research in social psychology indicates and as many budget officers would be able to confirm, negative reactions to small decrements tend to be much stronger than positive reactions to small increments[6]. Accordingly, the transition from stable expansion to selective contraction of government expenditures has thrown the budget office into a new and more exacting role. Instead of being primarily reactive and responsive to demands from others, it is now in the position where it must also formulate and campaign for its own demands. Failures in this pursuit are often explained in terms of insufficient political clout; guardians of the public purse have not been strong enough to resist the heightened pressure. Given this diagnosis, an obvious remedial strategy has been to boost the authority of the budget office.

Efforts to this end can be observed in many countries. A first step is often to strenghen the ties to natural allies within the government. A normal combination is for the minister of finance to rely on the support of the cabinet leader and for the budget office to seek the backing of the prime minister's office in its skirmishes with spending departments. This may be particularly important in countries where an active leadership of the cabinet is exercised. In the Federal Republic, for instance, the office of the federal chancellor has more than 400 employees organized in "mirror sections" corresponding to the various units in the departments. Many governments have taken measures to reinforce their instruments of central coordination and control. Special review bodies and advisory staffs have been attached to prime ministers in order to complement and scrutinize the suggestions of sectoral ministries.

Other frequent allies of the budget office include ministries of economic affairs and ministries of local affairs, which tend to reflect the concerns of subnational governments with costly initiatives by various sectoral ministries. In many cases, ministers of finance take steps to organize broader cabinet support for their proposals. Joint cabinet decisions on the government's economic strategy may serve this purpose, as may the decisions by different cabinet committees. Parliamentary decisions may be another source of support for the treasury view. Committees with comprehensive responsibility for the economy (such as budget committees, finance committees, general accounts committees, civil service committees, committees on government operations, etc.) tend to be particularly responsive to the concerns of the budget office and will often make statements and decisions that strengthen its position in the budgetary process.

In times of restraint, it is also customary for the budget office to set stricter standards for the spending units. Students of public finance in poor countries have noticed a tendency toward "repetitive budgeting": appropriations already granted are often withheld unless reconfirmed at later stages[16]. Business organizations in crisis often enter into a similar "control cycle" in which the grip is tightened and new restrictions are imposed on spending. Typical ingredients in such restraint packages are hiring freezes, deferral of capital expenditures, and postponement of cash payments. Levine[7] argues that retrenchment policies normally advance in stages, from a phase of denial and delay to a phase of stretching and further to a third phase of cutback planning. Jorgensen[5] distinguishes an "incrementalist phase" of retrenchment followed by a "management phase" and eventually a "strategic phase." In the latter two stages, organizational structure and processes are frequently modified to meet the new situation.

An important task of the budget office under austerity is to defend the discipline of the budget cycle. In times of economic crises, urgent demands are often made for immediate rescue operations for branches or regions in distress. Macroeconomic negotiations with organized interests may also entail concessions that disrupt the normal budget procedure. Such scattered decisions tend to reinforce the tendency to make the budget a summative rather than a formative document. As Jacobsson[4] points out, a large and perhaps increasing number of economic choices are now made outside the budgetary arena. This endangers the coordination of economic policy and can be particularly fatal in periods of governmental retrenchment.

Another threat to the authority of the budget office is posed by the variety of "off-budget" programs and institutions. Several governments have tried to take a firmer grip on such types of expenditure or "cost engines" in the economy. In many cases, semi-independent bodies have been brought under closer control. An Italian observer reports a policy "aimed at restricting progressively the residual autonomy of local governments with a cobweb of penetrating rules in order to keep their behavior within the path set from the top for meeting given financial targets." Legislation tabled recently in the Canadian parliament purports to enhance the government's direction of the activities of Crown corporations and to integrate their operations into the policy and expenditure management system through a system of "corporate plans." Efforts to extend government auditing and control to state-owned joint stock companies and other semi-independent institutions are under way in Finland, Sweden, and the United Kingdom. While many governments remain committed to a policy of decentralization and while strong centrifugal forces are constantly at work in our highly mobilized socieities, reorganization projects floated by the budget office frequently aim at the recovery of central control. Bringing the "uncontrollables" into the budgetary sphere is an important element in such efforts.

Conclusion

The three types of investment discussed in this paper are intertwined. By achieving some measure of agreement on their key targets and by expanding their resources for analysis and absorption of information, budget offices will also strengthen their authority. To what extent these resources really do enhance the capacity to budget is more difficult to say. The record of recent budgetary cycles must be assessed with an eye to the formidable obstacles that governments have been confronted with since economic growth began to falter. Programmed for steady expansion and exposed to an unprecedented range of public expectations bolstered by statutory entitlements and well-entrenched programs, the governments of the OECD area have been compelled to adjust to new realities. After a long period of incremental change, they are now learning to master the art of contraction. In this transition from one pace of development to another, the budget office has performed a particularly crucial function in providing inspiration, guidance, and control.

The structural and organizational changes undertaken to facilitate this conversion may seem limited, and their impact is certainly hard to assess. Yet the ambitions deserve to be noted. While the same annual ritual repeats itself time after time and the script of the budgetary dialogue does not shift very much from one fiscal year to another, actors do learn from experience and adapt their behavior to new circumstances. Faced with a growing divergence between government receipts and government expenditures and with a great many centrifugal forces jeopardizing the coherence and implementation of economic policy, OECD governments have taken many small steps to strengthen their capacity to budget. Central objectives have been to enhance consensus-building in the budgetary process, to expand and refine the analytical resources available to budgetary decisionmakers, and to boost the authority of the budget office.

References

[1] Connolly, William, ed., *Legitimacy and the State*, Oxford, Basil Blackwell, 1984.
[2] Habermas, Jürgen, *Legitimationsprobleme in Spätkapitalismus*, Frankfurt-am-Main, Suhr-kamp Verlag, 1973.
[3] Hirsch, Fred, *Social Limits to Growth*, London, Routledge and Kegan Paul, 1977.
[4] Jacobsson, Bengt, *Hur styrs förvaltningen?* Stockholm, Studentlitteratur, 1984.
[5] Jörgensen, Torben Beck, *När staten skal spare: Et studie i politiske og administrative problemer at fordele besparelser*, Copenhagen, Nyt fra Samfundsvidenskaberne, 1981.
[6] Kahneman, D., and Tversky, A., "Prospect Theory: An Analysis of Decision under Risk," *Econometrica*, 47, 1979: 263–91.
[7] Levine, Charles, "Organizational Decline and Cutback Management," *Public Administrative Review*, 38, 1978: 316–25.
[8] Light, Paul, *Artful Work: The Politics of Social Security Reform*, New York, Random House, 1985.
[9] Offe, Claus, *Contradictions of the Welfare State*, London, Hutchinson, 1984.
[10] Olson, Mancur, *The Rise and Decline of Nations: Economic Growth, Stagnation, and Social Rigidities*, New York & London, Yale University Press 1982.
[11] Saunders, Peter, and Klau, Friedrich, *The Role of the Public Sector: Causes and Consequences of the Growth of Government*, OECD Economic Studies, 1985.
[12] Schmitter, P. C., and Lehmbruch, G., eds., *Trends Toward Corporatist Intermediation*, Beverly Hills & London, Sage, 1977.
[13] Tarschys, Daniel, "Good Cuts, Bad Cuts: The Need for Expenditure Analysis in Decremental Budgeting," *Scandinavian Political Studies*, 7, 1984: 241–59.
[14] Tarschys, Daniel, "Curbing Public Expenditure: Current Trends," *Journal of Public Policy*, 5, 1985: 23–67.
[15] Thurow, Lester C., *The Zero-Sum Society: Distribution and the Possibilities for Economic Change*, New York, Basic Books, 1980.
[16] Wildavsky, Aaron, *Budgeting: A Comparative Theory of Budgetary Processes*, New York, Little, Brown, 1975.

Résumé

Dans une période de faible croissance, les bâtisseurs de politique doivent se battre avec des projections élaborées durant une longue période d'expansion sans précédent. Dans une large mesure, ces projections ont été institutionnalisées en droits statutaires et en investissements entraînant des coûts de fonctionnement élevés et croissants. Quand les gouvernements essaient de faire face à cette situation—allant de l'expansion à la restriction—ils trouvent peu de consolation dans des "approches systémiques", telles le PPBS, le MBO et le ZBB. A leur place, ils se tournent vers un large éventail d'innovations progressives dans le processus budgétaire. Sur la base de matériaux rassemblés à l'occasion d'un projet de recherches comparatives mené par l'OCDE, ce rapport distingue trois directions principales de réforme budgétaire au cours des années 1980 : investissements en consensus, investissements en analyse, investissements en autorité.

Anciens Dirigeants/Former Officers

Anciens Présidents/Former Presidents

Edgar Allix, France	1937
William Rappard, Suisse/Switzerland	1938–1940
Max Léo Gérard, Belgique/Belgium	1948–1950
Carl S. Shoup, Etats-Unis/USA	1950–1953
Ugo Papi, Italie/Italy	1953–1956
Fritz Neumark, République Fédérale d'Allemagne/Federal Republic of Germany	1956–1959
Maurice Masoin, Belgique/Belgium	1959–1962
Bernard Schendstok, Pays-Bas/Netherlands	1962–1965
Alan T. Peacock, Royaume-Uni/United Kingdom	1965–1968
François Trévoux, France	1968–1971
Ottó Gadó, Hongrie/Hungary	1971–1975
Jack Wiseman, Royaume-Uni/United Kingdom	1975–1978
Horst-Claus Recktenwald, République Fédérale d'Allemagne/Federal Republic of Germany	1978–1981
Jean-Claude Dischamps, France	1981–1984

Anciens Vice-Présidents/Former Vice-Presidents

Lord Beveridge, Royaume-Uni/United Kingdom
André van Buggenhout, Belgique/Belgium
D. Diachenko, URSS/USSR
Jean-Claude Dischamps, France
Francesco Forte, Italie/Italy
Victor Halberstadt, Pays-Bas/Netherlands
C. Lowell Harriss, Etats-Unis/USA
Lady Ursula K. Hicks, Royaume-Uni/United Kingdom
P. Jacomet, France
Fritz Neumark, République Fédérale d'Allemagne/Federal Republic of Germany
Ugo Papi, Italie/Italy
H. de Peyster, France
Helga Pollak, République Fédérale d'Allemagne, Federal Republic of Germany
Karl W. Roskamp, Etats-Unis/USA
Günter Schmölders, République Fédérale d'Allemagne/Federal Republic of Germany
E. Seligman, Etats-Unis/USA
Carl S. Shoup, Etats-Unis/USA
Nicolai Sichev, URSS, USSR
E. da Silva, Portugal

Stepan Sitaryan, URSS/USSR
Lord Stamp, Royaume-Uni/United Kingdom
Conte Volpi, Italie/Italy
Jack Wiseman, Royaume-Uni/United Kingdom

Anciens Secrétaires Généraux/Former Secretaries-General
André Piatier, France   1937–1948
Maurice Masoin, Belgique/Belgium   1948–1959
Paul Senf, République Fédérale d'Allemagne/Federal Republic of Germany   1959–1974

Présidents Honoraires et Membres Honoraires
Honorary Presidents and Honorary Members

Présidents Honoraires/Honorary Presidents
Jean-Claude Dischamps, France
Francesco Forte, Italie/Italy
Ottó Gadó, Hongrie/Hungary
Lady Ursula K. Hicks, Royaume-Uni/United Kingdom
Richard A. Musgrave, Etats-Unis/USA
Fritz Neumark, République Fédérale d'Allemagne/Federal
    Republic of Germany
Ugo Papi, Italie/Italy
Alan Peacock, Royaume-Uni/United Kingdom
Horst-Claus Recktenwald, République Fédérale d'Alle-
    magne/Federal Republic of Germany
Paul Senf, République Fédérale d'Allemagne/Federal
    Republic of Germany
Carl S. Shoup, Etats-Unis/USA
François Trévoux, France
Jack Wiseman, Royaume-Uni/United Kingdom

Membres Honoraires/Honorary Members
C. Lowell Harriss, Etats-Unis/USA
Motokazu Kimura, Japon/Japan
Paul Schütz, République Fédérale d'Allemagne/Federal
    Republic of Germany
Stepan Sitaryan, URSS/USSR